KT-447-013

Making Media

Practical Production in Media Education

David Buckingham, Jenny Grahame,
Julian Sefton-Green

British Library Cataloguing-in-Publication Data
A catalogue record for this book is available from the British Library

ISBN 0 907016 24 3

Designed and typeset by Elizabeth Elwin, London
Cover by Dave Bradshaw, Push Design
Printed and bound by Redwood Books, Trowbridge

Published by The English and Media Centre
136 Chalton Street, London NW1 1RX

Contents

Acknowledgements   vi

1   Introduction   1

2   Picture Stories: Investigating Visual Literacy with 7V   17

3   New Models for Old? English Goes Multi-media   47

4   Hangin' with the Technology:
    A Critical Investigation of Group Production   75

5   Original Copy: Re-selling Sounds   105

6   In Search of the Real Audience:
    The Limits of Self-evaluation   140

7   Do I Look Like a Prostitute?
    Soaps, Reality and Learning through Performance   169

Conclusion   199

Bibliography

Index

Acknowledgements

As this book was written by three individuals who worked in six different locations, there are inevitably a large number of people we would like to thank for their support, input and advice. The Gulbenkian Foundation funded the main part of this study, and we would particularly like to thank Simon Richey for his care and enthusiasm. Generous support for two of the case studies was also provided by the Central School of Speech and Drama. The British Film Institute also helped to fund a series of seminars on practical work in 1993, which informed our progress.

In many cases individuals and institutions helped us a great deal and entered into our inquiries with enthusiasm and erudition. We would particularly like to thank the following: Ros Moger, Rosie Mason, Tracey Jones, Claire Wilmer, Andrew Cox, Rob Burgess, Kate Chapman, Isabel Piachaud, Diane Marcus, Pandora Kay-Kreitzman, Elizabeth Kitcatt, Tim Brown and colleagues, Melanie Ancliff, Pete Fraser, Helen Bridge, Ros Davies, Bruce Wooding, Eugene Doyen, Fran Stowell, Tony Carroll and Tony Burgess. We would like to thank Dave Allen for his close reading of the whole manuscript and Michael Simons for his care and attention as our publisher.

Finally, we would like to thank the students who participated in these projects: we hope they find themselves and their work fairly represented here.

This book was collaboratively written although the research on which it is based was undertaken by each of us individually. We hope it is not too confusing for the reader that the case studies are generally written in the first person. For the record, David Buckingham was responsible for the research in Chapters 4 and 6; Jenny Grahame for Chapters 2 and 5; and Julian Sefton-Green for Chapters 3 and 7.

David Buckingham, Jenny Grahame,
Julian Sefton-Green
July 1995

Chapter 1

Introduction

Practical media production has become an increasingly popular activity in many areas of the school curriculum. Yet the aims and methods of such work are often quite diverse. Students might use photography as a form of creative expression in Art lessons, for example, or as a means of presenting data from their Geography field trip. They might use audio tape in producing a radio play in English, or to record interviews for an oral history project in History or Social Studies. Most students are likely to produce a class magazine or newspaper at some stage in their school career, not just in English, but perhaps also in Modern Languages or Social Studies, or even in History. Video is increasingly employed, both as a means of recording events for later discussion or analysis (for example in Science or Physical Education), and as a medium of expression in its own right (for example in Drama or English). And new digital technologies are now beginning to be used, not merely as means of accessing existing information (as in the case of CD-ROMs), but also in forms of media production that integrate many of the 'older' technologies we have mentioned here.

While at least some of these processes might be loosely described as 'media education', our definition of this term is a little more prescriptive. We would make a fundamental distinction here between teaching *through* media and teaching *about* media. In practice, a great deal of teaching takes place *through* media – not just through electronic media such as television or computers, but also through print media such as textbooks and worksheets. To risk a broad generalisation, we would argue that the media are often used here in *instrumental* ways – that is, as a means of teaching content or developing skills that are specific to the subject area. In the process, it is comparatively rare for the media themselves to be questioned: textbooks, educational television programmes and now CD-ROMs are predominantly regarded as neutral sources of objective information. There is, we suspect, very little attention to questions about why and how these texts may have been produced; about the particular points of view they may offer; or about how the formal characteristics of the medium may determine the kind of information that is presented. Educational media are largely designed and used as if they were transparent 'windows on the world'.

Many of the forms of media production described above could be seen to adopt a similarly instrumental approach. In using photography to record the school field trip, or in making a video recording of a science experiment, for example, it is unusual for teachers to draw attention to the characteristics of the medium itself, or to the different ways in which the event might be presented for different purposes. Indeed, we would argue that these kinds of questions are rarely raised even where the media are used as a means of expression in their own right. Many English teachers, for example, will have undertaken the production of class newspapers or magazines; yet in our experience, this kind of work is rarely accompanied by the sustained critical analysis of newspapers, and in some cases, there is often little systematic reflection on the form and selection of content in the finished product. Here again, the media are largely used as a means to another end.

Media education

By contrast, media education necessarily involves teaching *about* media. This is not in itself incompatible with teaching *through* media; although it must involve some kind of systematic reflection, not merely upon the content of media texts, but also on their form, and on the social contexts in which they are produced and consumed. The British Film Institute's influential summary of key areas of media education (see fig. 1.1) offers a clear indication of the kinds of issues and questions that might be raised here.

Media Agencies
Who is communicating what and why?
Who produces a text; roles in the production process; media institutions; economics and ideology; intentions and results.

Media Categories
What type of text is it?
Different media (television, radio, cinema, etc.); forms (documentary, advertising, etc.); genres (science fiction, soap opera, etc.); other ways of categorising texts; how categorisation relates to understanding.

Media Technologies
How is it produced?
What kinds of technologies are available to whom; how to use them; the differences they make to the production process as well as the final product.

Media Languages
How do we know what it means?
How the media produce meanings; codes and conventions; narrative structures.

Media Audiences
Who receives it, and what sense do they make of it?
How audiences are identified, constructed, addressed and reached; how audiences find, choose, consume and respond to texts.

Media Representations
How does it present its subject?
The relation between media texts and actual places, people, events, ideas; stereotyping and its consequences.

Fig. 1.1: Key Areas of Media Education
From the British Film Institute's *Primary Curriculum Statement* (Bazalgette, 1989).

Of course, these questions do not only apply to what are loosely termed 'the media'. They could easily – and indeed productively – be applied to many areas of culture, language and communication. Yet at first glance, it is far from clear what role practical media production might play in this approach. Aside from the brief reference to learning 'how to use' media technologies, most if not all of the areas identified here seem to imply an emphasis on the *critical analysis* of media texts, and of the processes of production, distribution and reception. Media education – teaching *about* media – would appear to involve a combination of techniques of 'close reading' drawn from literary criticism with the study of elements of sociology and economics.

In fact, however, the document from which this summary is drawn places a central emphasis on practical media production – as indeed do nearly all contemporary Media Studies syllabuses[1]. So what is the place of practical production in media education? What differences should we expect to find between practical production in media education and the more 'instrumental' approach identified above? What is the relationship between practical production and the critical analysis of the media? Is production simply a means of acquiring conceptual understandings of the media – or is it an activity that can be pursued in its own right? And, most importantly, what are students expected to *learn* from making their own media products?

Origins and disciplines

As might be expected, there are no single answers to these questions, not least because of the diverse historical origins of media education – and indeed, of media educators themselves. While the term itself is comparatively recent in origin, it is possible to identify evidence of media education in schools as far back as the early 1930s. Even here, one can detect a strongly practical tradition – principally, at that time, in the area of film-making – alongside the critical work being undertaken principally by English teachers[2]. While the main location for practical work appears to have been in extra-curricular Film Clubs, some of it was characterised by a strikingly 'technical' orientation. Rather than making complete films, students were given exercises designed to explore particular rules and conventions of 'film grammar' – an approach which partly derived from the work of the Soviet film-maker and montage theorist V.I. Pudovkin[3].

The 1960s saw the emergence of a more expressive approach, based on notions of creativity then current in the child art movement in Art teaching, and in the renewed emphasis on creative writing in English. Media production came to be seen here, not primarily as a means of encouraging a greater awareness or understanding of the media, or as a form of technical training, but as a means of self-expression and aesthetic exploration on a par with writing poetry or painting. Accounts of work undertaken at this time seem to adopt a view of production as an organic, almost intuitive process, in which formal instruction was at best a distraction[4].

Meanwhile, the critical orientation was developing rapidly beyond its origins in literary criticism, as the academic study of the media (or, more accurately, of the cinema) embraced successive waves of 'continental' theory. From this perspective, practical work in schools was implicitly seen as redundant, or at least as secondary to critical analysis. Indeed, as we shall see, many critics also came to condemn practical work as politically suspect, on the grounds that it encouraged an unthinking imitation of dominant media forms, and hence an uncritical acceptance of the ideologies they were seen to contain. From this perspective, production was seen to have only a limited role: it came to be regarded as little more than a form of 'practical analysis', in which dominant conventions were systematically exposed and deconstructed.

As specialist media courses began to emerge in the late 1960s, there was a clear polarisation between these two versions of the subject. On the one hand, there was Film Studies, which contained no practical component, and was examined at O-level; while on the other, there was Television or Media Studies, which generally contained a substantial practical component, and was only available at the lower level of CSE.

In some respects, this distinction has been sustained into the present. Most GCSE and A-level courses have in fact attempted to strike a balance between practical work and critical analysis – although practical work is currently under threat following government reductions in coursework[5]. Yet the 1980s also saw the emergence of pre-vocational media courses that were predominantly practical, and frequently offered very little opportunity for critical study or reflection. The divorce between 'theory' and 'practice' may thus have become institutionalised as part of a wider distinction between education and training – and, of course, between the students whom these different forms of provision are intended to keep apart.

At the same time, while Media Studies as a separate subject has continued to grow apace in British schools, increasing numbers of teachers in a whole range of curriculum areas have now come to refer to aspects of their work as 'media education'. While this is most explicitly the case in English and in Art and Design, it is also apparent in areas such as Personal and Social Education, History and Geography, as well as less immediately obvious areas such as Modern Languages and Science[6]. Furthermore, while most specialist Media Studies teachers were initially trained as English teachers, many come from quite different disciplinary backgrounds.

These various disciplines define the relationship between critical analysis and practical production in different ways; and this of course is bound to influence what teachers themselves define as the aims and purposes of media production. In English, for example, the systematic critical analysis of literature is largely confined to the upper years of secondary schools, and to post-compulsory education; while creative writing plays a much more central role with younger students. Similarly, most Art teaching is essentially based on practical production (drawing, painting, and so on) – although in recent years, the critical analysis of art has begun to emerge as a more important aspect of the subject[7]. Teachers in both areas are therefore likely to perceive practical production as a central aspect of media education, albeit perhaps in rather different ways. By contrast, teachers undertaking work on the media in Social Studies or in History are much more inclined to concentrate on the critical analysis of existing texts; although they might perceive a role for practical production as an alternative to written presentations, or as a different way of demonstrating students' understanding of the subject.

Versions of practical production

This thumbnail sketch illustrates the diverse ways in which the place of practical work, and its relationship with 'theory' (or critical analysis), have been defined. Broadly speaking, it is possible to make distinctions between four possible 'versions' of practical media production in education – although of course in reality these often co-exist and overlap[8].

1. First, there is the notion of *practical work as self-expression*, which derives largely from 'progressive' Art and English teaching. As we have seen, this approach emphasises individual creativity and the aesthetic possibilities of audio-visual media. Thus, Art teachers have tended to emphasise the formal exploration of the unique properties of the visual media: in the case of photography, for example, this has involved experimenting with light-sensitive paper, with photographic printing techniques, or with the conventions of perspective[9]. Meanwhile, some English teachers have been more inclined to emphasise the media's potential as a means of bringing children's 'authentic' out-of-school cultures into the classroom, or as an expanded form of creative writing – for example, through combining video and poetry or using montages of images in conjunction with autobiographical writing[10]. Both approaches can permit a form of experimentation with the possibilities of the medium, and with generic conventions, although the implications of this are not necessarily the subject of explicit reflection. A more overtly 'political' variant on this approach has been developed through the uses of photography and video in youth and community work, considered in Chapter 4.

2. The use of *practical work as a method of learning* comes close to the 'instrumental' approach identified above. Carol Lorac and Michael Weiss[11], for example, illustrate the ways in which practical production can help to develop students' learning in a whole range of curriculum areas, for example by developing their skills as researchers, and by enabling them to reformulate their existing knowledge in order to communicate with a wider audience. Thus, students might use video as a means of recording and presenting material from an oral history project based in their local neighbourhood; or they might use tape/slide or animation as a means of re-presenting their analysis of a scientific process such as photosynthesis or the transfer of energy. By virtue of the fact that it relies on small-group work, media production is also seen here to promote more general 'social and communication skills'. The question of how far these outcomes are specifically dependent upon the use of *media* – and whether they might just as easily have been achieved by other forms of group work – remains unanswered, however.

3. *Practical work as vocational training* is, needless to say, well-established in the media industries and in higher education; although it began to work its way down to further education and to schools in the mid-1980s, initially under the auspices of the Manpower Services Commission. In the contemporary context, this approach is most apparent in courses such as B-TEC National (examined by the Business and Technician Education Council) and GNVQ (General National Vocational Qualification). This approach is predominantly concerned with the acquisition of technical skills and with the replication of established forms of professional practice. In the case of most B-TEC courses, for example, it would include systematic training in areas such as camera techniques, editing, pre-production, audio mixing and health and safety. While GNVQ does require students to engage in systematic critical study of the media, it remains to be seen how effectively it will manage to combine 'theory' and 'practice'. In fact, even at FE level, such courses rarely offer sufficient training to qualify students for entry to employment, and might more accurately be described as *pre*-vocational.

4. The notion of *practical work as deconstruction* would appear to be fundamentally opposed to all the others identified here. While it has precedents in the 'film grammar' approach of earlier decades, it is essentially derived from the application of semiotic theories of 'visual language' which were popular during the 1970s. According to Len Masterman[12], deconstruction exercises involve the practical analysis of the dominant 'codes' of television: '[deconstruction] allows individual conventions (of framing, camera positioning, editing, etc.) to be isolated, experimented with and broken while variations in their meaning are explored'. Thus, students might undertake exercises on the conventions of TV interviews or news presentation; or they might be required to produce 'exercises in style' designed to demonstrate their understanding of a particular genre such as film noir or horror. Unlike the first two approaches identified here, deconstruction is not concerned with students' desire to communicate or to express themselves, nor indeed with finished products; and in direct contrast to the vocational approach, it explicitly seeks to oppose and subvert dominant notions of professional practice. The 'expressive' potential of practical work is thus very much subordinated to the demonstration of conceptual understanding.

Media education: the critique of practice

While all three authors of this book have experience of other approaches, our own perspective here derives primarily from that of Media Studies teaching in schools. Our point of departure, then, is from the fourth position here – and indeed from a strong sense of the inadequacies of that position. As we have implied, the establishment of Media Studies as a legitimate academic subject in schools has involved a troubled, almost schizophrenic, stance towards practical production. On the one hand, the inclusion of practical work has been seen to define Media Studies as an essentially vocational or creative subject. In the traditional academic hierarchies that continue to prevail, even in many of the inner-city schools in which we have worked, this has effectively marked it out as a low status subject for low status kids. On the other hand, for many students across the whole range of 'ability', it is the promise of getting their hands on cameras or of doing creative work with computers that often motivates them to choose the subject in the first place. Furthermore, it has largely been the practical work that has helped to keep *us* as teachers interested and enthusiastic in what have frequently been difficult circumstances.

Nevertheless, advocates of Media Studies as a specialist subject have traditionally adopted a sceptical, even hostile, attitude to practical work. The most influential writers in the field in the 1970s and early 1980s tended to condemn the majority of practical work as politically suspect and as educationally worthless. Len Masterman's book *Teaching About Television*, published in 1980, was certainly the most influential book for a whole generation of teachers. Yet its chapter on practical work was very much the shortest in the book, and much of it was extraordinarily negative. What happens, Masterman asks, when you give students video cameras?

> In my experience an endless wilderness of dreary third-rate imitative 'pop'-shows, embarrassing video dramas, and derivative documentaries courageously condemning war or poverty, much of it condoned by teachers to whom technique is all and the medium the only message.[13]

What is quite striking about this quote now, fifteen years later, is its reliance on precisely the kind of Leavisite critical criteria that the rest of the book sought to challenge. Students' work is condemned as 'derivative' and 'third-rate', in exactly the same terms that one might find Leavis condemning a novel that had failed to gain entry to the Great Tradition. Yet this tone can also be found in other writings of the period. Bob Ferguson, writing in *Screen Education* in 1981, condemned practical video work in similar terms:

> Many groups ended up just clowning around with the equipment... the camera was often 'squirted' at its subject and the dizzy, boring and incoherent results thus obtained could be justified as experimentation. When plots were attempted they were puerile and in further education often incorporated obligatory punch-ups in pubs and discotheques.[14]

Significantly, Ferguson's main criticism was directed against the notion of 'creativity' which he saw as deriving from Art and English teaching, and which he condemned as mystical and individualistic. This approach was seen to reflect a dangerous 'romanticisation of the working class': it led to work that was 'intellectually undemanding' and that merely institutionalised low expectations of students.

If we come forward to the mid-1980s, this kind of argument is still the dominant one. Masterman's *Teaching the Media*, published in 1985, gives over little more than a page to practical work, in what claims to be a comprehensive introduction to the field – and in this respect, it is similar to other handbooks for teachers published at that time, many of which simply neglect practical work altogether[15]. Again, most of what Masterman says is negative. The new concern here, however, is with what he calls 'the technicist trap'. In the wake of the 'new vocationalism', it seemed to be vital to challenge any attempt to reduce media education to a form of technical training. This kind of training, Masterman argued, represents 'a form of cultural reproduction in which dominant practices become naturalised'; it is a kind of ideological 'enslavement' which produces 'deference and conformity'. The alternative, it would appear, is to encourage students to produce 'oppositional' texts which directly challenge and subvert the norms of professional media practice.

As we shall see in more detail in Chapter 5, these criticisms were partly motivated by a fear of *imitation*, which in turn derived from a wider suspicion of the deceptive pleasures of popular culture. Imitation was seen to be an inherently *unthinking* process, through which the 'dominant ideologies' of media products were simply taken on and reproduced. An emphasis on practical work was therefore seen to be at odds with the radical political mission of Media Studies, and its struggle against the ideological hegemony of capitalism: except in the rigorously 'oppositional' form of deconstruction exercises, it was effectively marginalised or excluded altogether.

Along with many other aspects of Media Studies, this perspective on practical work has been substantially challenged and revised over the past decade. There are several possible reasons for this. As we shall see, this change has partly arisen as a result of a more wide-ranging reconsideration of the fundamental aims and methods of media teaching, in which classroom research of the kind represented in this book has played an important role. Yet it has also reflected the changing status of the subject, and its rather different location in the school curriculum; and it could equally be seen as a consequence of technological developments, and of the increasing accessibility of production equipment. It is these latter issues that will be considered in the following sections.

Changing status

As we have implied, debates about the place of practical work in Media Studies have been bound up with wider claims for its status and distinctiveness as a subject discipline. The emphasis on the primacy of critical analysis that emerged very strongly in the 1970s can partly be explained as a claim for academic legitimacy – albeit one made in highly traditional terms. On the other hand, the emphasis on practical work in CSE syllabuses appeared to confirm a widespread view of Media Studies as a 'soft option', suitable only for students who were seen to lack academic potential.

In presenting Media Studies as a vanguard political 'movement', it was also necessary to distinguish it from subjects or approaches which could be condemned as mere reproductions of the dominant ideology, or else as hopelessly liberal. Bob Ferguson's arguments, quoted above, are partly motivated by the attempt to distinguish Media Studies from 'progressive' approaches to Art and English teaching, of the kind we have briefly described above. Likewise, Masterman opposes what he terms the 'critical' approach of Media Studies to the 'technicist' approach of vocational training. Both writers appear to make an implicit claim for Media Studies as part of a high-status academic curriculum, as opposed to a low-status practical or vocational one – a rather traditional position in comparison with the political radicalism both appear to espouse.

In some respects, these distinctions have been superseded. At least in the case of Media Studies, the advent of a common examination in the form of GCSE effectively abolished the 'class distinctions' that had been enshrined in the polarisation between O-level and CSE[16] – even if, as we have argued, such distinctions may have been sustained in the polarisation between 'academic' and 'vocational' courses at 16+. Nevertheless, all the new GCSE Media Studies syllabuses introduced in the mid-1980s contained a substantial proportion of practical work, albeit defined and assessed in different ways; and the same is true of the A-level courses that began to emerge in their wake[17]. Meanwhile, contemporary perspectives in English and in Art teaching have moved well beyond the woolly progressivism which Ferguson condemns. In different ways, the notion of 'Knowledge About Language' in English and the emphasis on 'Critical Studies' in Art offer productive approaches to integrating critical study with practical production[18]. Meanwhile, recent debates on the 16-19 curriculum have substantially challenged Masterman's opposition between the academic and the vocational, and there are significant moves towards a more integrated approach[19]. And of course, academic Media Studies has itself moved beyond the emphasis on ideological critique favoured by both writers, towards a recognition of the complexities of young people's engagement with popular culture. While critical analysis remains a central aspect of the field – as of course it should – teachers in higher education have also had to adjust their approach in order to take account of the changing competencies and motivations of their students.

At the same time, media education has moved closer to the educational mainstream. While Media Studies as a separate subject has continued to flourish – most spectacularly at A-level – work on the media has inevitably become part of a much wider range of curriculum subjects. After a difficult and contested passage, media education is now enshrined as a dimension of the National Curriculum for English; and it also appears in some form in the documents for Art, Modern Languages and History. In most cases, media education is defined here, not merely in terms of critical study, but also as a matter of practical production.

More significantly perhaps, along with information technology, media education has become a prominent part of a much more far-reaching argument about the need for 'new literacies' that will be appropriate to the changing social and cultural landscape of the next century[20]. Crucially, this new literacy is defined, not merely as a form of defensive 'critical' reading, but also as an ability to *write* or produce in the new communications media. It is these kinds of arguments that will, in our view, inevitably come to supersede the limited compromise that is represented in the current National Curriculum.

As we move into the second half of the 1990s, then, the political purism of earlier advocates of Media Studies appears increasingly redundant. The emergence of classroom research and the development of a broad conceptual definition of the subject field (identified above) have increasingly focused attention on the need to integrate theory and practice. Practical production has now been largely accepted as a central element of the field, both in the context of specialist Media Studies courses and in other curriculum areas. Yet awkward questions about the aims and outcomes of practical work have yet to be fully addressed. While we do not share their conclusions, we do recognise the broader political and educational concerns of earlier media educators. We have no desire simply to validate practical work for its own sake, or to justify it through some form of vague romanticism – or indeed, to define it merely in terms of the 'mastery' of technical skills. Our intention here is not to sweep these concerns aside, but to rethink them in the context of our broader focus on students' *learning*.

Changing technologies

As we re-read earlier accounts of practical work in schools, we are struck by the enormously difficult and cumbersome nature of the process. While none of us is particularly long in the tooth, at least two of the present authors can recall the days when practical work meant super-8 cameras and reel-to-reel portapacks. Formidable obstacles were posed by video that was never really 'portable', by 8 mm. projectors that unfailingly chewed up your film, and by enlargers that were as easy to manipulate as dinosaurs. In the era of palmcorders, photo-CDs and cheap computer graphics, it is hard to conceive of how we ever managed to get anything done.

Yet these technological developments are only part of a wider series of changes that have fundamentally altered the entire landscape of the media over the past two decades. There has been a massive proliferation of media sources, with the advent of domestic video, cable and satellite, and with desktop publishing, digital audio equipment and multimedia. In the media industries, the dominance of large national institutions has given way both to multi-national corporations and to the artisanal economy of independent production. Media audiences are beginning to fragment, as 'mass' entertainment gives way to the targeting of specialist interest groups. Most obviously in areas such as popular music and children's television, individual media have become part of a much wider 'intertextual' system, in which any single text is inextricably related to other texts; and in the process, the boundaries between records, films, TV programmes, computer games, toys and other merchandise have become ever harder to define. For many critics, these phenomena have in turn been regarded as a manifestation of much broader processes of cultural change. Theories of 'postmodernism' have rapidly become one of the most tiresome academic pursuits of our time; yet they have offered a challenging account of contemporary processes of globalisation, of economic change, and of the blurring and fragmentation of established cultural identities.

These changes have inevitably had a substantial impact on the practice of media education, and particularly on media production, in schools. Of course, practical production does not need to rely upon 'high-tech' media. A great deal of interesting and valuable work continues to be achieved with scissors and glue, with simple cassette recorders and point-and-shoot cameras. Nevertheless, these technological developments have made more complex forms of practical production much more accessible and easy to manage. Significantly, they are also leading to a situation in which the experience of media production is less and less confined to the classroom. Children's first experiences of making videos, for example, are no longer so likely to take place in school; and students will increasingly be coming to the classroom with experience of video editing, image manipulation and digital music technology. The home is no longer a site simply of media *consumption*: it has also become a key site for *production*. Furthermore, as we shall indicate in Chapter 3, these new technologies enable teachers and students to have much greater control over the production process[21]. Digital editing on computers, for example, is now possible using equipment that costs a fraction of what it did ten years ago – and that can, of course, be used for many other purposes. The brave new world of digital multi-media may well take longer to arrive than some have suggested; yet if the impact of videocassettes and micro-computers over the past fifteen years offers any guide, it is likely to alter what we mean by practical production in very fundamental ways.

At the same time, the cultural and social developments which have accompanied these changes also have far-reaching implications in terms of how we might define the *purpose* of practical work, and hence evaluate its outcomes. For example, the distinction between 'dominant' and 'oppositional' practice that still characterises many rationales for practical work has become increasingly redundant. The aesthetic strategies of the *avant-garde* of the 1970s and 1980s have steadily been incorporated into the mainstream, most obviously in advertising and music videos; and while forms of 'oppositional' practice could be said to persist, many of the institutional and economic distinctions between 'independent' and 'dominant' production have all but disappeared. The notion that there are fixed professional 'norms' that should be contested and deconstructed has become highly questionable; and the requirement that practical work should represent 'oppositional' practice – which is still enshrined in some Media Studies syllabuses – would seem to be an increasingly impossible demand.

Perhaps more fundamentally, these changes also appear to challenge the notion of the 'text' as a self-contained object – a notion that is at the heart of most definitions of media education (including the conceptual definition with which we began). As critics have argued, the boundaries between texts and other texts, and between media, have become increasingly blurred. People no longer watch programmes, they watch television; and their experience of television is inextricably bound up with their experience of other media such as video, pop music and computer games, and with the merchandising that surrounds and permeates them. In this context, the traditional activity of textual analysis may well need to be dethroned from its privileged position in media teaching. Likewise, we may need to question the idea that practical work should involve the production of finished texts, or that it should entail a disciplined and rational progression from intentions to final results. With the capabilities made available by the new digital technologies, production may increasingly come to be seen as a matter of raiding existing materials, and manipulating and recombining them in new ways. In the process, the boundaries between critical analysis and practical production – between 'reading' and 'writing' – are bound to become increasingly blurred.

Media education: change and continuity

The implications and eventual outcomes of the changes we have discussed here are difficult to identify with any certainty. It would certainly be a mistake to assume that they will be uniformly positive; although they will undoubtedly be quite far-reaching. At the same time, however, media education has itself undergone some significant changes in its aims and methods over the past ten years. By addressing hitherto neglected questions about children's existing knowledge of the media, and about how they learn, we have come to question many of the grandiose claims about media education made by its pioneers. The notion that media teaching would 'liberate' students from the chains of ideology has given way to a more realistic – and, we would argue, more effective – approach.

Nevertheless, there are several emphases that remain central, and that serve to distinguish our own concerns from those that may be apparent in other areas. In this book, we discuss a series of practical projects that took place, not only in Media Studies lessons, but also in English, Art, Drama and Information Technology, as well as in a youth and community work setting. In each case, there is an encounter between our own perspectives as media educators and the established (although often largely implicit) assumptions and approaches of these different areas. In our view, media education has much to gain from this kind of dialogue with other subject areas; yet at the risk of over-simplification, it is essential to be clear about the distinctive nature of a media education perspective.

As we have indicated, contemporary media education places a central emphasis on *conceptual learning*. The aims of the subject are principally defined, not in terms of skills or competencies, or indeed in terms of a body of content, but in terms of areas of conceptual understanding. In this respect, there is considerable common ground between the British Film Institute's definition (quoted above), and those that are contained within specialist Media Studies syllabuses. The contrast with related subjects like English, which is predominantly defined in terms of *activities* (reading, writing, speaking and listening), is immediately apparent. While most media educators place a central emphasis on practical work, there is a further fundamental distinction here between education and training. The aim of practical work in media education is not primarily vocational: the acquisition of technical skills is seen as secondary to the development of conceptual (or 'critical') understanding. The *process* of production – and the conceptual understandings that can be acquired through reflecting on that process – are hence of much greater significance than the *product*.

As may already be apparent, there are several ways in which we would want to qualify these arguments. We would accept that it is undesirable – and indeed, practically impossible – for schools to offer vocational training in this area[22]. Yet we do feel that there are skills in practical media production that can and should be acquired by school students, just as we would expect them to learn to write. As we have argued, 'writing' in the new media will be an essential part of the new literacy of the next century – not simply for the world of employment, but also for leisure and for other forms of cultural expression and participation. Furthermore, we are not convinced that a distinction between 'theory' and 'practice' – or between conceptual understandings and practical skills – is necessarily helpful or meaningful. We would argue that there are conceptual understandings of the media that can *only* be fully developed through the experience of production itself; and that there is a fundamental difference between the 'passive' knowledge that is developed through critical analysis and the 'active' knowledge that derives from production. It is possible to come to 'understand' continuity editing, for example, through detailed frame-by-frame analysis of films; but the understanding that can be achieved through actually doing editing oneself is qualitatively different. 'Knowing why' cannot be separated from 'knowing how' – at least not without impoverishing both. Likewise, we would seek to question the apparent opposition between 'process' and 'product'. We would argue that products are a fundamental *part* of the process, although they should not be seen as the end of it.

In all these ways, the emphasis on conceptual understanding appears to raise as many questions as it resolves. How can we separate conceptual understanding from the exercise of skills – or indeed, from the knowledge of factual information? What are we to take as *evidence* of conceptual understanding? How can we 'read' conceptual understandings from the form of students' productions – or indeed from our observations of the process? Media educators have traditionally sought to resolve these dilemmas by recourse to spoken or written language. It is in the 'logs' or 'critical accounts' that accompany Media Studies coursework, for example, that we expect to find evidence of the connections between 'theory' and 'practice'. Yet as many of the case studies that follow amply demonstrate, this emphasis on a *written demonstration* of conceptual understanding has fundamental limitations. All too often, students seem to be required to regurgitate the critical analysis that teachers have fed them: what 'counts' as conceptual understanding is simply a replication of the teacher's discourse, a matter of artfully mobilising academic terminology for the purposes of assessment. As we shall argue, reflection of this kind needs to be seen as an integral and essential part of the process, rather than a mere bolt-on extra that is designed to meet the needs of examiners.

The crux, of course, is to discover ways of ensuring an *equal* and *dialectical* relationship between 'theory' and 'practice'. Practice has to be more than a mere application of theory, or an alternative way of demonstrating pre-determined theoretical positions. By its nature, practical media production involves areas that often cannot be adequately accounted for by theory – the display of the body, the subjective domain of relationships and identities, the realm of aesthetics and creativity, and of humour and the emotions. While many of these terms would be anathema to the theorists of the 1970s, we would argue that it is in the exploration of these areas – *and* in the attempt to reflect upon and 'theorise' them – that much of the challenging educational potential of practical work can be found. As we demonstrate in this book, practical production has its own dynamic: it is a social space in which students can be sanctioned to explore their own identities and emotional investments in the media, in a way that is much more subjective and 'playful' than is the case with critical analysis. Inevitably, this is a process that generates considerable anxiety for teachers, and it is unsurprising that they often respond by attempting to reassert their ideological control.

At the same time, we should emphasise that we are not arguing for a return to earlier notions of practical work as pure 'self-expression'. This is an approach we would challenge both on theoretical and educational grounds. What students do in the course of practical work is, of course, highly constrained by the social situation in which it occurs, and by their social relationships with the teacher and with their peers. The technologies and conventions they use are also already structured in specific ways, that inevitably serve to determine what can be said. Ultimately, the notion that there is a 'self' that awaits its 'expression' is one that derives from an individualistic (indeed Romantic) conception of creativity – a view that we would hope to replace with a conception of creativity as a form of *social dialogue*. In educational terms, we would also want to insist on the importance of students *reflecting* upon the processes and the products of their practical work. It is through this process of reflection – for example, through making explicit *why* particular decisions were taken, and what effects they may have had – that the connections between theory and practice can be forged. As we have argued, there is a distinct lack of effective strategies that might ensure this; and yet it is here that much of the most significant learning may occur.

Classroom research of the kind we describe in this book has played an essential role in this more wide-ranging re-evaluation of the aims and methods of media education. In this respect, this book seeks to build upon our earlier work in books like *Watching Media Learning* and *Cultural Studies Goes to School*[23], both of which grew out of collaborative action research by teachers themselves. In common with this earlier work, our aim here is not to provide rose-tinted accounts of 'good practice', but to explore some of the difficulties and complexities of real classrooms. In this respect, we are intending to do more than simply document or record what took place. Our accounts are inevitably descriptive; but we are ultimately concerned to develop a *theoretically-informed* interrogation of practice. Thus, while our analysis is 'grounded' in the data we have gathered, we also attempt to step back from immediate experience, and to develop a dialectical relationship between action and theoretical reflection[24]. It is only on this basis, we would argue, that more effective classroom strategies can begin to be devised.

An outline of the book

The six chapters that follow explore these broad concerns through detailed accounts of classroom practice. The research on which they are based was conducted in a number of London secondary schools, and (in one case) in a youth and community project. From our initial reading and discussion of previous work in this field, and of our own experience as teachers and as teacher educators, we began by identifying a number of broad themes which were then 'translated' into specific classroom projects. In choosing schools and teachers to work with, we also attempted to cover a range of age groups and curriculum areas. Each of us was responsible for two of the case studies, although we met regularly in order to share material, and to ensure a common approach. Although we have written the case studies in the first person, not least in order to avoid confusion, the book has been very much a collaborative enterprise. Each case study therefore attempts to address a particular area of concern, although (as is always the case in this kind of research) each raises a number of further issues and questions that we had not necessarily foreseen. Inevitably, there is a certain degree of overlap in terms of the themes that are raised by the case studies; although we have found it extremely productive to compare the different ways in which issues are raised in different contexts.

Our role in these situations varied on a broad continuum between that of teacher and that of observer. In most cases, however, we effectively initiated and planned the projects in collaboration with the regular classroom teachers; and in some, we took the leading role in teaching ourselves. We were therefore very much *participant* observers, and we must take full responsibility for the failings and limitations of the teaching we describe. Only in one case, for particular reasons, did we attempt to adopt the role of passive observer (Chapter 4). None of these studies attempts to offer a model of 'good practice', nor would we necessarily claim that they are representative – although we would argue that, in many ways, they could be taken as instances of *typical* practice in their respective areas. At the very least, we hope that readers will recognise these experiences, and find ways of relating them to their own teaching.

In Chapter Two, we describe a photography project undertaken with year 7 students in a culturally diverse inner London school. This chapter investigates the ways in which students may develop their understanding of the codes and conventions of 'visual language' through practical production. It focuses particularly on the role of activities such as image analysis and storyboarding, that are conventionally used to support the acquisition of 'visual literacy'; and it also considers the ways in which bilingual students from different cultural and artistic traditions compose verbal and visual narratives. Through the detailed analysis of the ways in which these texts are constructed, this chapter seeks to explore and extend the analogy we have drawn above between media production and writing.

Chapter Three describes two projects using digital multimedia production technologies within years 8 and 10 of the English curriculum of a multi-ethnic inner-city girls' school. The year 8 students used multi-media 'authoring' software, combining image, sound and text, to create non-linear stories or 'hypertexts'; and their work raises questions about the use of traditional and non-traditional forms of narrative. The year 10 students used image manipulation and video editing software to produce film trailers and posters, with the aim of developing their understanding of genre and narrative conventions. In addition to broader questions about the relationship between technology and 'creativity', this chapter considers the potential contribution of these technologies to new definitions of literacy.

In Chapter Four, we focus on the problems and possibilities of learning in the apparently democratic context of small group production. The chapter offers a detailed account of one group's contribution to the production of a rap music video, in the context of an intensive media production course undertaken within a youth and community arts project. It traces the ways in which groups resolve or avoid differences of opinion, and achieve a balance between creative ideas and logistical constraints. The central emphasis here is on the interpersonal dynamics of the group, and the ways in which individuals stake out 'subject positions' in the production process. This chapter raises fundamental questions about the limitations of group work, and of the broadly 'progressivist' teaching strategies which are seen to characterise youth work.

Chapter Five analyses practical projects on the reception and production of popular music undertaken by a group of A-level Media Studies students in an inner London school. Following an exploration of their personal responses to a range of musical genres, the class undertook a structured simulation on the music industry; and then went on to analyse, re-position and market music from the past for a 1990s audience, through the production of music videos, radio extracts, record packaging and music magazines. The chapter examines how the students drew on their own knowledge of, and pleasures in, the generic conventions of popular music, and appropriated them through imitation and parody. It seeks to challenge long-standing assumptions about the ideological functions and consequences of imitation, and to explore what is at stake in students' 'reproduction' of dominant forms.

Chapter Six analyses a unit of work undertaken with a year 10 GCSE English/Media Studies group in a selective North London school. The class worked to a brief which required them to produce a trailer for a new children's TV series, and to include an element of research with their target audience of younger students. The account focuses particularly on the relationship between practical production and written reflection, and the kinds of learning that might be involved in 'translating' between language modes. The potential and the limitations of using 'real audiences' in this context are also explored. How (if at all) do students incorporate the perspectives of audiences into the production process? And to what extent does this help to make the process of self-evaluation more 'spontaneous', and less of an abstract requirement on the part of teachers or examiners?

In the final case study, we offer an account of a unit of media work undertaken in lower school drama lessons at a mixed inner London comprehensive. This chapter follows the scripting, performance and filming of a school soap opera, focusing particularly on the subjective dimensions of public performance. This involves a consideration of how students understand what it means to act in the play/soap opera, and how they judge the 'reality' of the finished product. These issues are framed by a broader discussion of the contrasting aims and methods of drama and media education, and of the significance of 'play' in each area.

Our conclusion attempts to draw together the major theoretical issues that have arisen through the case studies, and to discuss these in the light of broader educational perspectives. In taking a step back from the particular issues and dilemmas raised by the case studies, we attempt to outline a new agenda for research and practice in this field. While our concluding arguments are necessarily more abstract, we trust that they are fully grounded in the concrete experiences we have described.

Notes

1 Throughout this book, we use the inclusive term 'media education' to refer to teaching about mass media (film, television, the press, advertising, popular music, etc.) irrespective of the specific curriculum location. Media education is thus a (potential) dimension of English, Art and Design, History, Geography, and a number of other subjects. The term 'Media Studies' refers to specialist courses, for example those examined at GCSE, A-level and beyond.

2 Evidence on this can be found in Miller (1979) and Donelson (1971). Roger Manvell of the British Film Institute was running film courses in schools in the 1930s and 1940s (see Whannell and Harcourt, 1964). The major inspiration for critical work at this time was, of course, the work of Leavis and Thompson (1933).

3 Notably in Pudovkin (1929). The analogy between film and language that is implicit in notions of 'media literacy' may also have its origins here.

4 See, for example, Knight (1964) and Lowndes (1968).

5 This is of course part of a wider move to re-introduce the polarisation between 'academic' and 'non-academic' courses - and the different clientele they are seen to serve.

6 The British Film Institute's Curriculum Statements contain numerous instances of media education 'across the curriculum': see Bazalgette (1989) and Bowker (1991). For strategies for implementing cross-curricular policies, see Grahame (1991a).

7 Critical work is now included as an attainment target in the National Curriculum for Art, and as a requirement at GCSE. For an account of contemporary developments, see Allen (1992a).

8 The following section is adapted from the more extended account in Buckingham (1987a), Section 4.

9 See Colledge (1984). Photomontage would be another example of media education practice within art: see Carroll (1992).

10 See Grahame (1991a).

11 Lorac and Weiss (1981). For a critique of this approach, see Buckingham (1987a). Many suggestions for 'media education across the curriculum' (e.g. Bowker, 1991) reflect aspects of this approach.

12 Masterman (1980).

13 *Ibid*, page 140.

14 Ferguson (1981), page 44-5.

15 Masterman (1985), pages 26–7. See also Alvarado, Gutch and Wollen (1987).

16 Although of course it has singularly failed to do so in many other subjects.

17 Quite how this will survive in the face of restrictions on coursework is not yet clear. Following rationalisation, the two remaining GCSE syllabi appear to offer very different definitions of the relationship between theory and practice: see Grahame and Blanchard (1992).

18 See Carter (1990) on Knowledge About Language; and Taylor (1986) on Critical Studies.

19 See, for example, Spours and Young (1990), Finegold et al (1990).

20 See, for example, Tweddle and Moore (1993) and Buckingham (1993a).

21 Some general implications of these developments are outlined in Buckingham and Sefton-Green (1993).

22 Although it is important to distinguish here between vocational and *pre*-vocational courses. As we have argued, most so-called vocational courses in this area, including BTEC and GNVQ, cannot be seen as adequate preparation for employment in the industry: see Buckingham (1995).

23 Buckingham (1990); Buckingham and Sefton-Green (1994).

24 This general approach to classroom research is explored in Winter (1989).

Chapter 2

Picture Stories: Investigating Visual Literacy with 7V

Many students' first experience of media education has traditionally taken the form of analysing a media *text*: a print advertisement, a news photograph, a movie still, a comic-strip frame, or a photograph – in other words, studying a single visual image. In English, this might mean investigating the narrative clues offered by a book jacket or the generic conventions of a children's storybook illustration. In Art, the focus might be on portraits or reproductions as a starting point for the exploration of shape, colour and tone; while in Humanities, the study of an archive photograph might initiate an exploration of sources of evidence, their function and validity. While the outcomes of such study are defined in different ways, this shared emphasis on the analysis of visual images reflects a common concern with what is often called *visual literacy*. In this chapter, I want to explore the meaning of this term in relation to the ways in which children learn both to 'read' and to 'write' images and visual narratives.

What is visual literacy?

The concept of visual literacy has its origins in the discipline of art history. In their discussions of Renaissance painting, scholars such as Panofsky and Gombrich showed how the mode of representation in Western art was founded on carefully constructed systems of codes and conventions[1]. If spectators were to understand art works, they would need to learn – and perhaps be explicitly educated – about these systems, and the cultural contexts from which they derive. For example, the concept of perspective is one which relies on a series of visual conventions in order to represent a three-dimensional world. As is clear from the two-dimensional drawings of very young children, these conventions are not natural or innate, but progressively *learned*.

A parallel argument can be derived from Saussurean linguistics, which offers another influential perspective here. According to Saussure, language conventions are arbitrary and culturally determined. Words are seen as signs whose meaning is only fixed by social usage. These ideas, the cornerstones of semiotic theory, were developed and applied by Barthes to contemporary visual material. Thus, the codes of framing, of narrative continuity or of genre recognition in media texts can only make sense within the framework of knowledge learnt within Western culture: such codes make meaning for us because we are already 'literate' in their use.

The early Russian film theorists such as Pudovkin and Eisenstein applied similar theoretical principles to their analysis of the moving image. They argued that film-making constituted a new visual language system which audiences must learn to interpret – although they would inevitably do this from the perspective of their own social and historical contexts. Nowadays, for example, we need some knowledge of both the historical context and the formal significance of montage editing if we are to make sense of a text such as Eisenstein's *Battleship Potemkin*[2]. The same theoretical approach has also been applied to Western cinema. Continuity editing, for example, is a highly conventionalised way of organising time and space in film, which evolved gradually in the early years of Hollywood. In order to be able to make sense of film narratives, audiences need to learn the conventions of continuity editing – such as the narrative significance of a close-up shot, or the 180° rule (whereby the camera following a character moving must stay on the same side of an imaginary line in order to preserve continuity). The key question, however, is whether audiences learn these systems simply through their experiences of viewing, by a form of osmosis; or whether media educationalists actively need to teach the 'rules' of film grammar and syntax.

The work of Golay and Gauthier in the early 1970s proposed concrete models for teaching these forms of film language[3]; and this approach fed into the highly influential teaching resources developed by the British Film Institute Education Department in the late 1970s and early 1980s. Teaching packs such as *Reading Pictures*, *Picture Stories*, and *Selling Pictures* provided accessible strategies for visual literacy education for young people. They drew on exercises developed from work on the psychology of perception in order to de-naturalise and thus deconstruct the 'multi-layered significance' of images[4]. They offered a framework for decoding images through detailed description of lighting, framing, camera shots and angles, to the analysis of the meaning of the image in its context. Such strategies – including close analysis, sequencing and cropping exercises, captioning and other 'anchoring' activities – were further adapted by another similarly influential teaching resource, *EyeOpeners*[5]. This was a series of activities around still photographs shot in familiar locations, and incorporating items of popular cultural significance. Along with the BFI packs, this material became the staple diet for the first term of many secondary school Media Studies courses, and was widely adopted by English teachers as a ready-made self-contained introduction to the reading of images.

Invaluable as these packs were for their structured approach to image analysis, they were perilously similar to the closed model of comprehension practised in English. As with English, the ability to apply closed analytic procedures to decontextualised texts may be helpful to those who have learned the rules of the procedures, but may not necessarily lead to more generalised conceptual understandings about the nature of visual images[6]. Furthermore, although lip-service was paid to the concept of active and participatory readership, little attention had been given to the ways in which audiences consume, make sense of, and construct their own meanings from media images. Defining visual literacy in terms of a fixed sequence of 'decoding skills' was an approach which, in retrospect, appears to have been fatally reductive.

From visual literacy to media literacies

At its simplest level, the term visual literacy has often been used very loosely, to refer to 'a broader visual education'. It is in such terms that the concept is now formally referenced in the National Curriculum for Art, where it is incorporated into Attainment Target 2 on *Knowledge and Understanding*:

> In order to develop visual literacy, pupils should be taught about the different ways in which ideas, feelings and meanings are communicated in visual form[7]

However, the concept of literacy is used here in a rather different way from its use within English teaching. In English, it is taken for granted that literacy is acquired and demonstrated through both reading *and* writing. Situating visual literacy within the more analytical *Knowledge and Understanding* end of the Art curriculum, rather than the more practical *Investigating and Making*, seems to imply that pupils can be taught how to *read* different forms of visual communication separately from being given opportunities to make them. This confusion is exacerbated by the fact that there is no formal definition of the term anywhere in the National Curriculum for Art. Indeed, Tony Carroll suggests that 'The kind of characteristic vagueness that typifies the inclusion of visual literacy in the National Orders for Art without a definition of what it might be, reflects the way the term has again come to serve political interests'[8]. In this case, Carroll implies, the phrase is a cipher for a merely 'aesthetic' appreciation of 'our cultural heritage'. By contrast, Dave Allen has suggested a more positive reading of the term, arguing that there may be a *plurality* of visual literacies, which are developed both through reading *and* making images and artefacts[9]. Either way, however, it is clear that the term requires a more complex and thorough discussion than a one-line definition will allow.

In fact, the use of the term literacy in this kind of context has become increasingly fashionable. We now have computer literacy and television literacy, not to mention economic literacy and even emotional literacy. Visual literacy is frequently confused with media literacy, an equally nebulous umbrella term, or taken to be a dimension of it[10]. This confusion derives from the fact that the word 'literacy' itself seems to have no exact definition except in relation to its opposite: 'illiteracy'. In its narrowest common-sense application, it means, of course, the ability to read and write; but we would argue that it could in principle refer to any form of social communication or practice which requires a form of language code, and which therefore needs to be learned. Nevertheless, this is implicitly to argue for a *social* rather than a merely *psychological* definition of the term. As David Buckingham has argued elsewhere:

> literacy cannot be reduced to an abstract set of 'skills' which can be studied in isolation from the meanings which readers (or viewers) produce, or the institutional and social structures in which they are embedded[11].

To be literate, therefore, does not mean simply to have acquired the technical ability to decode and encode signs and symbols. Literacy inevitably involves a much wider range of competencies which are entailed in making meaning. Reading or writing in any medium is bound to draw upon the reader's existing knowledge and previous experience, and on the social context, as well as on the ability to reflect, to evaluate, and to (re)produce.

Four key dimensions of visual literacy

In his comprehensive overview of research on literacy, David Barton defines the term as follows:

> a set of **social practices** associated with **particular symbol systems** and their related **technologies**. To be literate is to be **active**; it is to be **confident** within these practices[12]. (my emphases)

It is in the context of this pluralistic definition that I now want to ask what might it mean to be *visually* literate. How do children learn to 'read' and 'write' in visual images? Following Barton's definition, this question would appear to have four main dimensions.

1. **Social practices**
    A first issue to consider here is the function of the social and cultural context within which reading and writing take place. Given the global dominance of gigantic multinationals such as Time Warner, Rupert Murdoch's empire, or CNN, to what extent does children's understanding of the visual conventions of media texts depend on their familiarity with particularly Western forms and conventions? What other experiences, knowledge, or cultural understandings do children draw upon in order to make meaning from visual images? How are these influenced by social factors such as ethnicity, age, gender, and class? For example, one of the claims frequently made for media education is that its emphasis on primarily visual popular cultural forms is particularly empowering for students with limited spoken English. Yet as media teachers will testify, such students often experience enormous problems in making sense of unfamiliar cultural codes and practices; they may read media texts in diverse and often contradictory ways which challenge the conceptual frameworks on which orthodox media education is based. One aim of the case study described in this chapter, then, was to investigate these issues further by working with a group with a very diverse mix of ethnic backgrounds, languages, cultural experiences and academic abilities.

2. **Particular symbol systems**
    If, as has been argued, visual literacy depends on an understanding of a language system with its own culturally specific codes and conventions, in what ways is that understanding acquired and articulated? Some media teachers might argue, in ways not dissimilar from early Russian film theorists, that each genre has its own distinctive grammar and syntax which can be *taught* as a series of discrete skills – just as some English teachers believe that traditional grammar teaching is the best way to develop students' knowledge about language. On the other hand, it is often claimed that students bring with them to the classroom huge reserves of conceptual understanding and linguistic competence. How real is that understanding, how has it been acquired, and how effective are the classroom approaches we routinely use to extend it? For example, how effective are conventional approaches like storyboarding as a means of developing students' ability to 'think visually', or to construct coherent visual narratives? Or do such understandings develop invisibly or intuitively, as an inevitable consequence of the experience of production?

3. **The technologies of still and moving images**

   As noted above, it is common practice to introduce the key concepts of a Media Studies course through the close analysis of a photographic image. In fact, this may not be entirely for theoretical reasons; there are practical considerations as well. After all, the single image stays still, it is cheap, requires no black-out, no equipment or volume control. Yet in an era in which young people are familiar with a wider range of technologies than ever before, does this focus on the still image possess the same educational rationale? Does it actually make sense to start from the 'micro-discipline' of the photographic image – or would a simple video exercise provide equally valid learning experiences? The assumption that we *build up* meaning from still to moving images – recapitulating the history of technological changes – may well need to be questioned in the light of students' access to, and understanding of, the complex, visually dense narratives of the contemporary media.

4. **Active and confident practitioners**

   Finally, what should be the role of production in developing visual literacy? Barton's definition above suggests the importance of *active* and *confident* participation in literacy *practices*. It implies that literacy is an active participatory state which depends on the *interaction* between reading/understanding and writing/producing. This assumption is a cornerstone of good practice in mainstream English teaching, where the production of competent and confident writing is considered appropriate evidence of literacy skills. In media education terms, however, the active production of a final text is not always considered valid evidence of learning; as we have noted, students are generally required to articulate their conceptual understanding separately, and usually formally, in writing. So what kinds of broader media learning take place in the production of visual texts? In what ways might the production process actively *facilitate* visual literacy as opposed to simply *demonstrating* it where it already exists?

The school and its context

The case study described in this chapter was undertaken with year 7 pupils in a multi-ethnic inner London comprehensive. The school is set in the heart of a diverse community, located in a landscape of once-prized estates founded by the Church as an antidote to the Dickensian squalor of Nineteenth Century urban poverty. An experiment both in slum clearance and in social engineering, the area has always housed a traditional white working class community. Changes in immigration patterns and in the demography of the area are reflected in the school's intake, which is now substantially populated by Bengali children. Over twenty languages are represented, and there is a high turnover of refugee children, mainly from Somalia, many of whom enter the school with little or no experience of formal schooling and a bewildering diversity of learning needs and abilities. There is no tradition of core media work within the English curriculum, or a specialised Media Studies option within the school.

Framing the course

As a 'dry run' preliminary to the case study, I piloted a photo-story assignment with a year 7 group under the aegis of the Art Department. I wanted to observe the ways in which Art as a discipline – as opposed to English, or to Media Studies – might approach the task of story-telling through pictures. I was interested in investigating how far such work might either draw on, or seek to develop, a conceptual framework for the understanding of narrative structure, genre and film 'grammar'. I was also curious to see how far pupils' different cultural expectations and experiences might be visually incorporated into their work. I therefore tried to avoid conventional Media Studies-style preparatory work on genre and narrative. Over a single lesson, the group was shown a range of visual narratives from graphic novels, children's comics, photo-stories and cartoons, and we discussed the different forms of framing, graphic technique, and speech conventions. The students were then given a range of open-ended titles, and offered guidance on the process and function of storyboarding.

This class was smaller and less diverse than most others in the school. Their approach to the task was interesting because of the speed with which they identified genres in which they wished to work. The students in one group, working initially with the Art teacher, were determined to produce a horror story, and took their narrative cues from the visual sources and objects surrounding them in the art room. Thus, their fantasy narrative was woven, seemingly at random, around an iconic papier mache mask of a mythical beast, a huge plaster cast of a foot, and a variety of other non-naturalistic sculptures and artefacts. It was also ingeniously developed to integrate both the wheelchair of a disabled member of the group, cast as a witch, and the hyperactivity of a particularly mischievous pupil, who was wrapped from head to toe in bandages and cast as a mummy. The result was hilarious but incomprehensible, largely because the improvised nature of their narrative did not lend itself to the specific horror conventions within which they had chosen to work.

Another group set out explicitly to make a stalk 'n' slash movie ('We want it to be like *Childs Play 3*, Miss') but finished up with a classic gangster drama based on a revenge narrative. However, left to their own devices, despite their efficient division of labour, well-organised photo-shoot and apparently well-documented storyboard, they produced a final narrative filmed entirely and unintelligibly in long-shot.

Each group thus started off in a very different organisational fashion, but experienced similar logistical and conceptual difficulties – difficulties which many media teachers will recognise as typical of 'first-stage' media producers. These included problems of continuity from one shot to the next; an apparent reluctance to explore the potential of different types of shot and viewpoint; and difficulties in physically translating their understanding of formal conventions and generic codes into concrete camera shots, framing or angles. Although this group appeared to communicate well with each other, they also found it hard to 'anchor' their images with written text in the form of speech bubbles or captions, in order to clarify meaning and progress the narrative. Apart from the use of onomatopoeic sound-effects of the 'Bang!' and 'Aaaaaah!' variety, such written text as they used seemed to reflect the group's own internal understanding of the story rather than the need to explain it to a wider audience. There appeared to be a disjuncture between the acute observations about genre and form they were able to demonstrate in discussion and planning, and their ability to construct their narratives visually as they might be read and understood by others.

This pilot project was useful in confirming my own previous classroom experiences and identifying issues for further exploration. As a result I decided to focus the case study itself around a tighter structure with more explicit emphasis on concepts of narrative and genre, and to provide a more directive framework for plotting the production. Although I had tried (in vain) to leave behind my own background in the English curriculum, I was nevertheless conscious that my own preoccupations with genre, narrative, continuity, and audience were not familiar ones for my colleague from the Art Department. For her, the central emphasis was on the 'visually unique', the original or creative solution, rather than on ways of exploring, replicating, or consciously subverting the conventional[13]. Certainly there was an absence of analysis during the *process* of production which seemed to imply a different and more practice-led model.

Working with 7V

7V was a highly motivated class, with roughly equal numbers of boys and girls, and a vast diversity of learning needs – ranging from the academically able to recently arrived refugees with virtually no English, and a traveller child who had never attended school until the previous term. Bengali pupils were in the majority, although friendship groupings were not ethnically exclusive. Gender, however, was predictably a strongly divisive factor: only one working group in the class included both girls and boys, although girl groups 'borrowed' boys for their pictures and vice versa. Even here, though, Bengali groups were careful to recruit only non-Bengali members of the opposite sex. Despite a period of considerable unrest within the school, the class reflected a collaborative and supportive ethos, and considerable respect both for each other and for their work, reinforced by close and effective liaison between teacher and form tutor. The class's experienced English teacher was also supported by a student teacher who worked closely with a particularly disparate group of pupils.

My first priority, given the cultural diversity of the class, was to identify a base of shared experience. We needed also to focus on the concept of audience and readership, which had not been sufficiently foregrounded in the work with the Art group. In the previous term 7V had worked on the writing and illustrating of children's books. It seemed useful to build on this activity by focusing their production work explicitly around the concepts of *narrative* and *genre*. These concepts offered a clear context for the photostory task; and provided a basis for identifying the understandings and assumptions which were shared by the class.

The sequence of work

The unit began with some preliminary work from the English and Media Centre booklet *Making Stories* focusing on different kinds of written stories, drawing out ideas of genre, narrative structure, characters, places and events[14]. The students were then introduced to the idea of using pictures to tell a story, and the conventions of different forms of visual narrative. For this activity, groups of students worked on analysing single images drawn from sources ranging from Beatrix Potter, through American Superhero comics, to *Just Seventeen*. They were asked to analyse each picture in terms of the genre of story, intended audience, and what might happen next, drawing on visual and structural cues

– the framing of images, variations in scale and size of image, the direction of the eye across the frame, the shape and position of speech bubbles, etc.

They then progressed to a more extended photoplay narrative, using an example from an old *Grange Hill* annual. The task here was to read the first page in full, and comment on its conventions; and then to predict the remainder of the narrative from photocopies on which the speech bubbles had been blanked out, using the visual cues of body language and facial expression, eye-line and type of shot to help them read the meaning. Finally, the class completed the story by re-writing appropriate speech bubbles, and then compared their own versions with the original, finishing with a plenary report-back in which each group justified its predictions and explained the basis for their choices. They then progressed to work on their own photostories.

As with much introductory work of this nature, I had anticipated that its most important function would be diagnostic rather than educative, in that it would highlight or reinforce the pupils' existing understandings rather than teach 'new' knowledge. Despite some initial problems in finding terminology for the different genres of story we explored, it was clear that all the children in the group had a broad understanding of the concept of genre and related narrative conventions, and that this was largely due to their familiarity with televisual narrative. This was equally true both for prose extracts and for single images drawn from picture stories.

For the remainder of the unit, pupils worked in groups to script, shoot and mount a sequence of 16 photographs around a choice of pre-determined titles. These were chosen for their ambiguity and adaptability to a range of genres, and included topics like 'After School', 'On the Streets', 'Our Brilliant Adventure' and 'The Killers' – titles which suggested generic possibilities but were open enough to allow for the development of fantasy, autobiographical or thematic narratives. The students were inducted into the activity through a series of structured 'scaffolding' help-sheets which broke each stage of the task down into manageable steps.

The process

To begin with, the groups were asked to develop a very simple narrative outline and to identify characters, places and events which would feature in their story. Then they were required to break the outline down into 16 separate segments which would each represent a single shot. Finally, they were asked to storyboard each of their 16 shots in as much detail as possible, and to log on a separate sheet the components of each shot – who's in it, what they're doing, where it takes place, what sort of camera angle will be used, and whether any words are used, either as speech bubbles or as narrative comment. Each group would thus have a fairly comprehensive record of the thinking behind their chosen narrative, and a number of different opportunities to reflect on it or redraft it if necessary.

Having scripted in some detail, each group went off to shoot their storyboard as accurately as possible. They were also told that, should they need extra shots after the pictures were developed, they would have the option to take a few further fill-in shots. The thinking behind this latter option was to encourage students to distance themselves from their own familiarity with the plot, and to reflect upon how effectively the story had been told. I hoped that this would encourage a process of *re-drafting*, which is usually very hard to develop with visual texts. Interestingly, this option was not taken up, for reasons which will be discussed later.

Some initial reflections

While this scheme of work represents a fairly conventional English/media education approach to work around photostories, it differs in that the preparatory stages of scripting and storyboarding were unusually closely structured and monitored. I had originally intended to leave this process more open-ended, as with the Art group, in order to explore the students' generic and cultural influences. However, it soon became obvious that the diversity of linguistic ability and experience, and the dynamics of the class as a whole, would require a far more controlled and rigorous approach to the different stages of the activity. The process of transforming a simple narrative from third-person narration into a series of images which both internally embody appropriate generic conventions *and* function sequentially in terms of continuity and viewpoint is an exceptionally complex one for all children. We thought this might be even more difficult for pupils who were only just acquiring basic English language skills and who may have had very different understandings of genres and texts.

A further issue, which became apparent from the preliminary work with the Art group, was that the form of the photo-story is rather more problematic than I had imagined. While it has long been a staple part of the English and media teacher's repertoire, the photo-story is moving inexorably towards extinction as the *My Guys* and *True Romances* of the 1970s and 1980s have given way to more postmodern and post-feminist versions of narrative. Indeed, I had considerable difficulty in finding any contemporary examples to analyse. The nature of contemporary film and televisual narrative, and the digital technologies to which children now have access through computer games, are rooted firmly in the synthesis of sounds, images, and movement in time and space. Consequently the acquisition of skills employed in breaking down a visual narrative into individual components is not necessarily a 'natural' or logical process for young people whose media consumption is far more likely to involve multimedia experiences than the two-dimensional form of pictures and captions. In fact, most of the pupils in 7V had never seen a 'real' photostory before.

While I had anticipated that this might be a problem, I was also unsure what to expect of this particular age group, particularly when it came to reflection and re-drafting. There are, of course, no formal media education assessment criteria to apply to this age range. On one hand, I hoped that because the activity was undertaken so early in their secondary school career, the pupils might still be sufficiently uninhibited to respond positively to the opportunity to reflect open-endedly on their work. At the same time, the process of self-evaluation in media education is essentially a verbal one, and as such was likely to present considerable obstacles to many of the pupils in 7V.

Groupings and genres

7V formed working groups primarily on the basis of friendship, with minor intervention in order to ensure a spread of language ability and to avoid personality clashes. Five groups of varying heterogeneity emerged: two all-girl groups, one of which consisted entirely of close-knit high-achieving Bengali girls, two male groups, and a fifth, mixed, group composed of recent arrivals to the class, including three Somali refugee pupils and a traveller. The attendance of this latter group was erratic as all were withdrawn from the class at various points for individual language support.

This was 7V's first real experience of collaborative English work since entering secondary school. It was therefore a challenging and potentially intimidating experience which, as always with this sort of work, depended for its success on an effective group dynamic. Furthermore, the ability to agree on a genre seemed to be contingent upon shared understandings and experiences. Inevitably, right from the early planning stages, it was clear that the more homogeneous the group, the clearer and less troubled the decisions became. Finally, groups fared predictably better where there was fluent communication, whether in English or in their mother tongue, than those who had to negotiate language obstacles.

Perhaps more interesting than the ethnic or gender balance of the groups was the different processes by which they elected to work within a particular genre. One group of Bengali girls had determined to work on soap opera even before the project was fully under way, and unhesitatingly opted for a narrative based on their preferred characters in *Neighbours*. This was conceptualised in great detail:

> Hasnara: We could do like things happening around school, and someone gets a
>   low thing on her exam, and... OK listen, listen, listen. Now where do
>   you want it set? We've got four people, right? We've got Cody and
>   Debbie, we need a teacher, there's like this girl who's really mean, she's
>   trying to get the students to get low marks in their exams... So we're
>   going to have like Nazia, she's the naughty one, she can act like that.
>   We'll have some bits in the toilet because in Grange Hill and places like
>   that they all go to the toilets and smoke and that...

A second group, this time exclusively male, decided equally quickly to produce a vampire-style horror story, motivated initially by their own domestic viewing preferences and the recent availability on video of 'new wave' monster films such as Mary Shelley's *Frankenstein*, or Coppola's *Dracula*. This group had also shown considerable familiarity with the visual conventions of super-hero comics, which was to prove an important influence on their storyboarding abilities. Their choice was clinched by invaluable access to appropriate props and clothing provided by their unofficial leader (interestingly, the only member of the group who was not Bengali).

Each of these groups demonstrated a shared ability to conceptualise generic detail, whether in terms of characterisation or the appropriate use of visual conventions and iconography. In different ways, each developed a storyline which was both generically appropriate, yet also unresolved or incomplete – although a soap opera is of course an on-going narrative in any case.

For the remaining pupils the decision was more complex, though equally related to group dynamics and interpersonal relationships. Anne-Marie's all-girl group was dominated by her uneasy relationship with Natalie. Here, two assertive middle-class white girls with extensive reading histories and literary aspirations (Anne-Marie, a voracious reader and writer of romance, was currently writing a full-length pony novel reminiscent of Angela Brazil) spent several lessons wrangling over exactly what sorts of horror conventions they should aim for, and playing with a variety of options in terms of plot and mise-en-scene, the subtleties of which were not fully clear to the others in their group. Ultimately the ambition of their ideas exceeded their capabilities as producers, at the expense of a coherent narrative.

The 'language support' group had enormous interpersonal problems to negotiate, initially between the single boy, and the other two Somali girls in the group, whom he alternately teased, harassed, and flirted with. This unsettled grouping was further complicated by the prickly presence of an assertive girl from a traveller family who had entered the school entirely illiterate the previous term and was now approaching her work with ferocious pride. This group needed constant support from the student teacher. Initially it appeared that they would lack either the linguistic confidence or the negotiating skills to locate their story visually within any recognisable genre. However, they were eventually able to operate at the level of a simple kidnap narrative, and to demonstrate some understanding of the conventions of suspense.

The final group, to whom I will return later, constructed a narrative entirely around one pupil's basketball skills based on an amalgam of two school-based children's TV programmes (one British, the other the highly popular US sitcom *Saved By The Bell*), with heavy undertones of B-movie crime films. These students, who immediately conceived of the title *The Basketball Gangsters*, were unable to name any specific influences on their work, but quickly developed an extraordinarily complex plot with little apparent attention to any recognisable generic conventions. As we shall see, their final text reflects a serious attempt to represent sound and image in filmic ways despite the limitations of their given photo-story format.

From the very start, then, it seemed that choices had to be made between narrative and genre; either the genre came first, resulting in a partial or incomplete narrative, or the narrative was prioritised, with little apparent attention to generic detail. Meanwhile, the synopses themselves make interesting if elliptical reading. The italicised passages are extracts from the students' own written summaries; my comments simply fill in gaps.

The stories:

1. *Horror Begins After School* (Hana, Hana, Ruzi, Anne-Marie and Natalie).
   It all begins after school when all the children have gone home. One group gets locked in the school by themselves, and see weird events happenings, levitating chairs, etc. They then discover that a hundred years ago, something else strange happened... This sequence contains little action and even less dialogue, and many shots of a group of students hanging around the empty hall. The narrative hinges on a girl who was locked in alone and eventually died under the hall platform. This is finally revealed as a flashback by Anne-Marie, narrating in the year 2055.

2. *The Basketball Gangsters* (Mazid, Anru, Andre and Luke).
   Starring Anru as DJ, Luke as Ice, Mazid as Dick Tracy, Ruhal as Chink, and Andre as Criss Cross. Criss Cross, ace basketball star, is attacked and beaten up by a rival team jealous of his skills. They are caught by two female detectives, found guilty in court, and sentenced to prison. Meanwhile Criss Cross recovers and regains his strength. The villains are released in time to see him win yet again. They apologise and he agrees to coach them. This story incorporates an extremely ambitious range of live action shots and inventive use of mise-en-scene to recreate a chase sequence, the courtroom and a prison. The narrative begins and ends with a basketball game (we see the boys making peace, but no reference is made to the coaching arrangement)

3. *Kidnapped* (Martina, Abdo, Zam Zam and Amina).
   Tony, Peter and Lisa are friends. After school Lisa is kidnapped by the Coke machine and locked up in the old science lab. Tony and Peter search for her everywhere, and eventually ask a teacher to help them. They eventually find her. She is very frightened. The teacher catches the kidnapper. The search for the victim takes the boys from football practice to a variety of locations including the girls' toilets, the PE block and disused parts of the building.

4. *Dracula* (Justin, Abu, Akram, Khalique and Ruhel).
   Joe tells his mates Michael and David that he has found a haunted place. All three go to explore it and find themselves trapped in a sort of maze. They try to escape but behind every door there is a new monster. Their story deals with their successful confrontation with Dracula and Gruesome. To be continued. The encounter with Drac was shot almost entirely in semi-darkness in different parts of the school hall. Despite a definitive ending, the group saw this as an episode in a continuing story.

4. *Neighbours* (Hasnara, Bilkis, Nazia and Shahinoor).
   Debbie, Cody, Rick and Michael from Neighbours are revising for an exam. Meanwhile, another student, Hannah, is acting suspiciously. She follows them, and hides under the teacher's desk in the exam room. The pupils take their exam, and hand their papers in. Hannah steals Debbie and Cody's papers from the teacher's desk. She is caught by Sandra, who makes her return the papers. Hannah is scared. Meanwhile, the others are celebrating the end of the exam. What will happen next? This narrative existed in enormous detail in the group's heads, but was far more fully developed than the number of shots allowed. This led to some continuity problems, partly due to an unsuccessful attempt to represent parallel time and interwoven storylines.

In fact, despite our careful attempts to support the development of the narrative into individual shots, these synopses are hard to follow in written form, and are reconstructed from a combination of discussion, notes and storyboard description. For example, Luke orally described the opening of his group's narrative thus:

Luke:	Well, put it this way, us two are in one school and he's in another school. He keeps winning the tournament and our school gets jealous and they tell us that they'll give us money if we take him out. We knock out two kids that go to his school and we go into their class and take their language folders and all their books and go into their class so the teachers think we're in their school –
Andre:	and their uniforms, and their uniforms...
Luke:	and we go into the gym and we see you practising, and so he pulls out his gun, and he aims it at you.
Andre:	and he tries to shoot me, right, but I'm already up in the air and I just score –
Luke:	No, he throws a rope, and it catches you, and then when you come down he ties you up, and he aims a gun at your shoulder, so it won't kill you, and... and then you try to get up, and Amru blows your shoulder off, and you fall to the ground... and Andre loses a lot of blood, all guts spilling out...

Much of this personal investment in a classic 'boy's own' story failed to make its way into a written summary, let alone into the final photostory. Nevertheless, after some teacher intervention to clean up the bloodshed and break down the narrative, Luke's synopsis reads far more episodically and manageably:

> Criss Cross takes a 3-pointer in the match. Ice and DJ plan taking out Criss Cross. Beating up Justin and Masnu, sneaking round to the gym, and shooting Criss Cross, when detective comes. They are running from the detective, the doctors come, the criminals are caught. Criss Cross is in hospital. Trial for criminals; criminals in prison. Criss Cross comes back school and plays the big match. Criss Cross finishes his day with a lovely day (sic). Criss Cross gets his trophy.

This shift from spoken to written account demonstrates a classic distinction between the students' understanding of *story* – the events as they actually happened – and *narrative*, the re-ordering of events in sequence as they are to be told. Luke's original spoken account illustrates his abilities to tell the story – but not, as yet, to construct a narrative; while his written work certainly displays an increased control of the formal aspects of narrative: time, space and action.

Thinking in pictures: the storyboarding process

Although the guidance sheet we had prepared was undoubtedly valuable in helping the pupils to organise their ideas and break down their plot outlines into manageable visual segments equivalent to scenes, it was less useful in encouraging them to think in terms of concrete images. I had hoped that having to identify personnel, place, action and dialogue in each shot would help pupils to visualise more precisely the type of shot they wanted. Yet although they mapped out each segment conscientiously, it was clear they were thinking in terms of moving scenes rather than static images or freeze-frames which would represent them. Similarly, although we encouraged each group to go on 'recces' to seek out the exact location for each shot, they were reluctant to do this, instead citing broad areas of the school – the old Drama Studio, the Hall, the gym – rather than the precise geography and terrain of their mise-en-scene.

One example of this difficulty was the mismatch between the careful plotting of shots and angles logged on the planning sheets, and their actual visual reconstruction as the separate frames of the storyboard. However shots were described in writing, the storyboards themselves relied heavily on long shots, with tiny stick people lined up symmetrically in the far distance – a characteristic problem for first-time storyboarders. Even when this anomaly was pointed out, re-drafted storyboards rarely incorporated the use of close-ups, although they were frequently used in the actual shoots themselves

It was unclear how far this mismatch was simply down to the pupils' lack of confidence in their artistic abilities, or whether my supposedly reassuring protestations that artwork skills were not important in storyboarding were taken as license to ignore the rules. Alternatively, the act of storyboarding may just have been one process too many in a challenging sequence of activities; once the images had been mentally constructed, the fiddly business of sketching them out may have been redundant. Indeed, this reluctance is in many ways justified. However carefully images are planned on paper in low-tech work, a 'walk-through' on location with a video or still camera is

Fig. 2.1 *Dracula* storyboard: opening frames

often a far more effective and less tediously time-consuming way of revealing discontinuities, problems of framing and focus, and technical impossibilities[15].

I had also anticipated that there might be gender differences here. Would the girls' groups, who in discussion appeared to be paying far more attention to visual and narrative detail, be more successful in producing a functional storyboard? This was not borne out in practice. In fact, only one group did produce a series of anatomically accurate and lavishly detailed drawings, featuring not only highly appropriate use of camera shots and angles, but clear indication of different points of view, attention to light and darkness, and varied and interesting compositions within each frame. This was the boys' *Dracula* narrative, which, apart from continuity problems, seemed to represent a confident and sophisticated understanding of visual conventions and narrative momentum (see fig. 2.1). This was all the more notable because the group had appeared to negotiate so little during planning.

By contrast, the *Neighbours* group shared none of this visual confidence, despite their extensive and enthusiastic discussions of plot, personality and dialogue. Although their narrative was the most fully developed, they seemed to have little confidence in transferring their ideas into images, and made several false starts at their artwork:

> Hasnara: Do we really have to do this, miss? I'd much rather write it down like a
> story with words – we're good at that in this group!

While it could be argued that the horror genre is intrinsically more 'visual' than soap opera, the girls' reluctance to express themselves visually at this stage seemed less related to a lack of understanding of the visual codes of soap (the angst-ridden close-up, the two-shot and establishing cut-away), all of which did eventually appear in their finished text, than a lack of confidence in their own abilities to accurately represent a camera-eye view.

In a *real* school...

An issue which appeared to be a further complication, both at storyboard stage and later, was that of realism. Four of the five groups had opted for a school-based narrative, presumably because they thought it would make for an easier life; yet it was precisely this familiarity which they seemed to have problems in representing:

> Luke: In a *real* school people would be coming out of lessons and going to the toilet... How can we draw that? Anyway, if we show a body being dragged into the toilets, what if stupid people keep getting into our pictures?

In the same way, the *Neighbours* group went to great lengths to locate their story in a recognisable environment, including the school sign in their establishing shot, drafting in extras for background detail, and, in the sole use of close-up on their storyboard, reproducing a hand-written exam paper, captioned EXAM PAPER for authenticity. At the same time, they seemed unaware of the irony of a narrative involving the highly westernised teen personae of the *Neighbours* cast being played out by a mixed race group of whom half were wearing traditional shalwar kameez[16].

In this context, it is perhaps less surprising that the *Dracula* group were able to handle the storyboarding process more easily: their narrative depended on the suspension of disbelief rather than any requirement to reproduce the school environment realistically. Indeed, for this group, a Portacabin very easily became a haunted castle, a flowerbed the entrance to a dungeon, and the school hall Dracula's lair. What was interesting was the inconsistent ways in which they projected their own knowledge of generic conventions: props, lighting, body language and facial expression were all lovingly recreated, but within an entirely un-horror-like setting, which lent their work an almost surreal dimension. It would seem that the criterion of realism was applied very selectively here – an issue which will be discussed at greater length in Chapter 7.

Hearing the pictures

Another dimension of storyboarding is the construction of an aural commentary to accompany the images. This process is intended to indicate an anchoring soundtrack, rather than the accurate scripting and positioning of speech bubbles and narrative captions as for the production of the final photo-story. For 7V, however, the whole process of separating sound from image was fraught with difficulty. This was illustrated particularly by the basketball group's discussions in pre-planning, punctuated by bursts of rap and graphic sound effects:

> Luke: ...and Criss-Cross is going for the three-pointer and its a double-spin and – can he do it? –
>
> Andre: Boom shaka boom shaka (beat-box noises).
>
> Luke: ...and he's lost it – come on Crissy, neaooooooaw – and, YES!
>
> Andre: Yeaaaahhhh!

Here the students are clearly thinking in far more cinematic terms than this project requires. Each of their frames and its accompanying soundtracks – the running sports commentary, the cacophony of sound effects, and the additional use of music – is the equivalent to an extensive and action-packed scene: what this group is producing is a film-script rather than a photostory. So intertwined were sound and image that when they came to shoot their photographs, they insisted that a teacher drafted in to play the role of a sports reporter actually produced a running commentary throughout the first few shots – 'it kind of adds atmosphere if you can hear the pictures' (see fig. 2.2).

The shoot

While the storyboarding process clearly had considerable shortcomings in helping pupils to conceptualise the final product, it proved nevertheless a very useful preparation for the heart of the process – the photographic shoot. Indeed, so much of the thinking had already been done by the time each group went out with their SLR camera that even the most disorganised and unruly groups (the *Basketball* and *Kidnap* groups in particular) were transformed into efficient teams for the duration of the shoot. Three groups were each able to complete their 16 photographs within the space of a 55 minute lesson – a considerable achievement, given that these were Year 7 pupils with no previous experience of production work, nor an unblemished reputation for decorum. As Hasnara comments of the *Neighbours* shoot:

> It was difficult because it wasn't just drawing the pictures, everything had to be perfect, the right angle, the long shot... The difficulties were solved eventually, once it was on the storyboard it was easy to do when it came to the photo-session. I loved it, not disappointed!

On the other hand, the *Horror Begins After School* group, which had seemed so sensible and thoughtful in its planning, discovered they had virtually no story once they actually embarked on their shoot, and fell out over who should direct. The *Basketball* group, who for the most part restrained their more volatile excesses, fell prey to the seductive combination of an empty gym, a basketball and a seriously talented player, and insisted that all their photographs must be taken in action, necessitating repeated goal-scoring

Fig. 2.2 *Basketball Gangsters*: opening shot

and slow motion violence, which was predictably difficult to shoot. Nevertheless, the whole operation was unusually painless: the expected inter-group rivalry for access to the camera did not emerge, and even the normal peer group horseplay seemed curiously muted in the interests of getting the pictures done. I had anticipated some macho posturing and jockeying for camera use; but in fact all pupils of both sexes took at least one picture, and although no one single pupil was prepared to volunteer to be exclusive photographer, each group (with the exception of the *Kidnap* group) ended up with at least one 'expert' who could claim responsibility for a sequence of shots.

The ingenuity and speed with which each group was able to identify weaknesses in their original ideas when on location, and then find ways to re-frame particular shots was also impressive. Many shots had to be rethought because the photographer realised that the composition within the frame did not leave sufficient space for the insertion of speech bubbles. Huge swathes of the *Basketball* group's original narrative were axed without protest once they finally accepted that they were actually filming still images without sound, rather than the X-rated cinemascope production they had first developed. Where older students might have spent fruitless hours trying to salvage or reconstruct a misconceived image, 7V adjusted cheerfully to changes in scenario and personnel, recruited new classmates to replace absentee participants, and generally avoided the prima donna-ish responses which can make production work a teacher's nightmare at GCSE level.

Putting it all together: making meanings for readers or writers?

The developed photographs generated a huge sense of excitement and satisfaction. My worst fears – of illegible or unfocused prints, under- or over-exposure, mismanagement of the camera – were unfounded (and were actually almost impossible with the Year 7-proof equipment we used)[17]. Virtually none of the shots were unusable; many showed considerable ingenuity in exploiting inappropriate lighting, distance and perspective effectively; and many were very respectably composed. This was particularly true of the *Dracula* group's pictures, which had been shot in extreme haste in the wrong location, without the blackout they had originally planned for: as Justin said:

> We want it to look as if we're looming out of the darkness at them, and then the
> dawn breaks and it looks as if I'm just sort of melting away (see fig. 2.3).

We had arrived at an interesting and generally well-framed series of sequences; but would they tell their stories as planned? The task now was for each group to compare their sequence of photographs with their storyboards, identify differences, and point to areas where their original narrative was now unclear. At this point they had the opportunity to take more shots to re-establish their narrative, but this option was taken up only by Hana, who objected to her own expression in one close-up shot, and the *Dracula* group, who identified a missing 'establishing shot' too late to incorporate it. As a device to encourage critical reflection, this strategy did not work here: the pupils seemed far too proud of the transformation of their ideas from artwork to photograph to use this opportunity to re-draft their work.

This in itself was interesting on several counts. 7V seemed genuinely delighted with the results, despite initial embarrassment from several of the girls, and to want them to be shared with a wider audience. In my experience, this is less often the case with

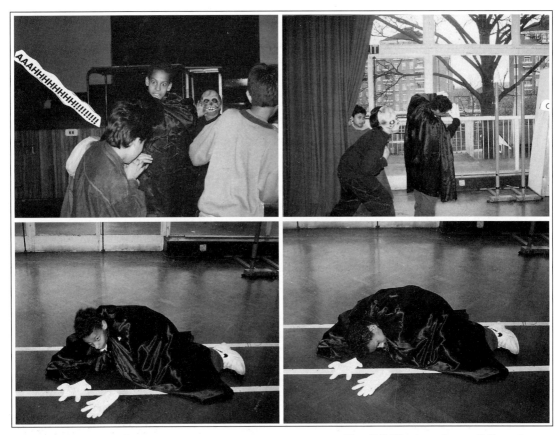

Fig. 2.3 Closing shots of *Dracula*

older students, who would inevitably have expressed embarrassment at the sight of their own images in contrived and melodramatic poses, and might have found ways of re-taking or subverting them prior to display.

Although it was apparent to us that in several cases there were serious flaws in the narrative which could easily have been rectified with the insertion of a few extra shots, or even judicious speech bubbles, these discontinuities were instantly dismissed by the pupils. This was particularly true of the *Basketball* story, which had been refined so much that it was incomprehensible in at least three places.

> JG: I'm not sure what's happening here – don't you think these shots are in the wrong order?
>
> Luke: No Miss, no, they're like that on the storyboard, see? Anyway, it makes sense to *us*, and we know what the story is, so it don't matter.
>
> Mazid: Anyway Andre's not here, and he's in that shot, so we can't change it anyway.
>
> JG: Well, I suppose you could get round it by putting in some extra speech bubbles here...
>
> Luke: Nah, we don't need 'em Miss. You said we have to try to tell the story without much words. Anyway we know what it means, leave it to us.

A reluctance to re-draft or to accept criticism is a common phenomenon with older students. While it may sometimes arise as a result of laziness, it can also reflect a sense of inadequacy or embarrassment; and in some instances, it seems to result from the way in which students' emotional investment in the production process leaves them drained. Sometimes, however, students are able to derive sufficient pleasure in their achievements, however imperfect, that they elect to preserve their work intact, whether or not it has meaning for a wider audience. My own sense was that this was Luke's response. His group was potentially the most disorganised and hyperactive in the class, incorporating an awesome melange of social disadvantage and learning and behavioural difficulties. Yet they were also the most noisily enthusiastic. The project as a whole was clearly an affirming and hugely enjoyable experience for them personally; perhaps it was asking too much to expect them to dilute its meanings in the interests of their readers.

Adding the anchorage

Similar issues arose when 7V began to lay out their photostories with speech balloons and captions. Although these had been fully positioned at the storyboard stage, there were many instances where the words – in conjunction with the images – simply did not work. In general, most groups significantly under-used verbal anchorage; compared to the examples they had studied in class, their own texts were remarkably thin on both dialogue and on the use of captioning devices. There was virtually no use of think bubbles, and such speech as existed was often unspecific, self-evident or redundant, as fig. 2.4 illustrates.

Fig. 2.4 Selected shots from *Basketball Gansters*

There seemed also to be a resistance to any form of anchorage which would distract from, or otherwise obscure, the composition of the pictures. This was particularly interesting in the case of the *Basketball* group, whose original narrative had been so filmic and whose images had been so integrally bound up with sound effects. When it came to representing sound in verbal terms, they categorically rejected the conventional option of producing sound-balloons or 'flashes' which visually represented aural effects. As Mazid argued: 'It would look too messy, Miss, we want ours to look really smart'.

Despite many suggestions for fleshing out dialogue in the interests of motivation or narrative clarity, few changes were made, even where groups tacitly acknowledged the shortcomings of their work. The students in the *Horror Begins After School* group were self-critical about their failure to construct a coherent narrative, and could see quite simple ways of salvaging their photostory with a different set of speech bubbles, but seemed to feel that deviating from their original narrative was a form of cheating:

Anne-Marie: Well, we didn't really know what we were doing; we hadn't really worked out what had happened properly, or what was going to happen.

Natalie: I think we did make it a bit better, but we couldn't really change the whole thing, it wouldn't have been fair.

The same was true for the use of narrative captions to indicate the passage of time, simultaneous events, or information unknown to the characters, which in several cases could have considerably improved the intelligibility of the product. It was not that Anne-Marie and Natalie failed to recognise the logic of such amendments: they were simply not motivated to make them.

One interpretation for this resistance to intervention might be that this project was one over which the pupils felt they could exercise an unusual degree of control and power. 7V had already become accustomed to regular and effective monitoring and support in English from a variety of sources. While they clearly welcomed this interest in their progress, the opportunity to perform on a non-verbal level may have been a liberating and empowering experience. It allowed them – possibly for the first time in secondary school – to concentrate on the process of *seeing*, and representing their own vision, rather than *being* seen.

Reading layouts

The layout and paste-up process was equally problematic. Earlier in the project pupils had seen a variety of layouts and formats, which we hoped might act as models or stimuli for their own finished work. These were entirely and quite consciously disregarded. While the images were mounted and annotated with extreme care and pride, there seemed to be very little reflection on the conventions or reading processes involved in making sense of photostories. While older students frequently experiment with overlapping or 'tumbling' images, three-dimensional graphics, or the use of colour, 7V categorically refused such suggestions. Apart from reading images from left to right with occasional arrows for support, they seemed to have little interest either in designing a format which guided the reader, or grouping the images in interesting or non-linear ways.

They did not ignore the reader totally, however. The two girls' groups both chose to lay out their images diagonally on the page, and to produce colourful title-pages lavishly illustrated with mini-icons and the names of the characters (though not the authors). The boys created eye-catching title captions presented in graffiti-like or horror-influenced scripts, complete with dripping blood or computer-game inspired cartoons – the sort of artwork which might be found on Year 7 exercise book covers and notice-boards anywhere in the country. There was thus a clear intention to attract readers in what seemed to be predictably gendered ways – even if the form of their appeal had little to do with mainstream examples of the photostory genre.

A lack of clarity about intended audience had emerged at the initial planning stage. Although we had talked at some length about different audiences for the examples we had considered in class, pupils seemed unable to conceive of appropriate audiences for their texts beyond 'people who like horror films' or 'students'. The *Basketball* group's confusion was typical:

JG:	Who's this story for, then? Who do you think would like it? What sort of people are you aiming it at?
Luke:	Somebody who's into sports and crime, who likes reading mystery books...
Andre:	No, boys between 12 and 19 who like sports and guns.
Luke:	What about girls? We need a girl in our group.
Andre:	No we don't. It doesn't matter if girls don't like it because you don't know if even boys are going to like it... we want to aim our story at everybody.

I would argue that for 7V the concept of a 'real' audience had little relevance to the project as a whole. Much as they valued the experience of production, the notion of amending their work to cater for an audience was an unnecessary additional diversion, possibly exacerbated by a lack of interest in the photostory form itself.

Reading the products

So far this account seems to have concentrated almost entirely on the enormous linguistic and conceptual challenges facing 7V. Yet to focus on the process without also evaluating the texts themselves is to underestimate the very significant issues raised by the work, and the diverse and interesting ways in which the pupils negotiated them. Four weeks of intensive, noisy and highly motivated work had yielded five entirely different photostories. All possessed some form of reasonably legible narrative and genre, and all demonstrated a considerable degree of technical competence. So what issues emerged from the products themselves, and what might they suggest in terms of the questions about visual literacy and learning posed in the introduction to this chapter?

Narrative structure: the sense of an ending

It is striking that only two out of the five narratives have a conventional beginning, middle and end; all the others are episodic and finish on cliff-hangers. While the option of a serial narrative was not originally included in the brief, it was an entirely appropriate device for the *Neighbours* group, working explicitly within the conventions of soap opera. The *Dracula* group, however, seemed to have constructed a reasonably 'finished' narrative based on binary oppositions, in which the 'good' youth overcome the 'evil' monsters. Yet they themselves seemed to see it as both complete – signalled by their end caption – and incomplete. They initially insisted on adding a 'To Be Continued' legend as if this was merely an opening scenario, a first stage in a continuing epic; we had to persuade them that in fact they had satisfactorily concluded their story. Conversely, Anne-Marie's group used the device of an unresolved enigma possibly to avoid confronting a lack of consensus in the group.

Interestingly, the two complete narratives were produced by the most disunited groups. In both cases, the existence of a conclusion was partly a reflection of a considerable degree of teacher support. Yet it is also related to the fact that, unlike the others, both these groups were working with 'mixed' narrative forms; and not within easily recognisable media genres. Perhaps, however, there are other hypotheses to be investigated here about the significance of completion. Is it an important measure of reassurance or closure for pupils grappling with language or conceptual difficulties? Could it be argued that more confident pupils may be more conscious of the shortcomings of their work, and that one solution is precisely to avoid narrative resolutions? What is the resonance of the sense of an ending for pupils at different stages of linguistic and emotional development? While major generalisations obviously cannot be drawn from the work of a single class, particularly one as atypical as 7V, the ability to construct – or, more importantly, to reject – an ending does seem to be a significant area for further research.

Gendered genres?

Unsurprisingly, 7V's narratives reflected gendered interests. In fact, these were less clear cut than usual in that the horror genre, traditionally seen as a male preserve, was adopted by groups of both sexes, although with rather different emphases. Both groups demonstrated considerable familiarity with formal conventions. However, the *Dracula* group concentrated on reproducing the visual iconography of classic Hammer horror – the use of darkness, stock Hammer characters, a highly traditional Dracula in full evening regalia complete with dripping fangs, elaborate make-up and dramatic posture; while the girls' group located the horror of their narrative in the contrast between the familiar environment of the school and mysterious events of the past. Their narrative seemed closer to the ethos of a children's television serial, comic or school story where 'normal everyday youngsters', meet the occult lurking behind the surface of 'normal everyday life'. Thus, other than the unexplained levitation of a chair, nothing explicit is physically revealed, and the suspense resides in the threats that are posed to an individual character in an isolated situation. There is little narrative action in the first four frames of their photoplay beyond constructing a sense of place and personalities; the middle section of the story focuses on one character's exploration of the unknown; and the final three frames establish a time frame and a narrative enigma, spoken direct to camera as if to subvert the expectations of readers. The *Dracula* narrative, on the other hand, avoids characterisation altogether, and focuses on the (undifferentiated) boys' quest and their struggle with evil – although they are untypically passive, and no physical violence is actually shown.

Elsewhere, gender almost over-determines narrative structure, most clearly in the work of the *Neighbours* and *Basketball* groups. Here, the predictably contrasting genres of soap and all-male action-adventure are linked by a shared theme – that of fair play. Both these texts are surprisingly moral; both deal with the implications of cheating. But while the *Neighbours* narrative focuses appropriately on the emotional dilemma, the solidarity of the friendship group, and the threat to their academic and personal well-being posed by an alienated pupil, the *Basketball* story is rooted in a male world of physical aggression, gangsterism, guns, and the strong arm of the law. Where the moral complexity of the *Neighbours* story remains unresolved – will Hannah get her comeuppance? – the *Basketball* scenario is neatly tied up, with Criss Cross miraculously recovering to reclaim his victory, the baddies well-punished, and peace made between warring factions.

I would argue that these are variations on recognisable 'school story' themes of loyalty, jealousy and honesty, tackled in typically gendered ways, from initial scenario to narrative resolution (or lack thereof). It is interesting to speculate where the students might have encountered such stories, since they seem in many ways to be closer to the traditional *Fifth Form at Mallory Towers* novels than the contemporary narratives from which most photostories are derived. Nevertheless, there are important questions to be raised here about the relationships between the students' understandings of genre and narrative form and their wider sense of social and cultural identity.

Identification – putting yourself in the picture?

As I have suggested, visual literacy is intimately related to the social and cultural context. So to what extent does 7V's work reflect the influence of their mother tongue languages and home cultures, and in particular their previous experience of media consumption? Several issues are particularly striking here. Firstly, it is notable that in every group, despite the diverse ethnicities of the pupils, the characters are all given Western names. None of the students was able to explain this fully, although Hasnara may have got closest in rationalising her group's choice of *Neighbours* characters:

> We just like them, but we don't want to *be* like them. That's why we're wearing our own clothes, not dressing up.

This is a familiar phenomenon which will be recognised by most English teachers with a high proportion of bilingual students. On one level, it may simply reflect the fact that working within the conventions of Western forms and genres naturally implies Western names and characters, as with the *Dracula* and *Neighbours* groups. However, it may also illustrate a more fundamental impulse to identify with – and to be *seen* to be identified with – the mainstream culture. After all, this project was undertaken in an *English* lesson, whose primary function as far as the pupils are concerned is to enable them to communicate sufficiently fluently to assimilate into the culture of the school. Indeed, at the start of the project, when I asked pupils why they thought we were doing this type of work in English, they automatically assumed that its function was primarily to develop their language skills; and although I spent some time with each group explaining my interest in their work from a media education perspective, I'm still not convinced that they entirely believed me[18].

What 7V's work does *not* appear to demonstrate is evidence of the pupils' conscious use or recycling of mother-tongue media genres or cultural influences beyond those of the mainstream Western media. I wondered, for example, how far the *Dracula* group's classic 'quest' narrative might also have drawn unconsciously on similar mythic elements in Hindi films; but they were adamant that their sole influence was their shared interest in horror. I talked with both groups and individuals about their home media consumption and its influence on their work; and they were offered opportunities to reflect on the significance of their choices of genre and narrative in a self-evaluation exercise at the end of the project. In all of these situations, they clearly saw the object of the activity as being to work within a particular set of media conventions, developing skills in story-telling, genre, and image construction.

Nevertheless there is also a sense in which each group seemed to appropriate elements of genre and recycle them imaginatively for their own purposes. During the course of the project the school was the focus of considerable racial hostility, which affected many of its pupils and their families. I was initially surprised that so little of this tension had apparently filtered into 7V's narratives. Indeed, we had deliberately selected titles which would allow them to draw on personal experience if they so wished. However, closer analysis of the work might reveal a deeper level of meaning and a reconfiguration of pupils' fantasies or fears.

It might, for example, be possible to read the *Kidnap* group's simple but poignant narrative as symptomatic of their own status as threatened outsiders. At the risk of psychodynamic exaggeration, it could be argued that their photostory is a metaphor for their own alienation as newcomers, disempowered by lack of access to the language of the rest of the class. This interpretation is strengthened by the careful plotting and framing of the individual images of their narrative, which more than any other group emphasised perspective, isolation and a sense of enclosure and claustrophobia. It's easy, of course, to mistake happy coincidences for intentionality, and it must be said that the group did not themselves photograph the majority of their chosen images. However, they were most vociferous about the elements and angles they wanted to include in each shot, and their locations – the toilets, doorways, stairwells and deserted corridors – were explicitly chosen to reflect the less acceptable spaces of the school environment (see fig. 2.5).

Indeed, I would argue that this work did offer opportunities for explicit emotional involvement. The most obvious example here is the *Basketball* group. Not only was the entire scenario built around Andre's prodigious sporting skills, but each member of the group developed a distinctive persona with which he came to identify totally – including the baddies, whose Tarantino-style performance was positively Stanislavskian. Their identification reached a point where the group claimed to be unable to proceed to the paste-up stage because Andre was temporarily absent and thus unavailable to script his own speech balloons.

However, one of the most striking absences in the work as a whole is that of parody. Although there are moments of (often unintended) humour and the occasional joke, what this body of work lacks is the sort of tongue-in-cheek pastiching of form, genre and characterisation which so often typifies the work of older students, and which is discussed at length in chapters 5 and 6 of this book. While the on-going planning and production generated a great deal of horseplay, mickey-taking and laughter, none of

Fig. 2.5 Selected shots from *Kidnap*

this surfaced in the final photostories. They are all about *serious* play – the positioning of the self in 'grown-up' stories with cause and effect and moral implications – but without the dimension of irony or critical distance. In general, the finished work shows little evidence of the de-centering or distanciation usually manifested in humorous or self-deprecating pastiche by Year 10 or 11 students. Again, this may be significantly related to the students' view of English as a 'serious' and worthwhile subject

What did 7V think they learned from the photostory project?

Ultimately, it may prove extremely difficult to identify the ways in which students learn to read and write in visual images. How do pupils come to understand what makes a 'good' composition? How do they acquire a visual 'eye' for detail and framing? How do they use their ability to read images in developing their skills as writers? In the last resort, it is impossible to know whether the Bengali boys' artwork skills in the *Dracula* storyboard were the result of some inherited visual sensibilities, culturally determined, or the product of sustained analysis of comic-book narratives and horror movies; the boys themselves simply accepted their skills and got on with exercising them. Similarly, it is tempting to reconstruct deliberate intention behind some of the strongest images produced – for example, the single close-up shot of Hasnara's hand stealing the exam papers in the *Neighbours* photostory, or the *Kidnap* group's image of the victim framed in the porthole window of the locked classroom (see figs. 2.6 and 2.7). In fact, however, the pupils themselves were unable to explain what motivated the composition and framing of these shots; they were produced 'intuitively' and from a position of experimentation rather than conscious knowledge.

It is primarily to the students' talk that we must look if we are to understand how they made sense of the project, and what they themselves felt they had learned from it. As the above extracts would suggest, the talk that took place was so wide-ranging and energetic that it is difficult to reproduce. Some groups conducted their planning and negotiation in mother tongue, others in the disorganised discourse typical of excited year 7s; while others were so locked into the specifics of their work that their discussion was unintelligible to the outsider. Yet across the range of 7V's unreservedly positive comments, several themes emerge. Firstly, enormous value is placed on the collaborative nature of the work, and the liberation and support provided by working with friends:

Fig. 2.6 Selected shots from *Neighbours*

Fig. 2.7 *Kidnap* victim

> One person didn't just talk and give the ideas, everyone distributed (sic)... I was
> so surprised that everyone was working extremely hard... so that was brilliant
> because if we didn't work together as well as this, we wouldn't have come this
> far.

This is of course a familiar refrain from students of all ages, but it was clear that for
many pupils in 7V the social dimension of collaboration contributed to a genuine sense
of empowerment.

Secondly, there is a major emphasis here on acquiring new technical skills and a
language with which to describe them; and of getting a handle on the ways in which
images work. Although this is again a recurrent response to successful practical work,
7V's enthusiasm initially surprised me, given that the technology was in fact a foolproof
SLR camera, possibly considerably inferior to the ones in their own homes, in which
they received very little formal tuition. Nevertheless, every pupil seemed to feel that
they had learned a great deal about photographic codes and techniques, and for them
this form of instrumental knowledge was the central focus of the exercise. My
hypothesis is that in fact it was the combination of access to camera *plus* friends *plus*
the invitation to structured play with preferred genres which so strongly captured their
imaginations – in other words, a curricular approach which simultaneously (and very
unusually) validated their own cultural interests, prioritised social interaction and
offered new status and knowledge on the basis of existing skills.

Perhaps the most revealing comment comes from Hasnara, one of the most
conscientious and academically able pupils in the class, and the lynch-pin of the
Neighbours group:

> Yes, I think I learnt a lot more about different types of story during the
> photostory, I've learnt how to tell stories in pictures, about the different types
> of shot and putting them together... but the best part of the photostory was the
> shooting, because it's *different from writing and reading* (my italics).

However limited, I believe these are the observations of an active and confident
emergent literacy practitioner. In a sense, the central task for media educators is to
identify the strategies which will help Hasnara reflect on and exploit that 'difference'.

Rethinking the photostory

We had chosen to work with the photostory format both as an example of conventional
practice in media education, and because it seemed to offer a way of investigating the
development of visual literacy. As I have noted, it became clear very early on that the
form in itself was problematic both in terms of its lack of relevance for the pupils, and
in the difficulties it posed for the exploration of genre. In effect, the activity required
three discrete sets of abilities: control of the photographic technology, and of the
various stages of the production process; an understanding of the photostory format,
and of the ways in which it is read; and the more general ability to construct an
appropriate generic narrative. Add to these the usual requirement to produce a text
which creates appropriate meaning for a specific audience, and it becomes clear that
these are challenging and complex demands, which involve a high order of critical
analysis, reflection and technical competence if they are to be effectively combined.

In this sense 7V's finished texts represent the limitations and weaknesses of the task. Each group was forced to make compromises, and to prioritise one or other of the variables at the expense of others. The *Neighbours* group, for example, constructed a narrative which demonstrates an implicit understanding of the conventions not only of soap in general, but also of their own chosen soap: the tight-knit friendship group, the naturalistic context, the moral dilemma, the cliff-hanger. Yet their soap bears little resemblance either to freeze-frame moments of an episode of *Neighbours*, or to a teenage magazine photostory based on it. At the other end of the scale, the *Kidnap* group produced a competent and concise narrative which cannot be precisely located in any particular media genre. None of the finished texts really took on board the visual coherence of the photostory – yet all incorporated selected conventions and reflected a degree of competence in photographic skills.

One possible conclusion here might be that the form of the photostory is in fact a kind of red herring – a diversion which is as distracting as it is empowering. As discussed above, the rationale for using the photostory form is based largely on the application of semiotic analysis. It might appear to make sense to work initially in a form which allows students to break sequences and images down into their basic constituent elements; and which offers them a degree of control and physical manageability. After all, movement, sound and editing can always be tackled later on, with more sophisticated technology. Yet this of course presumes that these elements are assembled in a particular sequence, as though they were a series of building blocks – a view which, as I have implied, is certainly questionable. Perhaps the main problem here, however, is that for many students there *is* no 'later on'. In many areas of the curriculum (English included), the photostory, image sequence or comic strip will constitute the sum total of their production experience. Students may never be offered the opportunity to *develop* the visual skills they acquire from these experiences in making media texts which more closely represent their own media and cultural interests. At best, the photostory should be seen as a first stage in a recursive process of visual investigation, which must be revisited and extended through production experience in increasingly complex technologies. Yet in retrospect, 7V might have been equally well served by the opportunity to produce simple video sequences, edited in camera, such as trailers or opening sequences. Despite its apparently greater complexity, this might have enabled them to explore generic and narrative conventions in a 'real' media form rather than confining them to the artificial language of a defunct and rather alien format.

Some conclusions: reading, writing and reflection

So how far did this project enable 7V to progress along the path to visual literacy? There is little doubt that the *process* of photostory production was valuable – not least in terms of the social benefits that derived from collaborative communication in a primarily non-verbal medium. It could also be argued that in terms of Barton's emphasis on 'particular symbol systems and their related technologies', 7V have come a long way. There is evidence that our scaffolding activities did seem to offer students a manageable route from devising a story to structuring a visual narrative. Similarly, the early work exploring the effects of mise-en-scene, camera angles and narrative continuity provided a useful framework for closer analysis, which in turn appeared to feed into their production work.

However, in terms of the other key issues raised in my introduction, a number of questions remain unanswered – questions which will resurface in different contexts in the chapters that follow. Firstly, there are significant questions to be asked about the concept of literacy as a *social practice*, and the influence of ethnicity, gender and other social differences, which this case study has only begun to explore. Issues such as the 'gendering' of particular technical competencies, from storyboarding to camera skills; the relationship between students' cultural backgrounds and their perceptions of genre; and the ways in which class, ethnic and gender interests might determine students' understanding of narrative structure, all demand fuller exploration.

A related issue which remains unresolved is that of audience, a concept with which 7V had yet to get to grips. Throughout their work, they showed considerable resistance to re-drafting and adapting their own shared stories for others to read. It could be argued that, with the perspicuity (or cynicism) usually shown by older students, 7V were aware that in a sense this work was not 'real' – that they were producing their photostories only for themselves and each other, rather than for a wider audience. They certainly seemed to have no problem with the unfinished 'look' of their final texts, nor with the fact that their work would never be circulated to a wider readership. By the same token, the question of progression and development in itself requires closer scrutiny. 7V's resistance to formal evaluation and redrafting suggests (unsurprisingly) that it may be harder for this particular age-group than for older students to 'de-centre' and read their own texts from an outsider's point of view. Are the processes of distanciation and objective reflection acquired simply through practice, over time – or can they be *taught* as a necessary adjunct to the 'technical' skills of image analysis and genre recognition?

In addition, we need to explore far more fully the sequence or chronology through which particular visual skills, concepts and understandings are developed, and the means through which students can best acquire them. It would seem to make sense to argue that visual literacy is acquired *recursively*: it involves drawing out and making explicit what students already understand, and then revisiting and reinforcing that understanding at different levels, across a range of different media, employing increasingly complex tasks and technologies[19]. The work with 7V would suggest that while there may not be an obvious sequence to the ways in which students come to understand concepts such as genre and narrative, the analytic and practical skills through which they acquire them do need to be developed gradually in a structured way.

What are we to make, though, of Barton's final claim that 'To be literate is to be active; it is to be confident within these practices'? In what ways can we see the evidence of active and confident practice in 7V's work? What these pupils clearly demonstrated in the final stages of their work was the ability to *read* visual images. For example, they were able to identify the appropriate point for a long shot or a close-up; to predict how a shot should be framed in order to allow room for the insertion of speech bubbles; to use or avoid the effects of dim lighting or bright sunshine; to identify the effects of a high- or low-angled shot; and so on. What their work did *not* necessarily show was how far they had actively become *writers* in images; and in part this was because they had not yet acquired an ability to reflect on, and to articulate, the reasons for their decisions or the consequences they may have had. This may in itself be unsurprising. As we shall see in later chapters, these analytic and discursive skills are often beyond the reach of much older and more linguistically competent students; and there remain considerable difficulties in ensuring that this kind of reflection is meaningful and effective. Nevertheless, we would argue that the requirement to be 'active and confident' in the practices of visual literacy must involve some form of explicit reflection, which goes beyond the text itself – reflection which, for 7V, was only beginning to emerge.

Notes

1   See Messaris (1994) for a discussion of this history.
2   The Odessa steps sequence in Eisenstein's 1925 agit-prop classic is frequently invoked in Film and Media Studies to demonstrate the ways in which cutting together disparate images can produce new ideas as a result of the 'collision' between them.
3   See Gauthier (n.d.) and Golay (1971).
4   See Donald (1977).
5   Bethell (1981).
6   See Moy and Raleigh (1984).
7   DfE (1994), page 6.
8   Carroll (unpublished paper).
9   Allen (1994).
10 One obvious – but often neglected – point here is that the 'media' are not solely 'visual'.
11 Buckingham (1993b).
12 Barton (1994).
13 This latter, more analytic, aspect of the Art curriculum might be located in other forms of practice such as Critical Studies (see Allen 1992b) tackled with older students, or restricted to a post-production de-briefing or 'crit'.
14 Mellor et al (1984).
15 The use of digital cameras such as the Canon Ion, which has recently been widely adopted by some media teachers for storyboarding purposes, demonstrates a combination of the recce, the storyboard and the Polaroid; instant, re-cyclable and accurate, it provides a series of frozen video images which can be immediately re-sequenced, edited or re-shot as a template for the 'real' shoot.
16 See Gillespie (1995) for an analysis of the special attraction of soaps for British/Asian communities.
17 The camera used here was a Canon EOS 100, an autofocus SLR with automatic zoom lens and flash. It was set up on full auto setting, which allowed instant point-and-shoot operation.
18 It's also interesting to note that when I tried out the project with the Art group, the pupils actually elected to give their characters their own names. See Gillespie *op cit.*
19 See the conclusion to Buckingham (1990); and Buckingham & Sefton-Green (1994), Chapter 8.

Chapter 3

New Models for Old? English Goes Multimedia

The relationship between technology and creativity is a key theme in all media work. Of course, the ability to undertake practical work in the first place is largely determined by the cost and accessibility of media production equipment. For example, technological developments in video at the end of the 1970s brought 'film' making within the reach of most schools; and subsequent technological changes have played a major role in the growth of media education in general. However, as we have argued, such technology is often used for instrumental purposes. There is an obvious temptation for schools to buy expensive equipment and then invent media projects in order to show off the special effects, rather than to develop students' understanding of the media themselves. By contrast, it is quite possible to do practical work that develops students' knowledge of the media without requiring sophisticated equipment at all – for example through 'cut-and-paste' activities like photomontage or the narrative sequencing exercise *The Visit*.

As we have noted, practical work in film education dates back at least forty years. However, even in the early days, critics were often suspicious of the ends to which technology might be put. For example, in 1964, Roy Knight, one of pioneers of this work, wrote: 'anything that savours of playing around with a camera or uncritical indulgence in the excitements of the beach movie is likely to be ... dangerous'[1]. While contemporary media educators might not use quite such loaded terms, a crucial distinction remains between popular recreational uses of technology and what are seen to be 'critical' and educational ones. At that time, such arguments were also motivated by a concern about whether media technology could allow for true 'creative expression'. While nobody would now dispute the 'artistic' dimensions of film and photography, there is also a widespread feeling that media technology is 'impersonal' and difficult to use. Focusing rings, switches and computer keyboards are not granted the prosthetic status accorded to the artists' sable brush or the writer's quill.

Whereas 'older' technologies such as film and video have gradually been granted due status as potentially creative tools, the computer has now become the contentious machine in this ongoing struggle for aesthetic recognition. In particular, the development of *multimedia* has made the computer less of a number crunching technology and more of a creative tool. Multimedia is one of the buzz phrases of the nineties. It is part of the broad convergence of information and communication technologies which has been growing apace in recent years. Essentially, multimedia offers the possibility of encoding different kinds of analogue information – written text, sounds (such as music and speech) and images (including moving images) – in digital form, so that they can be handled by the computer. Thus, it is possible to 'scan' still images or frames of video, or to 'sample' musical sounds, and then use the computer to edit, combine and manipulate them. Some programmes also make multimedia 'authoring' possible. This refers to the creation of 'interactive' products, such as CD-ROM 'books' or adventure games, which combine all kinds of multi-media effects in a single text[2]. Until recently, these possibilities were only available to professional media producers with access to expensive and complex technology. Yet they are now increasingly accessible to users of personal computers (PCs), both in education and in the home.

This chapter will consider production work using new multimedia technologies carried out in mainstream English lessons. We set out to explore students' uses of this new technology for a variety of reasons. First, long term trends in commercial media production indicate that the digital processes associated with multimedia are becoming the dominant production practice. For example, the editing skills of the film or video 'cutting room' are being replaced by what is known as non-linear editing. Instead of cutting together film on a frame-by-frame basis, the whole process of editing can now be done on a computer which can manipulate the images and sounds at the same time as subjecting them to a wide range of special effects. From a broadly vocational and skills-based perspective therefore, this kind of work could offer a useful introduction to current industry practice.

Secondly, we hypothesised that the technology itself might make explicit aspects of media production that are more 'hidden away' in conventional (analogue) technologies. For example, we wondered whether introducing students to non-linear editing might enable them to get closer to the actual decisions made in the editing process than they would through using conventional editing equipment. Similarly, because multimedia image manipulation programs allow for any graphic element of the picture to be manipulated, in terms of size, colour or text, we were interested in how this might affect students' selection and combination of images when it came to design work.

Thirdly, the computer screen is increasingly replacing the television screen as the place where young people *consume* media products, from games to 'interactive' books and films. Multimedia formats are a developing medium in their own right. And just as practical work in photography or video seeks to build upon young people's experience as consumers of those media, the same will increasingly be the case with work in this area. The question for us as media educators is how young people's experiences of being multimedia consumers might inform their work as multimedia creators.

English and new literacies

The fact that this work took place during English lessons also raises some fundamental questions about the relationships between media education and its 'parent' discipline. Teaching about the media has, of course, been an element of mainstream English for decades. Most English teachers are likely to teach about aspects such as newspapers, advertising, posters or magazines, using practical as well as critical approaches. The current National Curriculum for English also includes a small but compulsory component of media work; and there is a wide range of media education teaching materials specifically designed for English teachers.

Activities such as designing book jackets and posters, or genre studies of horror or romance, have become fairly commonplace in most schools as a result of the broader approach to the study of books described in the Cox report and disseminated through the LINC (Language in the National Curriculum) project. Although they are not always identified as 'media education', it is important to recognise that such activities are as much examples of media production as the more complex video work described elsewhere in this book. However, what is particularly interesting about these kinds of activities is the way their pedagogic focus is altered when they take place in English. Thus, producing book covers within English might be used as a way of focusing students on the content of the book under discussion – in effect, as another means of developing literary appreciation. By contrast, in Media Studies it would be used as part of a wider study of the processes of book production, and of the ways in which the publishing industry targets potential readers. In addition, we suspect that media teachers would be more likely to require students to *reflect critically* on their practical work in written form. By contrast, in English, as in Art, being able to 'do' the task is often seen to be enough[3].

Yet apart from the technology itself, the kind of work we describe here would not be out of place in any English department around the country. Indeed, while multimedia might lend a degree of superficial glamour, it too is in the process of becoming standardised. While it might seem advanced, the current rate of technological change means that work of this kind will most probably become commonplace by the end of the century.

As we argued in the introduction, practical media work can in itself be seen as a kind of 'writing'. Of course, the use of such linguistic metaphors is not without its theoretical problems[4], although in many ways it remains productive. For example, the processes by which students can take and mount photographs that reflect their perspectives and concerns are strongly reminiscent of the expressive purposes of creative writing[5]. The strategic construction of images has many parallels with the ways in which we invite students to consider the effect of voice and register on potential readers and audiences. And the talk that surrounds the photographs is very similar to that which accompanies the drafting and redrafting of written texts. In all these respects, we are implicitly regarding writing as an active, social process, whose meaning is located in specific social settings and relationships, rather than something confined to a particular technology such as pen and paper. Using English as the subject base for this work thus enabled us to explore further this expanded notion of writing.

There is, of course, a connection here with the notion that we are entering a new era of 'digital literacy'. While it is a much trumpeted phrase, the meaning of 'digital literacy' (like that of 'visual literacy'[1]) is still open to debate[6]. Nevertheless, as we have described in the previous chapter, recent research has pointed to the need for a broader definition of the term, which acknowledges that literacy is not a question of abstract decoding skills, but is embedded within particular social relationships and practices. The nature of literacy – or more accurately of litera*cies* – is culturally and historically diverse and changeable. Any contemporary definition of the concept must include the understandings and competencies that are developed in relation to 'new' communications technologies, in addition to 'older' technologies such as writing and print. We want to use this broader concept of literacy here in order to encompass texts in a whole range of media; and to include an equally wide range of interpretative processes, from 'reading' print to 'reading' images or 'playing' video games[7]. 'Reading' and 'writing' at the computer screen can therefore mean many things, from deciphering words to producing and manipulating moving images.

Developing multimedia in practice

The mixed ability girls' school in which this project was set had successfully applied for Technical and Vocational Initiative (TVI) funding to introduce Information Technology (IT) into an arts area of the curriculum. This in itself was considered an unusual use of IT within the borough. The English department and the IT co-ordinator wanted to devise work to meet objectives across a range of National Curriculum subjects and attainment targets. On the other hand, as the researcher, I wanted to implement projects that derived from the best tradition of practical media production work. The three post holders in the English department, the 'co-ordinator of resources', the IT technician and myself all devised the work together.

As the technology we used will be described in detail and is so obviously important to the purpose of this project, it is worthwhile briefly describing the school's resources. The TVI funding had supplemented a suite of Apple Macs with a range of software and a single more powerful machine. However, although the school's suite consisted of fifteen machines, only three were powerful enough for image manipulation work. Four others allowed for basic multimedia authoring. Despite all this, we were constantly aware that we had limited storage space (hard disc memory size); and although multimedia production is quite easy to carry out on Macs, images and sound are greedy for memory. A recent HMI/OFSTED inspection at the school had suggested that its 'below average' provision was a key area for action; so although the TVI funding had enabled the purchase of some dedicated equipment, this school did not have any special advantages with regards to IT.

Students were introduced to integrated packages, mainly word processing, from year seven, although as in most schools the teaching of such a cross-curricular skill tended to fall between departments. While the school is committed to delivering IT throughout the curriculum, students' experience of it was inconsistent and partial. Using multimedia in this project therefore raised the question of the *transferability* of computer skills across different curriculum contexts – and indeed across different software programs. For example, the commands 'cut' and 'paste' can be applied to words, images, parts of images and even movie clips. Within the context of the whole school curriculum, one might expect there to be some progression and commonalty in the use of a range of computer-based activities. This in itself is significantly different from the ways in which young people learn how to use other forms of media technology: for example, video cameras might only have been encountered in leisure contexts, such as making home movies, rather than elsewhere in school.

We worked with three age groups: years 7, 8 and 10. With the youngest age group, we decided to explore a program called *Morph*. This transforms one image into another relatively smoothly, thus giving the impression that faces or objects can metamorphose in front of your eyes (see fig. 3.1). This process is relatively common in Hollywood films and adverts: the special effects in the film *Terminator 2* and Michael Jackson's *Black or White* video are perhaps some of the best known examples[8].

Whilst we agreed that this process of transforming or merging images was highly suggestive, it was by no means clear *what* it suggested. The program can create eerie and subversive effects; seeing one's face metamorphose into an animal is bizarre, especially as the film can be stopped at any point leaving a mutation for all to see. However, we realised that special effects for their own sake, or even on the level of what is known as photo-therapy[9], do not necessarily serve any obvious pedagogical function. It was not easy to see how it could be used within, or in addition to, existing units of English work. Eventually, with some caution, we decided to include it as part of a standard year 7 unit, the *Myself* project.

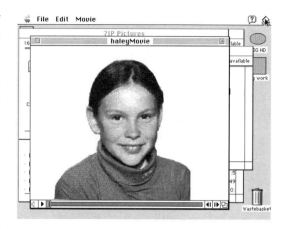

This project is composed of a series of activities all revolving around aspects of the self, from gathering factual statistics to writing memories and family histories. It is a popular topic which is common in year seven as a way of encouraging students to reflect on their growth as they start secondary school. We thought the morphing could be used in two ways: either getting the students to transform themselves into a fantasy figure, such as a loved pop star; or using the program as a way of exploring family resemblances. This latter idea derives from the work of *avant garde* artists and, as we subsequently discovered, has even been used in the American courts as a method of determining paternity. Our *Morph* activity required students to bring in images of themselves and members of their family. In pairs, they would be taught how to use the program and subsequently asked to write up a description of their features, in the mode of a nineteenth century novelist.

The second project was with year 8 students. Here we wanted to use *hypertext* as a way of exploring narrative. Hypertext is perhaps best defined as non-sequential narrative; but it also refers to the process whereby readers can determine their own

Fig. 3.1 Morphing in action

versions of a text by the routes they follow through it[10]. It allows for links to be made between virtually any point in a text and another, or even between text, sound, image or digitised film. Most hypertexts are, in a way, extended databases and are used for the storage of information. A good example of a hypertext on CD-ROM is the commercially available teaching pack *The Crucible*. This opens with an image positioning the reader in a theatre foyer. On the walls are posters advertising an interview with Arthur Miller or 'Smash Hits of the 1950's'. There is a foyer, bookstore and doors to the auditorium, the gallery and the dressing room. Click the mouse on any of these and the reader gains access to large amount of information about aspects of the play, the playwright, the fifties and so on. This kind of hypertext format is also distinguished by the use of multimedia, since image, text and sound can be all stored on the computer. Thus the section called 'the dressing room' introduces you to a screen on which are arranged portrait images of the characters taken from a recent production by the Young Vic. Click the mouse on one of the pictures and it is possible to watch and listen to pre-recorded interviews on film where the actors give their interpretations of their role.

The notion of hypertext fits well with projects that encourage students to write extended fictions and with assignments which focus on narrative structure. Indeed, many critics now claim that hypertext itself is a qualitatively new way in which narrative can be structured[11]. It is, they argue, a radical use of technology which is going to change conventional methods of reading linear narratives and accessing information[12]. It also relates strongly to other kinds of computer texts, such as video games, where the distinction between 'reading' and 'playing' has become increasingly blurred. The player of a computer game could be seen as both a reader and a writer; the 'reader' follows pre-determined narratives, while the 'writer' interacts with the text in order to influence the progress and outcome of the story.

We therefore developed a unit of work which required students to write extended choose-your-own-adventure stories in hypertext form using the programme *Hypercard*. This allows for sound and pictures to be set alongside written text. Above all, it is a program that requires authors to conceptualise narrative structure. One writes in it by means of *cards* and *buttons*: the cards are pages onto which one can put sound, pictures and writing and the buttons are devices that allow the reader to move, or 'navigate', between cards. Authors can put text, image, sound and even video clips onto cards and then build in buttons between cards that allow readers to move around at their own speed and according to their own interest. Although the use of video clips is still a little cumbersome, it is particularly easy to record sound directly onto a card and then 'conceal' it under an appropriate picture or phrase.

The project started with work taken from the widely-used booklet *Making Stories*[13]. This uses a structuralist approach to fairy stories. It gets students to think about the relationships between plot and story and encourages them to alter traditional tales as a way of drawing attention to underlying narrative conventions. We then demonstrated an example of a *Hypercard* story which we had written, in order to exemplify the possibilities of the program. As in the *Making Stories* booklet, we sought to emphasise the ways in which narrative offers choice within structural constraints.

The students were split into groups of three and asked to devise stories which: [a] had reader choice built into them – that is, points in the narrative where readers could choose what could happen next from pre-given options; and [b] included pictures and sound as equal mechanisms with written text as ways of telling the tale. The choice of content was left to them. Having produced diagrammatic versions on paper of the stories they wanted to create, they were taught how to use the program and make hypertext *stacks*, as *Hypercard* products are known.

The third project, with year 10, revolved around the study of the film *The Outsiders*[14]. The unit invited students to make posters and trailers for the film, as if repackaging it *either* for transmission on television in the near future, *or* for another audience which they had to specify (such as re-releasing it in another country). They also had to compare the ways in which narrative is related in the film and in the book on which it was based. In terms of assessment within English, the posters and trailers had to be seen as pretexts for oral work, since they could not be assessed in their own right; and the unit also included fictional and discursive writing. This work followed a fairly common model of syllabus organisation at GCSE, where material for coursework folders and oral assessment can be derived from extended study of a text or range of texts.

The media production activities (the poster and the trailer) are in themselves commonplace at every level of the English curriculum. However, we did teach about the way these kinds of texts are constructed more explicitly than is normally the case within English. The students had read the book and watched the film at the beginning of the unit. They were then given a range of posters and trailers to analyse with directed worksheets. These drew attention to the ways in which posters are comprised of a number of elements (title, background, critics' recommendation etc.); while trailers use voice-over and editing to create a mini-narrative of their own. The class spent some time considering how both forms of advertising target potential audiences and how both media employ specific strategies in order to do this, for example in the way the style of lettering on posters creates generic awareness. The class was then shown how image manipulation and video editing programs work. In groups of three, the students were asked to produce either a trailer or a poster for the film. They first had to input their chosen extracts from the film into the computer and then work with the digitised images.

This project was quite ambitious and intensive. Only three machines were available for poster making and one for trailers, so the class was split into groups. Whilst the media production was going on, the rest of the class either worked on pieces of creative writing, loosely derived from the storyline of the book; or on a comparison of narrative styles between the film and the book.

All three projects took place over half a term, with class sizes of between twenty four and twenty eight.

Introducing students to the work

Considering that the work took place within English; that students had no prior experience of media production in school; and that we were introducing them both to the practical and conceptual challenges posed by multimedia, the initial responses to all projects are worthwhile exploring. The nature of the technology used within each project is particularly significant here.

In many ways, the most conceptually demanding project was the year 8 hypertext work. Although students might be familiar with computer games, and expressed more than a working knowledge of the choose-your-own-adventure books, hypertext stories are not (at present) a common form of cultural product. As we shall see later, the most significant problem the students encountered was being able to distance themselves as writers of a text in order to imagine how different readers might read it. The project required them to make up stories with multiple routes through them. This was directly related to the choice of story genre. Making up stories is of course part and parcel of English, although in practice this only applies to certain kinds of stories. Being able to invent stories that focus on plot ingenuity – rather than 'rounded characters' or detailed description – requires a working knowledge of fictional genres that are different from those usually studied in English. While boys may be more frequent consumers of adventure narratives, the fact that this work was done with girls offered different and perhaps challenging possibilities.

We shall see later how the students 'solved' these problems. Yet the difficulties they faced in coming to terms with the technology reflected a conundrum that is common to many forms of media production. As first time users, students obviously do not know what the technology can do; and since it is unfamiliar, and perhaps daunting, it may be difficult for them to envisage all the possibilities. In addition, the students had to interpret the task we set them within the constraints of their prior knowledge of genre and narrative. There was thus a tension between the need to find a recognisable genre of writing and the external, and largely unknown, constraints of the new form.

We were therefore faced with a series of questions as soon as we described the task. Which comes first: the ability to write in non-linear narratives or the experience of reading them? Could the students invent non linear narratives without being competent users of the technology? These questions can be represented in diagrammatic form:

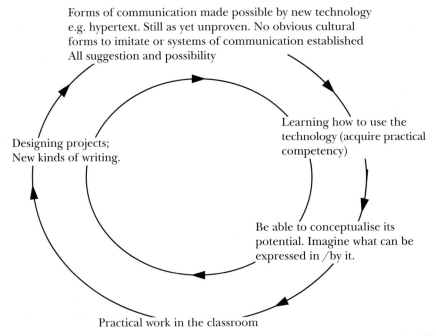

Forms of communication made possible by new technology e.g. hypertext. Still as yet unproven. No obvious cultural forms to imitate or systems of communication established All suggestion and possibility

Designing projects; New kinds of writing.

Learning how to use the technology (acquire practical competency)

Be able to conceptualise its potential. Imagine what can be expressed in /by it.

Practical work in the classroom

Fig. 3.2

Similar problems were faced by the year 10 students who had the task of making posters, and to a lesser extent by the year 7 users of *Morph*. The image manipulation program, *Photoshop*, which we used for making the posters, is industry standard software and is extremely complex. Because the students had no experience of the program, they found it hard to imagine its potential to 'ghost', 'fuse' or 'filter' images[15]. However, because posters are a recognisable cultural form, unlike hypertexts, this problem was less pressing, in as much as the students could easily design a model on paper to start off with. The hypertext students could only start with different models, like the choose-your-own-adventure book.

The students experienced this problem in a different way on the *Morph* project. While they might have seen morphing in the context of adverts or pop videos, they still experienced some difficulty in imagining what the final product might look like. They brought in a range of family photographs, some of which made no sense in terms of how we had set up the project. Of course, their choice of photographs was partly fortuitous in any case; and in the event, many brought in pictures which they did not appear to value. In the end, we could not communicate the point of using the technology as a way of exploring family identity *in the abstract* without being able to show them the possibilities we had imagined. The idea of 'morphing' between two contrasting images as a way of exploring more fundamental changes and tensions – for example, watching one's features emerge out of a composite family history – was almost impossible to explain. The activity thus became an opportunity simply to play with the technology for its own sake.

In addition, the project may have invaded the distance students understandably wanted to maintain between their family lives and the school environment. Several girls wanted to take the work home with them; and it is reasonable to infer that if they did get involved in the process of exploring family resemblances, they would have wanted to discuss the process within the family. The most notable example here was a girl who was persuaded by her mother to bring in pictures of her uncle and her father: morphing between each of these and a picture of the girl herself produced some interesting results! If this sense of personal space was important, it does suggest some important questions about the *Myself* project as a whole. Like a great deal of autobiographical work in English, it is doubtful whether this kind of approach does in fact offer an authentic opportunity to explore the subjective realm of individual identity[16]. While the use of *Morph* in this context may have offered significant pleasures and even insights of the kind we had hoped to achieve, these did not become the focus of explicit discussion. This in turn raises broader questions about the role of reflection within the production process, which will be considered in more detail below.

Hypertext: conceptualising narrative

The relative failure of the *Morph* project is instructive. By contrast, despite the use of complex technology, the year 8 and 10 work was completed more successfully. The most striking fact about the year 8 hypertext work was the range of different genres used by the students as a way of fulfilling the brief. Although not all the projects were completed in hypertext form, the eight groups in the class composed narratives which are summarised below:

1. *Michael Jackson.* An unpopular boy called Tony gets tickets for a Michael Jackson concert. He has to decide who to take with him: his sister, his best friend or a popular boy. Whoever he takes then has to repay the debt in various ways. His sister

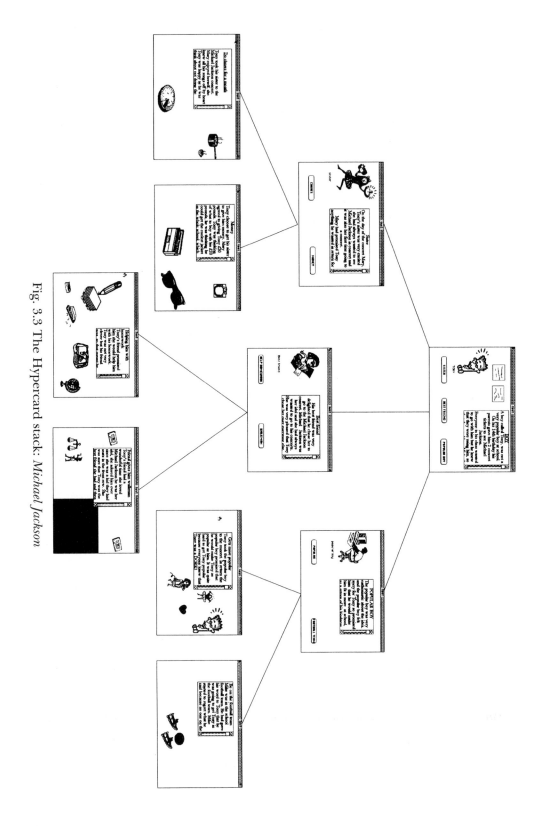

Fig. 3.3 The Hypercard stack: *Michael Jackson*

either has to do chores or pay him money. The best friend either does Tony's homework or gives him her walkman and the popular boy either makes Tony popular, or gets him onto the football team (see fig. 3.3).

2. *The Baker.* A lonely baker is given a magic potion. He knocks it into his dough by accident and then has to decide whether to make a cream cake, a sponge cake or a bun. The cream cake is either bought by a pop star or an old lady; the bun is either bought by a girl or it runs away and is squashed by a car; and the sponge cake is either bought by a boy or it meets a girl sponge and falls in love.

3. *The Boyfriend.* There are two friends, Sharon and Tracy: one is lucky in love, while the other is unlucky. The lucky one brings home a boy whom her friend fancies. She has to decide what colour make-up to wear. If she wears blue, she is fancied by the boy; and she then has to decide whether 'to style it out' or blush red and run out of the room. If she styles it out, she can either go shopping for more drinks or drink by herself. (Unfortunately the consequences of wearing green or brown make-up are not clear from the finished product!).

4. *Haunted House.* A boy gets lost in a forest. At a scary moment, he can either follow a beautiful ghostly woman or he can go through a mysterious door. If he follows the woman, he then has to decide whether to kiss her or not, the choice of which leads either to a 'sexy' death or to safety. If he goes through the door, he dies in a miserable cellar.

5. *Mary's Nightmare.* Mary goes to visit her grandmother's grave on a spooky night. By accident she falls into the grave. She has three choices: she can either go down a bright tunnel or a dimly lit tunnel or climb out. If she climbs out, she is pursued by a wolf, so she has to escape either by running along a road or through some woods, which contain further adventures. The bright tunnel takes her to a mysterious room with a weeping statue of her grandmother and a ladder. The dim tunnel takes her to a pit with goblins who offer her either a magic hat or a magic whistle.

6. *Halloween Night.* A rich girl and a punk decide whether to go trick or treating or go to a Halloween party. The first option leaves them with a choice of two doors: the first leads to a witch, the second a vampire. If they go to the party, they can either get drunk on beer or drink poisoned grapefruit juice which sends them to sleep for 1000 years until awakened by a punk's kiss.

7. *The Unsolved Murder.* The wife and best friend of Mr. Clinton Smooth want him murdered. If the reader gets the wife to do it, she will be a suspect; while the friend might not be strong enough and might confess. Alternatively a hitman would cost money. (See below)

8. *Paris.* A couple have to decide which pair of friends to take with them on holiday to Paris. Whichever pair they choose, the events of the holiday turn out differently. (Unfinished)

These brief summaries emphasise the ways in which the narratives are structured in terms of either/or choices[17]. At the same time, they tend to flatten out the subtlety of some of the work, whilst also disguising some of the more confused narratives. *The Unsolved Murder*, for example, does not give choices at the end of each page but it does have buttons, so the reader can move from page to page. The final page 'tells you the answer' as follows:

> TIME TO KILL HIM
>
> Now its time to kill him and who should do it Laura, Carol or the hitman, they have decided that Laura would kill him this is how it turn out.
>
> HITMAN = The hitman tried to kill him but he did not succeed because he didn't have enough strength
> LAURA = Laura tried to kill her husband but did not succeed because in a way she still loved him.
> CAROL = Carol did succeed and killed him in a very horrible way.

There is then an 'end' button that thanks you for 'playing our game', spoken by the students. The reference to the product as a game is revealing. At the beginning of the task, the same group had asked me whether they 'could do it like *Crime Monthly*, where you have to solve the murder' and suggested that they would make it 'like *Cluedo*'. However, the final product seems to have already 'played out' the game for future readers, thus making it more like a completed story. Games and stories appear to differ in terms of the illusion of control they give to consumers: stories explicitly guide the reader, whereas game players think they do it for themselves. The ability to think through the ramifications of an *interactive* product as opposed to constructing a fixed narrative completely baffled one group. The makers of *The Boyfriend* never seemed to grasp the point that they had to make an open-ended story, rather than solve the narrative problems themselves: they wanted to close off the narrative by making one of the make-up choices better than the others. This may derive from the kind of magazine story or advice column where there are clear right and wrong choices to be made.

This highlights one central difference between this project and a great deal of conventional writing in English. This kind of work requires authors to imagine in a very explicit way how a reader will interact with their text. Furthermore, the writer has to take account of the ways in which the reader changes and learns as they read. To write hypertexts, or interactive games, writers have to put hypothetical readers at the heart of the act of writing. In theory of course, this is true of all writing – from the writing I am doing now to the work children produce in English lessons. However, because the work is done in groups and because the technology forces authors to be explicit about the effects they want to achieve, it may encourage the process of 'de-centring' that beginning writers can find so difficult. This may be an important claim for practical media production in general.

Nevertheless, there are two important caveats here. The first relates to the ways in which these students themselves referred to hypothetical readers. The *Michael Jackson* group, who produced by far the most polished product, described how readers might interact on a 'micro' level:

> – Oh I know, you lot, you know Tony's hand? We could put a button on Tony's hand so when people press Tony, he says:

- Oh I know, *Good Morning*
- No. He says, *Hello* [heavily accented in a stupidly sexy way]
- Yeah, that's sweet!
- Yeah, that's good. Who's gonna do it?

They can clearly imagine how an outsider might derive pleasure and narrative information from responding to the textual cues they can build in. But when I asked them who might read their work or whether they could imagine books like theirs being produced in the future, one of the authors replied:

> You know children at the age of say, ten. They usually don't like reading that much. They find it boring. And this [Michael Jackson] makes them interested and try to watch it out and that. If you make it too long, then they'd find it boring.

The easy generalisations about younger children and the superficial reference to 'boredom' indicate the difficulty of imagining real readers – even though they clearly can conceive of how people in general might read their text. In the end, however, this may simply reflect the fact that so much students' writing is lacking in a 'real audience' – an issue we explore in more detail in Chapter 6.

Secondly, one should be cautious about the claim that it is the technology in itself that makes this process of de-centring possible. It should also be acknowledged that different *genres* 'inscribe' different readers within their typical narrative structures[18]. For example, detective stories may encourage us to identify with the protagonist's search for the solution to the crime; whereas in horror stories we may be encouraged to identify with the victims of the monster or killer. The range of genres chosen by the class clearly picks up from the earlier work they had done on fairy stories; and the mix of fantasy, social realism and horror is typical of most English classrooms. The horror and crime stories are closest to games – as indicated by the reference to *Cluedo* – and do already exist in interactive forms in the shape of the choose-your-own-adventure story. The different forms of address to hypothetical readers which characterise these genres are largely replicated in the students' work. Yet while their interpretation of the task may have begun from safe generic structures these became progressively mixed or 'hybridised' as the project developed and their familiarity with the technology grew.

For example, the *Michael Jackson* group moved beyond their initial concern with structure and began to consider the ways in which sound and picture could be combined with text. Having planned the narrative, they then used the potential of the program to elaborate and develop it further. For example, on the first card of their stack they pasted a picture of Tony (see fig. 3.4). This image is taken from a bank of clip art that comes with the program. However, it was their exploration of the program that suggested this image, not a pre-existent sense of the character in the first place:

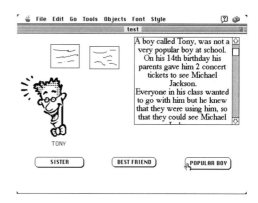

Fig. 3.4 'Tony'

> – Let's use that gimpy guy.
> – I love that gimpy guy!
> – [with an acted voice] Hiya Tony
> – Let's put a picture of him on page 1.

The more images they found, the more they used the ability to create parallel narratives in image and sound as a way of providing an ironic commentary on their original plot. Thus their discussion about the way he speaks was as comic as the picture they chose to represent him:

> – So when people press Tony he says...
> – Oh I know, *Good Morning*
> – No, he says *Hello* [heavily accented]
> – Yeah, that's sweet!

The tones of voice, impossible to reproduce here, make Tony a figure of fun. By using the sound track, the girls are able to create a more distanced perspective on the character.

It would seem that this process of transforming plot into a multi-levelled narrative is one that occurs *during* the production process and particularly through group discussion. This ability to add play-acted voices was used to send up other characters. Likewise, the snippets of songs sung by the girls or recorded onto the stack provide another form of authorial commentary. For example, the funky dance number, Stevie V's *Dirty Cash* was recorded over a picture of the money bag that Tony's sister gives him as a possible repayment for the Jackson tickets. The effect of this is to give the story a contemporary cultural frame of reference, even though this works against the tone and plot line of the story.

These injections of irony and parody are part of the way this group exercised control over their work and set out to entertain themselves and the friends who read it. For example, by the end of the piece, when the popular boy is trying to make Tony popular, they ended up writing: 'It was quite hard to get Tony popular because everyone knew that Tony was a DORK!' This comment was added in when they arrived at that stage, as their work on the earlier cards had led them to this inevitable conclusion.

All these subsequent re-workings of the original story derive quite clearly from the *social* nature of group production. The practical work becomes a kind of open-ended dialogue where opinions, feelings and jokes can all be shared and exchanged. Listening to them at the screen, it became impossible to distinguish individuals from a choric voice at work. Here they are talking about selecting an image to illustrate a card:

> – The jacket..
> – We can change it.
> – Yeah, put back...
> – Oh no, we pasted it
> – Who cares?
> [laughter]
> – Just do another one.

As students become confident about what they are doing, as they begin to share some of their work in discussion or with their peers and the teacher, other possible interpretations of the narrative become apparent and they act on these. The action they take may conflict with previous ideas, but because an attitude of experimentation (in this case) prevailed, they tended to go with the flow. Of course it is not unreasonable to expect students to change their minds: indeed, it would be worrying if they had such fixed ideas about the finished product that they did not develop them through the production process.

At the same time, these points might qualify any arguments we might wish to make about the 'subversiveness' of this kind of practical work – for example, on the grounds that the students were satirising and therefore somehow challenging the conventions of their chosen genre. In many ways, the tensions between generic form and narrative structure were inherent in the task set and may have encouraged this more ironic approach. Yet the girls' engagement with the activity clearly took it well beyond a mechanical exercise in narrative construction.

Selling *The Outsiders*

By contrast, the work undertaken by the year 10 students was considerably less free in its attitudes towards form and audience. Producing trailers and posters places the authors and readers of such products in a significantly different position compared with those established by the hypertexts we have just described. Considering this work also requires us to engage with the *simulated* situation, where students are invited to take on the role of media producers within the framework of the commercial marketplace, as opposed to the emphasis on individual expression typically found in the English classroom.

The film *The Outsiders* was made by Francis Ford Coppola in 1983. It is based on a remarkable novel by a teenage authoress, S.E. Hinton, which is relatively common in English stock rooms around the country. The girls had read the book in year 9, well before we contemplated using the film for this project. *The Outsiders* tells the story of inter-gang rivalry in an American town split along class lines: the working class kids are 'greasers' and the middle class kids, 'soc's'. The hero of the story, Ponyboy Curtis, is orphaned and brought up by his elder brother. Indeed, much of the story's appeal derives from its focus on orphaned inter-male relationships, a theme emphasised in Coppola's canny casting of 'brat pack stars' like Matt Dillon, Ralph Macchio, Thomas Howell, Patrick Swayze, Emilio Estevez and Tom Cruise.

Although the outcomes of this project – trailers and posters – are typical Media Studies products, I want to argue that using digital production processes significantly affected the kind of learning which took place here. As we have seen, our use of the *Morph* program only seemed to emphasise the superficial and redundant aspects of new technology: amazing but pointless. On the other hand, making hypertexts is clearly only possible using multimedia technology. However, the test in this case is whether the multimedia technology makes a *qualitative difference* to the learning. If the products had been made using conventional analogue technology, would the students have learnt 'less', or learnt something different? In this case, the technology clearly makes for 'better quality' products when compared with the results of drawing, storyboarding or cutting and sticking usually employed in media education or indeed in English – although this does not in itself tell us a great deal about the quality of the learning.

The fact that this work took place within English lessons and was also set up to meet attainment targets within IT further complicates the picture. As we have indicated, the primary aim of practical work in Media Studies is often defined in terms of conceptual learning. By contrast, English is essentially defined in terms of *activities* – reading, writing, speaking and listening – which are seen to be worthwhile in their own right: the aim of writing in English, for example, is primarily to become a better writer (and thereby, some would argue, a better person). Meanwhile, IT is characterised by a task-led model of skills development which is directly opposed to the notions of language and learning that underpin most English teaching. These contrasting models of the writing process clearly embody very different theoretical assumptions, and suggest quite different criteria for evaluation.

'It made you realise, just gets you deeper into the story'

This comment was made by one of the girls, Nuriye, who produced the trailer, and it refers to what she got out of the process of digitising the material prior to its construction as a trailer. Both the trailer and the poster group had to go through the same procedure in order to gather together the material they wanted to use in their respective products. This involved watching the film as a whole class and noting down the images or sequences they wanted. They then 'grabbed' these and put them in a bank to use for the construction of their posters or trailers. (The 'grabbing' is in effect the computer recording still or moving images and converting them into digital documents. This is achieved through a piece of hardware fitted onto the back of the machine known as a video spigot). What Nuriye's remark suggests is the way in which

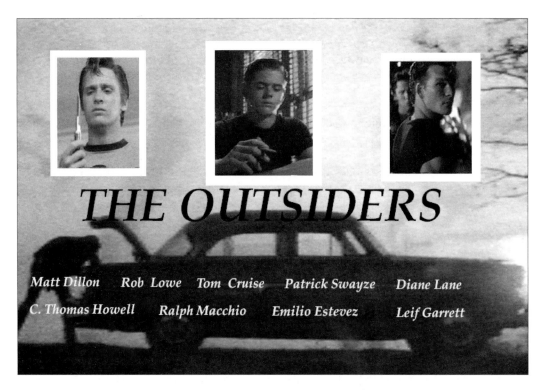

Fig. 3.5 *The Outsiders*: poster

this stage of the production (or pre-production) process focuses attention on the actual text.

Both projects required students to watch the film and discuss which extracts or stills they wanted to use. Yet unlike, say, drawing posters on paper, which in theory encourages students to think about the 'big idea' behind a film, using image manipulation programs requires an almost microscopic attention to detail that could easily obscure the conceptual intent behind the task. For example, one of the poster groups needed to use a still of Patrick Swayze. Having discussed in detail which sequence from which scene contained the image they wanted, they focused on a part of the sequence where he turns from right to left and then chose the exact profile they wanted from a second-long piece of the film. (see fig. 3.5, top right image). This process was interesting on two levels. First, it demonstrated an aesthetic awareness: they wanted him to look in a particular direction in order to ensure that all the stars on that poster were looking in the same direction. Secondly, it indicated a level of knowledge and recall that clearly derived from their viewing of the film outside school. Indeed, discussion about Patrick Swayze's movements was coloured by the film's cult status and the students' enthusiasm for its male stars. The fact that the three students making this poster could share this kind of detailed knowledge highlights a level of affective investment characteristic of media work of this kind

While it might be possible to access this level of knowledge and interest through critical analysis, being able to *control* the film and work almost directly with the images and sequences in this way allowed for a whole host of informal knowledge gleaned from home viewing of the film to be used as part of the task. Indeed, I would want to make the larger claim that being able to handle the film in 'virtual' form, frame by frame, or image by image, may transform the power relations that normally obtain between text and viewer. Academic debates within Media Studies have veered between an emphasis on the power of the text and the claim for the power of the reader. Yet however mentally active viewers may be, they are physically limited in terms of what they can *do* with the text. Image manipulation of this kind gives a physical control over the material far in excess of freeze-framing or fast-forwarding material on video.

Exercising control over the film in this way is akin to a kind of critical reading of literary texts, where one can extract quotations or mark the margins as a way of supporting one's reading and interpretation. Viewing and re-viewing, noting down shots, shaving frames off clips and simply poring over the desktop with its frame-by-frame representation of the film clip, the sound track or the kind of edit used (see fig. 3.6) forces the students to adopt a high level of concentration and attention to detail. One of the trailer groups made this point in discussion:

> Helen: You sort of notice, like say, what's he called? Johnny?
> Nuriye: Yeah, Johnny.
> Helen: Yeah, Johnny and the way he doesn't get on with his parents which
>   leads him to run away, and you don't seem to think about that so much.
> [...]
> Nuriye: Yeah, when you first watch it, the main story is about Ponyboy and his
>   brother. When you watch it again in this way, it's all together.

Nuriye's last comment 'when you watch it again *in this way*, it's all together' seems to refer both to the demands of the simulation (in that they have to watch the film for the

This is a collection
of all the clips from
the film to be put
into the trailer

One can preview
clips from the film
one is making

This is a selection of all
the possible editing
transitions

Clips can be put
in either of
these tracks

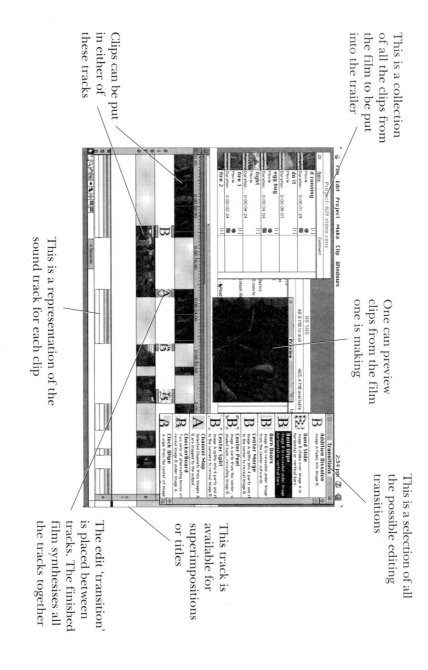

Fig. 3.6 Digital editing in action

This is a representation of the
sound track for each clip

This track is
available for
superimpositions
or titles

The edit 'transition'
is placed between
tracks. The finished
film synthesises all
the tracks together

specific purpose of making the trailer) and to the microscopic detail in which they work with the film text.

Of course, the same kind of concentration is necessary for media production on analogue equipment, such as conventional video editing technology. In a sense, the same kind of 'discipline' is required. Yet multimedia technology allows a level of virtual modelling and experimentation which enables ideas to be played around with almost immediately and, most importantly, to be *visualised*. This facility, of being able to test out ideas with no loss of final quality, to look at one person's idea and evaluate it within the group, is more than just a question of immediacy and access. By contrast, analogue processes require an ability to conceptualise the finished product, dependent on training, imagination and what is loosely called 'visual literacy'.

It is helpful to distinguish here between the conventional phases in media production: *pre-production* (planning and devising), *production* (in films this would be shooting) and *post-production* (again in films this would refer to editing, dubbing, titling etc.). Likewise, making posters in traditional ways requires a 'pre-production' level of competency: the whole finished product has to be conceptualised, either designed 'in the head' or in sketch form, before actually beginning the process of making or producing it. The digital processes allow real manipulation of actual images from the film (leading to a higher quality of product), whereas traditional work of this kind in both Media Studies and in English is likely to be drawn or sketched. More fundamentally, however, they support the design process through which students might actually conceptualise the product in the first place. This latter process is normally invisible to the outsider, or is often described in mysterious terms like 'creative' or 'artistic'. In effect, they blur all the traditional distinctions between the different stages of the production process.

The poster (fig. 3.7) is a case in point. First of all, using the actual images rather than requiring students to draw them (which in practice usually means referring to images recalled in the film) makes the task more 'real' in terms of the simulated production scenario. Secondly, the students can model their ideas at the screen. Such discussions might appear opaque to an outsider: phrases like 'move it there' or 'click' or 'smallen that' are external manifestations of a dialogue with the screen and they don't mean much beyond that context. Nevertheless, the kinds of narrative relationships established through the arrangement of the portrait shots of the cast or the positioning of those shots over the background can be discussed and negotiated by the group, rather than appearing as a product of individual artistic imagination.

However, if the process facilitates aspects of the construction, it does not replace the capacity to imagine the final product – even if one might expect students to do this more effectively as they become more familiar with the programs. This is apparent when we compare the different backgrounds the students chose for their posters. Several of the groups didn't actually put in backgrounds until we pointed out to them that they would need to colour in the spaces between the pictures of the stars or leave them blank. Whereas doing the process manually would actually require them to colour in physically, doing the work digitally allowed them to make good their errors. On the other hand, in fig. 3.5, the students selected a full screen image to use as their background. This is important on a number of levels beyond the immediate aesthetic effect. The image is golden in colour, which feeds off the poetic motif in the text where Ponyboy quotes a phrase from a Robert Frost poem about lost youth. It is also part of a flashback sequence about Pony's dead parents, an important emotional moment in the film. Their selection of it as the background image reflects its importance in their

Fig. 3.7 *The Outsiders*: poster

reading of the film. It also implies that the narrative function of the *background* has been understood in the first place: i.e. it establishes a frame against which other images (and events) can derive meaning. Because the program requires backgrounds to be positioned in the first stage of any complex montage, it also means that the students had to reach this level of understanding at the appropriate stage of the production sequence.

From storyboards to imagining film

This facility to construct work conceptually is nowhere more evident than in students' uses and abuses of the storyboard. Storyboards have always been used as a basic tool in cinematography. The Film Studies text book *Film Art* gives examples of the ways in which complex action and special effects sequences would be drawn frame by frame as an annotated script for a film crew[19]. The celebrated film maker and theorist Pudovkin refers to a *'working* – that is, a ready for shooting – form of scenario provid[ing] in itself the detailed description of each, even the smallest piece [of the film], citing every technical method required for its execution.'[20] Above all, he stresses the importance of *editing* in creating the meaning of film, the process most obviously made explicit in detailed drawings of this kind.

However, early film education guides did not necessarily emphasise the use of storyboards as a pre-production requirement[21]. These early media education programmes stressed the value of 'scenarios' and 'shooting scripts'; but it is only relatively recently that media educators have placed so much emphasis on the role of the storyboard. In practice, we suspect that storyboarding is often used as a form of classroom control, particularly where there is a scarcity of equipment: it is a way of finding something for students to do when it is not possible for them to make real films. Ideally, storyboarding should serve to develop students' ability both to visualise *before* shooting and to conceptualise how the film will be edited *after* shooting – although these two functions are often confused. Nevertheless, storyboarding is rarely taught as a discrete skill. In fact, it requires a high degree of 'visual literacy'; and unless students are already experienced film or video makers, aspects such as shot time or camera angle are rarely meaningful. In our experience, students often tend to use single images to stand in for whole scenes rather than accurately write down a shot-by-shot analysis.

The notion of 'scaffolding' is useful and appropriate here. This idea is derived from the work of Vygotsky and was subsequently developed by Bruner[22]. It refers to the ways teachers support students' conceptual development in a scaffold or structure, similar to the way buildings are erected. In other words, we hold up the student until they can stand for themselves. In media education, the storyboard is intended to fulfil that intermediate function – or so it would appear from GCSE and 'A' level syllabi. However, there is a Catch 22 situation here. In order for students to become fluent film or video makers, they would need to use the storyboard as a way of visualising and representing ideas; but they need to have some experience of video making in the first place in order to be able to *make use* of a storyboard in the actual production process. Rather like the use of a background images in the poster work, there needs to be an element of trial and error here. Here again, the relationship between technology and creativity is a circular one.

This is where the virtual storyboard on the computer screen can make a difference. The program we used allows for the video to be laid out frame by frame along a time line (see fig. 3.6 above). Whereas experienced film-makers can use storyboards as an economic way of drafting ideas, inexperienced students, who may well be fluent 'readers' of film, cannot make an automatic transition to being 'writers' of film. However, the desktop storyboard gives students a purchase on the editing process which is frequently absent from work of this kind. The key to digital editing is that it represents the ideas directly in front of you. Students can thus see immediately the consequences of their decisions about pace, shot selection, sound, editing transitions etc.. By contrast, unless (like Pudovkin) they have 'scenarists' who can envisage the detailed workings of final edited film, analogue processes require film-makers to imagine their ideas until they are realised in the cutting room.

This kind of project was deliberately not an 'open' creative or imaginative assignment; and as such, it aimed to provide the kind of scaffolding we have described. In more open-ended assignments, students are required to visualise the final product *and* to conceive of how it will be edited from the very start – which is clearly extremely demanding. Using the support offered by the virtual storyboard enabled students to learn explicitly about this stage of the process before moving on to the next. For example, students' discussions about the editing of the trailer illustrated the ways in which they were learning to articulate the conventions of continuity editing. For example, the following extract is concerned with the rules of 'match on action' and eyeline[23]:

Helen:	It's quite nice 'cos it's like him looking back and then someone's quite sharp.
Nuriye:	Oh yeah.
[...]	
Nuriye:	If we put the punch there it'll be like him, Johnny, him turning to look at Ponyboy.
Helen:	Ponyboy wants to get punched in the face.
Nuriye:	So shall we delete that?
Helen:	We'll change that.

Here, the students understand that the sequence of the punch will be read as if continuous with the following shot of Ponyboy, thus distorting the plot line of the film. It would also confuse the relationship between Johnny and Ponyboy.

Although these conventions can of course be taught through the use of written storyboards, the students' understanding here has come about through correcting a 'mistake'. This open way of working through experimentation is, one can speculate, a natural stage in the way experienced film-makers might experiment as they write their own storyboards. By comparison, when writing prose the developmental stage is invisible as we struggle to find the right word or phrase in our heads – although here again, there may be a difference between writing on paper and word processing on a computer. In this respect, the girls' work could be likened to the process of learning to write through drafting, crossing out and reworking ideas.

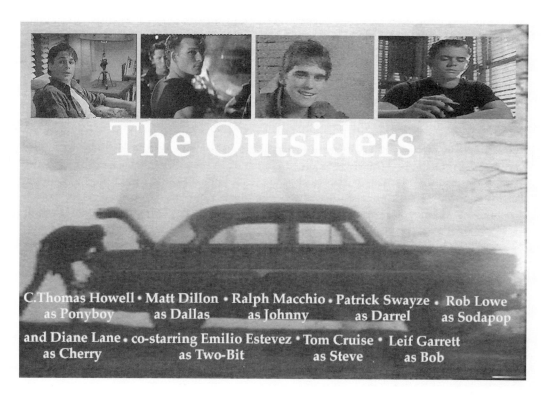

Fig. 3.8 *The Outsiders*: poster

Evaluating the products

As I have noted, one of the major aims of both the year 10 projects was to encourage students to think about the marketing of films to particular target audiences. In our preparatory work, we asked to students to analyse how both trailers and posters offer what John Ellis calls a 'narrative image'[24] – in other words, how the narrative enigma that is posed by the film is used to attract potential cinema-goers. While most of the work did succeed in creating some kind of narrative image, some of the posters were clearly more effective than others. There tended to be a certain amount of imitation of others' work, partially because the background to figs. 3.5 and 3.8 was so admired and partially because the second group of poster-makers used the bank of images provided by the first group rather than scanning the film for themselves. All the groups used portrait pictures of the stars, which is obviously a significant convention in film posters – although again, this is also indicative of their interest in the film. However, the most effective work (see fig. 3.7 as well) established a kind of tension between the images which does, in effect, construct a narrative within the frame of the poster.

The formal qualities are also instructive. Many of the portraits are carefully arranged so that the gazes of the stars to the left and right are centred on the viewer and the composition of the different elements is balanced. These compositional elements reflect the students' readings of the film. Another poster, for example, positioned the characters Dally and Johnny outside of the embracing family group. This balance reflects the salient oppositions within the original text; and if these students had expressed this structural awareness in prose as part of a discursive essay there is no doubt it would have been well received.

While the finished products appeared comparatively 'professional', this was not so obviously the case in the use of lettering, both for the title and other verbal information. Despite the equipment's facility for manipulating fonts and type sizes, and despite the fact that this part of the project could draw on competencies developed in word processing, none of the finished products were as confident in their use of written words as they were with the images. Our feeling was that this area could easily be worked on: we had demanded too much too quickly, given the level of difficulty posed by using the program. However, the kind of information that would have made the students' work look like the 'real thing' – giving all the details of the various production or distribution responsibilities – is pretty mundane. In practice, this would certainly have meant a lot of copying out. Judged either as expressive or critical readings of the text, the posters did their job; and in strict design terms, some of the posters clearly fulfilled the brief of the industrial simulation, which required them to re-package the film.

However, this is to evaluate the work in 'media education' terms. Within the comparatively open assessment framework of English, or even within the narrower skills-based approach to IT, the students were not actually required to fulfil the full terms of our brief. As we have noted, the principal aim of designing a poster within English would be to provide a new approach to reading the text: summarising the book in a single image would serve to focus students' attention on the key themes and relationships within it. By contrast, in a Design subject, the emphasis would be on replicating the formal elements that comprise posters, and on the display of technical competence. Within media education, however, students are generally required to be explicit about the audience they are targeting and to reflect *theoretically* on the relations between text and audience – although, as we have noted, evidence of this kind of reflection is generally expected to be contained in the accompanying writing[25].

In the case of these students, however, their writing did not contain evidence of this kind. The 'logs' they wrote answered some leading questions which we had set, but none of the students referred directly to the implied audiences for the film. This was partly due to the problem the students had in differentiating between themselves as the audience and other kinds of possible viewers. In addition, since the film already has a real audience, being asked to conceptualise a new one can appear redundant. However, what is really revealing about these accounts is the students' attitude towards the analytical work on posters which began the unit of work. Half the students justified their own work in these terms:

> The poster analysis we did came in really useful. We used quite a few ideas from 'real posters' and put them into our own. For example, we used a lot of ghosting effects which we would never have thought of before.

On the other hand, some were concerned about their inability to reproduce the 'real thing':

> The aspects of my poster that are unlike real posters are that my poster doesn't give any information about the ratings or the producers.

Part of the problem here is that in English, students are not generally asked to reflect on the writing process as part of a writing assignment. As we have noted, there is a sense in which writing in English is perceived as an end in itself, even where it involves the use of existing styles or genres: students are not generally asked to reflect explicitly on why they used particular plot formulae or stylistic conventions. In media education, on the other hand, this kind of explicit reflection is seen as an essential way in which 'theory' and 'practice' are related; and it is mainly for this reason that a piece of critical writing is submitted for examination along with practical productions. Meanwhile, the IT curriculum in schools is predominantly defined in terms of 'how to' skills. This leaves us with the products themselves, which is of course also where English teachers would begin their assessment of any piece of work.

Likewise, the trailer activity drew on a number of media production and reading competencies, although these were rarely made a focus for explicit analysis. For example, let us consider the use of transitions between sequences. Although in classic film theory there are four basic kinds of edits (cut, dissolve, fade and wipe), the editing program offered about fifty special effects which could perform this function. These are 'dragged' onto the virtual storyboard and manipulated to take the correct amount of time (see fig. 3.6 above). The temptation is to use all sorts of special effects for their own sake. However, after the initial rush of enthusiasm for pop-video-style effects had worn off, the students found the discipline of the advertising trailer a salutary corrective, and they economised on special effects to maximise impact. None of the trailers used more than three or four unusual transitions, and these were used emphatically to further the narrative. Thus, the effect in which one scene opens, iris-like, from the middle of another scene was used to convey the sense that the second scene emerges from the 'heart' of the first. This also drew attention to the core of the family grouping with their arms around each other.

These technical competencies were matched by the students' use of voice-over and in particular the pace and timing of the thirty or so clips that they used in their work. These qualities are notoriously difficult to define and they tend to be discussed by teachers as issues of taste and judgement[26]. We can accept that it is difficult to put into words why clips should be only three rather than four seconds long: yet one might have expected these students to be able to explain why the narrative structure of their trailer used the thirty or so clips it did and in the order it did. In particular, one might expect the task of *marketing* the film would force them to be explicit about defining the audience, and so affect the narrative that they actually constructed. Yet here the students resorted to the bland discourse of film criticism:

> Helen: It wasn't so much a story, it was just trying to fit all the scenes we
>   wanted in some order.
> Nuriye: We tried to balance them out.. not too much –
> Helen: VIOLENCE.
> Nuriye: – and not too much soppy stuff
> Helen: So we just spread it out easily.

The concepts of 'spreading out' or 'balancing' could be seen to reflect neo-classical values of harmony and balance; while the categories of 'violence' and 'soppy stuff' derive more from everyday critical discourse about the media. These judgments were given social credibility by the way in which both girls then hypothesised a 'parent' and a 'stereotypical teenage girl' watching their trailer: both, they argued, would find enough to keep them interested, without being offended by what they might watch.

Nevertheless, the girls' explanation here does not adequately account for the careful way in which the narrative of their trailer is structured; and it completely fails to account for its thoughtful reworking of the story. This can mean two things. First of all, it implies that however 'literate' their reading of the film and their creation of the trailer might be, they do not possess (and in fact have not been taught) a *meta-language* in which they can express their understandings – that is, a vocabulary with which they can analyse media language. Secondly, however, their comments reveal a way of talking about the media that continues to reproduce a sense of anxiety and fearfulness, that is typically bound up in arguments about taste. It may be that in talking to me, as a teacher, they feel the need to apply a level of self-censorship : they say what they feel people like teachers expect to hear. Nevertheless, given the level of understanding demonstrated in their work itself, these arguments appear depressingly simplistic. Here again, there is a need for students to be offered alternative ways of conceptualising the relations between media and their audiences – not least in order to take them beyond the easy assumptions that often dominate public debate.

Conclusion

In many respects, the projects we have described in this chapter represent familiar practice, both in English and in media education. Yet the technology and the curriculum location of this work have raised some larger questions about the relationship between technology and creativity. In particular, the work suggests a rather different approach to the relationship between 'theory' and 'practice' in media education – or, to use the metaphor that has been central to our argument here, between 'reading' and 'writing'. As we have indicated in our introduction, advocates of Media Studies as a distinct discipline have tended to regard these as contrasting opposites, and to privilege the former. By and large, the *purpose* of practical production in Media Studies has been defined in terms of conceptual learning, rather than in terms of 'self-expression' or in terms of technical skills. The contrast here with the notion of writing in English, *and* with the notion of using technology in IT, is striking: both, in different ways, privilege the activity as an end in itself, rather than regarding it as a means to another end.

On one level, the new digital technologies would appear to create significant new possibilities for media production. Great claims have been made about the profound impact of the digital revolution – claims which perhaps inevitably contain a degree of exaggeration. Yet technologies do not in themselves determine the ways in which they will be used. On the contrary, new technologies inevitably interact with existing cultural forms and patterns of social use. As the first two case studies in the chapter have shown, the abstract possibilities made available by digital multimedia are transformed into specific cultural forms in particular social settings. In some ways, *hypertext* does represent a new cultural form; yet the students appropriated and used it in terms of their existing cultural experiences and knowledge. By contrast, despite our enthusiasm, the potential of *Morph* did not appear to connect with these students' concerns and imaginations in any meaningful way. The technologies do undoubtedly offer new expressive possibilities; but these are not guaranteed outcomes or indeed inherent qualities of the technology itself.

On the other hand, the technologies do clearly make certain aspects of the production process much more accessible than in the past. Digital editing, for example, is significantly more flexible – not to mention much cheaper – than its analogue equivalent. In the case of image manipulation, the technical quality of the finished product is undeniably better than the results of more traditional cut-and-paste methods. Yet as we have shown, this is more than simply a technical matter. Bringing certain aspects of the process – such as editing – within reach enables students to acquire much greater control over the conceptualisation of the finished product. The systematic *experimentation* with a wider range of possibilities – and hence the *conscious* selection of a final version – are made much more explicit as a focus of discussion and debate.

At the same time, digital editing and image manipulation appear to enable students to work more *directly* with the media, and hence to work in an almost intuitive way. This is certainly a substantial advance, although it has ambiguous implications in terms of learning. 'Older' technologies establish barriers at many stages of the production process, not least to do with the skills that are required. For many years, these barriers certainly prevented school students from producing media work with which they themselves could be satisfied. Yet on the other hand, these barriers also represented points at which students were forced to be explicit about their aims, and to reflect upon what they had achieved thus far. As we have argued, this process of explicit reflection is an essential dimension of media education – although (as we shall see in Chapter 6), it is not without its difficulties. The fact that this process did not really take place in any of these projects may be partly to do with their location within English, where reflection of this kind is rarely a central concern. However, it may also be a consequence of the more 'intuitive' aspects of the technology. While we welcome the accessibility of the technology, we are wary that it might lead to forms of media production that regard the medium itself as transparent, and the production process as simply a matter of individual creative expression. Like the media technologies that have preceded them, these new technologies should give rise to a much more wide-ranging reconsideration of our fundamental notions of creativity.

Notes

1   Knight (1964).
2   See Sefton-Green (1994).
3   Buckingham (1990).
4   For a detailed discussion of the problems of the 'literacy metaphor', see Buckingham (1993b) chapter 2.
5   See Buckingham and Sefton-Green (1994) chap. 5.
6   See, for example, Barton (1994).
7   See Buckingham (1993a).
8   See *Edge* November 1993.
9   This is a term coined by Jo Spence (1986) which describes a personal use of images of the self in a variety of poses to act as a form of psychological or therapeutic analysis of individual development.
10 Landow (1992).
11 See Landow *ibid*.
12 See Poster (1990).
13 Mellor et al (1984).
14 Dir. Francis Ford Coppola (1983).
15 These terms refer to the processes that can be applied to elements of images within the program. They describe a number of 'transformations' that the computer carries out on the graphic element selected. The fact that they require use of a separate vocabulary as well as knowledge of their visual effect focused

attention on the relationship between the linguistic and the conceptual dimension when introducing students to the program.

16 See Moss (1989).
17 This issue has been explicitly addressed in narrative theory: see Rimmon-Kenan (1983).
18 Eco (1979).
19 Bordwell and Thompson (1993).
20 Pudovkin (1929).
21 See Peters (1961).
22 For other applications of Vygotsky's theories to media education see Buckingham (1990), Chapter 10, and Buckingham and Sefton-Green *op cit.*
23 Bordwell and Thompson *op cit.*
24 Ellis (1982).
25 See Grahame (1990), Buckingham and Sefton-Green *op cit.*, Chapters 8 and 9.
26 See Fraser (forthcoming).

Chapter 4

Hangin' with the Technology: A Critical Investigation of Group Production

The logic of small group work

Practical media production, both in schools and in less formal educational contexts, is almost by definition a group process. Most Media Studies syllabuses actually *require* group productions, even if marks are allocated individually. Group work is often regarded as an unavoidable consequence of the complex technologies that are involved: video production, for example, is generally seen to entail a number of distinct roles that will be performed by different students. It is this that has led some more utopian advocates of practical work to argue that media production inevitably challenges individualistic notions of authorship[1].

In fact, there is rarely any inherent technical reason why media production has to be a group process. TV studio work is perhaps the only context in which a group is actually *required* – and in this case, it is significant that the group is almost invariably structured in a hierarchical way. It is perfectly possible for students to produce videos or sound recordings as individual projects, although of course they may need to draw on other students as required. It is often quite hard, when following syllabus requirements, to devise ways in which photography and design work can meaningfully be carried out as collective activities[2]. Meanwhile, there is a long historical tradition of the individual artisan in avant-garde film-making; and the advent of the video diary effectively explodes the myth that video production has to be collaborative. Particularly with the advent of digital technologies, as described in Chapter 3, the potential for wholly individualised production cannot be ignored.

Of course, the argument for group production work may function partly as a way of rationalising the shortage of resources: if you only have one video camera, it makes sense to invent roles for everyone to perform, even if all they involve is standing around with a clipboard. Yet there are, of course, much stronger reasons for the emphasis on collaborative group work, although they will be inflected in different ways in different contexts[3]. Thus, in many areas of the school curriculum, group work is seen as a valuable means of cultivating 'life skills': even the more mechanistic advocates of 'communications skills' have emphasised the importance of learning to work in groups, and of respecting others' points of view, even if only to prepare students more adequately for the world of work. From a more radical perspective, however, the preference for group work is essentially ideological: collective methods are seen to be inherently democratic, or indeed to provide a working model of a society based on democratic principles.

Yet the fundamental reasons for media teachers' emphasis on collaborative production are, I would argue, to do with arguments about *learning*. It is perhaps in this area that the debt to progressive English teaching is most apparent. Following the enormously influential work of writers like Douglas Barnes and James Britton, small group work has been accepted as a fundamental principle of contemporary English teaching. Even apparently individualistic practices such as reading and writing have been transformed into collaborative activities, on the grounds that language and learning are essentially *social* phenomena. A co-operative learning environment, which is based on small group work, will (it is argued) make best use of the available class time, foster students' confidence and motivation to learn, and make room for more constructive and egalitarian relationships between teachers and students[4]. The focus here is clearly on the social and intellectual development that is seen to characterise the *process*, rather than on the need to generate finished *products* – although this is not to imply that process and product are necessarily opposed.

These are arguments we would very much support, although they may also gloss over some of the tensions and difficulties of group work, particularly in media teaching. For example, one of the most notable applications of these arguments to media education was in the Schools Council Project on Communication and Social Skills, documented by Carol Lorac and Michael Weiss[5]. This project, which was conducted in the late 1970s, used media production both as a means of facilitating subject learning in a range of curriculum areas, and as a way of developing the more general skills identified in its title. Perhaps inevitably, given the period in which it was written, Lorac and Weiss's account tends to suffer from an excess of self-justification. This is particularly apparent in their discussion of group work:

> [The students] were continually put into situations in which it would have been all too easy to feel a sense of personal rejection as the group rejected or modified suggestions, yet they very quickly came to accept this as a natural and necessary part of group work. Also, once they knew what it was like to have an idea of their own rejected, they were more sensitive to the feelings of others within the group... They became responsible to the group for the quality of their activity, for the speed and thoroughness with which they approached it, for justifying their choices and decisions and for organising an adequate presentation of their results to the group... Whatever form of organisation they chose, coping with disagreements was something which each group had to consider, In almost all cases this was managed with remarkable skill, and some individuals demonstrated quite advanced organisational skills...[6]

While this account might represent group production at its best, the reality is often significantly less rosy. It is very easy to think of situations from our own teaching in which the very opposite has happened. All of us have at some time set up projects which have foundered primarily because the students (in many cases adults) have been unable to agree with each other, or evolve a way of working through their disagreements. Simply putting people into groups obviously does not in itself guarantee that they will evolve democratic ways of working, let alone mutual respect or responsibility. Group work can easily become a power struggle, in which individuals pay very little regard for others' feelings, and may actively seek to disrupt the effective functioning of the group.

Of course, there are all sorts of reasons why this may occur. Individuals come to groups, not as blank slates, but with existing personal histories and with established social positions. The power-relationships that develop in groups are bound to reflect those which obtain in the wider society – and in this respect, differences of age, gender, ethnicity and social class are obviously of central importance. In the case of media production, for example, gender differences have frequently been seen as a particular problem in this respect: boys, it is argued, always hog the equipment, while girls are left in the more exposed position of performers. While it is important to avoid an easy essentialism here, it remains the case that boys and girls are likely to approach both the technology and the situation of small-group work with different expectations and orientations. If, as teachers, we wish to offer different possibilities, we have to ensure that they are 'written in' to the structure of the activities from the start, rather than emerging after the event.

Indeed, it may well be worth asking whether 'democratic' decision-making is necessarily the most efficient method of group organisation, particularly when it comes to media production. As I have implied, some forms of media production may be accomplished much more effectively on an individual basis, although of course this is not to suggest that they cannot be shared and made the focus for group work at a later stage. In the context of a group, however, the need to get things done – that is, to generate a product – may well conflict with the need to secure agreement or mutual harmony, and in some cases a consensus may be impossible to achieve.

In this respect, there is a striking contrast between the emphasis on group democracy in media education and the nature of professional media production, which is generally organised in an extremely hierarchical way. Media sociologists have often depicted this hierarchical structure as a means whereby centralised control is sustained within media institutions[7] Yet anybody who has attempted to produce a television programme in a studio *without* a director issuing instructions to the crew will confirm that, at least in this context, a hierarchical structure is simply the most efficient (some would say the *only*) way of getting the job done. On the other hand, of course, many individuals in such situations will learn very little, except perhaps the need to follow instructions – and to this extent, there may be a fundamental contradiction between the need for efficiency and the interests of maximising *all* students' learning.

Learning in groups: some fundamental dilemmas

As the above discussion suggests, group work – however it is organised – does not in itself necessarily promote democratic outcomes. Effective group work obviously requires considerable support and intervention on the part of teachers: students need to be *enabled* to work together, just as they need to be taught to use the equipment. Yet in devising effective group work in media education, the teacher has to face several fundamental dilemmas.

Some of these, of course, apply to group work in general. How do you ensure that everyone is equally involved, when it is clear that the task will require different levels of involvement at different times? Does it make sense to allocate roles to different members of the group, or do you wait for them to decide on this for themselves? Do group decisions need to be formally recorded or voted upon, not least in the interests of avoiding disputes? What do you do about more dominant students, or about those who appear to contribute very little? How do you make sure that the motivated students stay motivated, without losing those who may be less keen? When and how should you as the teacher intervene? How do you balance praise and encouragement with constructive criticism, in order to help students move on?

In the case of media education, additional dilemmas are posed, which may partly derive from the particular balance between process and product, and between content and technical skills, which characterises media production:

1. When and how do you teach *technical skills*? Particularly if this is the students' first experience of media production, do you begin with exercises explicitly designed to teach skills, or do you wait until the content is developed to a certain point and then teach the skills that appear to be relevant? And if so, how do you as the teacher tell what is relevant, and what constitutes a diversion from the aims of the group? As we have noted in previous chapters, this is somewhat of a circular argument. You can only know what can be said in a given medium once you are familiar with the potential of the technology; and yet technical skills cannot really be acquired in any depth until you have something to say. Teaching skills in the abstract can be meaningless and boring, but how do you know what is possible until you have the skills?

2. Similar questions apply to teaching *the 'language' of the medium* – for example, different camera angles or the 'rules' of editing. As we discussed in Chapter 2, there is a tradition in media education which teachs conventional principles like the 180 degree rule – for example through 'code-breaking' exercises. On the other hand, do we expect that students will discover these rules by themselves, through trial and error? Or do we refuse to teach them in the hope that they will thereby come up with 'oppositional' or formally experimental texts? Here again, the circular argument applies. The problem, of course, is that these distinctions between content and skills, or content and language, are ultimately false: but this kind of philosophical point does not exactly help if we are seeking to plan an effective sequence of activities.

3. How do you enable students to develop *content*? Arguably, most students will have chosen to come on a media production course (or indeed an academic Media Studies course) in the first place because they want to learn technical skills, rather than because they have something they are burning to say. They want to make a video, not a statement about the world. Yet if they are really going to learn how to *use* the medium, it is vital that the content is meaningful and important to them – even if this is something they discover during the production process itself. Learning to use a given language is more than just a technical process: it involves communicating meaning, and setting out to achieve particular purposes or effects. If the content doesn't really matter, then the technical (or indeed creative) skills that are developed will also be fairly superficial. Yet the content of practical production work is an issue that, at least in Media Studies, is often left to the students to decide; and as long as it does not violate the tenets of political

correctness, it is rarely discussed by examiners either. This may well make good sense, but *only* if we have ways of enabling students to develop and extend what they want to communicate, and thereby to move beyond the superficial and the obvious.

4. How important is the *product*? As we have noted in our introduction, media educators have traditionally insisted on the primacy of process over product. Yet the experience of process *without* product is at least demoralising, if not meaningless. Most of us would now accept that the product is important – although we would reject the idea that it should be seen as the end of the process. On the contrary, the product should be seen as a vital part of the process, and an important opportunity for further reflection. Yet the need to balance process against product raises several key dilemmas. Experienced teachers will have fairly clear ideas about what kind of product is realistic or possible given the constraints of resources, time and equipment. But how do you make these apparent without simply imposing your conception of the finished product? How do you scale down students' ambitions without destroying their motivation? How do you make sure that something actually gets done in the time that is available? And how do you enable students to evaluate and reflect upon their product in a way that does not merely result either in defensiveness or in disappointment?

5. How do you balance *intentions and results*? Clearly, students' intentions are likely to change as a production develops. They may not begin with clear intentions and only discover them once the work is under way – if indeed they do so at all. Yet Media Studies (and perhaps particularly Communications Studies[8]) has often seemed to employ a rather simplistic objectives-based model of communication, in which production is seen as an orderly progression from intentions to results. The question 'did you achieve what you set out to do?' is often regarded as the acid test; and changing your mind is implicitly seen as an admission of failure[9]. Yet in the vast majority of situations, the production process is bound to be much more complex, and indeed more messy and confused. While acknowledging this, it seems equally vital to ensure that the process does not become merely arbitrary. How do you ensure that students keep sight of their intentions, and review them systematically? How do you ensure that they consider their potential audience, and do not produce something that only makes sense to themselves? How do you enable them to reflect upon the ways in which their intentions may have changed, and how this is reflected in the finished product?

Media production and youth work

My aim in undertaking this case study, then, was to investigate some of the ways in which groups learn to work together – an issue which has been largely neglected by previous research in this field[10]. Of course, individuals often come to a group with an existing history of relationships, and (certainly in schools) with past experiences of collaboration. As a group production progresses, those relationships will be affected further by what happens, not merely within lessons, but also beyond them. Much of this is bound to be invisible to teachers and (even more so) to researchers coming in from outside.

It was primarily in order to get around some of these complexities that I chose to study an intensive production course, in which at least some of the participants would not know each other, and in which the work of the group would not be subject to the constraints of school timetables. The course took place in the context of a youth and community arts project, rather than a school, and as such it offered rather different possibilities from those described in the other chapters in the book. The young people who attended the course did so voluntarily. The course was not examined or certificated, nor was it constrained by the curricular requirements of another academic subject. It was not limited to fifty-minute lesson times, and it was extremely generously resourced in terms of technology and staff time. On the other hand, it was also subject to less immediately obvious constraints, for example to do with the expectations of the young people who attended and with the implicit assumptions of youth work itself – which in turn derive partly from its institutional location. It is this broader context which needs to be sketched in here.

From its inception in the late 1960s, portable video has been a staple tool of youth and community work. While the history of this approach has yet to be written, its origins probably lie in the much earlier use of film as a means of 'cultural animation', for example in some of the projects carried out in collaboration with rural communities by the National Film Board of Canada[11]. In common with much of the community media production that arose in the wake of the student activism of the 1960s, the vast majority of these projects were informed by the aesthetics of documentary realism[12]. The central preoccupation was with *content*, with 'giving a voice' to groups whose perspectives had hitherto been ignored or unrepresented. While there are some exceptions[13], there was often a distinct lack of the kind of formal experimentation that characterised the other main use of portable video at that time – namely, the fine art practice of video makers such as Nam June Paik.

Some very grand claims have been made in this context for the power of video as a means of democratisation and social liberation, although they have proven remarkably difficult to substantiate in practice[14]. Nevertheless, much of this work continues to be informed by a belief in the progressive political potential of media production, particularly with under-privileged groups. Thus, it is argued, enabling kids to take control of the 'means of production' can empower them in relation to the adult world, and in relation to the media themselves[15]. They become producers rather than 'mere consumers', able to give voice to their own concerns, and to offer positive alternatives to dominant representations. Yet the extent to which such work has ever successfully moved beyond the paternalism that it almost inevitably entails – and which is embodied in the notion that young people have to be 'given' a voice – remains an open question.

The most influential contemporary version of this approach – albeit one that was based primarily on photography rather than video – can be found in the work of the Cockpit Cultural Studies Department, and is documented in some detail by Andrew Dewdney and Martin Lister[16]. During the late 1970s and 1980s, the Cockpit undertook a series of projects using practical photography, primarily with working-class young people in schools and youth centres. Rather than emphasising the aesthetic or technical aspects of the medium, this approach sought to capitalise on the status of photography as a genuinely popular social practice. Building on everyday uses of photography (such as the snapshot and the family album), the Cockpit team sought to move beyond the limitations of traditional 'amateur photography', and to devise an approach which was based in the cultural forms which are most valued by young people themselves. The central focus of much of this work was the notion of youth culture as 'style'. Following the work of academic writers such as Paul Willis and Dick Hebdige, style was seen here as the terrain on which young people actively construct and explore their own cultural identities. This approach aimed to enable young people to investigate the relationships between who they 'are' and how they are represented; and as such, it clearly did attempt to move beyond the limitations of documentary realism. It was not simply about young people 'expressing themselves' or communicating their perspectives and concerns. On the contrary – at least in principle – it involved a self-conscious and reflexive emphasis on the *process* of representation itself.

In many respects, the work of the Cockpit team offers not just a developed alternative to academic Media Studies in schools, but also a direct challenge to it. Dewdney and Lister argue that Media Studies' drive for academic legitimacy has effectively undermined its 'best and most democratic elements': in the process, it has fallen prey to a didactic and schematic approach, and a form of 'theoreticism'. This is a critique we would broadly share. Both in this book and in earlier classroom research, we have drawn attention to the ways in which the radical aims of media education are all too often compromised by the institutional constraints of schooling – for example, by the narrow requirements of assessment, or by the exercise of teacherly authority over the potentially subversive meanings and pleasures of students. The logic of this argument would appear to lead inexorably to the view that media education would be able to fulfil its radical potential much more easily in a less restricted institutional context, and using much more open-ended teaching methods. Ultimately, perhaps, we should be abandoning the search for academic status, and seeking to define media education, not as 'work', but as an extension of leisure – as it is in fact defined in many other European countries[17].

To a large extent, the evolution of the Cockpit approach appears to follow through this logic. Thus, while some of the work took place in schools, it was largely consigned to the margins of the formal curriculum, for example in the form of 'life skills' work with disaffected school leavers. Even this work tended to import the ethos of youth and community work into the school: while the institutional apparatus of the school was largely perceived as a constraint that had to be resisted or evaded. Thus, Dewdney and Lister note 'the remoteness of the school as a social institution from the social worlds of young people' and argue for 'the need to look beyond the school to other institutions in the communities in which young people live as the next stage in building cultural practices with them'[18].

Nevertheless, the use of the word 'institutions' is significant here. The youth service – in which this kind of work has increasingly been located – is funded by local social services departments to provide institutionalised provision for young people, both in the form of youth centres and clubs[19], and by supporting voluntary sector projects. Yet it would be a mistake to assume that these are merely neutral spaces, in which radical interventions are somehow magically possible. On the contrary, the historical study of local authority youth provision would suggest that it functions primarily as a means of keeping troublesome youth off the streets – and in this context, the term 'youth' implicitly refers to young people who are working class, often black and predominantly male[20]. Of course, it would be simplistic to regard the youth service – or indeed schools – as simply a form of 'soft policing', but the arguments can clearly cut both ways.

In their retrospective account of the Cockpit work, Dewdney and Lister also identify a number of difficulties (or at least unresolved issues) in their approach. They acknowledge the dangers of focusing exclusively on 'spectacular' youth cultures, and the limitations of a simplistic validation of 'resistance' to middle-class authority. As they note, radical teachers cannot simply affirm young people's perspectives simply by announcing that they are 'on the same side'. Particularly within the context of school (although I would add not *only* there), young people may often reject the attempt to make their own resistance the obvious subject of educational intervention.

Ultimately, however, Dewdney and Lister fail to resolve the crucial question of what students might actually be *learning* from this kind of work, beyond merely acquiring technical skills. The danger of their approach is one that has been identified in critiques of 'progressive' pedagogy much more broadly. In seeking to validate students' perspectives, does it not end up simply leaving them where they already are? While this process of validation might prove to be progressive (or perhaps therapeutic) for teachers, it is more important to investigate what it might be doing for the students themselves. Advocates of the Cockpit approach have produced some persuasive analyses of students' work, which implicitly make use of semiotic and post-structuralist theory[21]. But the extent to which these insights were available to the students themselves, or in what form, remains highly debatable. Dewdney and Lister acknowledge the need to 'problematise', to 'make students think about what is being celebrated', and to enable them to be 'self-reflexive' about their own work[22] – an emphasis that we would see as crucially important. Yet they provide few indications of how this might be achieved in practice, without merely recuperating it back into the academic (or, in their terms, 'magisterial') mode of conventional schooling[23]. Indeed, the non-interventionist pedagogy on which the approach appears to be based would seem to preclude such 'teacherly' interference.

Many of the questions that will be addressed in this case study implicitly reflect these much broader criticisms of the progressivist approach. Does working with 'students' cultures' necessarily have progressive political consequences? To what extent does this apparently non-interventionist approach actually embody a 'hidden curriculum' – an unstated set of prescriptions and constraints? How far is it possible here to enable students to ask critical questions about their own work, or to reflect back on the production process itself?

An outline of the course

The youth and community project in which the course took place is located in a run-down industrial area in London's inner city. Using a range of funding sources, it has gradually become equipped with technology for sound recording and video production that is, if not state of the art, at least significantly better than that available within the formal education system. Most of the project's work is with groups of young people in youth clubs and on council estates, although it does undertake some courses in schools and further education colleges. In collaboration with such groups, it has produced some acclaimed documentaries, and recently won a prestigious award for its educational work with young people.

The course, which took place during the school half-term and on two subsequent weekends and evenings, was taught by five staff from the project, all of whom were present for most of the course. The seventeen young people who officially attended the course were aged between 14 and 24, and were drawn from two local youth projects. Some of them had attended evening classes on media production at one of the projects over the previous two terms, but many were new to the area. Young men outnumbered young women by ten to seven, and the course acquired several additional hangers-on, most of whom were male. There were four male staff, one female. Twelve of the seventeen students were black (Afro-Caribbean) or of mixed race; three of the staff were also black.

The course had a dual focus on sound technology and video production. Despite occasional protestations to the contrary, the staff had a clear end in view, which was that the group should work collectively to produce a music video combining these two main areas of work. In the event, the group split into a number of smaller groups. While the younger boys mostly worked on writing and performing raps, four of the girls opted to choreograph a dance routine, while another girl worked on a vocal chorus. One young man helped with the sound equipment, building up a rhythm track using digital samples. The video group, which I observed for the duration of the course, consisted of three young men and two young women, all of whom were in their late teens or early twenties.

These groups were formed at the end of the first day, following a series of sessions in which everybody was introduced to the equipment and given a brief hands-on experience. The four subsequent days were spent planning, performing and shooting material for the video. While there were occasional meetings to share ideas and to check on progress, and some individuals worked in more than one group, for the most part the groups worked independently. Following the week's production work, a small group then took charge of editing the tape, with some feedback from the others. For various reasons, this took longer than anticipated, and eventually came down to the work of one young man. The tape was finally presented at a public screening one evening approximately four weeks after the main course.

Focusing the case study

In line with the broad questions raised above, my intention here was to look at one group in detail, focusing not so much on the content of their work, but on the 'group dynamics'. For example, I wanted to look at how ideas were generated and decisions were made; at how the members of the group agreed to organise themselves and divide up responsibilities; and at how potential conflicts were resolved (or not). My intention was not to focus on the 'teachers' but on the 'students', and to observe as neutrally and in as much detail as possible.

To a great extent, the account that follows seeks to preserve this emphasis, although it also exposes some of the naivety of my initial thinking. While I was very concerned at the outset that my teacherly instincts would get the better of me, I did largely manage to restrain my desire to intervene. The students either ignored me or treated me as a strange outsider, which was certainly compounded by the fact that I said very little and frequently made notes or tape-recorded what was said.

My relationship with the staff, however, was rather more uncomfortable. Unlike all the other work described in this book, this course was not planned in collaboration with the staff. Far from being a teacher/researcher, I was very much an outside observer, and I was perceived as such. While I had gained access through a 'gatekeeper' – the director of the project, whom I have known for several years – the staff who were actually running the course were only vaguely aware of my intentions, despite my attempts to inform them ahead of time.

As I suspect we all quickly recognised, the notion that it would be possible to study the work of the group in isolation, without also considering the context in which it was expected to work, was disingenuous – or at the very least, a form of wishful thinking. It was of course impossible to focus on the 'students' without also considering the role of the 'teachers'. Both through what they did and through what they failed to do, it was the teachers who (however invisibly) defined the parameters of the students' work. My account of the course emphasises a number of dilemmas which I believe are shared by teachers of practical media production, and indeed by all teachers who use group methods, irrespective of the context in which they work. Nevertheless, much of what I have to say focuses inevitably on what I perceive as the limitations of the teaching, and it would be dishonest to pretend otherwise. My criticisms of the course and of the teaching come from 'outside' – and while this is a traditional position from which to conduct educational research, I would not generally see it as the best one.

Perhaps the most significant issue here is the fact that I write from the perspective of someone who is centrally involved with formal education in schools. Thus, for example, I will obstinately refer to the participants here as tutors and students; and my central concern is with what students learnt, rather than with whether or not they had a good time (although of course I acknowledge that these are often indivisible). Having worked in youth centres myself (and often found it frustrating), the course brought back unwelcome memories. In my experience, most young people who attend youth centres define them precisely in terms of their *opposition* to school: they are essentially about 'hanging out', and definitely not about anything that might possibly resemble 'work'. Similarly, the professional ethos of most contemporary youth workers is defined in terms of their *opposition* to teachers: they are generally keen to avoid the implication that they are authority figures, or experts, or indeed anything other than older friends. This may well be an unfair characterisation of youth work, and it is not one that could reasonably be applied to all the students and the staff on the course I shall describe – although it certainly carries more than a grain of truth.

Nevertheless, the questions and dilemmas that were raised in my observations here also connected with my own experience in teaching workshop-based production courses, and in observing such courses taught by my students, as part of examined curricula in schools. In the end, it may be that I am simply judging this experience by inappropriate criteria – bringing my equally narrow and institutionalised concerns with schools to bear on a context that is inherently and necessarily different. Yet the question of what students might *learn* from this kind of work is one that I would argue is of vital importance, irrespective of the context.

In the account that follows, I will be quoting extended extracts from my 'diary' of field notes and transcripts of group discussions, and to a lesser extent from interviews with the students, that were gathered as the course progressed. These extracts (in italics) will be interspersed with a commentary that seeks to draw connections with some of the underlying themes identified here.

Day 1: Finding a focus

As I have noted, the course had a dual focus on video production and sound technology. The staff anticipated that there would be one group working in each area, and that they would work in parallel, although with a theme that would be agreed early on. The day began with a screening of examples of work from previous projects, which were mostly rap videos, and an attempt to arrive at a shared theme. Given the disparate nature of the group, this attempt to arrive at a consensus was inevitably problematic.

The tutors seem to have a very clear idea of the kind of product they are aiming at – namely, a rap video – and showing examples of work from previous projects reinforces this idea. At the same time, they keep disclaiming this, and saying people can do what they like. James, Chilo and Frank (older students) all say they are interested in other kinds of music, and I suspect hard-core rappers are in a minority. In the plenary discussions at the beginning and end of the day, there are a number of people who clearly dissent from what is emerging, although they are unwilling to push themselves. Both James and Frank, for example, explicitly say they don't want to impose their tastes on the rest of the group.

Further difficulties emerge when we move on to a discussion of the theme. The idea is that the theme will be agreed upon as a basis for the work of each of the groups. Everyone is asked to come up with 'things you are concerned about'. This leads to the following list:

> *life*
> *girls (supplied by one of the younger boys)*
> *tales of the city*
> *environment*
> *drugs*
> *sexism*
> *racism and the BNP*
> *world issues: Bosnia, Europe, South Africa*

Once this list has been generated, there is something of an impasse. Nafeesa (an older student) says there is no hope of them doing such big themes. Eventually David (an older student) suggests 'Change in the 1990s', which gains some approval from others in the group – although largely because it is a compendium for all the other ideas, and thus effectively avoids the necessity of having to make a decision. This is explicitly recognised by people in the group.

Towards the end of the day, once everyone has been given a brief introduction to each of the technical areas and a chance for some hands-on experience, the students express further worries: how long is the video expected to be; who will be responsible for putting the whole thing together; and who will take charge of each bit. The major problem here, of course, is that the groups working in different media (musicians, dancers and video-makers) are expected to work in parallel. James and Frank point out that it will be hard to put together the music track until the lyrics are written, and impossible to find images until there is a complete song. There is an argument that some creative forms are essentially individual: writing a rap is something you do on your own, 'like writing a story' as Ivor says, and some people are urging that someone should go away and write one in order that everyone else will have something to work from. Helen suggests that everyone should write some lyrics, and these should be pooled and edited, although this idea is not pursued.

The atmosphere of this first day was inevitably wary. While some of the younger students, and the dancers, appeared to have come as a group, few of the others knew each other. However, the design of the course (with different groups working in parallel) meant that an agreement about the content had to be reached very quickly – although in effect the group managed to avoid this. Perhaps a further problem here, however, was what was defined as 'content' in the first place. Certainly in the case of the rap videos that were shown at the beginning of the day, the overt message seemed to be secondary. What is central in such material is the look, the dance, the body, the pose, the gesture – in effect, a bodily aesthetics, albeit one that is fundamentally concerned with group identity. By contrast, the content that was elicited in discussion read like a worthy adult's list of Young People's Concerns.

This design arose partly because of the need to work in smaller groups. But it also reflected an attempt to democratise the production process – to turn something that would in reality be organised hierarchically and sequentially into a collective endeavour. In the world of professional production, a number of people would be responsible for producing a music video, but they would be hierarchically divided in terms of conception and execution. An individual writes the song (or perhaps two people write the music and the lyric), and then either performs it or directs other people to do so: and while the other performers may contribute, they are not involved in defining the idea in the first place. Likewise, a video director then directs, and although the camera operator and the editor will obviously contribute, they are negotiating with a concept that is the work of one person. This is clearly a *collaborative* process, but it cannot really be seen as *collective*, let alone democratic.

In this situation, there appeared to be a very clear conception of the *form* of the end product which was held by the staff, and which was reinforced implicitly and explicitly as the course progressed – and indeed emerged relatively unscathed in the finished tape. While there were certainly good reasons for this, it was not ultimately a matter for negotiation, and individuals who dissented from the general direction could only do so at the risk of being seen to be difficult or selfish. As I shall argue, this choice of form had very limiting implications both in terms of 'content' and in terms of the potential for developing technical skills.

Day 2: Improvising images

After the introductory day, the group split into smaller groups who were opting to work with particular media. The choice of medium was difficult for some students, but most had come with a clear idea of which they wanted to learn. At the same time, it is significant that this choice was fundamentally determined by medium rather than by any concerns to do with content. Perhaps as a result, a clear gendered division of labour emerged very quickly here, and appeared to be taken for granted by all concerned: the boys were rappers or sound engineers and the girls were dancers or singers, and nobody crossed the divide. Only the filming group was mixed, and it was this group that I observed for much of the rest of the course. The group consisted of three young men (Ivor, James and David) and two young women (Chilo and Nafeesa). They were all in their late teens or early twenties, and hence significantly older than most of the other students. Two tutors, Anna and Nathan, were assigned to work with this group.

The day begins again with a meeting. Nathan emphasises that, while people will work in specialist groups, the production will be based on democratic decision-making. 'It's a collective thing basically, same with the music and the lyrics and everything, it's a collective *thing. Although we will need certain people concentrating on each one, everyone's involved in actually making the decisions as to what goes in.'*

The problem from the point of view of the filming group is that they don't really know what to film until they get the lyrics for the rap. There is a re-run of yesterday's debate, but the staff resist suggestions for alternative ways of working: it seems their major concern is that everyone should not have to 'wait around' until the lyrics have been written – in effect, a disciplinary issue. James, the most vocal critic, is ultimately silenced, and the group splits into specialisms.

Once more, the filming group is asked to generate some topics – the list of Young People's Concerns. 'Whatever's important to you,' says Anna, 'anything from the nineties'. Each individual is asked to identify a topic, and most seem to respond without much thought, simply to get out of the spotlight. I find this painfully embarrassing. Nevertheless, a list is generated with names attached.

Of course the problem with the list of Young People's Concerns is that it doesn't give much idea of what to film: Anna insists lamely that these ideas all suggest 'really strong images', but no-one seems to suggest what these images might be. The only person to suggest specific ideas is Chilo. She says she wants to film a sequence of herself walking on water, and then lifting rubbish out of the water: this is to be accompanied by a song which she sings to the group which includes the line 'river deep and mountain high' (borrowed, of course, from Tina Turner) – the mountain being the rubbish she has lifted out of the water. Nobody knows how to respond to this, so it goes down on the list as 'environment'.

James and others are adamant that they don't want to produce a conventional rap video, full of 'shitty clichés' – rappers posing, 'shoulders on, shots from under their chin, looking into the camera, that kind of thing.' Nathan supports this. James attempts to assert that they will have final control over the look of the thing – 'we're the visual directors' – but Nathan says they will have to acknowledge the performers' wishes to be featured.

Anna tries to generate a list of images we're looking for – derelict buildings, homeless people etc. – and we go off supposedly in search of them. It is a lovely day, and the dirty canal looks beautiful with the light glinting off the water. We are probably going in the wrong direction if we are looking for images of urban decay. A solitary dead fish is the best pollution we can find. We wander towards town, with individuals taking turns with the camera and Anna trying to ensure that the shots are logged (she eventually gives up). Shots are taken of graffiti, the canal, reflections of the water, lock gates, railway lines etc.. James gets excited by the patterns on the water under the bridge; and when we get to Whitton Hill, David spends a long time getting long-distance shots of children and Chilo whirls round with the camera on the top of the hill, getting dizzy shots of the London panorama. Much of this is random filming for the sake of it: there's no real mention of the 'themes'.

The results are viewed in the editing room. David's shots of children in the park are lopsided and wobbly. Some bits haven't come out because of the light (too bright) and others are out-of-focus. Nevertheless, there are some reasonable shots of the reflections on the water and the railway lines (mostly taken by James, whom the others have dubbed Steven Spielberg).

Outside, on a break, James and Chilo get into a long and circular argument. James says that what they have done is 'shit'. It's out of focus, the shots are badly composed, the lighting is wrong. Chilo takes him to task for being negative, and says she is offended by him slagging off other people's work. Michael (one of the tutors) also supports this, and argues that you will only encourage people by being positive. James says he was only giving his opinion when invited (by Chilo) and that he wasn't broadcasting it around; he insists he isn't negative, he's quite happy to go out now and shoot the material again, and he feels he has learnt from his mistakes. Chilo says the only way you can learn about this is by doing it, you can't get a pile of books and learn it. This is supported by Nathan, and James also agrees, although he still maintains that what they have done is shit.

However, back in the editing room, James and Ivor have begun experimenting with the effects – strobes, wipes, negatives, adding tints. There is some agreement that particular bits look good – or, as David puts it, 'eye-catching'. The music track is being assembled in the next room, and David remarks how some of the images look good against the music. James and Ivor experiment *by manipulating the effects in time with the beat. After a further meeting, James and Ivor stay on to 'analyse' (their word) the video: Chilo tells me that James is now saying that some bits of the tape look really good.*

The assumption that people will *only* 'learn by doing' seemed to be shared by staff and students alike – although it also appeared to sanction a kind of refusal of teaching on the part of the staff, which I have suggested is symptomatic of a great deal of youth work. Throughout this entire day, there was virtually no instruction on how to use the camera; and when it came to viewing the rushes, the staff made very little contribution. While the students were aware that they had made 'mistakes', nobody was encouraging them to think about why they had been made, and how they might be avoided next time. 'Learning from your mistakes' depends upon knowing what counts as a mistake in the first place, and *why* you made the mistakes you did – for example that shots are out of focus because you should zoom in, focus, zoom out to frame the shot, and then start the camera. It also depends upon you having certain intentions to begin with – and since much of the work at this stage was simply in order to provide 'hands on' experience for its own sake, there was very little that could reasonably been seen as a 'mistake' in these terms. On the other hand, when one does have clearer intentions, making mistakes can also be extremely demoralising, particularly when they could easily have been avoided. Yet if being self-critical is seen as merely 'negative', it is hard to see grounds for improvement.

The choice of genre also sanctioned this approach. At their worst, pop videos seem to rely on a combination of accidents, assembly and effects. Any footage will do, as long as it is vaguely related. The aim is to collect a great deal of it, much more than you need, and then assemble the best bits. And once you add the effects and the music, the chances are it will be bound to look good. Of course, this is not to belittle pop videos in general: the best pop videos are very carefully constructed, and there is very little accident. But it is possible to make something that *looks like* a pop video with very little sense of direction or idea of what statement you want to make. If the effects are good, and there are some cool poses, then it will look fine. Since most pop videos use montage editing rather than continuity editing, and many make a virtue of illegible images, it is not actually necessary to know much about the 'language of film'. Ultimately, it is hard to conceive of anything that would count as a mistake, short of filming someone wearing an anorak. Crucially, this choice of genre also enables the appearance of group democracy to be preserved: everyone's 'bit' can be included – dramatic scenes, performance sequences, location shots – albeit at the risk of incoherence.

Finally, the use of rap as a form may also serve as a way of avoiding the need to develop content, or move beyond superficial concerns. Again, this is not to belittle the achievements of the best rap artists, merely to question its function in this context. Rap, as a highly self-conscious public form, seems to invite a good deal of well-meaning personal statement; but it is no less conventionalised and generic than your average poem in an English class, and no more personal. What counts as an 'authentic' rap does so largely in terms of established generic conventions. Rap is very much favoured in this kind of context as the privileged form of expression for 'the youth' – but this is a construction of young people that verges dangerously on the patronising. For all its apparent authenticity and social commentary, rap may serve as a way of marginalising the question of content in favour of a limited and highly conventional repertoire of physical and linguistic gestures.

Day 3: Working groups

For the first part of the day, we split into two groups. Ivor and James are emerging (perhaps despite their own wishes) as leaders, and it is on their initiative that two groups go off to re-do some of the shots that were taken yesterday...

The rap is promised for 3.30, but fails to emerge despite some concerted efforts by the staff. Later in the afternoon, I am sitting in the studio with three of the younger boys aimlessly spinning on chairs while one of them randomly scratches and puts in interjections over the track. It is at this point that I think of the title for my piece.

Nathan suggests that Chilo and David should shoot some 'wild footage' of people at work: he clearly has a specific end product in view. Meanwhile, I am observing James and Ivor, who are now purposefully logging the shots they need. Again, none of the staff are around to help with this, or make suggestions. James suggests that none of this material 'has any meaning', but that it might come in useful for backdrops (at several points throughout the discussions, chromakey seems to be seen as a kind of magic that will make anything possible – as in Chilo's fantasy of walking on water). When I ask him about what he had filmed earlier, he says that it's 'shit': the camera was too wobbly and the pan was too fast. Again, it is not clear why they didn't review the shots in the camera viewfinder, or why they weren't encouraged to pan slowly.

James also talks a lot about the dangers of clichés. While David was very enthusiastic about the shots of a wire cage, filmed yesterday, James sees this as a cliché, and doesn't log it (and Ivor falls in with this). Likewise, when we get to David's footage of the children, he says 'scroll this shit'. He is dismissive of the idea of filming the dance sequence in a basketball court (as was initially proposed) on the same grounds: 'what are they going to call it, White Girls Can't Jump?'[24] Like a number of the others, he rejects the standard iconography of drug trafficking – 'zooming in on close ups of packs of white powder'. James's rejection of all this comes across as middle-class 'indie' cynicism, and it occasionally sets him out as a lone voice. In the final discussion of the day, it is notable how the staff frequently attempt to close down his comments.

Eventually, the dance sequence is filmed outside. James effectively takes charge, shouting instructions to the dancers. He is interested in filming from above, and getting shots of the shadows of the dancers, which is difficult as the sun keeps going in. The dancers do their routine, but few people are impressed, and the film crew are more interested in some freestyle dancing. Ivor and Chilo also do some filming, while David acts as a kind of floor manager, relaying comments to the performers. There is an ongoing debate between the film crew and the dancers about which version of the track they want to use. Ivor is annoyed: 'people are just pissing about, wasting time'.

Nafeesa points out that it might be nice to have some male dancers, although her comment goes unnoticed. Meanwhile, there are some boys – Skinny and Stefan – who clearly do fancy themselves in this department, and who hang around in the background of the shots posing with their hoods up, bogling enthusiastically – although they decline the invitation to be filmed. Display of this kind is OK for girls, it seems, but much more of a problem for boys. Jordanna's ragga dance, for example, comes close to simulated masturbation, and is enthusiastically received by the girls and the boys (if perhaps for different reasons).

Finally, a sequence is shot and then viewed on the edit suite. James and Ivor are disappointed – the video is 'no good', 'pretty shit'. Ivor says this is because the dancers 'look like match-sticks in a field'. 'We need to move the camera,' he says, 'get right in there'. Again, there is some learning by discovery here – they have found out that you have to choreograph for the camera – but this could easily have been pointed out at the time. When we get back for the second attempt, the dancers are less amenable. There isn't a chance to plan the sequence, so again some random shots are gathered.

Later, there is considerable complaint about the attitude of the dancers. Ivor says 'they've just got totally the wrong attitude, like they're walking away from the camera when people are filming, and they're saying 'oh, we've had enough, all right, let's go home now'.. they just walk on and off the set like they are calling the shots, and everyone is running behind them, but a camera operator can't be doing that. They've got some conception in their heads that they are some big superstars, and without them, things can't go on, and everyone is trailing behind them'. The tutors respond by throwing the responsibility back to the group. Nathan: 'you have to take some control in that situation, not just say 'come along, do this'. And you can't just bully them into it, you've got to talk to them and tell them how serious it is. I think once you do that, things happen... You've got to coerce them and show them it's a joint project where every bit is as important as every other bit, and show them that what they're doing is quite important for the overall project and how it's going to look'. David suggests they need two floor managers, organising the performers; and Nathan agrees that there need to be roles in the team.

Finally, at the very end of the day, some intense planning begins. The raps have been read; and they aren't exactly rapturously received. Again, James is the most vocal critic, although David also finds them hard to understand. There isn't much relationship between the initial agenda of issues (the list of Young People's Concerns) and what's turned up. The lyrics are written in generic rap style, with 'correct' generic spellings – 'yout' not 'youth', for example.

Anna makes an attempt to go through the list again, and James responds impatiently. Both he and Ivor point out that the 'interests' they identified in the earlier discussions were 'off the top of my head', and that they don't want to be held to them now. Ivor suggests they abandon the list, and try to work on images, 'little dramas', that emerge from the lines of the rap. Chilo says the rappers can be in the drama – 'they just want us to tell them what to do' – but Nathan is still urging them to make it a 'collective' project.

Ivor says they need to devise storyboards. Nathan produces a sample of a storyboard from an earlier project, 'just to give you a rough idea', and emphasises the importance of this kind of detailed planning. Yet while the staff offer generalised advice about how the group should be organised, and occasionally steer people away from ideas they obviously feel will take too much time, ultimately it is down to the group to devise its own strategy. James suggests they take the raps individually and generate ideas and then come together. Nafeesa talks about how she's done storyboards at college. Ivor eventually takes over as the teacher figure. He gives everyone five minutes to work on one of the raps, and then moves to the front, collecting images or scenes based on each of the raps and putting these up on the flip-chart. A large number of suggestions is generated, although they are extremely disparate, and each would take some careful planning and setting-up. Ivor is concerned that the video will be 'too jumpy', while James argues 'we've got to try and get a grand story line out of the four raps, make it a grand story line that ties it all together, then we can have a theme'. Various suggestions emerge here, particularly from Nafeesa, implying a transition from 'negative' images of the city – rappers 'standing on the corner, hanging around and not doing anything' – to more 'positive' ones: 'then you see all the rapping and stuff, 'cause that shows the whole transition straight away, that shows that they're not just in the city on the streets, they're in the city doing something positive.'

Towards the end, David asks Nathan what he expects of the group by the end of tomorrow, but Nathan is evasive – 'groups work differently' – but David insists 'we need to aim at something' David clearly expects Nathan to give them a shooting schedule, but he avoids this: he says 'it's your project', and passes this task on to Ivor. David tries to organise everyone into producing a schedule from their list of ideas, but the others argue that a storyboard is needed first.

Although discovery learning clearly does have certain advantages, here it seemed to be applied not simply to operating the equipment, but also to the process of group-work itself. With such a large and disparate group working on a single production, relations between the different specialist groups (and between younger and older students) were almost bound to be difficult. With some exceptions, the younger students seemed to have come with rather different expectations of the course from the older ones: they appeared to regard it essentially as a social activity, an opportunity to hang out and have a laugh with friends, and perhaps in the process to gain a shot at stardom. By contrast, the older students had more serious, and to some extent vocational, motivations. Ivor, for example, had already attended some media courses in a further education college, and wanted to go on to take Media Studies at university. David was a professional actor, Chilo had worked as a professional singer and James was a musician and music teacher: all of them saw the course partly as a way of extending their existing areas of expertise. While the polarisation between these two groups was unusual, this range of motivations is probably fairly typical of students who are likely to attend this kind of course. Although the younger students were perhaps more representative of youth work clientele, the vocational aims held by the older students are also far from uncommon.

Yet here it seemed to be left to the older students to find their own way through these problems, in a situation where they themselves had no authority, and where imposing deadlines or more structured ways of working was bound to prove problematic. In handling the younger students, the tension between encouragement and criticism appeared to be a particular problem. The staff consistently counselled the older students against a confrontational approach – suggesting, for example, that if they dared to criticise the raps, the kids would simply walk away and reject them. While this was almost certainly correct, it seemed to be symptomatic of a situation in which criticism could not be seen as constructive. As we shall see, the possibility of anyone publicly criticising some of the sexist content of the lyrics was never on the agenda.

Within the video group itself, a clear hierarchy began to emerge – not so much, I would argue, because of the assertiveness of 'dominant personalities', but simply because it seemed to be the most efficient and familiar way of getting things done. The group effectively re-invented what they knew or imagined to be the structure of a professional production crew: terms like 'camera operator' and 'floor manager' (although not yet 'director') began to emerge. On the other hand, it was interesting to note that when it came to generating the visual ideas, the group naturally reverted to an individualistic method of working – namely sitting down and writing in silence. One implication of this might be that there has to be a structured interplay between individual and group creativity – that ideas have to be generated personally first, and then negotiated, and then reworked personally, and so on.

On the other hand, both within the video group and across the course as a whole, the gendered divisions of labour became increasingly apparent. Left to their own devices, without intervention on this issue from the staff, the students clearly had little to be gained from rejecting or questioning the roles that 'naturally' appeared to be marked out for them.

Fig. 4.1 Stills from the rap video

Day 4: Taking charge

With two days of filming to go, the pace started to accelerate dramatically. While there were still vacant spaces during the day, the deadline seemed to have galvanised everyone into action. By the end of the day, it was as though the doing of the task has achieved a momentum of its own – to the point where a critical perspective or distanced reflection (or even disagreements among the team) had to be minimised. 'Getting it done' had become the overriding aim.

We start at 1.15, the earliest yet. Ivor is very much in charge. He sets a deadline for 2.30 – 3.00, by which time he says the group should have produced a storyboard for each of the raps. He uses the ideas agreed upon yesterday and takes the lead in turning them into images for a storyboard. One of his aims here is to amalgamate the ideas and collapse them together into a smaller number of scenes. Ivor is trying hard to involve the others, getting them to come up and draw scenes: 'we're working against time here, so you have to tell me exactly what you want'. But he is definitely directing the group, and the shape the storyboard takes is pretty much the one he envisaged yesterday. He is also introducing technical vocabulary and abbreviations (C.U. for close-up, etc). Nevertheless, a number of others do contribute, including one of the rappers, David O, who appears to have a very clear idea of how his sequence should look.

Space precludes a detailed account of how the ideas for each of the rap sequences were generated – ideas which, it might be said, only rarely found their way to the finished product. Through these debates, there was a clear attempt (led by Ivor) to temper the group's ambitions in the light of what was possible given the available time and resources. It was these logistical constraints that ultimately determined many of the decisions: a proposal to film a montage sequence of newspaper headlines was dropped because no-one had had the time to find them, while any suggestions that would involve distant locations were quickly rejected. Technical solutions were also sought – for example by suggesting that the faster rap sequences be strobed in order to overcome the difficulties of lip-synching. Potential disagreements were talked around, and occasionally dispelled by humour, although there was some attempt to remain faithful to the spirit of the lyrics. Disputes that continued for some time were simply resolved by suggesting that these sequences be cut, or dealt with in a quite different way, for example by cutting away to a dance sequence.

With the storyboarding completed on target, Ivor congratulates everyone – with some irony, as though he's accepting an Oscar – but also says 'really, you've all worked this morning'. This then leads into a discussion of the shooting schedule. As Ivor has been developing the storyboard, Anna has made David group the shots in terms of locations. The continuing lack of a recording of the rappers is a problem that has to be negotiated around. It's decided (on staff advice) that the shots that don't require lip synch should be done first. There is then a further debate about whether to do the exterior or interior shots first. This process seems to take a very long time – partly because it all has to be written out. Ivor, who has deliberately taken a back seat, now expresses some exasperation at the way the group appears to have stagnated:

> Ivor: *We seem to be running about in circles now, which isn't really going anywhere, and we seem to be just losing our touch that we had round the corner [doing the storyboard]... there's just no point in saying, oh should we do this, should we do that, why doesn't somebody just take charge and say things should go like this?*

> David: But I think what everybody says is really useful.
> James: It's democratic.
> Ivor: It is useful, but still nothing's getting written down.

Despite this, Ivor is increasingly seen by the others as the leader. Nafeesa later asks his permission to take some time out as she has to go to college. David keeps asking questions, and only makes assertions – for example about which sequence will be shot first – once Ivor has pushed him into doing it.

Meanwhile, it emerges that Jermaine has produced a second part to his rap, and a copy is passed round. It's about girls, and talks about how he likes it when girls wear 'batty riders' (tight shorts that ride up their bottom) and 'punny printers' (lycra shorts that print the outlines of their vaginas). James is dismissive. Nafeesa says 'it's boyish', and Ivor also takes an ironic distance – 'just by reading it, you can tell how old the writer is'. Once it's explained to Anna, she says nothing.

Various deadlines are arranged with the rappers, and a time is fixed for a general meeting. When I come back from lunch, I walk into a classic 'hanging with the technology' session. It isn't clear why the rappers can't record. In the sound studio, Aramis is playing aimlessly with the mixer. People are watching TV and reading music magazines. In the film studio, the dancers are practising their routine while the rappers sit around posing with their hoods on, miming to an existing rap track, Fuck Compton *by* Tim Dog, *which is a vicious dissing of the opposition, with plenty of 'fuck' and 'motherfuckers' thrown in. Some seem to be asleep. Meanwhile the staff wander in and out distractedly.*

Anna eventually tells the video group that the staff have decided there won't now be a general meeting in which they will present their ideas, as this would cause too much disagreement. The crew decides to film the dancers. James is attempting to take charge, but the rappers have followed the crew out and are now standing around. James keeps telling them to be quiet, but there is a lot of resistance, and some sexual abuse directed at the dancers. James again shouts for quiet and finally walks off indoors, disgusted. Ivor takes over the camera, and eventually Nathan takes the camera off the tripod and does some closer filming.

The film crew stay outside to film a sequence from the schedule, although the storyboard isn't in evidence. Nathan is effectively directing now, with David on camera. Various new suggestions are made and followed up, not least by the performers and the staff. David has decided that the roles should rotate, so that everyone gets a turn, and he now offers Chilo a turn on the camera. Ivor disputes this, saying he'd prefer people to stick with their roles as they are wasting time, and he wants someone who 'has got a feel for the shot'. So David does it. As this shot is taken and re-taken, the three women, Chilo, Anna and Nafeesa stand to one side while the boys direct (there is multiple direction here, by Nathan, David O – the performer – and Ivor). Chilo doesn't get a look in throughout this whole episode of filming. Later I overhear her being counselled by Anna: she is bemoaning the fact that she isn't assertive enough, and resolving to do better next time. While the male members of the group move on to set up the party scenes, she goes to watch TV.

Following another 'hanging out' interlude, Chilo's song is recorded (largely according to her direction), followed by a party scene. Ivor occasionally consults the storyboard as this happens, although he now maintains that some of the shots are 'not needed', and so they aren't filmed. Shooting these scenes is an exercise in crowd control, particularly when it comes to the scene in which everyone is involved. The rappers and dancers are wild, posing with their shades, headsets and mobile phones (!). David acts as a bouncer, trying to keep them out until they are needed. Michael is doing a lot of the filming. Ivor eventually loses his rag and bawls out Skinny, and there is a nasty silence, James then takes over, while Ivor sits fuming. The film is eventually screened in the editing room, and there is general approval.

Amid some exhaustion, there is a final crew meeting to plan the following day's schedule. There's a review against the storyboard of which scenes have been shot and which haven't. Some scenes will need to be re-shot, although the staff try to dissuade them from re-shooting because of the lack of time. A schedule is generated for tomorrow, with everyone contributing suggestions for the easiest way of getting it done. David is again asking questions, and Ivor is providing lots of the answers.

Group work is inevitably characterised by ebbs and flows. In this case, periods of intense activity were interspersed with periods in which the group seemed to stagnate, and appeared unable to move ahead. Occasionally, there would be an energetic pursuit down a blind alley, followed by a humorous release of tension. Potential disagreements were more often avoided than faced directly, however, and often devolved down to a kind of easy consensus, almost by default. The logic for this avoidance was largely because disagreements came to be seen as obstacles: the task had acquired a momentum of its own, in which the fact of getting it done was more important than how it was done. As Nafeesa explicitly noted, the group was bound to opt for 'whatever makes it easier'.

Despite the apparent agreement that was reached during the storyboarding, there were many further changes at all stages of the process. Much of what was included in the storyboard didn't get filmed in that way, and much that wasn't did. Some scenes that were discussed in detail were summarily dropped. This was partly because what had been drawn up was not in fact a detailed storyboard; but it was also because the storyboard was effectively forgotten. Only Ivor appeared to consult it occasionally, and he appeared to be using it more as a checklist than a blueprint. It was also partly a result of logistical constraints: there simply wasn't the time to shoot each of these scenes as planned, and so makeshift alternatives were devised, often without being discussed by the original group. When it came to the filming, however, there was often some uncertainty as to who was in charge: at times it seemed as though three people were directing a scene, and yet it was often the camera operator whose decision was final.

What became particularly notable as the shooting progressed was that the staff (or, more specifically, the male staff) began to intervene quite heavily, often taking hold of the camera – even though none of them was referring to the storyboard. Like the video group themselves, they appeared to be motivated by a desire to 'get the thing done', although their use of the camera was quite different from that which had been envisaged in the planning. On the other hand, they were sometimes rather less in evidence when it came to the more urgent tasks of crowd control.

As the course progressed, the hierarchies within the group also appeared to become more fixed. While Ivor and James alternately took control, Ivor did so more consistently, even though he frequently appeared reluctant. Ivor seemed to carry more weight with the other students than James, partly because of James's 'negative' persona, but also perhaps because Ivor is black (as were all of the younger students). Ivor is the oldest of nine children, which may well give him some skills in that area too. By contrast, David tended to do what he was told and fit in with the general drift, looking to Ivor for guidance: he took charge of planning the shooting schedule or (occasionally) using the camera, but he was willing to let himself be directed by others. Nafeesa tended to look for spaces in which she could intervene, and contributed a number of useful suggestions, without ever really appearing to take charge – although the fact that she was absent on the second day meant that she came late into the group dynamic. Chilo was largely on the margins: she managed quite successfully to carve out the piece she had originally planned, but it was hard to see what else she contributed.

As I have noted, this dominance of the men in the video group was replicated across the course as a whole, yet there did not seem to be strategies that might have prevented it. Chilo's discussion with Anna about her failure to gain control of the camera was largely a matter of mopping up after the event: there did not seem to be a structure that would allow for equal participation, and although David eventually suggested one, this was easily overruled. Anna (the only female on the staff) rarely took charge of the camera either, and never did so in the more difficult situations, for example where there was a crowd of performers – although it is unreasonable to expect any individual to have to shoulder the burden of being a 'role model' in this way. What was most worrying, however, was that Chilo saw this as her *own* failure, a result of her own lack of assertiveness, and as an issue that she had to resolve personally. This was certainly confirmed when I interviewed her towards the end of the course: she said she was concerned that the more important roles had been 'hogged' and that she had been 'treated like a skivvy' – but that the solution to this was 'to stand up and say what I think'.

What were the implications of these shifting relationships in terms of the product itself? Most of the grand themes that emerged in the early discussions were never mentioned again, perhaps for very good reasons. But what emerged instead was largely what seemed obvious – the party scenes, for example, which dominate the final tape, effectively replicated scenes in the videos that were shown at the beginning of the course. It was particularly noticeable how the product became much more straightforwardly generic as it developed. Despite James's resistance to clichés, which was partly shared by Ivor and Nafeesa at least, and Chilo's individualistic approach, what emerged was full of little boys posing as gangsters. Jermaine's rap, which I would describe as offensively sexist (albeit in the time-honoured tradition of rap and ragga), was certainly perceived in this way by a number of the other students, but they appeared unable to challenge this. To do anything different would have involved working against the grain, and risking the possibility of ending up without a product at all.

Day 5: Getting it done

Again, space precludes a detailed account of the filming of each sequence, so I have included one that I feel is representative.

Jermaine's rap sequence is filmed. Ivor is clearly directing. He and James work on positioning the camera, while the others set up the tripod. Jermaine wants to be in front of the decks. Ivor says he'll be better behind, but he remains in front. (Here again, the shots that result are very different from those planned, which had Jermaine testifying to a group of gangsters from behind the decks.)

James also proposes various additional shots, and the sequence is shot a number of times, so that they can edit between. This becomes the standard approach, almost as though filming a live event rather than a storyboarded sequence. Nathan tells them they have to move the camera, and demonstrates the MTV 'ducking and weaving' style that he and Michael were using in the dance and party sequences yesterday.

Chilo asks to take over the camera, and does so, also attempting the MTV duck and weave. James re-arranges the backdrop to eliminate shadows. Ivor says maybe the over-the-shoulder shot isn't needed. There is an attempt to rearrange the lighting, as James in particular isn't happy that it's so yellow. The performers also contribute suggestions here. Ivor is concerned (as before) about continuity – he wants to make sure the lighting is the same as yesterday – which reflects a conception of the finished product than nobody else appears to share. Through this sequence, Ivor and James direct; Chilo films, David operates the tape deck. On the second and third takes, James films, getting wilder with the duck and weave.

The group decline to do Jermaine's second verse, the one about girls: Ivor says 'it's not needed', and David says 'there's enough'. This verse isn't yet recorded on tape anyway. As this scene finishes, Ivor goes back to the storyboard to see where to go next. He is having a passing anxiety about being too directive: 'I think everyone's getting sick of me now'. He moves out into the foyer with the storyboard, leaving Nafeesa and David to re-shoot Chilo's song sequence. But the foyer then becomes the production office: Nafeesa and then David come out to receive instructions from Ivor, who is planning 'filler' (cutaways) for David O's sequence and trying hard to find ways round the rain. He is still concerned with continuity, and about whether David O had his hood on yesterday or not, so that there isn't a mistake when they film the reverse shot for this sequence. Ivor consults with Nafeesa over this scene, and she takes instructions, as though an assistant director. David eventually films these shots (again, three versions for later editing), although he asks Ivor to make all the key decisions.

What became increasingly striking in such situations was how (by a process of trial and error as much as personal dynamics) the group came to replicate the structure of a professional crew. While the individuals occasionally changed roles, at any one point it was usually possible to identify a director (Ivor, sometimes James), a floor manager (nearly always David), a camera operator (most people, including Nafeesa and sometimes Chilo) and sometimes an assistant director (Nafeesa). Whether this simply represents the most efficient way of getting the job done is another matter, however. To what extent are such structures determined by the technology, the genre, or simply by a received sense of how these things should happen? Either way, the group appeared to run much more smoothly once roles became more established: as Nafeesa later observed, there was a much more developed sense of collaboration as the deadline approached.

By 6.00, all seems to be done except for sequences of James and Frank in the studio. However, Ivor is being pressured by the rappers and dancers to do a second party scene. Jermaine in particular wants to include his second verse to be included, as this is about 'the positive things of the 90s' (namely, girls in revealing shorts). Ivor wants to go home, and won't decide: he tells them to talk to Nathan, while Nathan tells them to talk to Ivor. Jermaine complains 'someone's got to decide, someone's got to take some responsibility here'. Finally, the decision to film the second party scene is taken by the staff – not least, I suspect, to pacify the rappers.

The scene has been set up by Ben (the head of the project), who now seems to be taking over as director: I wonder how far this scene is a last minute salvaging job. The lighting has been arranged much more effectively than was possible this morning, using colour gels. Ben tells James where to point the camera, while Michael works as crowd controller – 'don't all look in the same direction, it looks silly', he says, and 'if it was a real party, you wouldn't all be crowding together'. Ivor, who is still nominated by the staff as director, has slightly abdicated by this stage. Two takes are done, with Michael on camera for the second, using the now obligatory MTV duck and weave. The room is now incredibly hot, and there is a pause for air before the third and final take. Ivor is on camera now, Nafeesa and Chilo are performing. The rushes are immediately reviewed, amid great laughter, cheering and banter.

Group dynamics: some reflections

As we have seen, Chilo's resolve to be more assertive did pay off, in that (however temporarily) she did get to use the camera the following day. Nevertheless, as she explained when I interviewed her towards the end of the final day, she clearly resented the way in which the group was being run, and particularly Ivor's behaviour. This was partly, she felt, a matter of different expectations: she felt that Ivor was taking the course too seriously, and that most people were attending the course not to 'work' but to 'have fun'. However, it was also a matter of 'personalities':

> I personally think someone like Ivor would like to say 'I did that, and I shot that bit, and I shot that bit, and I shot that bit, and I edited that bit, and I edited that bit, and I did that bit, and if it wasn't for me that bit wouldn't have been there', like that, you know. And it may well turn out to be like that, but that's because that's the way he sort of like took control and designed it. And there's a way of taking control and having leadership qualities, but I just think in this sort of situation, you've got to share the power if you're going to have any kind of, and communicate to everyone, not exclude people... It's a group, a community thing... a group project. It's a matter of sharing the power. It's the way anyone's a good leader, is to share the power, not to hog it.

Ironically, of course, Chilo was the only person in the whole group who came with something definite that she wanted to do – namely, her 'walking on water' theme – and ended up having done it. As she said:

> Others may have wanted to blow it out, but I didn't want to. So I thought if there is anything that I am actually going to do, it's that. 'Cause I know how I want to be portrayed, you know. It's like when I do the vocal, they're not going to lay down a vocal that I don't like...

For his part, Ivor was aware of some of these resentments, and of the danger of being seen to dominate. As we have seen, he attempted to handle this tension in a variety of ways: through irony and humour, by explicitly inviting others to participate, and at times by deliberately taking a back seat.

> DB: Did you feel awkward about being seen as the leader?
> Ivor: Yeah, I did feel like that at times, because I didn't want to be seen taking a leading role. I mean everyone is a leader in their own sense, and everyone has had like an input into the production, but maybe I was just more... but maybe I just came across in a more domineering way, in a more dominant way.

As we shall see, he was even more cautious about this when it came to post-production, although by this stage the potential for taking control of the finished product was in fact much greater, as fewer people were involved.

The abiding contradiction throughout all these interviews, however, is that surrounding the notion of group democracy. On the one hand, everyone was keen to claim that the group had generally 'worked well together', pointing to the comparative lack of overt disagreements. The rhetoric of group work recurred throughout the discussions (for example in Chilo's comments above). Even James, who was most direct in his criticisms of the organisation of the course, felt obliged to disclaim his views by saying that they were merely 'personal'. Yet on the other hand, the need for leadership was accepted as inevitable by all, both for reasons to do with efficiency, and as a means of reducing uncertainties. Even Chilo, despite her resentments, said she felt that Ivor had 'done quite a good job in getting things done' – and that this would have been impossible without him taking charge. This ambivalence is most apparent in Nafeesa's response:

> DB: Do you think there are people who have been making more decisions
> than others?
>
> Nafeesa: Yeah. But I think you have to have that because it will all end up 'oh, if
> you like that, then I like that', you end up not really making a firm
> decision about anything... You need to have somebody who's got a
> clearer idea, not a clearer idea, but can be a bit more definite, because
> we all don't want to upset anybody, and you all don't want to say kind
> of 'I want to do this, so you can't do that', kind of thing. I think you
> need it to a degree. Obviously you don't want someone saying 'look,
> you've got to do this'. People who have taken more of a lead have
> always said 'well what do you think?' and it should be like that... But
> whenever you work in a group, you're always going to have leader
> figures, or people who are a bit more dominant...

In the light of research on group dynamics, such tensions are familiar – and perhaps ultimately unavoidable. Theories of the 'psychodynamics' of groups, for example, have emphasised the ways in which such authority relationships serve as a means of dealing with uncertainty and insecurity. From a Freudian perspective, of course, authority figures (like parents) are bound to serve as a focus for ambiguous feelings of dependency and resistance[25]. More prosaically perhaps, research on the development of groups has shown how they gradually devise norms and rules as a means of getting things done, and in order to overcome differences and conflicts[26]. Difficulties are almost bound to arise, however, when such structures – or indeed the resentments and emotional responses that they may provoke – are not explicitly revealed and discussed.

Post-production: democracy by remote control

Although the production week itself had ended on a positive note, very few of the students seemed to be prepared to see the video through the post-production stage. One week later, six students met to begin to devise an edit list, which would then be presented back to the whole group at a further meeting. Ivor again took charge, although he was also concerned to preserve a space for democratic decision-making, and to delegate tasks to others. While this meeting was comparatively brief, the issue of content – what the video was actually 'saying' – did begin to resurface. Ultimately, there was insufficient visual material to support the theme which had been agreed upon early on, and hence it was bound to prove difficult to produce a coherent product. If the original intentions had been lost, however, this could not be put down simply to organisational or circumstantial factors – to poor time management, unsatisfactory group dynamics or equipment failures, for example. On the contrary, it would be false to pretend that there were ever very strong intentions to start with: the 'theme' of the video was so vague and all-inclusive, and there was very little sense of anybody (except perhaps Chilo) having a 'statement' they really wanted to make. For everyone concerned, the main point was to make a video for the sake of making a video. The fact that the chosen genre was a pop video was (to say the least) extremely fortuitous, as it seemed to allow the freedom to change your mind at any time, or just to make it up as you went along.

One week later, there was a short meeting at which the editing group presented their ideas to some of the rappers and dancers, where this question of content became a significant point of tension.

Ivor says there is material to make a 'gangsta' video, using the party scenes and some footage of the raps that was shot in a warehouse. Kelly and others clearly approve of this, but Ivor says this is 'not what everyone was aiming at'. He says they are going to try to use some of the other material in an attempt to 'steer it away from the image it's got at the moment.' Helen (who was mainly responsible for the vocal chorus, but has now joined the editing group) also supports this:

Helen:	*It just looks like a rap video*
Kelly:	*That's what it is!*
Chantel:	*That's how we wanted it.*
Helen:	*But no, no, you're saying that's what you want, but it is a group project. So it's not what you want, it has to be a whole group thing.*
Kelly:	*Yeah, but if it's a rap tune, why are you going to have a classical video?*
Helen:	*No, that's not what I'm saying. We need a purpose for this video, that is why we wanted to do the editing, and I mean we don't just want to have a straight rap. I mean I thought videos kind of like have meanings to them, do you understand?*

The staff try to cool this down, and an uneasy compromise is reached, whereby everyone is encouraged to 'make an input'. It is suggested that two versions can be made, although this is rejected on the grounds of lack of time. The staff are equally aware of the limitations of simply imitating a 'gangsta' video, but they are also concerned about potential objections when the final product is screened. Nathan says the video should have 'all the influences... the people who are into it and people who are not into it'. Michael agrees: 'the video's got to represent everyone, as much as we can... if you have a bit of everything, then no-one can complain'.

In the event, and perhaps predictably, it was Ivor who pursued the production to the very end. Various technical mishaps and a considerable amount of discovery learning meant that the editing took him four further days. While some other students came round to offer advice, for much of the time he worked alone, or occasionally with a member of staff. Ultimately, many of his decisions were determined by the lack of adequate footage: they were made as much by default, as through any positive choice. Some sequences could not be used because the lip-synching or the miming or the lighting were poor, while others had sections missing. Editing became a matter of patching together the best visual material from a pile of fragments in order to cover the sound track. In the case of each rap, a basic version of the sequence was chosen and assemble edited, and extracts from other versions or other material were then inserted, not least in order to cover the mistakes. The audio track itself proved to be less than adequate, as the rappers had not been sufficiently tight to the rhythm, and some of the articulation was poor: even they did not seem to have acquired some of these basic skills.

Ultimately, Ivor's willingness to see things through did not seem to be motivated by any commitment to the content of the tape. While he did regard this as an opportunity to learn more about editing, what seems primarily to have led him on was sheer determination to get the thing done. As he put it: 'I think I've learnt to be more persistent, and not to give up when everything seems to be going the wrong way' – a sentiment that was also echoed by James in his final evaluation.

The finished product that emerged was extremely fragmented, although it appeared that everyone was represented. Ivor's 'dramatic scenes' particularly suffered: they were there, but only in short snatches that would probably have made little sense to an outsider. Some of the shots that were eventually inserted had not actually been filmed by the group, and seemed to have come from found tapes. Ivor also seemed to have used the full potential of the effects panel: there was a great deal of squeezing into wide-screen and venetian blind effects, and some cosmic overlays generated by the computer. Chilo did indeed walk on water (though not the water filmed by the group), but she also walked on a cosmic Dr. Who-style background, and her environmental 'message' failed to come across. In general, there were very few moments where the content of the lyrics was reflected in the visuals – although Jermaine's sexist rap was accompanied by some faintly embarrassing shots of the girl dancers (see fig. 4.1 above).

Back to reality

The final screening, held almost four weeks after the filming had been completed, was a somewhat inconclusive event. The group's response to the tape was fairly half-hearted, although everybody was concerned that they should receive a copy. Although the students were invited to make some evaluative comments about the tape, none were forthcoming. Instead, the proceedings were handed over to a panel of professionals from the media industries, who had been invited to answer questions from the group.

There is an interesting moment at the very start, where James asks them directly what they thought about the video. Alec (one of the panel) says the video is 'experimental', it's a 'learning process', and that it's not 'up to scratch' in terms of quality: they would be wrong to think they could go to a record company and get money on the basis of this...

The overall drift of the panel's comments is about the hard realities of the music business: Keith in particular talks in detail about how you have to work out where you fit in the market, how it's important to learn about the roles of DJs, distributors, promoters etc. Success isn't a matter of how good you are, it's about who you know. He's quite pessimistic about the prospects for British hip-hop/rap acts, and points out that most records don't sell in sufficient quantities to get the money back, and that even big hits do not generate massive amounts of income. 'You've got to be a salesman', he says, 'it's just like selling soap or any other product.' The woman from the BBC urges them to think about getting their music into different outlets – as background on EastEnders, or on children's TV. By this time, the younger kids have all left, and are wandering about the building, although the older ones are staying to listen.

This session, while somewhat marginal to the course itself, did raise some awkward questions about the potential vocational relevance of this kind of work. Phil Cohen, for example, has argued as follows:

> ...the growth of the cultural industries in the last five years has created the only major new source of job creation for young people in the inner city. Moreover these new media technologies are based on skills which are accessible to considerable numbers of working class youth, since they are closely related to their own cultural forms and practices.[27]

Yet it is important to avoid an easy optimism here. While the industries are undeniably changing and fragmenting, not least with the impact of new technologies, the chances for relatively 'unskilled' young people to find employment there remain minimal. There is a yawning gap between the work that may be done on these kinds of courses and the 'real' world of the media industries. Any pretence that they might be offering vocational training would seem to be more than a little dishonest.

Conclusion

My account of this course has been broadly critical. Yet with some notable exceptions, the students themselves were much less so. While evaluation forms (produced by one of the youth projects that funded the course) were not received from all the students, those completed by the performers were almost uniformly positive. Among the video group, James was predictably scathing, although Ivor, David and Chilo were on balance fairly supportive. Ultimately, I have no doubt that all the students learnt from the course, both positively and negatively – not just about how to make a video or record a track, but also about how to work in a group. It would have been surprising if such a generally talented and well-motivated group had not done so. My concern in this respect is simply that they could have learnt so much more than they did, and done so much more efficiently and productively.

Of course, the students could hardly fail to learn from such an extended opportunity to use the technology, although in the absence of much explicit *instruction* a great deal of this was achieved through trial and error. At least in the case of the video group, the choice of genre meant that very few 'errors' could be made in the first place, and in most instances did not need to be corrected. Nevertheless, I do not doubt that the majority of the group did become more proficient in manipulating the camera, and (at least in Ivor's case) in operating the edit suite. By contrast, in the case of the sound technology, where the equipment itself is much more complex, I had very little sense that any of the students had become sufficiently skilled to use it independently.

The situation with the rappers was different again. Of course, there are significant problems in making popular cultural forms such as rap the subject of educational intervention. Yet it would be a mistake to fall for the mythology of rap as some kind of authentic expression of oppressed youth, that emerges spontaneously and somehow without form or structure from their experiences on the street. This is, it seems to me, extremely patronising. It ignores the considerable skill and artistry of the genre; and in this context, it leads to an educational strategy that sells students short. Learning to rap well is just as much about discipline as learning to sing well, or indeed learning to use a camera and to edit: as rappers are fond of declaring, it is something that needs practice and dedication. Given that rap was so central to the students' work, it was disappointing that (as the staff were bound to admit) the technical quality of the rapping was so poor.

Collaborative group work can offer many positive educational outcomes, but it does not in itself guarantee them. To leave groups to their own devices in the hope that they will find their own ways of working, and to assume that these will necessarily be constructive and egalitarian, is not to delegate responsibility, but to abdicate it. For example, the tensions that were apparent here in relation to gender were familiar ones; and steps could have been taken to prevent them from occurring in the first place, rather than simply attempting to deal with them once they had arisen[28].

Similar arguments apply to the 'media learning' that may or may not have taken place. If it is to be anything more than a form of technical training, media production work of this kind must inevitably be 'student centred'; but to imply that this is somehow incompatible with direct instruction, or with clearly structured group activities, is to take the lazy way out. Furthermore, to focus primarily on the technology, or to begin with prescriptive ideas about the nature of the finished product, is almost bound to preclude the necessary investigation of students' aims and motivations, and what exactly it is that they wish to communicate. Without ways of developing and challenging the *content* of students' work, their learning in all areas is bound to be superficial and accidental, rather than directed and purposeful. Simplistic notions of group democracy and collective endeavour, or indeed of the inherent authenticity of young people's culture, may leave many students unsupported, while simultaneously undermining any grounds for critical reflection.

Notes

1 This issue has of course been a major focus of debate in Film Studies, particularly in the 1970s: see Caughie (1980).
2 Dewdney and Lister (1988: 76), for example, consciously set out to construct group practice and a sense of collective purpose while using a medium (photography) that is usually employed by individuals working alone.
3 Some of these arguments are summarised in Reynolds (1994) and Jaques (1991).
4 A clear statement of these arguments, together with a compendium of constructive advice on managing small group work, may be found in Reid, Forrestal and Cook (1989).
5 Lorac and Weiss (1981).
6 *Ibid*, page 162
7 See, for example, Burns (1977) and Schlesinger (1987).
8 I am thinking particularly here of the practical project component of the AEB Communications Studies A-level. A useful discussion of some ways around these problems is offered by Alistair Smith (1988).
9 This is apparent, for example, in the defensiveness of students like Nicky (see Chapter 6).
10 This issue is raised in passing in a number of contributions to *Watching Media Learning* (Buckingham, 1990), particularly those by Roy Stafford and Jenny Grahame.
11 For a brief outline of this history, see Sue Braden (forthcoming).
12 And, it would appear, much of it still is – see Goodman and Tandy (1993).
13 A film like the Berwick Street Collective's *The Nightcleaners* (1976) for example. More recently, the black independent video movement has offered numerous instances of work that appears to combine documentary aims with formal experimentation – for example Isaac Julien's *Who Killed Colin Roach?* and *Territories* or the Black Audio Film Collective's *Handsworth Songs*.
14 For an example of this argument, see Willener et al (1976); and for a critique, see Heller (1978). This work is discussed briefly in Buckingham (1987a).
15 See Dowmunt (1980).

16 Dewdney and Lister, *op. cit.* These comments on the Cockpit approach were pursued in more detail in a review of the book (Buckingham, 1988).

17 See, for example, the account by Drotner (1989).

18 Dewdney and Lister, *op. cit.*, p. 112.

19 Youth 'centres' and youth 'clubs' are different types of institutions, in that the former are more likely to run formal classes. Nevertheless, these and related terms are used in different ways across the country.

20 See Nava (1984).

21 See particularly Cohen (1990); and Chappell (1984).

22 See particularly Dewdney and Lister, *op. cit.*, pages 99–101. Cohen, *op. cit.*, pp. 44-5, seeks to distinguish between this approach and what he terms an 'experiential' pedagogy, although the grounds for this remain unclear.

23 This is precisely the dilemma about the relationship between practical work and writing posed by Grahame (1990) and pursued by Buckingham and Sefton-Green (1994), Chapter 8.

24 A reference to the basketball film *White Boys Can't Jump*.

25 See Jaques (1991).

26 This is summarised in Reynolds (1994), pp. 50–2.

27 Cohen, *ibid*, p. 45. For a less sanguine view, see Buckingham (1995).

28 One strategy that is frequently adopted here is to use single sex groups – as was the case in the video production work to be described in Chapter 7. On the other hand, it should be acknowledged that, with the exception of the video group, all the groups here were *de facto* single sex, and in very stereotyped ways (boys as rappers, girls as dancers) – which would suggest that additional strategies might need to be adopted. This issue will be discussed in our conclusion.

Chapter 5

Original Copy: Re-selling Sounds

Some definitions (from Webster's Dictionary):

Imitation (n): Resembling something else that is usually genuine and of better quality.

Imitation (adj.): The assumption of the modes of behaviour observed in other individuals.

Imitate: to follow as a pattern, model or example.

Parody: 1. A literary or musical work in which the style of an author is closely imitated for comic effect or in ridicule.
2. A feeble or ridiculous imitation.

Almost inevitably, practical production in media education is bound to involve elements of imitation and parody. Students' earliest attempts at video production, for example, are very likely to include pastiches of news interviews, advertisements or pop videos. As they gain greater control and fluency with the medium, their use of dominant forms may well become more self-conscious and elaborate. Yet as we have indicated in our introduction, this process has often been a focus of considerable anxiety among media teachers. The emphasis in a great deal of media education has been on producing 'oppositional' texts, which challenge or subvert dominant media forms. By contrast, using popular genres and conventions has frequently been seen as little more than a matter of ideological reproduction. Imitation, it is argued, is an essentially 'uncritical' – indeed, unthinking – process.

In fact, the question of what students might *learn* from imitation has rarely been addressed in any detail. This chapter seeks to investigate the functions of imitation for students, particularly in the context of classroom practices such as role-play, simulation, and discovery-based learning. In the process, it will question many taken-for-granted assumptions about the relationships between media production and the conceptual understanding of media forms and institutions. More speculatively, it will explore the tensions between our desire as teachers to facilitate original and creative production work, and the demands of a curriculum which explicitly privileges critical analysis over self-expression. Finally it will consider what and how the process of imitation means to students, its ideological implications, and the ways in which it might be re-evaluated as an important educational practice.

Pop, parody and practice

The work described here focuses particularly on popular music. In common, I suspect, with many other Media Studies teachers, my experiences of teaching with and about pop music have been instructive and challenging, if not entirely unproblematic. Conventional wisdom has tended to assume that the more relevant and pleasurable the area of study, the greater the engagement and creativity of students' responses; but with popular music it is precisely those aspects of relevance, pleasure, personal investment and cultural status which can militate against successful teaching. You have to be pretty confident about your own authority and relationships within the class to take on a subject about which you are invariably both less informed than your students, and likely to adopt a rather different discourse; and you need steel nerves and a good sense of humour to negotiate the minefield of personal taste, sub-cultural affiliation and street credibility generated by different musical preferences. As has been argued elsewhere[1], it is often hard enough to persuade young people even to *listen* to music they don't like, let alone to engage in critical discourse about it; but to encourage students to publicly analyse its meanings and significance – personal, emotional, ideological, industrial, economic – is a hazardous enterprise indeed.

Practical work is often seen as a potential antidote to some of these problems. Many teachers use the simulation of industrial practice – the signing up and promotion of a new band, for example – as a safer way into a more distanced investigation of music promotion and institutional power. The risk here, however, is of defusing the contentious issues of taste, style and pleasure – in other words, the subjective and emotional aspects of music – to such an extent that what remains is merely a mechanical and ultimately cynical exercise in marketing. Alternatively, the practical production of pop videos and other secondary texts about pop music such as record covers, fanzines and PR material can allow students to explore aspects of image construction, audience and meaning in a less threatening or exposing way. Here again, though, lurks danger. Music is perhaps one of the most gendered forms of all popular culture. It has been argued by many classroom teachers that to explore it in a mixed group through conventionally male-dominated technologies such as IT and video may compound its gendered nature, doubly handicapping if not disenfranchising young women. Equally disturbing, as many critics have disdainfully noted, this sort of activity frequently results in *imitative* rather than original imagery, adulatory pastiches of existing musical genres, or, worse still, parodies and piss-takes, the epitome of all that is seen as suspect in practical work[2]. Indeed, the tensions between young people's intense personal involvement both with music itself and with the approval of their peer group may actually inhibit the production of 'authentic' or original material, so that parody or pastiche becomes an inevitable defensive response.

The problem is compounded by the fact that pop music is in itself a hothouse for the recycling and imitation of previous musical forms, obsessively ransacking its past to re-invent itself with a complicated mix of affection and irony. Issues of parody and pastiche are never far from its surface; indeed, many would argue that all pop is ultimately parodic, or at least ironic, even when it appears sincere. It is hard to know whether to define the streetwise cheekiness of mid-nineties groups like Blur or Oasis as reverential homage to mid-sixties groups like the Small Faces, as cheap rip-off, or as knowing pastiche. Even more problematically, what sense can we make of the success of explicitly imitative bands such as Bjorn Again (the Abba clones) or the various Pink Floyd sound-alikes, let alone the fact that there is now actually a 'real' Spinal Tap? And can we realistically expect originality from an industry where 'living legends' such as Gary Glitter, Slade and Madness, whose heroic status has always depended on their tongue-in-cheek humour, are repeatedly resuscitated in ever more cynical, self-parodic ways? Yet these examples are perhaps only the most spectacular instances of a general tendency in all forms of popular music. Pop, it could be argued, is always the sum of a body of 'influences': it is always strongly generic. Even jazz, which is often surrounded with highly romantic arguments about individual genius and spontaneous creativity, relies heavily on a shared body of stylistic motifs which are drawn from previous performances. In post-structuralist terminology, this could be seen as a form of *inter-textuality*: each text inevitably refers to and draws upon other texts, to the point where no text can be seen as 'original'[3]. As these questions suggest, the area of popular music is a particularly interesting one in which to address questions about the educational potential of imitation and parody, and to begin to reformulate the debate.

Production work and the problem of imitation: lost in the endless wilderness?

By the late 1970s, when many teachers came to Media Studies for the first time, the whole question of imitation was already seen as a contentious area. While it was widely acknowledged that students needed to make their own media texts in order to fully understand how the 'real' media constructed meaning, there was little consensus as to what constituted appropriate practice, what order of technical, conceptual or authorial skills might be involved, or which criteria – professional, aesthetic, or theoretical – might be employed to evaluate it. Amongst the small but significant number of classroom practitioners and the clutch of Mode 3 Media Studies CSEs they taught, 'the practical project' (as it was – and still is – frequently known) was often valued more for its motivational benefits for 'lower ability' or alienated students than for its educational rigour or its ability to provide insights into professional practice. At a time of scant resourcing and unwieldy technology, when production usually meant expensively-processed fun with a super-8 cine camera or laboriously typed class magazines, it was often marginalised – an end-of-course treat, a time-consuming diversion from the real (analytical) work of the course, or an opportunity to record a school play or journey whilst satisfying course requirements.

As we have indicated (Chapter 1), this uncertainty about the place and purpose of practical work in Media Studies was partly resolved by the emergence of 'deconstruction exercises' – an approach which has informed the rationale for practical production in GCSE and A-level examination syllabuses, and has dominated the field ever since. This approach sees practical work primarily as a form of 'applied analysis' – a way of experiencing, and thus laying bare, the processes of production in order to reveal the ideological forces which are seen to determine them. From this perspective, the prime rationale for media production is as a tool for ideological demystification.

As we have noted, this approach was explicitly recommended by Len Masterman in his seminal book *Teaching About Television*[4]. Following Enzensberger's claim that amateur media-making is inevitably demeaned by comparison with professional production, Masterman mounted a virulent attack on the limitations of most student-centred production work, which he perceived as 'an endless wilderness of dreary imitative third-rate pop shows'. According to Masterman, practical work was little more than 'doing your own thing with a Portapak', and could lead only to products that were 'alienated and humiliating'. Only through emphasis on fostering 'a genuine group culture and an awareness of the possibilities of group action', and a process of 'conscientization' would students be able to find an 'authentic' voice[5]. Meanwhile, such production work as was necessary should take the form of sound-vision experiments, simulations and code-breaking exercises – approaches which reveal the constructed nature of televisual conventions. Perhaps surprisingly, however, Masterman argues that 'the *systematic* and *detailed* study of codings is perhaps too abstract and specialised for schools, and may best be left to college and university students'[6].

At around the same time, Bob Ferguson[7] offered an equally scathing critique of the notions of creativity and self-expression which had previously been used to justify media production work. Ferguson attacks the 'liberal progressivist notions of pedagogy' which he sees as implicit in much practical work, on the grounds that they reflect patronising assumptions and low expectations on the part of both teachers and students. Like Masterman, he argues for practical work as deconstruction, which is defined as:

> ...*a means of activating the process of consumption*. It is a process of interrogation which asks the students to refuse the production style and message construction which is presented to them as normal, desirable, transparent. It is an act of dissection with a double purpose. The first is concerned with code-breaking and the second with the realisation that the possibility exists of code *construction* ... based on a rational and conscious assembly of images and sounds to achieve the desired effect[8].

As this quotation implies, 'deconstruction' is seen – at least in principle – as a first stage in the move towards more consciously 'oppositional' forms and production practices. Thus, Ferguson argues that

> it [is] important to show how practical work can extend comprehension of the structures, practices and production values of the broadcasters, while at the same time opening up a potential means of communication which allows for the development of oppositional, informational and expressive message-making.[9]

Although quite how this 'expressive message-making' might be different from the work he condemns is far from clear.

Ultimately, however, his final comments underline a fundamental distinction which characterises a great deal of subsequent thinking about the nature of practical work:

> The development of language skills parallel with a cognitive awareness of the functioning of the media is probably the most important aspect of practical

work in media studies. ...the way to undertake such a task is to concentrate
upon *cognitive rather than experiential development*[10] [our emphasis].

Ferguson's opposition between cognitive and experiential learning is a crucial aspect
of his argument, yet it is also highly problematic. As we have seen, Ferguson argues that
practical work must be based on the 'rational and conscious', as opposed to the more
expressive and perhaps intuitive models traditionally identified with English or Art.
Both Ferguson and Masterman tend to describe these more 'experiential' versions of
practice in their least effective forms, and to discount them more by means of
anecdotes than detailed evidence. Ultimately, what emerges here is a fundamental
distrust of the emotional, subjective dimensions of students' engagement with the
media. It seems to be assumed that these can simply be cast aside once the tools of
rational analysis are placed in students' hands. Perhaps the most crucial concern here,
however, is with the possibility that students will merely replicate the conventions of
dominant media genres. These formal conventions are seen to contain an ideology
which is somehow invisible, and which students will unconsciously absorb if they are
not protected by the cognitive armour of critical analysis.

My personal interest in these issues dates back to 1980, when as a 'beginning' media
teacher, I had just experienced my first year of practical work with my first-ever Media
Studies CSE group. This was a typical 'sink' group of 'lower ability' inner-city students,
with a smattering of disruptive underachievers who constituted a physically
intimidating and pedagogically challenging presence. They had just completed a
lengthy video narrative based loosely on the TV spy series genre, involving large
quantities of camouflage, military hardware, uniforms, tomato ketchup and skilfully
choreographed (though less successfully framed and focused) fight sequences,
culminating in a heap of corpses. Despite obvious misgivings about the gendered
nature of its content, I was utterly captivated by the group's problem-solving skills,
unparalleled motivation, and technical ingenuity in the face of mind-bogglingly limited
equipment. My ambivalence towards their *Boys Own* feats of typically British heroism,
in which they played out male fantasies within the conventions of a specifically male
genre was underpinned with a glorious sense of irony given the group's racial diversity,
known villainy, and unsavoury reputation both academically and socially within the
school. In retrospect, the work now seems to me a classic example of subversive
pastiche, albeit only 75% intentional, and perhaps one of my proudest moments. At the
time, however, I was discovering *Screen Education* theory and Len Masterman; and my
encounter with Ferguson's scepticism sent me frantically to hide the tape in the stock-
room, suffused with embarrassment and guilt about the dubious ideology
underpinning what the boys had produced and my own role in condoning it. The fact
that the production was perhaps the most memorable, pleasurable and affirmative
experience of the students' entire schooling seemed to compound my anxiety: surely
pleasure would only exacerbate the ideological flaws and confuse the argument?

Yet the critique of imitation outlined above has remained a dominant orthodoxy
among media teachers, which is enshrined in assessment criteria and examination
requirements. Just as subjective pleasure in production is seen as somehow unsound,
so imitation is frequently perceived as an *unthinking* process, despite the fact that it can
demand a high order of analytic, observational and technical skills. Thus, it is generally
considered good practice for students to produce an exercise which deliberately mis-
frames and subverts the visual codes of a TV news broadcast in order to reveal the
'invisible' authority of its presenter, or the way an interviewee is set up and

contextualised. On the other hand, a seamlessly constructed version of a 'straight' news report, however skilful technically or conceptually, may be seen as plagiarised, derivative, uncritical and reactionary – all adjectives which continue to be used frequently by teachers and examiners in assessment meetings. Ironically, the more professionally polished the product, the harder students may have to work to justify their thinking. Where such work is produced as part of an examination syllabus, students are invariably required to support the work with a critical production account spelling out precisely the conventions, codes and stylistic features which characterise the form within which they have worked, however clearly they are encoded in the work itself. It is as if the more competent and convincing the production within its chosen parameters, the more evidence is required to prove that the producers consciously (or *cognitively*, according to Ferguson) understand what they have produced.

There seems to be an unspoken assumption here that using popular cultural conventions must involve a process of ideological contamination – that in tackling well-trodden dominant media forms, students must necessarily become complicit in their values and condoning of their ideologies. This tendency ultimately derives from a kind of formalism espoused during the 1970s and early 1980s by the highly influential magazine *Screen*. *Screen* theorists argued that it was the form in itself that determined the political status (and indeed the political consequences) of a work. Their espousal of the work of auteurs like Godard, and of both the artistic and the political avant-garde, reflected a belief in the radical potential of form as opposed to content, a perspective echoed in contemporary debates about realism, most notably in the dialogues between Colin McCabe and Colin MacArthur[11]. Thus, *Screen* theory would argue that without formal innovation and departure from realist narrative there can be no potential for radical content; and it is this strangely purist position which still finds expression in many current Media Studies syllabuses.

It is as if the *forms themselves* – of genres such as soap opera, crime series, youth programming or situation comedies – possess intrinsically reactionary values which may be rationally unpicked through classroom analysis, but which are somehow less easy to resist when approached 'experientially' through the processes of practical production. The fact that such forms are often highly pleasurable to work in, and generate a lot of fun for students, merely compounds the argument: surely in constructing their own version of *The Bill* or *Beverley Hills 90210*, however parodic or pastiched, there is a risk that young producers may be swept along in the momentum of their own pleasure, unable to distance themselves sufficiently to question or challenge the seductive ideology of the form. Ultimately, this fear of imitation seems to be based on the premise that media forms are all-powerful and irresistible – an argument which effectively ignores a great deal of the research and debate about media audiences which has taken place over the last two decades.

This argument takes a particularly acute form in terms of the power-relationships of the classroom. Imitation is often seen as a threat to classroom hierarchy and to the notions of ideological control to which many media teachers still aspire. Teachers whose primary aim is to change students' political beliefs by asking them to 'refuse the production style and message construction which is presented to them as normal, desirable, transparent', will inevitably find the process of working within mainstream forms problematic. The debate about imitation thus invariably poses questions about the ways in which 'political' issues are defined and addressed in the classroom – and indeed about the different ways in which they may be perceived by teachers and by students themselves. As accounts of anti-racist and anti-sexist teaching have increasingly acknowledged[12], strategies for confronting, challenging, or refuting students' positions on these issues often entail a reinforcement of classroom power-relationships in ways which are not always straightforward or productive.

These problems were particularly apparent in the early days of A-level Media Studies, where the syllabuses required practical work to be explicitly 'critical' and 'self-reflexive'. From my early experience of assessment, it seemed that the production of popular cultural forms was regarded with particular scepticism; chief examiners frequently appeared to favour work which resembled Godardian 'counter-cinema' or Channel Four small-hours experimental programming, with a further sub-text privileging originality and creativity over parody or pastiche. Recently, however, examiners and teachers have identified and challenged the hidden agenda of the assessment criteria, with some success. They have argued that this implicit bias towards innovative and oppositional production makes demands far beyond the means of all but the most able undergraduates, let alone A-level students, and that such work is both inappropriate and disempowering.

A case for imitation and parody

Clearly the distrust of imitation which has been identified here requires further scrutiny. Why are mainstream moving image texts so often reviled as sources for production work where other popular print forms are welcomed? For example, in English teaching, the concept of writing within a popular genre such as horror, romance, or science fiction might be seen far more positively, as a means of consciously acquiring and appropriating dominant forms of language[13]. Indeed, protagonists in the genre debate would argue that students need access to, and instruction in, dominant language genres: to deny them this access on the grounds that such genres are ideologically tainted would be selling them short in the interests of the most sloppy and ill-conceived liberalism[14]. On one level, this argument could be seen to reflect a more general commonsense wisdom, which is that children 'learn through imitation'. Research on language acquisition, for example, shows that young children learn to speak partly through 'parroting' adult speech. A great deal of educational practice is of course based on such assumptions – for example, as in the case of life drawing in Art. Yet when it comes to the media, this argument is almost exclusively phrased in negative terms; and in this respect, the concern about students imitating popular forms could be equated with popular anxieties about the 'effects' of the media on children – for example the argument about 'copycat' violence, or about the influence of 'poor role models'.

As this implies, the possibility that learning 'media language' – like any other kind of language – will *inevitably* involve a process of imitation is one that has been rather too easily discounted. As Jane Arthurs argues[15], students cannot be expected to deconstruct or subvert until they have got to grips with the forms they are deconstructing. Yet according to Media Studies orthodoxy, producing a horror or soap opera sequence would be acceptable not in terms of developing visual techniques or mastering technology, but only as a means of demystifying intrinsically corrupting material. On the other hand, teachers appear to be much less critical of imitation when the forms students are reproducing are the *avant-garde*, non-linear narratives of the Black Audio Film Collective, or the work of 'photo-therapists' such as Jo Spence[16]. A

111

pastiche of Godard is likely to earn good marks; while a pastiche of an Arnold Schwarzenegger movie will be condemned as derivative and ideologically unsound.

One of the most problematic assumptions here is that imitation is necessarily 'slavish', in the sense that it attempts simply to reproduce an original. Yet a brief glance at even the most outwardly 'imitative' student productions would suggest that there is nearly always an element of parody in students' uses of dominant forms – for example, in the spoof crime series trailer, the role-reversed Levi's ad, or the tongue-in-cheek rendering of *Blue Peter, Top Of The Pops* or *Middlemarch*. It is worth remembering that we are as likely to see parodies on our own domestic screens in programmes like *The Day Today, KYTV, Drop the Dead Donkey* or *The Word* as in the classroom, and that the form is as appealing to adults as to adolescents. Here again, parody is widely accepted within the English curriculum as a challenging and appropriate writing activity – which of course reflects its status as a literary form, from Greek comedy to Pope and beyond. Parody could be seen as a highly powerful and pleasurable means of developing students' mastery of form, in a similar manner to genre writing in English; and indeed, could be considered to have a potentially 'critical' or deconstructive role. Yet, as with more straightforward imitation, parody of media texts is ignored or dismissed in most of the critical writing about classroom practice.

So can it be argued that parody is, on the contrary, an empowering and enriching process? If it is, what makes it so, and how does it position the writer or producer? One answer might be that parody allows students to articulate their own ambivalence about the media: it gives them licence to *play* with a genre without necessarily having to conform to its values. In pastiching *Die Hard* or *EastEnders*, students can acknowledge their pleasures in the form and their ability to play with conventional expectations – for example, to do with representation or 'stereotyping' – without being obliged to take responsibility for their less acceptable characteristics. On the other hand, parody also has an in-built 'face-saving' function for students as a means of salvaging an embarrassing or unsuccessful product. If it looks naff, they can rationalise after the event that they intended it as a parody; and if it goes wrong half way through, it can be swiftly re-invented as an ironic pastiche. In an area so dependent on performance, self-exposure and technical skill, the potential for parody provides a safety net which students may find it hard to resist. This does of course beg serious questions about where imitation ends and parody begins, and at what points the distinction between them is made. This in turn raises the question of how we 'read' parody. Can a product intended as a straight performance be read as a parody – or vice-versa? Is parody simply a matter of the intention of the producer, or is it in the eye of the beholder?

Ultimately, we would challenge the view that parody or imitation in media production is necessarily an 'unthinking' or mindless process, as critics usually claim. Rather than seeing this simply in terms of copying or reproduction, it would be more productive to consider the diverse ways in which students *use* and *re-work* dominant media forms. It will become clear in the course of the following case study that these are complex processes, whose educational and political consequences cannot be determined in the abstract. The crucial issue, we would argue, is to identify the sorts of *learning* that might be taking place here. What do young people themselves think they are doing when they appear to be engaging in 'imitation' or 'parody' – and indeed, how would we know? What are the social functions that are served by this use of dominant media forms – and what precisely are the pleasures which are at stake?

Introducing the case study

The students with whom I worked on this case study were members of a large and successful Sixth Form consortium in a North London borough. The consortium is served by four contributing schools, and housed in pleasant Victorian buildings and newer teaching blocks on the edge of extensive park land. Despite its elegant and largely middle-class setting, the school recruits widely from all areas of the community, and the sixth form in particular is extremely diverse in social, ethnic, cultural and academic terms.

The seventeen students were in their second term of the course, but had previously come from a range of backgrounds, and were still negotiating their relationships with each other and with the staff. The majority had attended the four contributing consortium schools; two boys had come in from a public school outside the borough; while the rest had come from a range of other London comprehensive schools. They were typically diverse, with eleven boys and six girls; perhaps half were from comfortable professional environments, with a smattering of parents working in the media, whilst others came from local estates or from the predominantly Greek-Cypriot neighbourhood. Surprisingly for an inner city school, there were only two black students. Throughout the early stages of the module, friendships and allegiances were shifting and re-forming. However, because the nature of the production work involved groups with similar musical interests working together, by the end of the term they had welded into very coherent friendship groups; and indeed these groups remained close and continued to work together throughout the rest of the course.

The work was produced for the 'Basic Production' module in the Cambridge B syllabus. As the name implies, this module is undertaken early in the course and is largely practice-led; however the students are expected to show their understanding of a variety of media debates and concepts both implicitly in their finished production, and explicitly in an individually written commentary which accompanies the products. In the previous term, students had completed two textual analysis pieces, on men's magazines and on advertising, which had already been moderated with marks upheld. The students were therefore confident that they had started off on the right foot, satisfied with their grades, and aware that they already had a sixth of the entire course under their belts.

Selling sounds: marketing pop music

The unit of work followed by the students was devised specifically for the 'Basic Production' module. Used extensively on INSET courses and training sessions for A-level teachers, this unit has now been adopted by at least half the A-level centres in North London; although in the event I adapted it to include a brief simulation and to trial materials from a classroom pack I was producing at the time. Another account of this basic unit focusing on different issues in another North London school has appeared elsewhere[17]; and the classroom materials for the final brief and preparatory simulation exercise have since been published by The English and Media Centre[18].

The module lasted for an entire term of 10 weeks, with a final evaluation/ moderation session with the two regular class teachers (Penny and Eleanor) a fortnight later. Its central premise was that students' own expertise and subjective responses to music must be foregrounded. However, it was also acknowledged that they would require a degree of critical distance, some understanding of the music industry itself, and a structured framework in order to be able to talk about music and work creatively with it. The sequence of work was as follows:

Week 1: Semiological analysis of different styles and sub-genres of popular music and their associated cultures, followed up by more personal presentations of students' musical preferences.

Week 2: Close reading of secondary texts such as promotional material, the music press, reviews and album covers, in order to explore concepts of audience targeting and niche-marketing. These areas related to some of the media debates included in the terminal examination, such as the relationship between mainstream and independent music production, ideology and popular culture, and the 'authenticity' or 'commercialisation' of popular music[19].

Week 3: An 'unseen' storyboarding activity, creating a storyboard for a new video for Wilson Pickett's *In the Midnight Hour*. This was followed by analysis of a range of pop video material, and a lightning tour through different theoretical models which we hoped students might reflect upon critically in the course of their own production. There was a further double-session using a tightly structured simulation in which groups selected a music track for re-packaging from a selection of lesser-known talents from the 60's to the 80's, and then presented their ideas for a full promotional campaign re-launching the artist with an image and cultural identity for the 1990's. The function of this session, to which I will return in depth later, was pragmatic and two-fold: partly as a means of identifying what, if anything, students had been able to transfer from their previous terms' experience in advertising and marketing, and partly to give them an industrial context and structure for the more open-ended nature of their final brief. This whole lead-in to the production work took three weeks in all, leaving seven to complete the brief and its accompanying commentary.

Weeks 4 – 8: The central brief for the module was to produce secondary promotional material around a selection of artists, including those they had been invited to re-launch in the simulation. Students were offered a choice of four different media:

- photography/artwork for the production of album covers;
- the construction of 15 minutes of a radio programme featuring their chosen track in some form;
- creating a music video;
- producing a pilot version of a music magazine.

This last option was the only one which did not retain some element of the previous re-packaging; although in the event, at the request of the class, we relaxed the rules in order to allow groups to re-package music of their own choice, provided that it was sufficiently elderly (i.e. pre-1986) to be justifiably re-cycled. The productions were to be accompanied by a substantial production report or commentary in which students were expected to reflect explicitly and critically on their work, in the light of media theory.

Interestingly, although we had anticipated that the main interest would be in video production, this option was chosen by only two students, one of whom left the course halfway through production. Lottie, the remaining student, produced a complex narrative version of the Doors' *Roadhouse Blues* single-handedly – a feat of considerable courage. Chrissie and Gina chose the artwork and photography option, producing album covers re-packaging Jefferson Airplane's *White Rabbit* and a Bob Marley compilation. An all-male group, James, Matt and Brian, produced *Stompin' Groove*, a new music magazine targeting young people with an interest in jazz, blues and funk; while the remaining three groups opted for radio, producing extracts from stations entitled *Love FM*, *Rainbow Radio*, and *PMT* (People's Music Transmission).

Weeks 9 – 10. The final products were reviewed and evaluated in a plenary session, where each group presented its work and was interrogated by the rest of the class and staff. Students then worked on production reports, with supporting guidelines from staff.

Rationale

We had deliberately adapted the brief to focus on the concept of re-packaging for a variety of reasons. First, we wanted to ensure that students worked at a distance from their own immediate preferences, partly to avoid being over-influenced by existing material, but also to minimise the potential for uncritical hero-worship – although our own motivation here will be investigated more fully later. Gender was definitely an issue here, both in view of the dynamic of the group, which was dominated in the early preparatory sessions by two rival factions of highly vocal boys; and in the choices of music selected by the students themselves.

We also wanted students to focus more closely on concepts of audience and image construction, and to think about the social and cultural context of different musical genres – ideas which are hard to apply in practice to one's own preferences. For this reason, the brief required an unspecified degree of audience research, which to our surprise the students took extremely seriously and approached both professionally and enthusiastically. This may have been because the formal processes of organising questionnaires and surveys, and then analysing and interpreting results, felt like a reassuringly safe way in, and allowed a let-out clause in the event of peer-group ridicule. After all, as Dorian pointed out, 'if we end up producing rubbish, it's not our fault – we're just doing what our target audience wants'.

By insisting on recycling existing music from the past, we hoped to encourage students to reflect more analytically on the original audiences for their chosen music, and on how issues of style, genre, and representation of the image or attitude of the artist might be reconstructed and inflected for new listeners, and for different moments in time. Our original selection of texts included a range of music which we felt was both representative of different historical periods and subcultural groups, and might also have some interest for the students[20]. However, as we shall see, it was perhaps ultimately more useful as an opportunity for subversion and play than as a critical strategy.

The preparatory work

For the first sessions we played a compilation of un-credited samples of music from as wide a range of popular genres as possible, which students described and analysed, with some difficulty, using a framework derived broadly from semiotics. For the following session, they were asked to bring in and analyse music of their own choice, this time also discussing its subjective appeal – how it spoke to them, why they chose it, and their feelings about it. This was a fascinating exercise for us, but predictably awkward for the group: in general, they found it far easier to deconstruct other people's choices than to do justice to their own, which they seemed either unable or unwilling to discuss in any detail. While many of the students had clearly taken considerable care and time in making their selection and preparing an analysis, in the event it was clearly 'un-hip' to seem to be too well-prepared. We had predicted this; the students had only worked together for a term and were still uneasily forming alliances and testing out their status and credibility, so that any excess of personal commitment or enthusiasm was decidedly uncool. At the same time, they were having to confront the problem of finding an appropriate vocabulary for analysing an essentially non-verbal aesthetic form. Simultaneously, we were asking them to expose personal choices in a very public way. And there was the additional irony of having acquired the academic status of A-level studenthood in order to be able to legitimately enjoy aspects of popular culture which only six months earlier would have been seen as the exact antithesis of the school ethos.

The range of student preferences was interesting, from crusty-ish folk rock to grunge and garage, with a strong dance bias, including 'really hardcore' hardcore and ambient tapes recorded live from raves. There were only two tracks by black performers and one by a woman – a predominantly white, Western, male collection. This issue of the male-dominated Eurocentric nature of their preferences was discussed at some length. So too were the selections of the young women in the group, which demonstrated a softer, more mellow appeal (Maxi Priest, Soul Asylum and the Levellers): these were referred to, apparently disingenuously, by James, the most vocal male student, as being 'for young girls in bedrooms' – a remark for which he was later challenged. More surprising for us, however, was the inclusion (by males) of several vintage Dylan, Zappa and Van Morrison tracks, apparently inspired by parents or childhood memories – although there may also have been some opportunistic sizing up of teachers' and researchers' cultural histories, both in order to please us and to display their own compendious musical knowledge.

Throughout the session the students demonstrated both familiarity with a predictably broad range of genres, and polite curiosity about each others' selections (if a little knowing and weary at times). One group of male students, James, Marek, Matt and Tom, were particularly vocal in discussion. They were clearly highly knowledgeable about a broad range of musical genres and forms, and apparently *au fait* both with the marketing strategies of branches of the music industry, and with the divergent discourses of the music press. However, their interest and knowledge was of a somewhat different order than the more streetwise enthusiasms of the rest of the group. Not only were they keen to demonstrate detailed familiarity with forms of music beyond their own peer group and subcultural affiliations, but this familiarity was expressed in more erudite and critical terms, verging on the academic. For this group, there was more at stake than the exposure of personal taste; there seemed to be an assumption of authority and expertise which also perhaps implied a degree of contempt for more populist forms of popular music – although this was never fully articulated.

Interestingly, this symbolic muscle-flexing was picked up by the teachers from another perspective, and the session concluded with their intervention. At the end of the lesson, Penny kept James, Matt, Marek and Tom behind, and reprimanded them for their vocal dominance and sexist analyses in discussion, and for intimidating the other students with their obvious expertise. This chastisement was accepted gracefully but with some ill-concealed pride; after all, it's not unflattering to be told off (especially by a young female teacher) because you know too much about one of the more 'sexy' areas of popular culture. I could identify only too well with Penny's concerns, both to defend the interests of the less confident young women in the group, and to foreground issues of sexism within the music industry. Nevertheless, I felt that this intervention was potentially counter-productive: it seemed to impose constraints too early in the process of investigation, thereby closing down opportunities for debate and challenge which the group as a whole might have reached of its own accord, perhaps with more empowering consequences for the young women themselves. This episode raised a number of familiar questions about the function of such interventionist strategies, and indeed the whole problem of 'policing' students' attitudes[21] – an issue to which we will return in this and the following chapter.

Having tasted, with partial success and some discomfort, a subjective and affective approach to matters of musical taste and personal identity, we progressed to a more distanced analysis of PR material. This included close linguistic and image analysis of record covers, posters, advertising and display material, focusing particularly on visual and street style, dress and image construction; and deconstruction of the music press, in terms of concepts of audience and readership. These were practices with which both students and teachers clearly felt more comfortable. The formalised academic approach seemed to come as a relief after the more open-ended subjective aspects: it felt 'safe', constrained and familiar. Exploration of taste requires a degree of personal honesty which is not only exposing and un-school-like, but also difficult to achieve in the context of an implicit agenda of political correctness. Analytic procedures can displace and de-fuse these bigger questions of personal identity; but they can also lead to superficiality and cynicism. Thus, when we asked the group to summarise the viewpoint and style of a variety of extracts from music magazines in the form of a hypothetical mission statement, they were able to demonstrate an uncanny familiarity with the strategies of niche marketing and the jargon of readership profiles – features which were to recur disturbingly throughout their practical work and resurface in their final evaluations.

Storyboarding Wilson Pickett

A similar level of competence emerged in the first activity which required the group to create their own texts. As a warm up to pop video, we asked them to storyboard a promo for Wilson Pickett's *In the Midnight Hour* – a track we had chosen for its 'classic' status, simple musical structure and lyrics, and familiar genre. I wanted to know what pupils would do with a mainstream vintage track verging on cliché which might not lend itself easily to the style and imagery of current pop video. Although the group had already had experience of the process of storyboarding in their 'Textual Analysis' module, I was nevertheless surprised by how unproblematic and unthreatening they found the exercise. Despite the recent revival of interest in 60's Soul, and the inclusion of this track on a heavily promoted best-selling compilation of music from that era, not all students knew the song. Nevertheless, there were no grumbles either about its genre, nor about the dearth of live footage of the original performance. Instead, nearly every student reconstructed the song as a narrative, drawing on a wide range of both visual and symbolic conventions. Unsurprisingly, most produced pastiched versions of a similar theme; the repetition of the chorus was represented figuratively by repeated images of the moon, the hands of a clock approaching but never reaching midnight, and circling shots of the night sky. These were woven into a variety of 'waiting' scenarios – from the soldier on leave desperately trying to get back to his girl, to the waitress in a red dress in a smoky bar-room. Tom provided a variation in the form of reconstructions of old black and white footage, both of live performance and of the storyline, shot in the style of grainy 60's *Ready Steady Go* re-runs. James subverted the song by transmuting the singer into a vampire in the closing chorus, *Thriller*-style. Only Ian, himself heavily into techno-dance and ambient music, avoided the narrative format, and went for an imaginative montage featuring rapid cuts and mixes between an innovative range of motifs, including astrological phenomena, headlights, numerals and patterns, impeccably presented in post-modern fashion as cut-and-paste rather than drawn artwork. In his case, as in several others, there was a clear connection between his own musical and cultural affiliations, and the pace, rhythm and iconography through which he interpreted the song. Gina and Lottie, both studying A-level Art, provided highly stylised and lovingly detailed representations of Norman Rockwell-style 50's diners and London rooftop cityscapes respectively. In this way, the 'meaning' of the song was reworked in each student's version to reflect both autobiographical and analytic elements; and in discussing the results, the students' understanding of the polysemic nature of music was clearly articulated.

On paper, at any rate, there was little evidence of Masterman's 'endless wilderness' of dreary images. While the ideas were certainly not 'original', they were at the very least appropriate, and at best inventively reworked. On the back of these storyboards, we took the group on a lightning tour of different academic accounts of pop video, using highly simplified versions of analyses by E. Ann Kaplan and Simon Frith[22]. We were able to point out that each and every issue such critics touched upon was represented in some way in their own work, and to highlight yet again their considerable expertise, which by now was becoming something of a cliché in the class. This attempt to introduce basic theory by grounding it in the students' own 'un-theorised' practice was a deliberate reversal of normal Media Studies procedure; on this occasion it seemed an empowering and thought-provoking strategy.

It was clear from this exercise that the students were already thinking in terms of concrete images, and were able to draw on rich reserves of visual and aural experience. It is hard to say how far this is simply a symptom of their 'media literacy' in general, or related more specifically to the allusive nature of music texts and intensive music consumption in particular. Similarly, we can so far only hypothesise about whether students respond creatively to music storyboarding because of its rhythmic and narrative structure and (usually) concise format; or because of the dimension of marketing, which invariably links sound and image in highly visible and inescapable ways.

What was clear however was how much pleasure they took in this work. Although this had only been intended as a brief ice-breaking activity, it was completed without prompting in the students' own time and involved some high quality artwork. The activity seemed to provide opportunities for the students to reflect upon and deconstruct musical forms that were far more convincing than those that had been offered by the more explicitly analytical work. However, I found myself wondering here exactly what I was looking for, and why. In terms of artwork, this was in general competent and skilful, even from the most laid-back of the group. The concept of storyboarding and the relationship between sound and image was clearly well-established; and ideas of musical genre, narrative and style were well-realised and explained. In syllabus terms, this activity in itself encapsulated many of the criteria demanded by the module. Yet I felt there was something missing, which I found hard to define. Perhaps it was personal investment – a sense either of subjective pleasure or of dissatisfaction in the music itself, as opposed to the activity around it.

The music simulation: putting the industry into practice – and practising the industry

By this stage I had already begun to suspect that even the limited and cursory preparatory work we had undertaken so far was beginning to impose an implicit agenda of formal and conceptual analysis which might constrain the sorts of work the students were likely to produce. There was, however, a feeling, from both students and teachers, that up until now we had been skirting around the edges of an industry which could not be fully understood either through semiotics or through personal response to music. We therefore decided to go ahead with the institutional simulation which we had planned as the final stage of preparation, but confined it to an intensive half-day activity which would be the starting point of their own original work.

The simulation was a condensed version of a sequence of role-plays I had developed for a forthcoming publication, heavily indebted to an earlier teaching pack, *The Music Business*[23]. The first stage (about 45 minutes, exclusive of a brief listening period) involved students acting in groups as record company A&R personnel, debating which of a selection of little-known classics to re-release. The choices, as described above, came from a range of music genres and periods. A central aspect here was to encourage students to consider the original audiences for each artist/band, a potential target audience for the 90's, and the sort of image and cultural identity they would construct. During their deliberations, the students were offered a range of data about the music industry. This included information about the working practices of major and independent record companies; the economics and politics of recording, touring, promotion, and video production; and analyses of the importance of the charts, radio playlists, plugs, etc.

Having selected what to re-issue and how, each group briefly presented its suggestions for development and promotion. Their action plans were now rotated around the room as each group assumed a different role for Stage 2. Here, for an hour, they became marketing departments, charged with producing an overall campaign plan and promotion schedule based on the suggestions of the A&R team, within a fairly tight budget.

'We never knew there was so much to learn...'

Perhaps the most fascinating aspect of this activity was the almost imperceptible process by which vague discussion yielded creative ideas, which finally became concrete and rationalised action. Equally striking was the professional confidence and competence with which each group presented its final action plans, and the extent to which they played ball with the demands and conventions of the industry – and simultaneously with us, as representatives of their exam syllabus.

James, Tom and Marek, marketing a virtually unknown bunch of weedy art-student types of the mid-80's called Total Strangers, produced artwork and a video storyboard uncannily close to the real thing, even down to their vision of black and white torn-edged publicity shots and aerial views of the band doing wacky things under Brighton pier in Dick Lester-style speeded-up action. In discussion, their willingness to identify and exploit an image for a band they had never seen and certainly did not like, and to predict its doomed trajectory so accurately, was quite impressive:

James: Well, they're never going to make it just on the record, are they? It's just too soft and art-schoolish, too mid-80's. But we could build on their popularity in Brighton and focus on their image using the beach and the pier, 'cos that might give it more of a fun holiday feel...

Tom: I reckon it's a lost cause – we'll do another couple of records for them and they'll disappear. None of them has a strong enough personality... No stars.

Two groups chose to re-launch a South African band called The Mahotela Queens. In their discussions, both had a clear sense of the ideological implications of their task, and of the political importance of representing South African Black culture positively. Both were also sufficiently cynical to reject overtly political imagery:

Lottie: There'll be lots of red, gold and green and black repeated symbolically, and we'll be showing images of the townships and everything, but positively, nothing too controversial...

Ian: 'Cos we don't want to get up anyone's noses and put people off.

Dominique: And anyway we might offend someone in the company or mess up other deals.

Lottie: And we want it to get played, so it'll be really colourful and good-time-ish.

The debriefing session was notable on three counts. Firstly, we had not anticipated the ease with which the students adopted the personae and language of their institutional roles for their presentations, nor the competitive rigour with which they interrogated each other after each one. While some aspects of the task (identification of appropriate sales outlets for target audiences, and the problems of getting the products' radio air-play in particular) had suffered from the time constraints we had imposed, in general each group presented logical, well-argued and convincing campaigns, which they defended vigorously and confidently, firmly rejecting any potential criticism:

Matthew: But don't you think all these images of colourful black women dancing, little kids and so on, don't you think that's a bit sort of patronising?

Lottie: No.

Dominique: Well, the artists are happy with it, and we think it's an image which students and people like that will relate to.

Under different circumstances, this intransigence would have been a problem, given the requirement of the syllabus for reflective analysis; but in the context of institutional role-play, in what students clearly perceived as a cut-throat and highly performance-oriented industry, there was no room for doubt or reconsideration. This was serious games-playing, in which the newly acquired discourses of marketing appeared to be embraced uncritically, and only rarely with tongue in cheek. I began to feel uneasy about my own expectations of the activity. In requiring their involvement in an explicitly exploitative marketing exercise, had we effectively 'sold' them the very values we had hoped they would critique? Had I secretly hoped that they would find the whole process so ideologically distasteful that they would subvert the exercise through humour or parody? I found myself wondering at what stage and by what means students are able to dissociate themselves from their elective roles and objectively evaluate both their own decisions, and the process itself. This of course is precisely the sort of work which Len Masterman and others have advocated as a way of 'demystifying' the industry – in preference to the mindless reproduction of dominant ideology which is seen to dominate more open-ended projects. Yet our experience here would suggest that the use of this kind of simulation as a means of 'demystifying' the operations of the media industries can be undermined by the intensity of the situation[24].

Secondly, the concept of *audience* remained frustratingly unclear in each group's account of their campaign. Drawing on the previous work they had done on advertising, audience segmentation and market research categories, there seemed to be a disjuncture between the students' subjective perceptions of the diversity of audiences, and the demands of the simulation. Each group presented a detailed audience profile based on lifestyle, values and attitudes which bore an astonishingly convincing resemblance to advertisers' demographics, but which they totally disowned in relation to themselves and their peer group. Such manipulative marketing strategies invariably influenced other people – but never themselves.

Thirdly, the response of the students to the simulation in their subsequent evaluation was unreservedly positive. Although we had repeatedly warned them that this was only an approximation of professional practice, they saw it as a highly purposeful activity with an almost vocational status – something we had taken great pains to avoid:

Dorian: I thought it was really really useful.

Matthew: I'm doing Music, but I never knew there was so much to learn, especially all the stuff about plugging, getting records on air, and all that. I always thought it was just like a matter of having talent and being spotted...

James: It was really good being able to work so hard in such a short time, and to have to promote things we don't really believe in. Good practice.

Matthew: And doing all those different jobs – I reckon we could do just about anything in the business now. (Laughter)

James: Do we get marked on this? (More laughter)

These representative remarks suggest a further dimension to the students' perceptions of the simulation. They understood its function as a way of acquiring hands-on experience of a complex economic system and its professional practices. Yet they also identified it as an area of knowledge on the syllabus, and as a lead-in to the production module on which they would be assessed; and they were proving to us (in the nicest possible way, of course) that they had learned a lot. They were playing ball with us (and the syllabus) in much the same way as they had accepted the constraints and parameters of the simulation itself.

The main issue in this instance is whether consideration of the industry inevitably means privileging the *status quo* – things as they are – and therefore pre-empting the possibility for alternative or oppositional models – things as they might be. In fact, the very concept of an 'alternative' or 'oppositional' music promotion campaign could be seen to be pretty bizarre in an industry where generic categories have been so segmented and crossover forms so multiplied that even the most inaccessible musical form can be recycled, sampled and repositioned for a variety of audiences and contexts. Ultimately, the students' experience of the simulation was far more directed towards the development of marketing skills and economic strategies than towards an understanding of the music texts themselves; and this tension was to prove an inescapable influence on their own productions.

Getting down to 'the real thing'

The group now had about five weeks to produce their practical production, as described above. The groups were scattered around, working in the IT Department, at *Melody FM* (a local radio station), on location and in each others' homes; and a great deal of the work took place outside school hours. The production was to be undertaken with minimum intervention; the assessment criteria for the module included marks for research, analysis and planning and production organisation, and it was agreed that apart from technical support and supervision, the two class teachers should act merely as facilitators so that the bulk of the work was entirely the responsibility of the students.

It is worth pausing here to consider the conflicting interests which determine the production and reception of group practical work – at A-level in this instance, but also more generally. In many respects, the minutiae of assessment seem to reflect the uncertainties and anxieties outlined at the beginning of this chapter. The assessment of collaborative production work for Syllabus B is problematic and complex. Teachers are required to complete two assessment reports on each candidate, one in the early stages of the module, the other at the end. 15 marks of a possible 70 are allocated to criteria associated with group work – here defined as listening, co-operation, communication, negotiation, moving the group forward constructively, leadership skills, arbitration. In the final assessment, marks are divided equally between 'analysis and planning', 'technical expertise', and 'imagination and inventiveness'.

Where does this form of assessment place both student and teacher in addressing the priorities in production? If the product itself is to be excluded from the assessment process, as it effectively is here, then its status is questionable. Yet this is clearly not the case for the students themselves, for whom the 'quality' of the finished product is a crucial concern. For them, the experience of production is often the most significant and memorable aspect of their course, in which they invest enormous reserves of time and energy. Certainly our students looked to the practical work with huge excitement and apprehension; although at the same time they were constantly reminded of the need for their production to deliver the right kinds of evidence, and to meet a mixed range of criteria, many of which appeared to bear little relation either to the content itself or to concepts that have informed the critical debates around popular music.

Under these circumstances, a tendency to go for the safe or uncontentious option would be understandable. On the other hand, however, the syllabus also awards marks for 'imagination and inventiveness', which is defined in terms of 'willingness to learn, explore, challenge and be inventive with chosen medium'. Meanwhile, the teachers would be required to report back on the following questions: 'How successfully has the candidate applied mainstream conventions and challenged them within the practical work? What flair has been shown?' This seems to be a classic double-bind situation in which students need to 'read the examiner's mind' and tread a fine balance between creativity and conservatism, between demonstrating an understanding of the industry, and a willingness to challenge it. It is in this demanding context that I want to explore the outcomes of the students work.

Researching the market

The initial research was the first of many occasions on which the preparatory work we had done returned to haunt us. Over and over again we read mission statements and proposals voiced in the bland and confident tones of the industry, internalised from the audience profiles and publicity literature of the many radio stations and music journals explored by the students in researching their audience. Here, for example, is Irene's proposal for the radio group:

> From the market research carried out, we discovered a visible gap in the range of music available from the national radio network. There is no existing station which caters exclusively for Love music, and therefore having found from our research that over 50% of respondents were in favour of such a station, we decided that timeless love music would be the predominant theme for our radio network... We feel that this station would be the first of its kind – providing just one theme of music, but at the same time catering for all tastes, social classes and groups... the scope for our target audience is extremely broad, however from the market research we know that the majority of our listeners would be mainly female between 14 and 35, of working and middle class. Love FM will be the first radio station to allocate transmission time to the other 10% of the British population- the Gay and Lesbian community. We also have plans for new and original features such as radio Karaoke and Blind Date competitions. We have great aspirations for this proposed Love Station.

We were consistently impressed by the rigour of the research, and the professional ways in which it was analysed and incorporated in order to justify each group's production. Yet I also had a faint sense of unease about the students' superficial mastery of marketing-speak and research data. Yes, it provided ample evidence of the success of our preparatory work in developing understandings of the many levels of the music industry; but what implications would it have for the productions themselves? Our briefs had been about re-packaging and reconstruction, with the aim of providing opportunities for innovation and originality; but it looked at this early stage as if our emphasis on institutional issues might have hijacked or neutralised students' chances to engage creatively with their tasks. Would playing marketing games work against the possibilities for playing with the texts themselves? Would we end up with dreary, poorly conceived imitations of professional practice – and if so, what would our students have gained from the process?

The productions

What resulted was as follows:

1. *Record Covers* – Gina and Chrissie: two sets of album covers and PR material re-launching Jefferson Airplane and Bob Marley. These both make different and distinctive use of montage, including found imagery, recycled publicity pictures, literary illustration, pen and ink drawing, and the girls' own photography. Both packages draw extensively on the iconography and historical context associated with each artist, reinforced in sleeve notes: 'Welcome to the weird and wonderful world of Jefferson Airplane... This album is a haunting emotive experience, and an essential listening for understanding the 60's and 70's...' (see fig 5.1).

2. *Stompin' Groove* – James, Matt and Brian: a new magazine reclaiming Jazz in all its diverse forms for the 16 – 24 age-group, which claims in its editorial:

   > We're just as sick of that bourgeois, sophisticated, elitist attitude to Jazz as you are. Well, not only are we going to break through the myth that Jazz is this way, but also we're going to take it right through the spectrum of our imagination, aren't we? And if we don't, well we're going to die trying.

   The 8-page publication included a full colour cover design using the students' own photography; opinion columns, including a lengthy critique of Jazz FM and of jazz club exclusions policies for under-18s; reviews of albums and gigs; an interview with a (student-created) rising young jazz star, and advertising material (see fig 5.2).

3. *Pop video* – Lottie: A narrative video promo for The Doors' *Roadhouse Blues*, intended originally as live action but reduced (due to Tom's sudden departure) to an ingenious and innovative juxtaposition of still images, cutting backwards and forwards between drawn storyboard, photographic stills, live action and montage. This is certainly the text which takes most risks with its form, and represents the most imaginative recycling of the original imagery.

4. *Rainbow Radio* – Jan and Robbie: a programme of trance-techno music representing 'the current psychedelic movement', and featuring the re-launch of Jefferson Airplane 'to give a retrospective look back to the beginnings of psychedelia'. More specific than other texts in its audience address. It is intended to attract:

   > mainly young people who have adopted an alternative lifestyle in which they are accepted for what they are, without the need for any masks. Their style of clothing will be colourful foreign (i.e. Asian) import clothes. A more frequent number than usual will have dreadlocks, yet it is a predominantly white audience (not implying that ethnic groups aren't welcome). Many listeners will have had contact with other religions than Christianity, and will have made some progress on a spiritual level.

Fig. 5.1 Jefferson Airplane and Bob Marley album covers

5. *PMT* – Ian, Ron and Dorian: an extract from 'Slater's Paradise', a programme specialising in worst-choice music, broadcast by the unfortunately (but deliberately) acronymed People's Music Transmission station, *PMT*. Presented by DJ's Ron and D, this unashamed parody features an ongoing phone-in debate about the relative ghastliness of New Kids on the Block as opposed to Take That, the Top Ten Worst Singles and Albums charts, and concluded with Jefferson Airplane in the Listeners' Choice Worst Ever Request spot. Lots of fun was had with funny voices at the expense of Kylie, Take That and other old un-favourites.

6. *Love FM* – Marek, Irene, Nicola, Hollie and Dominique: this opens with the re-launch of the Raincoats' cover of *Lola*, hailed as 'going to be a hu-u-u-u-uge success', and is followed by Exclusive Agony Aunt and Uncle Doctors Loucas and Johnson dealing with callers from the gay community (a Brum Lesbian in love with her best friend); a request spot featuring *Unchained Melody* ('for my boyfriend, tell him I love him lots'); the five most popular Love albums of the month, from Barbra Streisand to Mariah Carey; a trailer for the Gay Blind Date slot, and the winner of the Karaoke contest (Marek, tunelessly warbling *Color Me Badd*). The extract fades out with a half-hour of Motown classics; it also includes a professional sounding station indent *One Love* (Bob Marley followed by the seductive slogan 'There's only One Luuurrve'), and a hilarious Sharon and Tracey ad for *Ann Summers* sex shops.

Fig. 5.2 *Stompin' Groove* magazine cover

The above summaries obviously cannot recreate the flavour of these texts. Nevertheless they demonstrate that imitation in a variety of forms was unquestionably and inevitably a feature of what we ended up with. Of all the texts, Lottie's video is the only one which is formally innovative, and that was more by default – in that she had to salvage a half-finished product single-handedly – than by intent. Gina and Chrissie's artwork is beautifully produced, showing a sophisticated understanding of musical and cultural influences and an ability to represent them visually through the juxtaposition of found and original material (see fig 5.1). Nevertheless, it is more notable for its technical competence than for any intrinsic originality. Similarly, *Stompin' Groove* has a fresh and personal (if occasionally pretentious) address, and considerable style and energy, but is less innovative in form and content than its editorial team claimed. On the other hand, *Rainbow Radio* is particularly interesting in that both producers would specifically identify themselves with their chosen audience, and have adopted a tone of voice which is unpretentious and conversational. Both students were also in some ways isolated within the group (one is a newly arrived American, the other is dyslexic). Unfortunately theirs was also the only text which was unsuccessful in terms of production values; despite extensive work, their equipment let them down, resulting in an almost inaudible tape. In contrast, *Love FM* was an extremely competent piece of work, recorded on professional equipment and remarkably convincing. It was also the only text which involved any form of dramatic or performance skills: contrary to expectations, the group demonstrated considerable skills in their use of adopted personae, accents, and sound effects, and an acute sense of where to draw the line. It would be difficult to define this work as out-and-out parody. It was delivered with panache and totally convincing authenticity, from cod American accents to seamless editing; yet in the context of its production team, it was impossible to read it as an entirely serious concept.

So, given this diverse range of products, how far were our fears of unthinking mimicry or humourless pastiche realised? How far had our over-conscientious preparation set an economic and industrial agenda which inhibited rather than facilitated creative responses to the assignments? And how far could we feasibly expect students to reflect on the ideological sub-texts of what they had produced?

Firstly, it seems clear that the structure we had adopted for the module imposed constraints which were only partially helpful. While the concept of repackaging pre-selected music genres had the effect of reducing the number of options available to the group and thus speeding up what might otherwise have been a hideously drawn-out and intimidating production experience, it also pre-empted opportunities for the students to engage creatively with their own cultural experiences. Although it encouraged some reflection on the iconography and potential meanings of different musical genres, it simply did not leave enough space to challenge or debate those meanings explicitly. Similarly, it was useful to demystify industrial practice through simulation, not least to challenge the mythology of artistic success as a product of individual inspiration irrespective of economic and institutional context. Yet by leading straight into production immediately afterwards, it may also have implied a cynical acceptance of the *status quo* – a 'hidden agenda' which any student who knew which side her assessment bread was buttered would have found hard to dismiss.

On the other hand, there was very little sense from the students' commentaries that they had felt either unfairly railroaded into choices not of their making, or cheated of the opportunity to produce work in which they could have invested more of their personal identities. On the contrary, the commentaries were lovingly detailed, and appeared to reflect considerable pride in the ability to interpret a quasi-professional brief quasi-professionally:

> Dominique: We wanted to create something which was *a bit* different, which would fill a gap in the market, One of the main points in the criteria was to find something there was a niche for, so that was our main aim. We wouldn't have wanted to do something a whole lot different from real radio. We wouldn't have had anything to compare it to.

Mis-reading audiences?

A further problem surfaces in terms of the syllabus criteria which refer to 'the application of techniques' for targeting the audience. For example, in justifying the content of *Stompin' Groove*, James argues that there is 'a massive cross-section of music in this magazine, so it's going to appeal to a wide range of people'. At the same time, he also claims both to represent the interests of the minority (i.e. young jazz fans for whom no publication or appropriate club exists) and to demystify for unconverted audiences 'a style of music that is essentially looked upon as being old, for older people' He argues that 'jazz has been stereotypically represented with that sort of sophisticated image, you know, it's cocktail bars and a hell of a lot of money, whereas there's loads of people that are listening to jazz and where it's going that are younger, instead of keeping it back in the 30s and 40s...' On the other hand, he refers despairingly to the research they obtained from the radio station Jazz FM which was

> full of statistics about how they had the highest proportion of listeners going to the theatre more than twice a month, and how they had the highest percentage of people who had mobile phones and had bought a new car in the last five years and things, and basically portraying their listeners to be middle and upper class people... so we were trying to have the opposite effect, for middle and lower class.

And yet he concludes 'we're not really singling out one specific group, we're trying to make it accessible for everyone, so if you do want to listen to it, you can.'

James's determination to refute one-dimensional notions both of his preferred music and of its listeners is undercut by his inability to reconcile the economic profile of industry-generated data with his own social and cultural experience. He has not yet acquired a theoretical framework which will allow him to make sense of this disjuncture, and his confusion surfaces both in his comments and in his contributions to the final product (see below).

This was not an isolated phenomenon. For all groups, the concept of audience remained confused and stereotypical. *Love FM* defended to the death its belief in a community of Luurrve Music listeners, which it defined as '14 – 35 year olds and mainly women of working/middle class'. Later on, however, their typical listener emerged as

> a 17 year old female who is studying. She would be aiming for a career in journalism and she would wear clothes from Top Shop and Miss Selfridge which

are fashionable clothes aimed at fairly young girls. Her hobbies and leisure time
activities would include reading, going to the cinema theatre and clubs.

Every group reported an audience profile in similarly lifestyle-influenced ad-speak
terms; yet at the same time, with the exception of *Love FM*, each group claimed to be
producing the sort of text that 'people like us are interested in', and vociferously
testifying to the intelligence and taste of their audience. No-one was quite able to justify
this curiously schizophrenic conception of audience, nor to challenge some of their
more outrageously stereotypical assertions. Here again, our misplaced emphasis on
marketing strategies and industrial practice, following on from the work they had
previously done on advertising, was problematic – but perhaps the outcomes were
closer to professional practice than we intended.

Writing about music – a literary genre, or a defensive reaction?

The problem of audience address highlighted another, contradictory, influence which
we observed particularly in the work of the *Stompin' Groove* group. James's comments
(quoted above) about demystifying the image of jazz and repositioning it for younger,
more working class people are undercut by the tone, register and style of his writing.
For example, his 'Opinion' column, which mounts a swingeing attack on Jazz FM,
adopts a florid, almost poetic, literary quality, laced with in-yer-face direct address:

> Don't get me wrong, they are the best radio station in the country, its just...
> well, I've said it, haven't I? Oh but to dream, eh? Years and years of hope put to
> rest and shattered in one week. It glimmered and shone like a fire, and then
> some bastard threw a bucket of water on it. So leave me now, I'll be back when
> the next shimmering of Jazz rears its magnificent head, even though only to
> have it chopped off by its supposed lovers. Thank you and good-bye.

The rest of the magazine suffers from a similarly split personality; the articles (which
are impressively lengthy for 17-year-old boys, albeit A-level English students) alternate
between street-cred laddishness and the reverence of the dedicated music expert.
Written text (again unusually) is privileged over visual images – uncharacteristic in a
magazine targeting young people – and there is much carefully considered wordplay:
for example, an historical review is described as 'an hors d'oeuvre before the main
course of the rest of the magazine' There is a sense of enormous pleasure here in
playing with language, style and ideas; but the overall impression is that of young men
self-consciously aspiring to the more mature reflection of older, more sophisticated
writers – occasionally with unintended parodic effect.

While this literary approach is most noticeable in the case of *Stompin' Groove*, it
recurs in a variety of ways throughout all the writing produced by the class. Indeed, for
a practical module, the unit yielded a surprising amount of written text, from initial
project proposals, mission statements, and audience research summaries, through
interim work-in-progress statements, to the final commentaries. This is due in part to
the two class teachers' backgrounds as English teachers; they work within a well-
established department with a strong tradition of learning support, emphasis on
redrafting, and high standards, and it may be that in this first, anxiety-inducing year of
teaching an unfamiliar syllabus in an unfamiliar discipline, these influences were

unconsciously foregrounded because they were safe and familiar. But I would also suggest a further dimension: that in dealing with the threatening areas of popular music, pleasure and production, we were all anxious to justify the work, render it respectably academic, and to cover ourselves in the event of unsound or unacceptable products. How far the dominance of the written word exerted a limiting and ultimately uncreative influence on our students' work is unclear. I have argued elsewhere that the emphasis on formal evaluation-writing in much practical work can have a deadening and un-motivating effect, and can devalue the status of the production process and product[25]. I would like to think that this was not the case with our students, but the evidence remains ambiguous.

Researching 'originality'

It could be argued that within the constraints of the assignment, several groups demonstrated considerable ingenuity and inventiveness in turning the task around to conform to the version of the text they wanted to produce (in a similar way to the hypertext work described in Chapter 3). Jan and Robbie, for example, were able to use their choice of Jefferson Airplane as a form of historical and social comment on a musical genre with which they closely identified; *PMT* not only used it as the rationale for their whole 'critical' approach, but were also able to marginalise it by fading out on it at the end of their segment. *Love FM* explored another rationale for their use of the Raincoats' *Lola* – despite their unfamiliarity with the song's origins:

> 'We chose 'Lola' as we felt it conveyed many factors which were ideal for a 'Love' station. We felt it displayed nostalgia... it has a strong appeal to the emotions and this combines well with the element of nostalgia. 'Lola' is dealing with the issues of sexuality and gender as they are a female group singing of another woman, this links into the other elements of gay issues we include. They are projecting a controversial and shocking image which we feel will attract positive attention for Love FM'.

I would also want to argue that a great deal of critical thinking went into aspects of the work which, as with so much practical media work, are either invisible or only tangential to the final product. The radio groups in particular developed elaborate policy statements for their stations which were discussed halfway through the proposal and surfaced intermittently in the commentaries, but were represented in their broadcasts only through previews and trailers. This was also true of the research element of the assignment, which involved the design of surveys, audience profiling, analysis of existing provision, etc., as well as investigation of the appeal and reach of the original source music they had chosen. As Chrissie described:

> We worked together to construct a questionnaire, which we then used to identify our target audience. We studied selective tracks from both artists in depth, collecting mental images which we felt were conveyed through their music and lyrics... I then constructed questions and observations for visits to major record shops... I also researched magazine advertisements for music albums, so as to get an idea of the sorts of design which work in marketing terms. Gina wrote to the record companies...

Most of the students felt that the research element was a challenging and creative aspect of the assignment. They referred to it extensively and frequently, both in discussion and the production reports as a formative influence on the final product, particularly the three radio groups:

> The original point of that show was because everyone we talked to – a very high proportion of them – said they wanted news and reviews, information about what's coming on, what's good and what's not. So rather than insulting their intelligence and sitting there saying, yeah, we think this is great, we prefer to say, well, this *isn't* good, this is what this is about, and do you really want this?
> (Dorian, *PMT*)

There were certainly variations in the ways in which such research was used (as Dorian's rather glib rationalisation suggests), and it would be unwise to take such assertions entirely at face value. Nevertheless, there was undoubtedly a sense of purposeful pleasure and pride in the design and analysis of the research, which often yielded unpalatable truths – such as Dorian's discovery that his habitual street style was a major deterrent to serious interviewing, and Ian's mortified realisation that 'his' musical preference, hardcore, was far less elite than he had imagined.

Alternative or political?

In the post-production debriefing session where the students critiqued each other's work, there seemed to be a disjuncture between what students intended as 'new' or 'alternative' in the interpretation of their brief, and what others felt they had in fact achieved. There were definite, though confused, distinctions made between notions of the 'political' and the 'alternative'. For example, *PMT* argued vociferously for the subversive element of their work:

> Ian: We identified with an alternative culture because the programme we did was unique, different, and we didn't want to be a commercialised station.
>
> Dorian: We wanted to be un-commercialised in the way that *they* promote whatever the music companies say they want to sell. We want to play what listeners want to hear, not what the companies want us to hear, so that's kind of alternative.

At the same time, this group denied strongly that they were 'political': 'we don't want to alienate any sort of person'. This antipathy to the 'political' seemed to be shared by all groups. James, for example, asserted during debriefing:

> We're not political, we don't want to get all 'right-on' – and we're not over-cool – although I suppose we are because we're trying to do something that's never been done... we don't want to be so anti-this, anti-that, we're not trying to be political at all, but we are trying to be alternative.'

There seems to be a clear distinction here between Politics and Being Alternative: the second is implicitly cool, the first is definitely not. This view is expanded and defended, somewhat awkwardly, in his production report:

> Our articles took hold of affairs in an a-political way, so as not to seem too 'right on'... Obviously they did adopt a slant, for instance the main article was directed from a 'rights for the young', deliberately approaching a young audience, thus, in the same breath, alienating the older audience. However, Jazz has evolved from a long history of black oppression and discrimination. In respect to this factor, we didn't pick up on this. Jazz is a music in its own right, to constantly re-hash its evolution, needlessly, is probably much to the downfall of its commerciality. Not to say that commerciality is what music should be about, in the slightest. Though I do feel it's hindering its popularity, thereby stopping its message being conveyed to the degree that it wants to.'

Clearly Politics is an area in which James can't afford to mess; although he acknowledges its significance in the development of jazz, he also recognises its threat in marketing terms. It is largely for this reason that he would prefer to represent *Stompin' Groove* under the much hipper 'alternative' umbrella

A certain amount of retrospective debunking and post-hoc rationalisation is inevitable when students are under heavy fire from their peers in a semi-formal plenary discussion of this kind. Like James, Dorian was reluctant to admit to political intentions; however, running through his contributions to the discussion there is an implicit (albeit simplistic) understanding both of the institutional danger of *PMT*'s venture, and also of their (political) challenge to the power structure:

Ian: We're going to need revenue.
Dorian: That's why we wanted the majority of the station to be run by the
          suggestions of the people. Because if we're running off their
          suggestions, then they have the power, and no matter what the industry
          says, the people are their power as well because they're the people
          going out to buy the stuff, so the companies have got to take notice.

As in the case of *Stompin' Groove*, the analysis is confused and contradictory, although it is no means mindless or arbitrary. There are, I would argue, subversive implications in both productions but neither James nor Dorian have yet acquired the political or ideological discourses through which to articulate them fully. In the context of competing youth cultures where to admit political commitment is uncool, the debates become increasingly complex – although this is perhaps not surprising in a culture where the official discourses of politics appear specifically designed to exclude young people. If we add to this the need to conform to an assessment process which seems to require both specific evidence of ideological 'challenge', and explicit justification of it, it is hardly surprising that students use a vague concept like 'alternative' in an attempt to justify their ideas and to defend their social identities.

On the other hand, we frequently noticed marked divergences between individual students' comments on these issues in discussion and in their written production reports. Not surprisingly, the reports represent the reflective and sanitised side of the coin, while the debriefing discussions, frequently heated, critical and anarchic, were the site both for play and for serious struggles for meaning. A recurrent feature here was the wind-up: there was a great deal of interrogation and debunking, both of themselves and of notions of political correctness, often directed as much at us as at each other. For example:

Irene: Would you say your audience was predominantly male? Because I really felt that it was like a really male programme and although the callers were female, both the DJ's were male and it was called *PMT*, and that's like taking the piss out of female problems. And that's alienating women as a whole, isn't it?

Ian: We don't believe that would alienate women, 'cos we believe women are intelligent and they can understand a joke. (Applause from all males in the group). If you believe women are immature and not intelligent enough to understand the subtle humour, then that's your problem.

Dorian: We chose the title 'cos it would give us attention, and automatically we would be recognised. But anyway it stands for People's Music Transmission, which is different.

James: I thought that would be a good idea because if you sort of appeal to people's pretensions, they'll listen cos they think it's a good idea.

Such discussion clearly needs careful teacher management to avoid marginalisation or intimidation, and to sort out genuine conviction from *post-hoc* positions adopted for the sake of argument – or indeed for examiner-pleasing. Nevertheless, it also provides a safe and potentially empowering space for testing out ideas and for assessing the limits of ideological debate. As Dorian commented afterwards,

> One of the best bits was being able to pull everyone's work apart and fire questions at them, especially things like ideas and politics. But no-one got really upset. *We were only practising.*

Playing with form

At the level of form, there was a contradiction between our view as teachers of what might constitute a subversive or original text, and the students' perceptions of what they had achieved. There was limited opportunity to play creatively with the forms within which the group was working, and as I have suggested, the institutional inflection of the task militated against serious innovation. Despite this, we felt a frisson of disappointment in discovering the limits of their radicalism; in most cases, the conventions of the chosen medium were minutely replicated bar the specific reversals and reconstruction of content which characterised each text. The *Love FM* DJ's made a conscious decision to play their roles with professional smoothness rather than *avant-garde* zaniness; and even the agony slot was handled entirely un-pruriently (much to our surprise and relief). Chrissie and Gina, who are clearly both creative and talented artists, researched and juxtaposed a whole plethora of interesting and lovingly observed imagery but were unable or unwilling to break out of the physical constraints of the album-cover format.

In fact the only product which demonstrated formal experimentation was Lottie's Doors video, which played on the concept of the storyboard by dissolving from hand-drawn frame to still photo to live footage to symbolic montage of images of Jim

Morrison, edited tightly to the beat. Ironically, this was a case of necessity being the mother of invention, and resulted from the way in which she was left single-handed with half-shot video footage and a looming deadline. Nevertheless, one might well ask whether its arbitrary nature makes it any the less original. In my experience, the most formally and visually innovative student video work is often a product of the creative problem-solving which arises from equipment breakdown, random accident, or failure in group communication. On the other hand, work which consciously aspires to the *avant-garde* – perhaps the sort of work sought by the examiners of the original A-level syllabuses – is frequently tedious, pretentious and unconvincing, however courageous its intent. Nevertheless, I would argue that genuine formal innovation is one of the hardest and most inappropriate requirements of the syllabus – and that our expectations here may well have been unrealistic and misplaced.

However, a closer look at both the products themselves and at students' perceptions of them, suggests a more complex evaluation. *Stompin' Groove*, for example, looks at first sight like a conventional early effort at DTP, under-exploiting the column format and combining a variety of unobtrusive fonts with cut-and-paste photography. The group's commentaries provide a series of retrospective rationales, often conflicting. James, for example, comments:

> The layout of the magazine, looking at it now, is much different to most magazines on the market that are aimed at a young audience. *Melody Maker*, for instance, has a very compact set-up, it seems chaotic, because everything is so closely packed together, with things that are essentially space-fillers. We as a group felt that was immature. So on laying out our articles, we left the spaces clear, so the overall image was of relaxation, nothing confusing or mind-scrambling, so that the messages we wanted to say, fundamentally, wouldn't get lost amongst mindless jargon.

Matthew, in contrast, claims: 'I think the layout could be improved, there is too much space at the side of the articles on some pages. This could have been filled up with artwork, as I think that there was not enough in the magazine.' This is a typical instance where written self-evaluation provides an opportunity for post-hoc self-justification, as will be described in more detail in Chapter 6. On the other hand, all three boys offer similar comments on the thinking behind their cover:

> Matthew: The words *Stompin' Groove* reflect the type of music in the magazine and how it is covered. The words are 'groovy', reflecting the music, and the typeface is bouncy and upbeat, representing the styles of writing in the magazine. The front cover is full of colour to make it stand out on the shelves. The red background to the main picture makes it prominent: the connotations of the colour red being wild and interesting... the model's clothes are also representative of the magazine – interesting and chaotic but serious as well.
>
> James: You see – most magazines – and this is another sort of subversion – most magazines have a very strict heading and a very strict layout about where the pictures should go, and it's sort of over-calculated, and they've spent years researching it, whereas we thought we'd go for a spacier image ...

Here, as in every group, there is evidence of conscious negotiation and decision-making based on analysis of existing conventions, even if this only occurs at the level of *post-hoc* rationalisation – or, as with *Love FM*, as an opportunistic acceptance in the interests of ratings:

> Irene: We aren't anti-establishment, and we don't pretend we are. We followed those conventions purely for marketability. Unlike *PMT* we want to get listeners and draw them in... But we are different too. We *are* quite mainstream. We found *Capital* was the most popular station anyway. Why are they popular? We did try to follow some of those conventions...

In fact, of all of the groups, and in spite of its mission statement, *Love FM* was the one which most successfully met the 'imagination and inventiveness' criterion in the Tutor's Assessment Report. It did indeed apply mainstream conventions *and* challenge them, with considerable flair.

Playing games with the production process

If playing with form proved problematic, this was in part due to the fact that in terms of popular music, almost all the games have already been played. From Smashey and Nicey, back through Lenny Henry, *This is Spinal Tap*, Sid Vicious, Captain Sensible, Jonathan King, Screaming Lord Sutch, et al. – even the Chipmunks and the Sesame Street Crew have been at it. In some cases the parody or pastiche is indistinguishable from the real thing: where does Barry White end and Theophilus P. Wildebeest begin?

One of the most positive features of the assignment was the fact that in all cases (apart from the unfortunate Jan and Robbie) it did yield technically competent products which demonstrated sophisticated understandings of the conventions and potential of their chosen medium. Given that we had done little analysis of radio, it might be inferred that the groups working with sound had done little more than reproduce their own listening; but the notable differences between the three final texts, and the evidence of the commentaries and debriefing discussion, would suggest that the industrial context, and in particular, the research, had focused their performance, particularly in terms of continuity, links and production values.

All groups shared a real satisfaction in play through performance, even where that performance was found to be lacking. Dorian, with aspirations to DJ-ing, was disappointed by his own contribution to *PMT*, as were Jan and Robbie, whose gentle, and utterly sincere *Rainbow Radio* ended up practically inaudible; yet they all commented on the opportunity to explore, and perform, under safe (i.e. non-public) situations, roles to which they aspired. In these cases, they were roles synonymous with their own personae. The *Love FM* group, on the other hand, required considerable acting talents, which they assumed entirely straight-faced, and with enormous professionalism.

Matthew and James, of *Stompin' Groove*, were also conscious of playing with language, form and voice, in ways which directly benefited from the process of imitation:

> Matthew: You get into a way of thinking when you write, you get a bit stylised. That was fun to do, to try and make it like what you read in other magazines.
>
> James: It wasn't a reflection of our thinking about jazz. My bits, especially the editorials, were though, it was like my feelings presented in someone else's voice. Its like when people do impressions, there'll be certain sort of mannerisms their voice will adopt, certain cliquey phrases... It's the same in writing. It was definitely conscious.

This issue of play and performance will be discussed in more detail in Chapter 7.

Conclusions

In this chapter, I have argued that imitation and parody were inevitably and inextricably bound up in the students' media production work. While this was partly a consequence of the structure of the assignment, it was equally determined by their own interests and pleasures. In many respects, what took place here cannot be seen as a matter of unthinking reproduction. These students were not slavishly copying dominant forms. On the contrary, they were actively using and re-working them for their own purposes. As I have argued, this process is recognised as an essential phase in many models of learning. Yet in Media Studies, it is often condemned as 'mere imitation', in ways that are almost invariably value-laden and derogatory. As this case study has shown, the process of imitation occurs in many forms and serves a range of important functions; its implications are diverse and open-ended, both in terms of students' learning, and ideologically. In exploring its many formal meanings, it is possible to identify at least six possible definitions of imitation, which seem particularly relevant to the work I have discussed.

1. *Imitation: to follow as a pattern, model or example.*
    This is perhaps the definition which is most frequently invoked in Media Studies: it implies mere duplication, if not fraudulent plagiarism. Yet the notion of the model or exemplar is, in other educational contexts, perceived to be a positive and beneficial one, from which people learn and develop skills. In Art, patterns and models are used to develop technical skills, visual and spatial awareness, and formal techniques; students are encouraged to draw from life, make observational sketches, and interpret existing objects. The process of imitation is seen as an essential stage in the mastery of form and the acquisition of 'visual literacy', before students move on to more interpretative or innovative work. I would argue that this is precisely what Gina and Chrissie are doing with the loving visual recreations of musical genres on their album covers; so too with the gentle subversion of mainstream form produced by *Love FM*. Here examples are indeed followed, explored, adapted and repositioned; and the students have acquired a great deal of skill and conceptual understanding.

2. *Imitation as non-authentic.*
    Imitation is most frequently defined as 'a copy of something else that is genuine and usually of better quality'. This could be seen as an entirely accurate description of all production work undertaken in the 'unreal' context of a Media Studies

syllabus. Of course the texts students construct are not 'genuine' in the strictest sense; they are often undertaken in the knowledge that they are simulations which are only very rarely seen by the audiences for whom they are notionally intended. And of course they are likely to be inferior to their models: given the type of equipment normally available in schools, it is inevitable that their production values, finish and sheer professionalism will measure up unfavourably to broadcast or published texts. What might James and Matthew have done with expertise in, and access to, the Apple Macintosh, colour reprographics, professional artwork, let alone more sophisticated industrial processes? To this extent, all but the most well-resourced of students are 'guilty' of imitation – although this is surely not a fault for which they should be condemned.

3. *Imitation of an artistic work for comic effect or ridicule: parody.*
This is the second most feared of all forms of imitation in Media Studies, although it is hard to know why this variation is so despised. Perhaps it is because bad parody is so often indistinguishable from unskilled imitation, and tends to highlight, rather than deflect from, that lack of skill. It is certainly extremely difficult to produce good parody, as *PMT* demonstrates. On the other hand, parody usually implies that formal conventions have been understood and are being interrogated; it is what students do when they have mastered their technology and form, and are trying to get their heads around its ideology – a way of exploring its ironies and ambivalences. The surprising absence of sustained parody in our students' work may partly result from their determination to take the brief seriously for assessment purposes; or because they were too new to the experience of production to feel that they could take risks with it.

4. *Imitation: a rehearsal for the real world.*
From this perspective, imitation is 'the assumption of the modes of behaviour observed in others' – for example in this context, the adoption of production roles and professional practices. This was clearly the thinking behind the pre-production simulation and research which seemed so dramatically to influence our students in their own production work, in particular *Love FM* and the Stompin' Groovers. In all cases, this was an element which was perceived as rewarding and important, despite the fact that it limited their choices, and despite their own recognition that it could only simulate 'real' professional practice. It is significant that in pre-vocational media courses, this function of imitation is not only viewed without suspicion but positively encouraged, and in some syllabuses, actively demanded. It seems a curious form of inverted academic snobbery that potentially life-enhancing vocational skills are so often denied to A-level students. By contrast, academic discourses are highly privileged, even though they are often perceived by the media industries as vocationally worthless.

5. *Imitation: the sincerest form of flattery.*
It is here that we may be getting to the root of the problem. Flattery is usually assumed to be fawning, sycophantic, even morally suspect. And it is precisely in this way that critics of practical work often represent students' use of dominant cultural forms – the 'endless wilderness' identified above. As I have argued, production within mainstream forms is often equated with ideological complicity. Yet in practice, imitation can *never* be unthinking. The use – whether unadorned,

pastiched or parodic – of mainstream conventions does not in itself imply an unquestioning acceptance of the 'dominant ideology' – any more than the acknowledgement of economic and institutional constraints means an internalisation their values. In their products, our students demonstrated a realistic awareness of the tensions between creativity and marketing which is anything but unthinking; and the attempt to make sense of these contradictory discourses was clearly apparent, both in the products themselves and in their subsequent reflections upon them.

6. *Imitation as celebration.*
   Celebration might be seen as the acceptable face of flattery – although in Media Studies it has increasingly become a dirty word. As I have argued, imitation frequently involves pleasure, both in the forms and meanings of what is imitated, and in the process of the imitation. It is of course equally easy to pastiche or parody a text you dislike, but it is likely to be a less satisfactory experience for students, and yield cruder and less well argued products. As our students testify, there is real fun to be had in pastiche, in acquiring (or at least practising) the conventions, vocabulary, and rhetoric of their favourite texts or genres. Yet words like 'fun' and 'pleasure' have often been critically reviled in Media Studies, as though they were fundamentally incompatible with critical awareness.

Perhaps the ultimate fantasy here, however, is that there is ever such a thing as the truly 'authentic' or 'original' work, which is somehow free from all conventions – whether 'dominant' *or* 'oppositional'. In this respect, the post-structuralist notion of *inter-textuality* may prove to be a more useful one than that of imitation[26]. It implies that any text is inextricably bound up in its relationships with other texts – and indeed, that it is partly through those relationships that it is possible for it to acquire meaning. From this perspective, the question is not so much to do with whether students either *imitate* or *challenge* dominant forms – as though there could ever be an either/or choice. On the contrary, it is to do with the ways in which they *use* dominant forms, and with the purposes (both educational and political) that such uses may have. This issue will be considered in more detail in the following chapters, and in our conclusion. Perhaps it is appropriate here, however, to give the last word to the students themselves:

James: You've got to understand the grain, the genre, before you can go against it. Like, in the work we've just done (for the 'Advanced Production Module', around notions of realism), you have to base anti-realism on realism. You have to understand the established genre first. You have to start with guidelines to go against, otherwise you'd just be freewheeling. And you'd end up producing something really bad.

Dominique: Also you have to work a lot harder if you're trying to compete with something. And you're learning more because you're really having to analyse and think about what you're doing. I think now we could go back to music and do something more original and it would be entirely different, and it *wouldn't* be bad.

Notes

1 Buckingham and Sefton-Green (1994), Chapter 4. See also Richards (1994).

2 It is worth noting here the withering contempt for the music show *Top of the Pops* which is displayed by both Len Masterman (1980) and Bob Ferguson (1981), whose arguments about practical work will be considered in more detail below.

3 Of course, this argument does not only apply to popular music. It could equally be applied to 'classical' music, and indeed to cultural production in general. As we have argued (Chapter 1), contemporary 'children's culture' is heavily intertextual.

4 Masterman (1980).

5 Aside from the Freirean rhetoric here, it is notable that Masterman (*ibid*) retains an opposition between the 'imitative' and the 'authentic'. This is an issue to which we shall return later in this chapter and in our conclusion.

6 Masterman *ibid.*

7 Ferguson (1981).

8 *Ibid* p. 47.

9 *Ibid* p. 53.

10 *Ibid* p. 53.

11 This issue was debated at length by Colin MacArthur and Colin McCabe in a series of analyses of the polemical BBC series *Days of Hope,* reprinted in Bennett, Boyd-Bowman, Mercer and Woollacott, [eds.] (1981).

12 See, for example, Williamson (1981/2), Buckingham (1986), Richards (1986), Donald and Rattansi (1992).

13 Although the status of students' use of popular forms in English is not without its problems: see Moss (1989).

14 See, for example, Cope and Kalantzis (1993). In practice, however, the genre theorists' repertoire of 'dominant forms' is rather limited: it would almost certainly not include the popular forms we are referring to here.

15 Arthurs (1987).

16 See Spence (1986).

17 Buckingham and Sefton-Green (1994) *op cit.*

18 Grahame [ed.] (1994)

19 Buckingham and Sefton-Green (1994) *op cit.*

20 It included The Yardbirds (mid-60s R 'n' B), Jefferson Airplane (late 60s psychedelia), Madness and The Beat (70s Two-Tone), The Raincoats (feminist-punk), an unknown Brighton band representing mid-80s indie-pop, and the Mahotela Queens, early 80s world music from Southern Africa. On reflection this selection says far more about our own musical histories and agendas than we realised at the time.

21 See Williamson (1981/2); Buckingham (1986); Turnbull (1993).

22 Kaplan (1987), Frith, Goodwin & Grossberg [eds.] (1993).

23 Blanchard, Greenleaf and Sefton-Green, (1989). This is now out of print.

24 These issues were initially raised in an earlier study of the use of industrial simulations in production work: see Grahame (1990).

25 Grahame (1990) *ibid.*

26 We would particularly like to thank Dave Allen for his observations on this point.

Chapter 6

In Search of the 'Real' Audience: The Limits of Self-evaluation

The evaluation of practical work has proven to be one of the most problematic aspects of media education. In some respects, this is inevitable. It is in the process of evaluation that one has to look hard at one's aims and methods – and in doing so, fundamental contradictions and limitations are almost bound to emerge. It is here that we have to identify what students are *actually* learning, rather than what we think they *ought* to be learning – a process that is often far from straightforward.

My argument in this chapter is based on a crucial distinction between *evaluation* and *assessment*. Assessment, as I shall define it here, is the process whereby teachers make comparative judgments about students' achievements in relation to external norms or criteria. It almost invariably involves the allocation of grades or marks. By contrast, evaluation focuses on the relationship between intentions and outcomes. Both for teachers and for students, this is likely to involve an element of *self*-evaluation – a process which we would regard as a crucial means of forging connections between 'theory' and 'practice' in media education[1]. While evaluation often accompanies assessment, it should not be reduced to it. Indeed, as I shall argue, the two processes may in some respects prove incompatible.

Assessment might appear to be a comparatively straightforward activity, yet even here there is often a considerable degree of uncertainty. Despite the apparently unambiguous nature of examination syllabuses and programmes of study, the criteria that are used in assessing practical work are often confused and contradictory. All sorts of different educational and ideological assumptions – many of them quite alien to media education – may be at stake in this process, yet they are rarely made explicit or debated[2].

Perhaps the most fundamental problem in assessment is in the relationship between the process and the product. As we have already noted, media educators have traditionally emphasised the former at the expense of the latter. Assessment criteria for practical work generally allocate a comparatively small proportion of the marks for the technical quality or 'polish' of the finished product, and often explicitly ignore it altogether[3].

The reasons for this are diverse. On the one hand, it could be seen to derive from the suspicion of imitation discussed in the previous chapter – from the misguided notion that copying 'dominant' forms is somehow inevitably unthinking and ideologically corrupt. From this perspective, technical quality often seems to be regarded as politically suspect in itself: the 'polished' production is often condemned as an uncritical replication of professional practice. On the other hand, it may also derive from an acknowledgement that schools have very different resources available to them: it is clearly problematic for an examination syllabus to prescribe a high level of resourcing, for example by requiring all students to have experience of video editing or photographic processing. From this perspective, to insist on technical quality may be actively to exclude particular groups of students.

Above all, however, this focus on process rather than product reflects the broader emphasis within media education on developing conceptual understandings rather than technical skills. The central aim of practical work, from this point of view, is defined in terms of its contribution to developing students' *theoretical* understandings – and it is predominantly in these terms that it is assessed. Yet perhaps the fundamental difficulty here is in deciding how (or indeed whether) these different elements can be separated. How can we assess the conceptual understandings that may be involved in practical production without also taking account of the effectiveness with which they are communicated?

In a sense, this debate about process and product could be seen as an epistemological one: it is, at least partly, a debate about what would count as *evidence* of students' learning. The product is clearly one major form of evidence, although it is not always easy to read in its own right. How, for example, does an examiner compare a production that is technically competent but conceptually vacuous with one that is a technical disaster but conceptually advanced? Yet this kind of debate, which often takes place at examiners' meetings, seems to beg a prior question: how is it possible to read practical work as evidence of conceptual understanding in the first place?

Part of the answer to this dilemma in media education has been to use writing – or the form of writing that, with shades of *Star Trek*, is often termed the 'production log'. It is this written account that represents the major form of evidence for the examiner of the conceptual understandings that were entailed or developed in the production process. Yet most media teachers would probably agree that this is a practice that is rarely done well. Reading logs at GCSE or even written accounts supporting practical work at A-level can often be a dispiriting experience. Most teachers will have read logs that make *The Secret Diary of Adrian Mole* look like Proust. One recent Chief Examiner's report for GCSE, for example, notes that the log is the assessment category in which the lowest marks are registered, and that candidates 'are often misled into substituting inordinate length and detail for genuine investigation'[4]. Yet candidates could well be forgiven for asking what might constitute 'genuine investigation' – as indeed could their teachers.

As an assessment practice, the reliance on a written account rests on all sorts of assumptions. It implies, for example, that the thinking that counts is the thinking that can be made self-conscious – whereas of course one would not assume that an artist or a musician or even a writer was necessarily the best person to explain their own work. It implies that what took place in a collective process can (and should) be individualised; and that the writing will be somehow honest – that it will serve as a true reflection of what really went on in the writer's mind, rather than as an exercise in self-justification designed to maximise marks in the examination.

One might go on from here to develop a strong critique of this approach. Thus, it could be argued that the written account is simply imposed by the institutional practices of examining – by a system that seeks to individualise and thereby to discriminate between students, that values writing above other forms of expression, and that sees learning as a matter of students regurgitating what they have been fed. As Jenny Grahame has argued elsewhere[5], a great deal of what is most valuable about practical work may be lost in the transition to writing. Many of the students who contribute most to practical production, for example in terms of their technical or 'artistic' skills, or their role in group work, tend to lose out when it comes to writing. One could well argue that, like other forms of examination, the primary aim of insisting on writing is to discriminate in favour of students who have skills in particular forms of communication, and against those who have other abilities; and that this serves merely to perpetuate existing social inequalities.

While there is certainly some truth in these arguments, we also need to look more positively at the functions of this kind of writing in terms of students' learning. In doing so, we will need to take a broader view of evaluation – as something that is not confined to the assessment of students by teachers, but that also includes self-evaluation by students themselves.

In previous publications[6], we have begun to develop a theory of learning in media education that draws critically on Vygotsky's analysis of concept formation. One of the key points here is the emphasis on the importance of reflection and self-evaluation. The aim of media education, we have argued, is not merely to enable students to 'read' – or make sense of – media texts, or to enable them to 'write' their own. It must also enable them to reflect systematically on the processes of reading and writing, to understand and to analyse how they themselves make meaning as readers and as writers. In the case of practical production, this means asking students to reflect back on the process in the light of their own and others' readings of what they have produced. Did they communicate what they set out to communicate? Why did they make particular choices, and what effects did they have? How does an audience read what they have produced, and what can they learn from this?

In this context, writing would appear to have a distinct purpose – which derives at least partly from the fact that the reflection takes place in writing rather than in talk, or some other form of communication. Elsewhere[7], we have studied the development of two students' writing in GCSE Media Studies, and have argued that much of the value of writing in this context derives precisely from its individual, private nature. This is not, however, to suggest that it is somehow a-social: on the contrary, it functions as a form of dialogue with an imagined other – or what one of the students in that account, Michael, aptly called a 'conversation with yourself'. Michael argued that, while he found writing difficult, it did serve as a prompt for reflection – that it helped him to discover things that he didn't know he thought[8]. On the other hand, of course, Michael wais also telling us what he thought we wanted to hear: his writing wass partly a form of self-presentation, and it would be a mistake to see it as purely 'personal'.

A further argument for the value of writing in this context can be drawn from recent work on the development of 'Knowledge About Language'. In his theoretical overview of the area, John Richmond[9] argues that self-conscious reflection upon the characteristics of language can be developed through the 'translation' between language modes. Writing about talk, or talk about reading, for example, can make the specific qualities of these different modes much more explicit, and thus contribute to the development of a systematic understanding of how language works. A similar argument could be made about the relationship between practical work and writing, which effectively involves a similar form of 'translation' between one language mode and another. In the process, it could be argued, students are inevitably forced to make their implicit knowledge explicit, to make it systematic and thence to question it.

Yet while this argument for written self-evaluation may be a powerful one, we should not lose sight of the social contexts in which it occurs. Ultimately, the major problem here is that self-evaluation is also nearly always a form of assessment. While it may serve as a valuable means of developing students' understanding, it is also a device whereby teachers gather evidence about students in order to allocate grades. As a result, in our experience, it is often seen by students as an artificial, abstract requirement on the part of teachers or examiners. Rather than being integral to the process, it is seen as something extraneous to it, that is merely tacked on at the end. It has no *motivation* other than to please the examiner. In this context, writing can easily become an exercise in self-presentation rather than self-evaluation. As 'process-oriented' styles of pedagogy have become increasingly popular in recent years (most notably in the wake of TVEI), it is clear that students can develop a facility in using the *discourse* of self-evaluation which may in fact say little or nothing about their learning[10]. The most successful students may be simply those who are best at presenting themselves; and in the process, educational evaluation becomes little more than a form of public relations.

Towards the real audience

To a greater extent perhaps than any of the other case studies in this book, the project described in this chapter began with a hypothesis. We wanted to see what would happen if we encouraged the students to address their work to a 'real audience', whose responses would be incorporated into the planning and evaluation of the project. Our aim here was to *motivate* self-evaluation by giving it a sense of purpose beyond that of formal assessment – and thereby perhaps to make it a more 'spontaneous', or at least less artificial, process. The acknowledgement of a 'real audience', we hoped, might make it easier for students to 'decentre' – to see their own work through others' eyes, and thus to adopt a more distanced perspective on what they had achieved.

The notion of 'real audiences' is of course imported from work on writing in English teaching. While there are obviously problems in extending this analogy between practical work and writing, there do appear to be some useful parallels here[11]. Probably the most significant starting point for this work was the Schools Council project on *The Development of Writing Abilities*, undertaken in the early 1970s. Here, the notion of audience is a crucial dimension in the move away from notions of creativity espoused by the 'personal growth' school of English teaching, towards what could be termed a social theory of writing:

> One important dimension of development in writing ability is the growth of a
> sense of audience, the growth of the ability to make adjustments and choices in
> writing which take account of the audience for whom the writing is intended.[12]
> (p.58)

The authors argue that writing cannot be seen merely as a 'soliloquising monologue': it is also constrained by an 'invisible audience', an internalised representation of the reader. They suggest that written genres have ground rules through which this relationship with potential readers is managed and regulated. However, their empirical analysis of school writing across a range of subjects found that it was largely directed towards an audience of one, namely the teacher – and more specifically, the teacher acting as examiner. While this was true of the vast majority of writing in all subjects, it was found to be particularly the case in factually-based subjects like history, geography and science (and if the research had been done in contemporary classrooms, one might well include Media Studies here too).

While this argument was contested by some at the time, it did lead to an emerging emphasis on 'writing for real audiences' in English, most influentially in the work of Donald Graves[13]. This approach has experienced something of a revival recently with the advent of E-mail and other means of 'electronic writing', which have made it much easier to reach real audiences beyond the classroom. While some of this work might justifiably be accused of a kind of naive progressivism – for example, in its implicit view of the classroom as a neutral space in which true communication can simply happen – contemporary accounts of this process are more complex. For example, the notion of genre as a shared social contract between reader and writer, which is implicit in the work of the Schools Council project, has resurfaced much more explicitly in recent debates about genre, as part of a wider social theory of textual production[14].

Inevitably, however, the notion of a 'real audience' raises as many problems as it appears to solve. We did not honestly expect that our attempt to introduce a 'real audience' would magically provide our students with the sense of motivation we acknowledged had been lacking in past attempts at self-evaluation. More fundamentally, we doubted whether *any* audience could justifiably be seen as 'real'. As I shall indicate, the tensions and ambiguities that surrounded the notion of audience in this project can partly be traced to the constraints of the classroom context, and beyond that, of the school as an institution, and the examination system in which we were working. Our teaching was based on a conception of the audience that was partly real and partly simulated, partly concrete and partly quite abstract: the 'real' audience was, in this sense, already rendered 'unreal' through our own attempts to construct and theorise it. Similarly, the students' perceptions of audience were also highly mediated, and very much determined by their own concerns. Like much of what normally goes on in classrooms, what happened was a very long way from free, natural communication – if indeed that has any meaning. Yet in this respect, we have to ask whether that makes it any less real than what happens in the 'real' world of media production. To what extent does media production *ever* relate to a real audience, and how does it do so? As I shall argue, we may be operating – however inadvertently – with inappropriate models of media production, which are much too challenging for students at this stage, if not completely utopian.

An outline of the project

The project described in this chapter was undertaken in the first year (year 10) of a double certificated English and Media Studies GCSE course. The course was taught by Pete Fraser, and this unit of work, which occupied approximately 22 hours of class time, was planned in collaboration with him. The school in which we were working is a mixed, grant-maintained selective school in North London. The school has a strongly academic ethos: students have to pass a highly competitive entrance examination, and public exam results are among the best in the country. Media Studies has been established at the school in various guises since the 1970s, and there are large A-level groups in addition to the joint GCSE course. This academic context is important in the light of the focus on evaluation and assessment, introduced above. At the risk of stating the obvious, there is a sense in which the institutional practices of academic assessment exert a 'much more powerful influence on these students' lives than would be the case in an 'average' London comprehensive school.

The work undertaken for this project counted as 30% of the final assessment for these students' GCSE in Media Studies. The Southern Examining Group syllabus we were using identifies a number of criteria which might be used in assessment. Some of these are purely descriptive: students are expected, for example, to engage in 'pre-production activities, such as research, scripting, organisation.' Other criteria are essentially concerned with technical ability: the top grade candidate will demonstrate competence in 'bringing the project to a full and complete realisation, and with a high degree of finish'. However, there is a major concern here with integrating theory and practice: candidates are expected to consider the appropriateness of the chosen medium to the content, and of the product to its intended audience; and they have to produce a 'log book, evaluating both the finished product and the chosen medium, and making connections with theory-based coursework'. Of course, as with all assessment criteria, there is considerable room for interpretation here, and not all will be relevant in any given case. Particularly when it comes to the more theoretical dimensions of the project, it is far from clear what might count as evidence of the candidate's competence in these areas, *other than* the written log.

In the first lesson, the students were provided with an overview of the project as a whole, which is reprinted below.

Reaching Your Target Audience

Over the next five or six weeks, you will be doing an extended practical project which will form part of your assessed coursework in Media Studies. The main part of the project involves producing a short trailer for a new TV series to be piloted on the children's satellite channel Nickelodeon. However, there are other important aspects to the project which will help you to plan and evaluate your work: this will be particularly useful when you write the final account of the project, which is also submitted with your coursework. All this work will be carried out in groups of five or six – apart from the written account, which is an individual piece of work.

Stage One
You will be given a brief to produce short outlines of *three* possible programmes within a particular genre (e.g. game shows, documentaries). You will then present these to a small 'focus group' of 11-year-olds, who are representative of your target audience.

Stage Two
Bearing in mind the responses of your target audience, you will choose one of the ideas to develop into a script for a trailer. The trailer will be around 3 minutes long, and will be designed to attract viewers by giving a good flavour of the main themes of the series. You will need to have a detailed shooting script for the trailer before you move on to production.

Stage Three

You will then shoot and edit the trailer, using locations in and around the school. At this stage, you will need to plan very carefully to ensure that you meet your deadlines, and that you are ready to use the equipment when it is available.

Stage Four

You will then evaluate the project, in three different ways: through considering the responses of another 'focus group', again consisting of members of your target audience; through reviews written for the daily press or for specialist TV magazines; and through your own written evaluation.

The class was then divided into groups and given a brief for their particular genre. Owing to the under-representation of girls in the class, we had decided to have one all-boys group and three mixed groups in order to ensure that girls were not marginalised. Different briefs were produced on situation comedies, adaptations, documentaries and game shows. In each brief, we had included the findings of a fictitious audience research study as a means of stimulating more concrete discussion of the possibilities. The following brief, which was given to the all-boys group, is indicative of the general approach:

Serious Productions
Innovative Independent Television

From: Julian Slyme, Managing Director
To: Creative Team

We have been approached by the programme production department of Nickelodeon, the new children's channel that has just begun broadcasting on the BSkyB satellite. Nickelodeon are looking for innovative independent companies like Serious Productions to put in bids for new programmes. This is where you lot come in.

As you know, Nickelodeon is an American channel, but they are keen to develop a British profile. They want programmes that reflect British children's interests and enthusiasms, rather than more copies of American shows. They are particularly concerned to target the upper end of their age range, which is around 10-11 year olds.

One area in which they are seeking bids is situation comedies. Their research has pointed to the success of Channel Four's early evening 'comedy strand', which features mainly American sitcoms, some of them quite old. They have found that most British children prefer the American shows to British sitcoms, which are generally aimed at an older age group. However, they have been struck by the popularity of such 'off the wall' British shows as *Desmonds, Red Dwarf* and *Absolutely Fabulous,* even with comparatively young children. What they are looking for, then, is a series *designed for children* within their target group that can rival the appeal of these shows. It will need to have a strong central situation, and a powerful cast – which might include comedians already popular with young people.

We'll be running some focus group discussions with children in this age group next week, and we'd like you to present them with *three* ideas for possible comedy series. They needn't be very long, but you do need to be able to say what you think the main interest of each series would be. You should try to think of three *different* ideas, so that you can get a clear idea of what the target group prefers. We'll then want you to develop one of these ideas into a trailer in the light of your discussions.

The approach adopted here is probably a fairly familiar one for Media Studies teachers. The brief assumes that the students will already be reasonably aware of the broad characteristics of the genre, if not with all the examples cited, and that they will be able to adapt these in the light of their knowledge of a given audience. (It is worth emphasising here that the students were thrown into the exercise 'cold', without any prior critical study of children's television, or of the particular genres we had selected.) Yet the aims of the exercise clearly go beyond the specifics of the particular genre: the point is not primarily to teach children anything about sitcom, but to develop their conceptual understandings about the constraints and possibilities of genre more broadly. Thus, our brief required students to come up with an idea that was both generic *and* original. What we were looking for was not an imitation or even a parody of a dominant generic form, nor yet an ideologically correct alternative. However implicitly, we wanted a product that would observe the 'rules', both of the genre and of the institutional constraints we had sketched out; but that would also offer something 'innovative', particularly in terms of its address to children. In terms of genre theory, the product had to manage a complex balance between similarity and difference[15].

Likewise, despite the emphasis on a 'real' audience, the exercise is very clearly a simulation (and this is a potential contradiction to which I shall return). Here again, the aim is not primarily to teach students about what eleven-year-olds like to watch, or indeed about what goes on in independent television production companies. The fundamental aim is to encourage them to think in more *conceptual* terms, about the relationships between institutions, texts and audiences. The choice of a trailer (rather than a complete programme, or an opening sequence) reflects this emphasis – as well as making for a more achievable outcome (although of course a real trailer would be significantly shorter than three minutes).

Perhaps the only more original aspect here is the dimension of audience research – although, as I have suggested, this kind of contact with 'real' audiences would not seem particularly novel to many English teachers. Indeed, when we asked the class if they had ever undertaken a project like this before, a couple said they had written stories for younger children as part of their primary school language work – and, it must be said, had been rather unimpressed by the audience response. The extent to which the audience research actually influenced the students' planning and evaluation of their work is an issue to which I shall return in due course.

Targeting the audience

The class had little more than a week (four hours) to devise their three ideas before presenting them to their focus groups. In doing so, a number of potentially contradictory criteria had to be held in the balance. The genres we had chosen clearly presented different challenges. In some instances – notably game shows – it seemed harder for the students to think beyond existing programme formats. In others – particularly documentaries – the genre itself was seen to be somewhat too 'adult' for the target audience, although it was partly our intention to create this problem in selecting that genre in the first place. Inevitably, group dynamics played an important part here: most groups split into pairs to develop their ideas, although when suggestions were pooled, dominant personalities tended to win out, regardless of the originality or quality of their ideas. Finally, there were also logistical considerations, to do with the known limitations of the equipment, of the possible locations, and of the budget (there wasn't one). As a result, when it came to the focus group discussions, most groups already had a favoured idea that tended to be promoted more enthusiastically than the alternatives.

I will return to most of these issues in due course, although I want to focus primarily here on the ways in which the students' assumptions about their target audience, and their brief encounter with a 'real' audience, influenced what they eventually came to produce. 'Audience' is invariably included as one of the key aspects of Media Studies syllabuses, although it is perhaps one of the most difficult to conceptualise. When asked to define their target audience, students will often resort to formulations like 'young people aged 16–25' – categories whose apparent demographic credibility barely disguises their lack of precision. Syllabuses themselves often take the easy way out, by equating real audiences with target audiences: the study of 'audience' often comes down to identifying who a particular text is 'aimed at', rather than attempting to test such hypotheses through empirical investigation.

On the other hand, everyday discussions of the media are of course suffused with implicit assumptions about audiences, even if they are rarely questioned or made explicit. Quite young children, for example, will engage in sometimes heated debates about what constitutes a 'boy's programme' or a 'girl's programme'; and while the markers of gender may sometimes be more explicit – as in the case of toys, for example – it is not always straightforward to determine the 'gender' of a text. Thus, a 'boy's programme' may be a programme that is mostly watched by boys; or one that mostly features boys (or men); or one that can be allocated to a genre or that features themes that are seen to be somehow inherently male. These criteria may overlap, but they may also contradict each other, and their application is certainly open to debate; and there are many programmes whose 'gender address' is recognised by children to be ambiguous and problematic[16].

Gender and age emerged as major issues in the students' attempts to define and reach their target audience. In the case of gender, a kind of equal opportunities logic often appeared to resolve the problem. The adaptations group, for example, rejected the idea of a *Sweet Dreams* romance on the grounds that it would have excluded male viewers: as Grant noted 'we didn't think boys would be interested in romance (or at least not admit to it)'. Likewise, this group attempted to revise *Malory Towers* by adding in boys. Sport, which featured in a number of programme ideas, was a particular problem area. It seemed to be generally accepted that a programme featuring football would only attract a male audience, and that more 'uni-sex' sports would guarantee a larger audience.

These comparatively essentialist assumptions about gender preferences were rarely challenged by the students themselves, even where contradictions were clearly apparent. For instance, the game show group rejected the idea of a programme based on computer games, on the grounds that this would exclude girls – although it emerged that Rebecca, the girl who had made this argument most strongly, was in fact a fan of computer games, and particularly of 'beat-em-up' games such as *Streetfighter*. When it came to the focus groups, these contradictions were sometimes more apparent: in the case of the adaptations group, for example, Nicky was surprised that the girls in his focus group were the ones who were interested in the idea of adapting a *Point Horror* book, since 'we expected the boys to be more interested in horror books'. In many instances, however, the compromises that were reached here were also compromises in terms of the relationships within the groups themselves. In the case of the documentary group, for example, there was considerable disagreement between the boys and the girls, and the majority of ideas were rejected on the grounds that they were too explicitly 'gendered'. The preferred compromise was a documentary series that combined 'male' and 'female' preferences – sport, 'idols', music and fashion – in a somewhat uneasy way, and that met with a mixed response from the focus group. The younger girls in particular challenged the implication that they should be interested in fashion: one girl said 'you put clothes on the list, which is what people *think* girls like – but you can strike it off!'

The issue of age, however, was perceived in rather more complex ways. However it might appear to us, the difference between eleven and fourteen years of age appeared to be seen by many of our students as a vast, unbridgeable gulf. In some instances, they appeared to feel that their ideas were pitched too high. This was acknowledged most explicitly in the case of the documentary group, where a number of ideas were rejected in the planning stages on the grounds that they were seen to be more suited to older children. In other cases, however, there was a fear of talking down to the audience: the game show group, for example, had numerous debates about whether to drown their contestants in large amounts of 'gunge', which they identified as a key generic characteristic of children's game shows, and eventually chose to avoid this on the grounds that it was patronising.

Likewise, Jonathan, in the sitcoms group, was concerned that too many of their ideas concentrated on 'role-reversal' situations where children were in charge – such as a series about a school run by children, or another about a boy who inherits his father's business. As we shall see, it is significant that the idea that was eventually selected here was the one that seemed to make least concessions to the younger audience – although this in turn invoked the possibility of parental prohibition. Similar issues were raised in the case of the *Point Horror* adaptation, where a fine balance had to be struck between being 'too scary' – and hence invoking parents' disapproval – and 'not scary enough' – and hence appearing too bland to interest the target age group. Another related issue that was raised in a number of groups was that of 'identification': it was argued, for example in the documentary group, that a programme featuring an older teenage presenter would be more likely to appeal to the target audience, thus overcoming the perception of the genre as too 'adult'.

In many instances, it was the encounter with the focus group that forced the students to reconsider their assumptions about the interests of their target age group. Again, this was clearest in the case of the documentary group: as Daniel acknowledged, 'we thought the kids would be interested in things that they weren't... we were thinking that they were older than they were'. Similarly, in the case of the adaptations group, a version of *Malory Towers* was chosen on the grounds that a school story would hold a particular appeal for younger children, although this was explicitly rejected by the focus group as too familiar and 'boring'; while the adaptation of a book of Roald Dahl stories was rejected on similar grounds.

In addition to these more specific assumptions about the audience, the discussions also invoked more generalised notions of audience 'appeal'. This was partly a matter of originality, an issue which will be considered in more detail below: many ideas were rejected on the grounds that they were too close to existing programmes, and would therefore not appear sufficiently 'fresh' to attract the audience. Yet in a number of cases, this was seen specifically in terms of a 'market'. Joe, in the adaptations group, who had proposed using the Roald Dahl stories *Ah, Sweet Mystery of Life*, suggested changing the title to include the words 'Roald Dahl', on the grounds that this would help the programme to 'attract a lot of attention'. Ultimately, however, it was the *Point*

Horror idea that was preferred, not least on the grounds that, as he noted, 'it would fill a gap in the market *and* have no competition', as well as gaining an early 'boost in the ratings' by drawing in existing fans of the books.

The 'real' audience

How might we assess the value of the students' encounter with a 'real' audience? Perhaps the most obvious way of answering this question is to look at the outcomes – that is, at the ways in which the focus groups' responses were incorporated into their decision-making. Particularly in their written accounts, many students argued that the audience research had contributed very little to their planning, and in some respects at least this is undeniable. In many cases, they seemed to ignore or tried to discount what the focus groups had said; while in others, they clearly manipulated the situation in order to arrive at the outcome they had already decided upon.

This was particularly the case with groups that already had very definite preferences. In the case of the sitcom group, for example, there was never any real contest, for reasons that will be discussed below. With the adaptations, the group's preference was also confirmed – albeit somewhat unexpectedly – and a straightforward vote appeared to decide the issue.

In the case of the documentary group, however, who had encountered some difficulties in adjusting their programme ideas to the target age group, their expectations were not wholly confirmed:

> Amit: Our [focus group] was pretty good, though, seriously. 'Cause we had three ideas and we preferred one, we thought it was like much better than the other two. But we realised that they thought that one of the other two ideas was better.
>
> Emily: The one we wanted to do, when we put it to them, and after they told us ideas, we realised that it was, we'd sort of made it for more our age group.

Nevertheless, the idea that was eventually chosen here was the one they preferred, and not that favoured by the focus group – a choice which was made primarily on the basis of what they felt would be 'easier to film'. However, the focus group discussion did seem have alerted them to the need to adapt their idea by featuring more younger people. Thus, the final product intersperses found footage of adult 'professionals' (models, footballers, pop groups) with filmed material featuring themselves and their peers. In the case of sport for example, Daniel argued that the aim was to 'tell how young people of that age can get good, till they become a kind of professional standard.'

It was primarily in the case of the game show group that the focus group discussion appeared to alert them to some of the limitations of their own ideas. As Tina said: 'we found out in the end that all our ideas were pretty similar... we found out that, like, after we'd read them out, they seemed, like, the same.' And Rebecca concurred: 'We thought our ideas were really good but they're not...I think you remember yourself being more intelligent than you really are'. In this case, the focus group discussions sent the students 'back to the drawing board', to devise new ideas from scratch. Yet while it was acknowledged that the focus group had provided some interesting new ideas –

'forfeits', for example – none of these were eventually taken up. According to Tina, 'They suggested some good ideas to us, because they're the age group that will be watching it. So they know more about what they like than we do. So they suggested some things and, you know, what they suggested would probably be good even if we didn't think it was.' However, there were significant differences here between the students' immediate responses in the discussion that followed and what they eventually wrote in their coursework, where they were generally much less willing to admit to such uncertainties (this issue will be pursued below).

If we simply consider the outcomes, therefore, we would have to say that the focus group discussions were fairly pointless. By and large, the students went on to do what they would have done anyway. Nevertheless, I think there is a case to be made for this kind of exercise, which is partly to do with being realistic about what it can achieve.

As many of our students were quick to point out, the actual discussions themselves were very much constrained by the context. We had invited groups of year 7 pupils to attend at lunchtime, with the minimal incentive of a chocolate snack bar – which, as some of the class suggested, might well have ensured an unrepresentative and only partially compliant sample. On the other hand, of course, accusations of unrepresentativeness provided a useful means of discounting the focus' groups criticisms. In addition, many students commented on the way in which the responses to their ideas depended upon the quality of the presentation, or even on the order in which the ideas were presented.

Perhaps more significantly, the encounter between year 10 and year 7 students was bound to be an unequal one. Many of our students acknowledged that they were somewhat intimidating towards the younger children, and that the latter were unduly reticent for this reason. Many suspected that the younger students 'were only saying what they thought we wanted them to say'. Daniel, for example, said: 'they didn't really know us, and I don't think they wanted to say anything really bad'. Joe commented: 'If they disagree with you, they know you're going to go "*Why* don't you like it?" So they think the least they say, the better... It was almost as though they were afraid of us...' Some students also acknowledged that they had been 'showing off' and accused others of being patronising; while others frankly admitted that they had intimidated the younger students in an attempt to get them to confirm their own preferences. The more extrovert students in the game show group, for example, used the occasion as an opportunity for some mutual joshing and witty repartee, in which the younger students were often the butt of their humorous attempts at intimidation. Rebecca, in particular, adopted a jokily dismissive tone, at one point rounding on one of the hapless group, saying 'have you got anything to say, or have you lost your voice box?' and later reassuring them 'don't think we're going to take any notice of you!' By contrast, in the case of the documentary group, the students' attempts to get the focus group to agree with their preferred idea were comically desperate – particularly insofar as they eventually failed to succeed. On the other hand, Nicky argued that his group's most effective presentation was the one in which these differences were minimised:

> 'John spoke to the year 7 like they would speak to each other, which made the
> year 7 open up to us...'

Of course, it would be unrealistic to expect fourteen-year-olds to be any more skilled than adults in interviewing eleven-year-olds, simply on the grounds that they are closer in age. Despite their occasional displays of arrogance, our students were themselves somewhat intimidated by the situation, preferring to stick rigidly to the sample questions we had provided, and often failing to follow up the younger students' responses. They discovered how much easier it is to close down a conversation than it is to facilitate it. Many commented afterwards on how 'disorganised' they had been.

On one level, this raises some quite fundamental questions about the nature of the audience, and the extent to which it can ever be 'known' – questions that have been raised in a very direct and challenging way in academic debate[17]. Ultimately, there is a definite limit to which *any* audience can be said to be a 'real' audience. Even for professional broadcasters, it could well be argued that the audience is little more than a notional construct – or even a sentimental conceit. There is evidence that broadcasters pay very little attention to audience research – at least apart from the crude measure of the ratings – preferring instead to trust their professional or creative 'intuition'[18]. Of course, it is possible to argue that this is profoundly undemocratic – that despite their lip service to notions of 'public service', broadcasters actually know very little about their audience, and therefore can hardly be in a position to respond to its needs. Clearly, our activity 'positions' students as producers, although it does so in a context where there are distinct limitations on believability (and 'Julian Slyme' and 'Serious Productions' reflect our acknowledgement of this). In such a situation, it might well be unrealistic to expect anything more than a token response to the observations of a 'real' audience, that is itself an unwitting part of the simulation.

In some cases, the students were quite cynically aware of the opportunities for falsification that were presented here:

> Rebecca: We'd all got in our minds what we wanted to do, and generally, nothing's going to change that, because I thought, they're only first years, they're only a small minority, the other people will like it... If it was going to work properly we should have asked a broader audience... because we didn't have a tape player or anything, we thought, maybe we could make up what they said, no-one would know the difference... or maybe [we could] twist what they said.

What is particularly important here, however, is that the students were inevitably forced to reflect upon the social dimensions of the situation, and hence to question the value of the 'data' they had gathered. In effect, they had to consider the *methodological* dimensions of audience research, in a way that some academic audience researchers have only recently begun to do themselves[19]. Even in attempting to discount what their focus groups had said, they were bound to address questions about representativeness, and about the 'truth status' of individual responses. While the audience may not have been straightforwardly 'real', it did represent an external constraint that somehow had to be negotiated.

However brief and artificial it may have been, the students' encounter with a 'real' audience did seem to have forced them to justify their ideas, if only to themselves, and to *make explicit* why they were making particular choices. Even if the content of their ideas remained unchanged (and this was not always the case), their own relationship with the ideas was definitely altered. In this respect, the act of having to present their ideas publicly to an audience, and hearing the words come out of their own mouths, seemed to be more important than what that audience actually said in response. As in the arguments about 'Knowledge About Language' described above, 'translating' ideas from one context to another, from the more private context of the peer group to the more public context of the whole class and thence to the focus group discussion, seemed to enable the students to adopt a more distanced, 'decentred' approach.

Ideological dilemmas: the case of *Flat Broke*

As space precludes a detailed examination of each group's work, I am proposing to concentrate here on one of the productions, namely that of the situation comedy group. This production was the most problematic (at least from our point of view) but also (by common consent) the most 'successful'. The group consisted of six boys: Nicky, Jamie, Jonathan, David, Daniel and Ian. Jamie describes the three ideas that were presented to the focus group as follows:

> Our first idea was to have a very poor football team that centred around one outstanding player, without whom they couldn't win a match. In their eventful season, they get relegated and have a good cup run. We got the idea off *Jossy's Giants*, an old comedy football programme on children's television. We thought that we could make it funny by the team being so awful, and other disasters going on off the pitch as well...
>
> Our second idea... was to have a series based around a flat with four different people that didn't get on. This idea was similar to *The Young Ones*. The four people would be: a feminist, a tart, a sexist, rude Greek, and a gay. The gay would keep making passes at the Greek and become very unpopular. The Greek would be very sexist, think a lot of himself, and not get on at all with anyone. The tart would go out looking for men with the gay, and not get on with the feminist. And lastly the feminist would be anti-social and unfriendly. We thought this was a very good, bizarre mix of people, and would be very popular...
>
> Our third idea was to have a small child put in charge of a very big business, because his father, the previous owner, had died. his father left the whole company to him in his will, and then unexpectedly died in a car crash. The child would be around 10 years old. We thought it would be a good idea to have a child of similar age to the audience running a big company, to see what it would be like for them...

It may come as little surprise to the reader that it was the second idea, which eventually came to be called *Flat Broke*, that was most favoured among the group, and by the year 7 focus group. The final version of the trailer as filmed is outlined on the storyboard on pages 156 and 157.

Quite what was at stake in adopting this idea will emerge as this account progresses. To judge from the students' writing, it would seem that the other ideas were rejected at least partly on the grounds of their lack of originality (a feeling that was confirmed by the focus group). Yet in a sense, there was never any competition: there was too much invested in the production of *Flat Broke*, both 'personally' and in the social context of school, for it to be rejected in favour of something safer. In terms of personal investments, what is interesting even from this brief summary is how it positions the different characters. It is worth noting here that Nicky, who was the originator of the idea and the prime mover in the group, is of Greek Cypriot origins himself, and eventually played the part of the Greek in the video. Significantly, while the Greek is defined as 'sexist', he is also 'fancied' both by the gay character and by the feminist – which, while it may simply reflect a degree of vanity, also seems to suggest that both these 'deviant' characters can be recuperated into a form of normality.

This group clearly had to negotiate some difficulties in presenting their ideas to us and to the rest of the class. On the one hand, there were the constraints of the activity itself, with its emphasis on balancing innovation and generic expectations. In an initial 'rehearsal' for the focus group discussions, there was some concern about the originality of the idea: Rebecca, for example, said it was too close to the MTV series *The Real World*. Nevertheless, *Flat Broke* was generally seen to be the most original of the group's ideas, since both the others derived more clearly from specific children's programmes.

The question of audience, however, also invoked broader moral issues. In the 'rehearsal' discussion, Amit suggested that the programme would not really be suitable for children, and that some parents would dislike it – although Nicky countered by arguing that parents would be 'open-minded' and would probably like it too. Nevertheless, this concern did generate some discussion among the group, as Ian later wrote:

> At one stage we thought we would reject *Flat Broke*. This is because we thought that children's parents would not allow them to watch it as it has a gay and a bimbo (as Nicky said 'a bimbo who wears tight tops and short leather skirts') and I did not think that my parents would have let me watch it when I was eleven. However, we thought that if we toned it down and concentrated on making it funny without involving the gay all the time, then it would be more acceptable.

It is significant here that it is the gay character who is seen as most problematic from the point of view of parents – although of course he is also the most interesting and problematic character for the group as well. Indeed, the programme was repeatedly referred to by other students in the class as 'the gay one'.

Daniel was also concerned about this issue, although as we shall see, his concerns had other motivations:

> I felt *Flat Broke* wasn't really appropriate. The subject matter of gays and flirts would be disapproved by many parents. However, the others disagreed and felt it was fine for 10-year-olds. So we went ahead with the idea.

Nicky, by contrast, was much more forthright, dismissing the concerns raised by his teacher as those of 'the censors' (although the inverted commas in the original point to a degree of irony here).

Nevertheless, the dismissal of this objection was also supported by the responses of the focus group:

> Jamie: The only question hanging over the wonderful idea was whether it would be suitable for a 5 o'clock slot on tele. Anyway, after lengthy group discussions, we decided that as long as we kept it clean, it would be okay. The focus group's opinion was also pleasing. They all said they could watch it and all thought they'd be allowed to watch it.

On the other hand, Daniel dismissed this research 'finding', arguing that the younger students were simply 'trying to act all tough and grown-up'. Significantly, however, Daniel's attempts to discount the younger children's enthusiasm for the idea also reflect his own awkward position within the group. A few weeks into the project, he tried to change to another group on the grounds that much of the content of the sitcom idea – and particularly the gay character – was against his religion as a Jehovah's Witness. It was on these grounds that he later refused to take part in much of the filming and editing, generating much hostility from the others. (While we might want to object to the negative stereotyping of the gay character, the official position of Jehovah's Witnesses is that homosexuality should not be shown 'as a normal part of society', to use Daniel's words.)

Interestingly, this argument was carried further in the final debriefing. Here, Nicky mocked Daniel's concerns about the 'innuendo' in the programme, and argued that the notion of the 'watershed' was simply hypocritical: 'there's loads of violence on the news, that they show before nine o'clock, and nobody ever complains about that!' Yet despite Nicky's confidence, the issue of the programme's appropriateness to its target age group was also raised in the final focus group discussion, albeit in a slightly different way:

Daniel S:	In our group, I thought they would like the comedy one a lot more than they did. They thought it was a bit too old for them.
Tina:	They thought it was for teenagers.
Jamie:	It was good, but it was aimed at an older audience, and when we were going 'do you know what feminism means?' they were just going [blank]. They were laughing at the time 'cause other people were, or there were funny things that they understood, but other times I don't think they understood it.

However, perhaps the most significant problem the group had to negotiate here was an ideological one. Even in his initial presentation of the characters, Nicky hesitated when it came to the 'tart'. The word 'slag' was also used here, although eventually the group had recourse to the (perhaps less overtly objectionable) term 'bimbo'. (Even in the marked version of Jamie's account, quoted above, the teacher has inserted inverted commas around the word 'tart'.) At the same time, the terminology varied according to the context. In less guarded moments, the 'gay' was occasionally termed 'the queer' – and not, it might be added, in response to the advent of 'queer politics', which has yet to make much impression on North London adolescents.

Yet these difficulties with terminology were only a part of the ideological policing to which the students felt themselves to be subject. The question of the programme's stance towards the characters – all of whom could be seen to represent 'minorities', albeit of different kinds – was raised consistently, both by us as teachers and by other students. While the group occasionally sought to ignore such concerns, they generally confronted them directly, by insisting on the even-handed nature of the humour. In our initial 'rehearsal', for example, Pete Fraser sought reassurance that the programme was not just about laughing at the gay character, to which Nicky responded by saying that it was about laughing at *all* the characters. Ben (a student from another group) added that 'a lot of people that age like to laugh at homosexuality' – reflecting a sense of disavowal, and an attempt to claim a degree of 'maturity'.

[Male voice-over:] Where would you expect the following four people to live?

Name: Dino Papadopolou. Occupation: part-time helper in kebab shop. Likes: jewellery, easy women, Mercedes and Cyprus. Dislikes: gays, feminists, English people and fish and chips.

Dino enters room. Girls' screams are heard. Dino exits, smiling. The door closes to reveal the sign: 'Girls' Changing Room'.

Name: Emma Frazer. Occupation: suffragette. Likes: long skirts and non-sexist men. Dislikes: bimbos, short skirts and washing up.

Emma talking with boy in bedroom. She walks to the bed, he follows. They sit on the bed. She pulls a machine gun from under the pillow and points it at him, saying 'you've got three seconds'. He exits hurriedly.

Name: Leonard White. Occupation: entertainer. Likes: men, flowers, rubber trousers and wrestling. Dislikes: nothing.

Two boys are in bed. There is a knock at the door. Boy 1: 'Do you want to answer that?' Boy 2: 'Yeah, I'll get it'. He exits to open the door, then returns hurriedly.

Fig. 6.1 *Flat Broke*

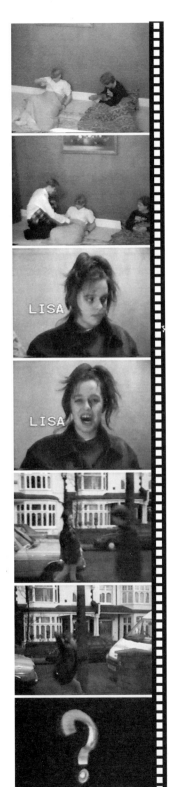

Boy 2: 'It's Leonard!' In fright, they strap themselves into their beds. Leonard enters, flapping his wrists.
Leonard: 'Are there any boys here? Oooh, I like it!' He kneels at the bed of Boy 2, only to discover that he is strapped in.
Leonard [weeping]: 'Oh no!'

Name: Lisa, last name unknown. Occupation: none. Borrows money to pay her rent. Likes: men, short skirts, tight tops, expensive jewellery, men who will buy her expensive jewellery. Dislikes: feminists, Greeks, men with no money.

Lisa is walking along the street. She turns her head to look at a man and calls out 'allo, darling'. Not looking where she is going, she walks into a lamp-post and falls to the ground.

Under normal circumstances, as far away as possible.

The four characters emerge from their bedrooms onto the landing of the flat. They look at each other, scream and rush back to their rooms.

Unfortunately, under these circumstances, they live together.

Kitchen. Dino and Emma are arguing. Emma: 'You pervert!' Dino: 'It's not my fault you're frigid!' Emma picks up a glass of water and throws it at him.

Join them in *Flat Broke*, weekdays at five.

[Group voice-over, American accents:] Only on Nickelodeon!

Similar objections were raised in the focus group discussion. One girl argued that 'Greek people could think it was racist' and that 'gay people might think it was against them', but her objections were laughed off. Jonathan insisted:

> ...it's going to be laughing at the whole cast, not just the gay. There's the feminist and... It's like it's from all extremes of society.

Interestingly, the focus group's suggestion of including a 'posh' character was also dismissed, on the grounds that this would not be as funny or as 'perfect' as their own characters. This is important because, as it stands, all the characters are in some way deviant: the norm is not being satirised, only the margins, and to introduce a 'posh' character might subvert this.

Quite where the programme might be positioned in terms of debates about stereotyping is hard to identify, however. In our initial 'rehearsal', for example, Rebecca described how *The Real World* 'uses stereotypical characters', and implicitly pointed to the tokenism of its approach ('they've got one gay, one feminist...'). This kind of comment suggests that she has moved on from a notion that stereotypes are simply 'wrong' and need to be replaced with 'reality', to the notion that they might be consciously *used* – and even that they might be necessary[20]. Yet for the boys themselves, this boundary between using (and even parodying) stereotypes and simply reproducing them was not always clear.

In their written work, four of the six in fact used the word 'stereotype' in describing the aims of the programme – although significantly Nicky was one of the ones who did not. Jonathan, for example, notes the objections of the focus group, but argues that parents would be unlikely to worry about a programme featuring 'such exaggerated stereotypes'. Even Daniel, who (as we have seen) disagreed with this, argues that the programme will attract a 'cult following' because of its 'outrageous stereotypes'. Even where the word 'stereotype' or 'caricature' is not used, there is a sense in which the programme is seen to be playing with conventional expectations, and is in some sense consciously 'over the top' and parodic. Thus Nicky, with characteristic modesty, described the responses of the focus group as follows:

> They thought it was funny, bold, outrageous, rebellious and a dozen other things apart from offensive.

Quite who is being 'outraged' and amused here, and with what effect, is of course the key question. However self-conscious the stereotypes may be, they are undeniably offensive: a gay child-molester, a violent, man-hating feminist, a lecherous 'ethnic minority' and an intellectually challenged nymphomaniac can hardly be counted as ideologically progressive representations. On one level, it is tempting to dismiss them simply as evidence of the insecurities and delusions of male adolescence – although it is worth remarking how such delusions and insecurities seem to feature so frequently both in mainstream and in so-called 'alternative' comedy.

Yet the 'outrageous' nature of the production also needs to be set in context. For the people who are being outraged and rebelled against here are of course ourselves as teachers, and the wider institution of the school. (It is perhaps notable here that the feminist character is given the surname of the class teacher.) To be sure, our own attempts at ideological policing were fairly minimal, particularly given the ambiguities I have identified above. Our brief did not require the students to produce an ideologically progressive situation comedy (and one might well ask whether such a thing were possible), nor did it imply that what they produced would be taken as evidence of their own personal beliefs. In a sense, the students saw the project as an opportunity to speak the unspeakable – to unleash the 'unpopular things' that are normally restrained by the institutionalised discourse of the school[21].

This is not to offer an apologia for the work that was produced by this group, or to attempt to reclaim it in terms of some simple-minded notion of resistance. The leaders of this group – and particularly Nicky – were classic adolescent homophobics, and to this extent they can hardly be seen as untypical of heterosexual adolescent boys in general. This is most apparent in Daniel's written account, where he notes bluntly that 'we were all similar people in the way we were boys who hated gays and so the opinion for taking the mick out of gays was unanimous'. My parting memory, as the students left the classroom at the end of the concluding lesson of the project, is of Nicky sticking a label on Daniel's back saying 'I'm a queer – shaft me!' While it is possible to deal with this kind of behaviour as an infringement of discipline (as we did in this case), quite how one responds to the ideological dimension of the students' work in the context of an examined course of study is more problematic.

One of the most significant difficulties, as I have implied, is that they are able to co-opt the arguments that one might use to challenge them. In his written account of the project, David even describes Dino, the Greek character, as 'homophobic' – implicitly distancing himself from this affliction – while Daniel suggests that a 'liberal' station like Nickelodeon would be unlikely to show a series that is so 'politically incorrect'. Yet the fact that the activity is a simulation is also relevant here: by virtue of being placed in the role of *fictional* producers, the students can effectively disclaim the suggestion that the programme represents their 'own' views. The fact that the programme is targeted at a young audience also allows some room for manoeuvre: in his magazine article describing the series, Jonathan suggests that 'although it's aimed at children, it's worth a look for any adults who can put up with the slightly immature jokes'. In effect, the ambiguous nature of the production – as simultaneously fictional and real – enables them to have their cake and eat it. And given that we had established these parameters in the first place, we were hardly in a position to complain about the consequences.

Ideology, evaluation and audience

To what extent did this group learn anything from their encounter with the audience? On one level, the answer would have to be very little. From the very start, *Flat Broke* was the unavoidable choice; and in the first focus group discussion, one of the group was heard to say 'who cares about the others, we've already decided what we're going to do'. Nicky, who effectively led the group, was particularly defensive throughout. His account of the initial focus group discussion, both in his written work and in discussion, effectively ignored the criticisms that had been raised:

> Nicky: We thought the first years would agree with our idea, cause we thought
>   that was the best, and so did they. They thought it was quite a laugh.
> PF: How did you know they were going to agree with it?
> Nicky: It was just outrageous.
> David: 'Cause it had a gay in it, they would think it was funny.

Nicky: Not just a gay, there was also loads of others, and they thought it was quite original, quite funny. And we said 'do you think your parents would let you watch it?' which we didn't think they would, and they said 'oh yeah, of course!'

When it came to the final focus group discussions, some of the students in this group appeared to re-think their approach in the light of the younger students' criticisms (for example, in the case of Jamie, quoted above). Some quite constructive comments were made here, for example about the need to sustain the series by introducing additional characters. Yet Nicky seemed unable to accept even these comparatively neutral critical comments, or the reactions of his peers, and eventually walked out. While he was not alone in this respect, his defensive approach was commented upon by other students:

Tina: Nicky kept forcing them, he was saying 'oh you think ours was the best advert though, don't you?'.
Nicky: They asked questions, and I answered them. They gave criticisms, I gave counter criticisms...They weren't saying what they thought, they were just criticising for a laugh, just to put us down.

The sole 'ideological' objection made by the younger students in this group was one which Nicky was in an ideal position to counter: when one boy dared to suggest that Greek people might be offended by the programme, Nicky responded by pointing out that the boy was not Greek himself – and thus, by implication, that he had no right to make a judgement on the matter.

While the reasons for Nicky's defensiveness are obviously hard to identify, two possibilities are relevant here. The first follows directly from the last point, which is to do with his perception of his 'ethnic' identity. Nicky certainly took the lead in the group in defining the negative qualities of 'his' character as distinctively Greek. The character's lechery, his liking for kebabs and his macho, 'medallion man' persona were seen as inseparable from his Greek nationalism and his tendency to 'babble on' in Greek. In creating this character, Nicky both inhabits this persona and distances himself from it: it represents a form of ethnic disavowal that only he is in a position to make.

The second point here, which I will consider in more detail below, relates to the issue of assessment. Nicky's behaviour in both focus group discussions, and in subsequently describing these, suggests that (like many others in the class) he perceived them partly as a form of assessment. It was important to gain the endorsement of the focus group because this would serve as a vindication of his ideas, and hence serve him well in the final assessment. Admitting to self-doubt, on the other hand, was a good way of losing marks.

The question of originality was also a major preoccupation here, for similar reasons. Nicky was particularly resistant to the implication that *Flat Broke* bore any relation to other sitcoms: it was, he wrote, 'a totally original idea, totally unheard of before'. The next (unfinished) sentence in his account is crossed out: 'Some of the other ideas were influenced a little by pre-existing [programmes]'. Instead, we have:

None of our ideas were influenced by pre-existing programmes. We just sat down and one by one as ideas just came up between our 6 minds we wrote them down and elaborated on them. This way we thought they would be totally original.

On the other hand, the others in the group did acknowledge the influence of a wide range of programmes, albeit not always the same ones in each case. Their final programme *Flat Broke* is variously attributed to *The Young Ones, Bottom* and *Red Dwarf* – none of which, interestingly, feature female characters, which *Flat Broke* does. While complete originality was not in fact one of our criteria in assessing this project, it clearly carries a considerable premium within the wider context of school work – and it may be this that accounts for Nicky's insistence on it here.

While not all the students were as defensive or impervious to criticism as Nicky, this group was certainly the one that was most dismissive of the focus group discussions. On the other hand, however, they were very well aware of their audience – and in a sense were more aware of the *actual* 'real audience' of peers and teachers, rather than the somewhat hypothetical 'real audience' we had created for them. As I have implied, the whole production could be seen as a very knowing move in a debate about representation, and a conscious subversion of the 'official' approaches of teachers, which are reinforced by the disciplinary structures of the school – although this is not in any sense to imply that it is therefore politically radical. The tortuous negotiations that had to be gone through in order for this act of transgression to be committed do in fact reflect a considerable degree of awareness of the potential audience, and of the politics of representation – even if this was more explicit in some cases than others (the price of Nicky's defensiveness is that he was one of the least willing or able to articulate this in his writing). In terms of assessment, this creates an interesting dilemma: however much we might wish to mark this work down on ideological grounds, we cannot really do so on the basis that it shows little awareness of the conceptual issues contained in the syllabus.

Returning to the audience

Nicky's feelings about the value of the final focus group discussion were not generally shared among the group – although, here again, I would argue that the value of the exercise lay more in the act of doing it than in what the younger students actually said. One issue that inevitably emerges in such situations (and that was raised in all of the groups here) is that of the technical quality of the product, and the comparison with 'professional' standards. The tapes had been shot on domestic camcorders and 'crash' edited, and the students had not had access to adequate lighting equipment. The time available for the actual filming and editing was probably in the region of fifteen hours, including time taken at weekends. As a result, the comparison with professional products was bound to be disappointing, particularly where the tapes combined original and found footage, as in the case of the game show:

> Ben: When you think about doing them, you always think about relating it to what it actually looks like on TV, like a professional look... and then you actually look at it, and it's sort of like, it's a different colour, the colour isn't quite what you expected, the sound quality isn't as good...
>
> Rebecca: You expect it to be done like with professional camera equipment, with trolleys and everything, but it's done with a camcorder and a tripod and it just really doesn't look the same. I think everyone's expectations were really too high.

> Ben: 'cause when you compare like some of the clips, some of the clips of actual shows we've put in our thing, to actual ones we've produced ourselves, it's like completely different, it looks so different.

Likewise, in the final debriefing interviews, when I asked the students what they felt they had learnt from the project, most agreed that they had learnt how much 'work' goes into professional production – a fact which they all agreed they needed to find out for themselves, rather than something they could simply be told about. (As in the last chapter this of course raises the awkward possibility that, far from encouraging students to be critical of dominant practice, the experience of practical work might in fact lead them to be more in awe of the achievements of the professionals.)

Interestingly, however, the implications of this seemed to change with time. Our first screening – which had taken place several weeks previously, when some of the tapes were still in 'rough cut' form – had met with general feelings of disappointment – with the possible exception of the sitcoms group, whose production was described by Nicky (with characteristic modesty) as 'better than everyone else's'. Yet when it came to the focus group screening some weeks later, reactions were less negative. A number of students argued that this degree of distance had enabled them to come to a more realistic evaluation of their work. In some cases, of course, they were painfully aware that the final product had not lived up to expectations: what had seemed funny at the time of shooting looked pretty lame in the cold light of day. On the other hand, however, some productions were received more positively than expected. Liz, in the documentary group, was not alone in being surprised by this:

> Basically, I thought it was really rubbish and there was no way they were going to understand it, but they did, and came up with like, they knew this was supposed to happen, and I didn't think they would... such as, what we tried to do, we tried to get the difference between amateur like football stuff and then get professionals, and they noticed that, and I didn't think they would.

Here again, the students were aware of the ways in which the social context constrained what they could find out. In some cases, it was felt that the younger students were inclined to be too polite, and that they were unwilling to challenge the older students, or indeed their peers. As Grant subsequently wrote: 'The focus group were easily swayed, You could put words into their mouths. You could say "our trailer was the best, wasn't it?" and they would all nod in unison' – although in fact the response to his group's trailer had been less than positive. Nevertheless, the process was generally considered to have been a useful one:

> Tina: Because we sort of understand it anyway, because we know what it's meant to be. But if the focus group can't really understand it, then it proves that it's not what we thought it was.
> Daniel: Like when you've just done it, and you've got all the ideas, you understand it perfectly, and you think it's a lot better than it normally is. So really it's good to have a period between.

Nevertheless, this kind of frankness did not necessarily emerge in the final written accounts. Even students who were most disappointed with their finished product were keen to emphasise the positive reactions among the focus group, or at least to omit or discount the negative ones, for example on the grounds that 'they didn't understand' or that they were unrepresentative. Many concluded with the bland observation that their project had been 'a success'. Nevertheless, these final discussion groups did appear to have encouraged the students to take a closer look at their own work, and to come up with some detailed suggestions for improvements – which would almost certainly have been more difficult to achieve without having had to submit it to a 'real' audience.

Evaluation and assessment

In conclusion, I would like to return to some of the broader questions about evaluation and assessment which this case study was designed to investigate. I want to suggest that, for various reasons, written evaluation may simply ignore many of the more important aspects of the production process. And I want to conclude by arguing that assessment can prove incompatible with effective evaluation, and that it may even actively prevent it.

Few of these students could be said to have problems with writing. On the contrary, most produced fluent written evaluations that were in excess of two thousand words. Yet particularly when it came to describing the production process itself, many of these accounts displayed the problems identified in the examiner's comments quoted above. There is an enormous amount of detail here about who did what and when and how, but very little about *why*. The logistical difficulties, the problems with faulty equipment and booking the editing room, the dramas of wiped tapes and the vagaries of the weather, are all described in considerable detail. Only in discussing the 'audience research' dimensions of the project – where students were automatically forced to justify their decisions in the light of the available alternatives – was a more evaluative and reflective approach adopted.

One important dimension here is that a great deal of what may be learnt in practical work can prove very difficult to put into words, and particularly written words – even for comparatively academically 'able' students such as these. This is because much of the learning is inherently enactive and non-verbal. Listening to tapes of students setting up shots or editing is often frustrating, precisely because the verbal dimension is so closely dependent upon what can be seen, what is physically there in front of you.

This was particularly apparent here in the case of the adaptation group, whom I followed closely through much of the filming. This group's production was very different from the others, insofar as it took the form of a sequential narrative, rather than a collage of 'highlights'. In the process, the group engaged in some very detailed discussions about camera angles and movements, and about the sequence of shots in editing. I would contend that these students effectively taught themselves many of the basic principles of continuity editing – principles which they knew 'passively', but which they had never been explicitly taught[22]. As we have argued this cannot be learnt in the abstract, simply through critical study; and advance planning (for example in the form of storyboards) is not always a guarantee of a coherent finished product. While most groups did draw up storyboards, few of them were found useful in the actual filming: if anything, they served primarily as a means of enabling the group to clarify their ideas – although it was acknowledged that these ideas were often revised as the filming proceeded. In the case of the adaptation group, the fact that they were able to have three attempts at the filming and evaluate each of these in the light of their initial intentions contributed a great deal to the coherence of the final product.

Clearly, this kind of learning did involve considering questions about the audience – albeit more in the sense of an abstract 'implied reader' than the 'real audience' we had identified. Thus, there were quite intense debates about how shots should be framed or linked together, in order to convey particular information to the viewer: 'you need to see her looking now, otherwise you won't know that she's seen him'; 'we mustn't give the title away until the end, otherwise people will be expecting things to happen'.

The crucial difficulty here, however, is that much of this learning did not find its way into the students' writing. In the case of this group, Grant (who had largely monopolised the camera) was the only one who referred to camera positions in his written account, while the students who produced the storyboard effectively ignored this whole dimension of the process. Like the pupils in Chapter 2, these students may have learnt a great deal about 'film grammar' – but at least for the moment, it appeared to remain passive knowledge[23].

Yet this kind of 'media knowledge' is only part of what may get lost in the translation to written assessment. When I asked the students, in their final debriefing interview, which part of the project they had enjoyed the most, the response was unanimous. It was the filming, and particularly the filming they had done outside school, that was far and away the most pleasurable activity. This certainly coincides with my own observations, both of the filming inside school, and of their editing of material they had shot over the weekend. Play-acting, dressing up, putting on wigs and your parents' clothes, 'having a laugh', making a fool of yourself, fluffing your lines, wandering freely around parts of the school that were normally off limits – these were, for the students, the most important elements of the process. And while these pleasures can be gained irrespective of the context, they also carry a particular resonance in the highly regulated environment of the school.

This was most apparent in the case of the documentary group, who had taken the camera one weekend when they went ice-skating, and subsequently to what looked like an impromptu party. The pleasure was particularly evident for the girls:

Liz: Lots of people have cameras at home, but I haven't got one, and it's just so funny acting in front of a camera, just being really stupid and seeing what you sound like and look like on tape...

However, they also acknowledged the problems that this later caused them:

Liz: We filmed so much stuff we knew we weren't gonna use, it just got in the way in the end, but it was fun anyway... the things we did were just so stupid. They were funny at the time, so we did them, we thought, we might be able to put that in, but they were too long, or just irrelevant, really...

Their finished tape did include some extracts from this material, particularly in the section on 'idols', where members of the group and their friends all named their favourite pop and movie stars. Nevertheless, much of the 'private' appeal of this material seemed to be lost in the more 'public' context of the finished product: as Liz acknowledged, 'it just looks like two girls having a laugh with the camera, not like a TV programme'. While the girls had to be coaxed to talk about this dimension of the work in our final debriefing discussion, it was effectively absent from their written work.

This mis-match between the 'private' nature of the production process and the 'public' nature of the finished text is, I would argue, a very common experience in practical work; and yet it leads to a rather different perspective on the notion of audience. A whole series of meanings are created in the shared social experience of production that rarely find their way into the final product – and in this sense, the production group is itself an audience for its own work. For example, the question of who plays which part is often particularly significant, yet in ways that are only ever apparent to those 'in the know'[24]: Nicky's performance as 'Dino Papadopolou' is an obvious example. As I have noted, many students commented on how 'what seemed good at the time', in the context of the production group, somehow lost its edge on subsequent viewing – and from my own experience as an occasional home video maker, I would have to confirm this.

In a sense, however, this suggests that we may be attempting to throw students into a form of 'public communication' much too early: we are expecting them to jump hurdles before they can even crawl. We seem to assume that they will be able to move easily from the stage of 'home video' – where it's all about social relationships and mutual understandings, about the thrill or the embarrassment of seeing yourself on screen – immediately on to constructing a controlled, purposeful public statement for an audience that can only ever be partially known.

To return briefly to the analogy with writing, we might choose to see this in terms of James Britton's distinction between 'transactional', 'poetic' and 'expressive' writing[25]. In a sense, we seem to be requiring a kind of facility in more 'public', and more consciously controlled, forms of transactional writing before we have given students an opportunity to develop a fluency in the more private expressive writing from which the public forms ultimately derive. There are clearly problems with this analogy (and indeed with the theoretical distinctions Britton makes) but the questions it raises are worth taking seriously. Unless students have substantial opportunities to explore the medium on a 'private' level, it may simply be unrealistic to expect them to achieve the level of technical, artistic and conceptual control that our teaching appears to require.

These arguments might usefully be related back to the question of audience. In this project, there would appear to have been several 'audiences', all of them more or less 'real'. In addition to our (simulated) real audience of eleven-year-olds, there were also different audiences made up of teachers and of peers. To complicate matters further, each of these might be seen to occupy 'official' and 'unofficial' roles: for example, students might make particular kinds of judgments about other students' work in their role as students (as is the case with many of the comments recorded here), yet they might make quite different judgments in their role as peers, friends or enemies. What is judged to be conceptually inadequate in one role might be perceived as a 'right laugh' in another. Finally, as I have suggested, the production group itself is its own audience – in the sense that there are meanings and pleasures which are only available to those who have shared the experience of production. It may well be that much of what is most significant about the production process takes place among these more private, 'unofficial' audiences; yet it is as though this cannot be acknowledged, or does not count, when it comes to the public, 'official' process of evaluation.

Yet if a great deal may be lost in the transfer to written form, the institutional context of assessment may also actively prevent effective evaluation from occurring. As

I have noted at a number of points, there were often contradictions between what students did in class, what they said about what they had done, and what they subsequently wrote about it. Students often ironed out the doubts and contradictions in their writing, in favour of a presentation of themselves as wholly rational and single-minded. It was as if marks might be lost for indecision or uncertainty. With few exceptions, the planning process was described as an orderly and structured progression from storyboard to shooting script to filming – 'like a machine', as Nicky wrote.

This was certainly the case with the game show group, whose doubts following the first focus group discussion were recorded above. When it came to the final debriefing interview, and particularly to their written work, there was very little recognition that they might have been confused about what they wanted to do, and hence that they might have learnt anything from the younger students' comments. Only Tina appears to acknowledge the focus group's contribution:

> Talking to our focus group inspired us quite a lot. Before, we hadn't had many good ideas to work on and we hadn't settled on anything definite. Because our focus group was the age that our task was aimed at, we valued their opinions... The type of things they told us we should have, we hadn't even thought about so it was obvious either people of their age would know about these things or our group hadn't thought about ideas deeply enough.

By contrast, Rebecca describes the same discussion in a completely different way:

> The first time we had presented our ideas to the focus group, we had already chosen our ideas in our heads, and we really were only looking for their approval... The focus group's ideas to us completely trashed our plans and we didn't like them so we went ahead with our former ideas anyway so the focus group didn't change our ideas at all and to us it was unnecessary.

While Tina's account is perhaps unduly positive, it coincides more closely with my own observations of this discussion group than Rebecca's. Yet it was Rebecca's account of the process that appeared to be shared by the rest of the group. Ben, for example, confidently states: 'we had already planned out what we intended to do' – a statement which is blatantly false, although one which a busy teacher might well accept at face value.

The dimension of group dynamics was also subject to this kind of *post hoc* self-presentation. Most of the written accounts are keen to emphasise the effectiveness of the group work, and to minimise the 'occasional' arguments. In general, however, the more argumentative students tend to paint a less rosy picture. Thus, while most of the members of the game show group emphasise the way in which decisions were reached 'democratically' by voting, Rebecca offers a detailed description of the arguments that took place, concluding 'I would never work with them again'. (Paul meanwhile notes 'the continuous arguing that Rebecca would have with a different member of the group each lesson'.) On the other hand, Daniel's account of the sitcom production repeatedly emphasises how well the group worked together; while a number of his fellow group members single him out for criticism because of his failure to participate.

The fact that, as we have seen, the issue of *originality* became a major preoccupation in the students' written work is also relevant here. While our brief explicitly required a generic product, and hence something (at least partly) 'unoriginal', many of the procedures of educational assessment would appear to value uniqueness and originality. Under this regime, the most heinous sin is that of plagiarism, or what school students are more likely to call copying. For students who are less familiar with group work, collaboration is often regarded with considerable suspicion, precisely for this reason – 'miss, he's stealing my ideas!' School students are still routinely exhorted to 'write it in your own words', as though paraphrasing were somehow a higher form of expression, and as though words could somehow unproblematically be claimed as 'your own'. And particularly in the more 'creative' aspects of subjects like English and Art, there is a rhetorical commitment to personal creative expression, which clearly entails a notion of individual originality.

Perhaps the ultimate irony here is that many of the students seemed to perceive the final audience focus groups – which we had hoped would encourage a less teacher-focused form of evaluation – as yet another means of assessment. Nicky was not alone in his attempts to get the younger students to acknowledge the superiority of his group's production, although some of his questions were perhaps the most leading: 'didn't you think that was the most best pieced together advert you've seen?' Nearly all the groups were keen that the younger students should vote to determine the best trailer. Here again, my taping of the discussions was regarded as a form of covert assessment: Amit repeatedly asked the younger students 'can you just confirm for the tape that you liked that one best'. Of course, a degree of rivalry of this kind might well be inevitable, but the overall context of assessment certainly encouraged this. In this respect, Rebecca's analogy is perhaps the most revealing: '[the younger students] were sort of like examiners, and their verdict was final: if they liked it, we had passed, but if they didn't, we had failed.'

This is perhaps to end on an unduly negative note. I have no doubt that the written evaluations, and particularly the 'audience research' dimensions of the project, did encourage the students to justify their decisions and hence to formalise their understandings. As I have argued, our 'real audience' was far from real in the eyes of our students, for a number of unavoidable reasons. In a sense, as the sitcom group implicitly acknowledged, their *real* audience remained that of their teachers and peers. Yet however limited and constrained it may have been, the students' encounter with our 'real audience' seemed to enable them to take a distance from their own work, and hence to evaluate it more readily and effectively. This is particularly apparent in their written accounts of this part of the project, which are much more reflective and thoughtful than their accounts of the production process itself.

Assessment is an inevitable part of the educational process, and it is perhaps unavoidably reductive. Yet it seems vital that students' experience of self-evaluation should not be confined to situations in which they are also to be assessed. Self-evaluation is bound to be less than effective if it is perceived (by teachers or by students) as merely a covert means of allocating grades. If students' only experiences of evaluation are so over-determined by the institutional imperatives of assessment, significant opportunities for learning may be lost.

Notes

1   See Buckingham (1990), Chapter 10; Buckingham and Sefton-Green (1994), Chapter 8.
2   See Fraser (forthcoming).

3   There is an interesting contrast here with art education, where the product is much more straightforwardly privileged: see Allen (forthcoming).

4   Southern Examining Group GCSE Media Studies: Chief Examiner's Report 1993. Recent examiners' reports at A-level have explicitly sought to warn teachers off the 'log' format.

5   Grahame (1990).

6   Particularly Buckingham (1990), Chapter 10; Buckingham and Sefton-Green (1994), Chapter 8.

7   Buckingham and Sefton-Green, *ibid.*

8   See also Burgess et al (1973).

9   Richmond (1990).

10 This approach could be seen to reflect a broader *psychologistic* orientation, which is designed precisely to deflect attention away from the social causes of underachievement and unemployment: see Cohen (1984).

11 See Buckingham (1989); and Chapters 2 and 3.

12 Britton, Burgess, Martin, et al (1975), p. 58.

13 E.g. Graves (1978) Thanks to Tony Burgess for his help with some of these arguments.

14 This is most explicitly debated in the work coming from Australia (see, for example, Reid 1987), although this approach is also implicit in Britain, for example in the work of the LINC Project or the National Writing Project.

15 See Neale (1980).

16 See Buckingham (1993b), particularly Chapters 3 and 6.

17 See Hartley (1987), and Buckingham (1993b), Chapter 11.

18 See Burns (1977), Ang (1991).

19 For a discussion of these issues, see Buckingham (1993b), Chapters 3 and 11

20 For useful discussions of the limitations of conventional criticisms of 'stereotyping', see Perkins (1979) and Barker (1989).

21 See Britzman (1991).

22 Arthurs (1987) makes a useful argument for practical work in similar terms.

23 This is not to imply that the rules of continuity editing could not be taught at this level, for example through detailed textual analysis - although I would argue that this comparatively formal approach is more appropriate at A-level.

24 See Buckingham and Sefton-Green, *op. cit.*, particularly Chapter 5.

25 Barnes, Britton and Rosen (1969).

Chapter 7

Do I Look Like a Prostitute? Soaps, Reality and Learning through Performance

Lights, camera, action!!

Despite the fact that their rehearsals had been videotaped for the previous five weeks, on the day we were filming the first episode of the class soap *Johnswood Heights,* there was a palpable sense of excitement. The students were, for them, uncharacteristically divided into single sex groups, clustered around the large and tatty space of the drama studio in what looked like focused and intense discussion. A large group of boys suddenly and purposefully moved away from the window and began following an enormous spider that seemed to occupy their attention. The camera crews carried on pretending to focus on students they wanted to annoy, draining precious battery time for no good reason. The girls were intensively applying make-up, sharing mirrors and running in and out of the drama office with bits of wardrobe. The drama teacher and I wandered around trying to encourage them all to get ready so we could start. I went over to two girls in order to try to prise them away from the lipstick when Saheda, one of the girls who had most impressed me with her concentration and organisational skills, looked up from the mirror, straightened her dress, checked the mirror again and then asked me, 'do I look like a prostitute?'.

There are pleasures for students doing practical work; and, it would seem, there are also pleasures for teachers. My retort was to ask Saheda why she thought I might know; but in many ways her question encapsulated the issues which are the concern of this chapter.

Leaving aside the touching faith in the omniscience of teachers, the question implies two fundamental concerns. First of all there is the issue of what a 'real' prostitute might look like, how we might know, and whether Saheda could look like one. This in turn begs questions about the nature of the soap genre and especially the idea of *modality*. Modality is a term derived from linguistics which refers to the level of the reality we ascribe to texts. All readers make judgements about how 'realistic' they find a given text. Cartoons, we might agree, have low modality status; cats and mice are not made of elastic and do not survive *Tom and Jerry* antics in real life. The News, on the other hand, has high modality status: we tend to believe that what is reported has actually happened. In general terms it is acknowledged that soap operas have a mixed modality status: at times they are seen to be 'realistic', while at others they stretch the viewers' credibility. As viewers watch soaps they typically move between a position of close involvement and one of critical distance: at certain points, they may be highly convinced of the reality of the characters' feelings or dilemmas, while at others they may dismiss them as too incredible to be 'true'. What Saheda was trying to determine by her question was whether her dress and make-up would have *sufficient* modality to convince within the conventions applying both to 'real' soaps and to the class soap. In particular, she was attempting to identify whether she might appear 'realistic' in terms of how prostitutes are conventionally represented in soaps – although whom she might be attempting to convince is another important question that we also need to address. Indeed, we might also ask why or what a prostitute might be doing in a class soap in the first place.

The second concern that is being invoked here is a more specifically educational one. In terms of our interests, we have to ask what Saheda thinks she is *learning* from dressing up like a prostitute; and in what ways acting the role might contribute to her understanding of, amongst other things, acting, making soaps and even being a prostitute. The issue has a certain frisson given Saheda's character, but even if another girl, such as Tamara, who was playing a teenage girl, had asked if she looked like a teenage girl the issues would still have been the same – although they would have sounded more confused!

The issue of how and in what ways students might be learning about characterisation and genre through the process of performance is strangely neglected in writings about media education. Some attempt has been made to explore the ways in which the content of the subject relates to concepts of subjectivity: for example, Chris Richards has written about the ways in which the formal study of the explicitly adult and sexual nature of much media output sets up contradictions for teachers and students[1]. However, despite the large amount of practical work in which students are the models, performers or characters in invented fictions and simulations, little attention has been paid to how this dimension – in effect, *the dramatic* – might affect or influence the nature of the learning that is involved.

It was primarily my experience as an examiner for A-level Media Studies[2] that threw this issue into sharp focus. I began to get the impression that there was a significant amount of media work produced, especially on video, that relied heavily on its dramatic qualities to give it meaning. For example, many exam centres produce work on *film noir*. This can vary from posters with images of men in trilby hats casting shadows across smoke-filled rooms to five minute dramas in which young people dress up in what look like their parents' suits and party frocks. I have examined many videos which feature hard-boiled 18-year-olds following strangers through the housing estates of Basildon, or murder chases up the stairs of 1980s furnished houses in Haywards Heath. This concentration on acting out whole scenes from genres far removed from contemporary youth culture drew my attention to the *performed* nature of media productions.

Obviously I find much of this *film noir* kind of work faintly risible, but that is not the point. The issue at stake here is the extent to which the nature of the performance – the delivery of the dialogue, complete with cigarettes and Bogart voice, the characteristic poses and gestures – make any sense in terms of Media Studies concepts.

What does dressing up and acting out *film noir* videos contribute to students' understanding of the genre? It is clear that students are really investing more than their pride in these activities; yet it is as if all the elements of play acting count for nothing when students are required to describe the learning that is supposed to have taken place in the context of their written assessments. Of course, such writing typically emphasises the ability to analyse elements of form and style, rather than acting.

There are two theoretical reasons which might explain this absence in accounts of pupils' learning. The first stems from the way in which media education seems to privilege rational thought over feeling. In most of the writing about the subject and especially in the descriptions of assessment criteria, media education courses emphasise the values of the rational and the analytical, as opposed to the affective and the expressive[3]. We have argued throughout the book that this model of learning, with all its trappings of 1970s deconstructionism, is an inadequate account of the range of meanings and pleasures that students derive from practical work. The second explanation for this lack of attention lies not in Media Studies but in the body of educational writing around Drama and Drama in Education. These more general educational philosophies, particularly those concerned with role play and simulation, also inform many of the most familiar teaching strategies in media education. As the two preceding chapters have argued, media educationalists may need to question many of the underlying assumptions of these practices in our interpretation of students' practical work.

My interest in performance in this context also derives partly from my role as a lecturer in media education within the teacher training department of a Drama school. This aspect of my job takes me into many Drama lessons where I often observe young people acting out improvisations based on media texts, particularly soaps; but in ironic contrast to Media Studies, such work in Drama appears to pay little attention to the concepts and purposes prevalent in media education. Given the similar positions media education and Drama now seem to occupy on the margins of the English curriculum, and given the alliances teachers of both subjects traditionally make within schools, it seemed important to explore the possibilities for establishing some common ground.

Drama and media

There are several reasons why we selected work around soaps in order to explore these themes, not the least of which is that they occupy a special place in the 'anti-canon' of right wing educationalists. 'There'll be no GCSE's in *Eldorado*' (hoho!) thundered John Major to the Tory faithful. Indeed if one genre seems to symbolise all the debased values of 'mass culture' it would have to be the soap[4]. Yet in English, soap operas are studied by between 40 and 50% of schools at Key Stage 3 and 4; and in Media Studies the figures are slightly less high[5] – which might be seen as a crude national curriculum of sorts. Obviously soaps are used in different ways for different purposes; but whether they are used as stimulus material for discussion of social issues or as a focus for practical work, it is likely that students will at least touch on the genre at some time in their formal schooling. On one level of course, this simply reflects their status as a core experience, a kind of 'common culture' in which virtually all the children of the nation participate[6].

The second reason we wanted to research students' learning about soaps is that (as I have already suggested) the topic inevitably raises questions about the construction of social reality. Because the dominant mode of most present day soaps – *EastEnders, Brookside, Home and Away* etc.- is that of 'television naturalism', asking students to work within the genre requires them to engage with debates about the nature of realist representations which have been a central concern in media education. Such work also focuses attention on the *content* of media production – that is, the reality, or lack of it, of the worlds soaps purport to represent. In Media Studies, this aspect is often seen to be secondary to the analysis of the formal elements of media texts – codes and conventions, audience address and so on.

Thirdly, making a class soap forces the issue of characterisation and performance into the open. Not only do students have to adopt various roles, they also have to perform them credibly. And as we have discussed in the previous chapter, the idea of credibility raises questions about the way students conceptualise the *audience*. After all, the notion of credibility comes down to whether a particular audience for the performance is convinced by that performance's claim to be real – in other words, its modality. Modality, credibility and audience are thus interlinked concepts in this way: each defines the other.

Finally, we wanted to use a creative arts subject like Drama as a subject base for this case study as it would draw upon students' conceptions of that subject, which would inevitably be different from their expectations of media work in other areas. Drama has a distinct pedagogy and philosophy of learning; and these values (amongst others) have been inevitably internalised by students. We hypothesised that if students were to undertake media work from a different perspective, their reflections about the project may well cast an interesting light upon the methods of learning common to both areas.

Teaching soaps

There is, however, a dilemma facing all attempts to teach about soaps. If virtually all children watch soaps, then they must clearly 'understand' them at some level or another; and if this is the case, then we have to question what the formal curriculum can add to that understanding. Perhaps the question is not so much *why* teach about soaps, but *what* can we teach that they don't already know.

This problem is apparent in many of the teaching materials available on the topic. The unit produced by the BFI as part of their *Media in English* pack (and for which I take some responsibility as a contributor), is typical of this[7]. Also aimed at year 9, the age group I worked with in this project, the unit aims to 'develop pupils' knowledge of the specific forms and conventions of soap operas [and] to investigate how soap opera narratives are structured'. (Rereading this, I suspect that the emphasis on 'forms and conventions' and the structuring of narratives represents an attempt to objectify and make educationally respectable the popular pleasures associated with watching soaps). The work in the unit entails a mixture of analytical work – for example, constructing diagrams and charts to follow the interaction of characters and plot lines – and comparative activities defining the characteristics of the soap genre. The practical assignment in the unit requires students to script a new soap based on stimulus material provided. This activity is set up as a simulation which requires students to make up their new soap in the form of a 'treatment' for a TV company.

I want to make several points about this kind of approach to soaps which will explain the different way I worked on this topic in Drama lessons. First of all, although this BFI unit acknowledges the pleasures and popularity of watching soaps for this age group, those pleasures form the background rather than the central focus of the unit. The fact that young people watch soaps, and the associated pleasures they must give, are not in themselves the kind of knowledge the unit sets out to investigate. On the contrary, this prior enthusiasm is used to motivate students to complete the charts and diagrams; and it also ensures that students will know enough about the characters and their histories in order to be able to complete such tasks. But other than that, the *kind* of popular knowledge students might have about soaps is set aside in favour of academic knowledge such as that contained in published accounts of the genre.

Secondly, the storylines within the simulation preempt too much. Students are provided with a small cast list of multi-ethnic characters living on an estate, and a rather politically correct series of storylines. However, the actual *content* of these plots is not the focus of study. Thus, we have 'Elena ... She has a Geordie accent and wears different clothes to the other young people on the estate'; and Tony who 'has been unemployed since his YTS for some time'. Both these descriptions imply a specific version of social reality. However, this fictional world is only intended to be of peripheral interest; the students are to be steered towards more central questions about audience or narrative structure. The simulation is perhaps fundamentally untenable in that it blithely requires the construction of a soap aimed at a youth audience. This is a complex task that television companies would approach with a great deal more caution. Indeed, as we shall argue in the following chapter, the unreal constraints of many simulations are often self-defeating. In my experience of using these materials, students are able to produce reasonable ideas for soaps, although they invariably move outside the initial brief.

The third problem with this kind of approach is that of progression. Virtually the same assignment is recommended in the Cambridge A-level Media Studies (syllabus B) as an assignment for the 'Textual Analysis' module. Obviously similar work can be set at a number of levels and is differentiated in the ways it might be assessed. However, getting students to produce scripts for soaps frequently results in lengthy pieces where the emphasis seems to on the imaginative process of character and plot generation. This is as true for year 9 students as it is for A-level students; and yet it implies that students have an agenda to explore that is *in excess* of the requirements of the media curriculum. Within Media Studies this 'excessive' creativity has traditionally been contained, not least by requiring students to evaluate their work in academic language and in terms of underlying theories or concepts. Leaving aside the problems that this approach raises – problems central to this book and others[8] – work on soaps seems to exacerbate this issue. Our impression is that students' 'creative' energies go into the careful construction of a fictional world, often with complex narratives full of social problems; whereas teachers, in English and well as Media Studies, use the topic to explore underlying formal structures. This clash of interests not only suggests that work on soaps may not be a terribly successful activity *in our terms*, but also that we may be neglecting the reasons why students are so attracted to soaps in the first place.

Improvisation

I worked alongside the Drama teacher in a mixed ability year 9 class in a working-class, multi-ethnic inner city school. Drama has suffered badly under the National Curriculum, but this particular class was lucky in that they had a single eighty minute lesson once a week. The problems of continuity in Drama with once-weekly lessons are often difficult and should not be underestimated. In the end, the project took nine weeks, although for one of these when we were filming a small group of students substantially overran into the following lesson. The editing took a whole day and was completed off site with two students. The drama room was a large and typically run down space with torn black drapes and various prop and wardrobe resources secreted away in cupboards and inner offices.

The students clearly enjoyed this project for a number of reasons, one of which was that we used video in a 'big production' way, as I was able to bring in two camcorders and take students to an editing suite. Although the school considered this the height of luxury, such facilities are not by any means extravagant or unusual in many schools these days. Nevertheless, there was a certain novelty value to this as well. The drama teacher, Bruce Wooding, had used various media forms in his lessons but the class had not carried out systematic video work before. It is fair to say that much of what we achieved was made possible by the students' excitement and enthusiasm about working with video in this way.

We modelled our approach on typical 'impro' work in drama, mixed with a version of the working method favoured by the film director Mike Leigh. Leigh uses a development of the 'method' promulgated by Stanislavski. He gets his actors to develop characters initially by themselves. The actor works on a fictitious biography and devises the full gamut of expressions associated with his or her 'personality'. These 'characters' are then introduced to each other in different settings and their interaction becomes the substance of Leigh's films. This process of interaction and change is a version of 'forum theatre' (developed by the radical Brazilian practitioner, Augusto Boal), and popularised in contemporary drama education theory[9].

This was in any case only a slightly different version of what happens in many Drama lessons. The school subject Drama has developed a model of teaching and learning which revolves around improvisations rather than performances. As has been somewhat cynically observed by David Hornbrook, too many Drama lessons take the form of getting kids to improvise and then show scenes, lesson after lesson[10]. I will return to theories of drama education towards the end of this chapter; but for the moment I want to signal the problematic relationship this 'impro' tradition has with the discipline of theatrical performance, with its emphasis on skill and technique. This discipline is almost diametrically opposed to the idea of intuitively adopting improvised personae; although on the other hand it is closer to what is almost a 'pedagogic' tradition in the training of actors. There, the strong humanistic tradition in the theatre implies that actors have to learn how to *be* other people: learning to be an actor means learning about people as much as about technique.

Briefly, we set the scene by eliciting which soaps the class watched. It is worth while noting that *EastEnders* was by far the most popular – an influence which will become apparent when we look at what they actually produced. The class were then told that they were going to make their own soap. This was not in the form of a brief or simulation, so it did not specify potential audiences or describe institutional constraints. Whilst such an approach may seem to go against common practice within media education, and run the risk of not drawing attention to the ways that media texts target audiences, making dramas is a 'normal' activity in Drama – like writing stories in English. The class were quite happy to set about the activity despite possible anomalies in the task. In groups of three they came up with the following list of likely characters and storylines for their soap:

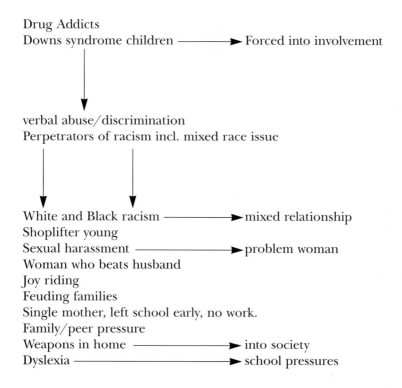

It is worthwhile trying to locate the generic antecedents for these ideas. Some clearly reflect the explicit interest in 'social issues' that can be found both in soaps (certainly of the *EastEnders* variety) and in drama education. In Drama, personal issues of this kind are often the implicit 'content' of the curriculum. Like other subjects, such as Personal, Social and Health Education (PHSE), with which Drama is frequently associated, it is often assumed that studying social problems will in some way stop students from becoming the victims of such problems. Thus, 'drugs, verbal abuse, family/peer pressures', and 'dyslexia leading to school pressures' are all instantly recognisable plot lines from the kinds of dramas that students are used to producing. Similarly 'joyriding' and 'weapons in the home' had recently been identified in the news as 'youth problems'; and racism was a particularly acute topic of conversation in the school at the time, as it had recently suffered a spate of racially motivated gang violence. The idea of a disabled character seemed to come straight from a topic in PHSE which the class had been studying at the time. Finally, topics like feuding families belong to the 'classic' themes of drama in general and soaps in particular.

Although this might indicate that the subject Drama was the dominant influence on the students' formulation of their soap, the genre itself is equally important. As has been observed, *EastEnders* also has a public information function. Both the didactic way in which it treats topics like AIDS or racism and the frequency with which such issue-based narratives are developed out of certain characters, such as the positive representation of Colin, 'the homosexual', also derive from the same model of socially responsible drama[11]. The idea of a woman beating her husband seemed to be both a subversion of traditional representations of domestic violence, current in the Jordache saga in *Brookside*; and at the same time to suggest a *Coronation Street* style of comic melodrama[12].

If the school curriculum appeared to be perhaps the most influential force at this stage (and it is worthwhile mentioning that the students may well have been on their best behaviour in order to impress me, the new 'teacher' in the classroom), I do not want to be unduly cynical about this. Although students do reproduce ideas to please teachers they are not necessarily uninterested in the ideas they suggest. The disabled person plot line, for example, generated much serious and thoughtful discussion as to how someone who had a mental handicap could be performed and might appear convincing.

However, further development of the characters started to owe more to soaps than to the hypothetical world of the 'social problem'. Having thought up the storylines, the class then had to work them into scenes in larger groups. The brief was to introduce the characters in a typical setting, at 7.00 in the evening at home, and ensure that their distinctive plot line would be established. They came up with the following improvisations:

1. A black man in his 30's, having split with his wife, meets an old white friend in the local cafe which is run by a new owner. He and his friend have a row with a mixed race customer who has recently moved into the area.

2. A black single mother has two teenage daughters, 15 and 17. The younger one has become a crack cocaine user. She is in debt to a heartless dealer; and after her mum flushed her 'stash' down the toilet, she robbed a shop. However, both her mum and the dealer are on her case.

3. An older boy (18) is looking after his younger brothers (twins of 8). Their parents are away and suddenly they have to look after their cousin after his mother had to go into hospital. The cousin was born with Downs syndrome.

4. A couple who met at college are having difficulties; the wife is beating the husband who has run up a large phone bill. The neighbours are powerless to help.

5. The mother of two boys (15 and 8) is a prostitute who is beaten up by her drug-dealing pimp. The elder brother gets hold of a gun to take revenge on her behalf. The younger brother finds the gun.

6. The Christian son of an alcoholic mother gets a Muslim girl pregnant and does not want to marry her.

The ethnicity and age of the characters began to be specified at this stage in order to give the dramas authenticity. Of course, although the students used such facts to make their portrayals more 'realistic', the characters were still being played by 14 year olds. This tension between the authentic and the play-acted raises a number of questions about the portrayal of realism, or modality, which we will return to in due course.

The fundamental differences between these improvisations and the earlier plot lines is, as one might expect, the increased level of drama: violence, drugs and pregnancy now have entertainment as well as 'moral' value. However, some of these improvisations were still schematic. The first story, for example, was rather absurd. The central character (whose only personality trait seemed to reside in the fact that he was black) simply picks a row with a mixed race customer on the similarly tenuous basis that he was of mixed race. As drama, this was quite bizarre and clearly showed the dangers of improvising likely soap stories from a politically correct menu.

The next stage was to work on the characters in more detail. The students had to write up 'fact files' on the characters they were playing in order to make explicit crucial details about physique, personality and family relations, all of which make soaps seem real. Here the influence of actual soaps was even more evident, as characters were named Fowler or Beale – after the families in *EastEnders*. However, the students completed these fact files in the first person, as if they, the students, were the character. This is a written form of the drama education device known as 'hotseating' which requires the student to imagine 'in role'[13]. The rest of the class direct questions to one student about that student's character, his or her past, or how they might respond to given situations. In answering those questions the student thus devises further aspects of the character through identifying with the fictional role. The device is rather like writing stories in the first person; and it is significantly different from other ways of devising characters in simulations. Typical media education simulations, for example, create character through description from the outside, as it were. Students are given roles like advertising executives, or BBC producers; 'characters' whose personality resides in their social role, not in the ways they might feel or act because of an individual history.

This point is worth explicating in detail because as we have seen throughout this book, there is an element of role playing in nearly all forms of student media production, particularly where they attempt to simulate 'mass' media. After all, asking students to make media texts like adverts or magazines is asking them to adopt the perspective of the media producer – the magazine editor or TV executive. In this respect, the student is expected to sublimate their own character to the social role they are adopting. It is not clear if this happens in practice; and if it does, it seems theoretically at odds with any idea that students might be being individually expressive in their production work. This whole dimension of learning in role, and the place of 'character' and identity in the learning process is one which drama educationalists have taken up in some detail and to which we shall return. At this stage, however, it should already be evident that drama education can offer a rather different perspective on media production as well as offering insights into the specific pleasures of soap.

The character profiles the students produced show an intriguing range of approaches to the construction of 'personality'. A number of characters were given performative traits; biting lips, saying 'you know', scratching arms (to indicate a drug habit), biting nails, chewing gum, tapping feet and being obsessive about wearing clean clothes, wearing bags over the left shoulder and so on. This kind of detail derives from the Stanislavskian method of 'emotion memory', in which the actor's body 'learns' aspects of the character's personality through muscular tricks[14]. This technique was further emphasised in the ways in which the students recounted their characters' past lives. In some cases this took the form of oblique and suggestive remarks: 'I got sexually asorted when I was livin rough. Never fought the person'. Elaine's victim status is only implied here. On the other hand, we also received mini-stories:

> My past history is that when my mother was pregnant my father had done a runner and when I was born I only had my mum and I never saw my father again, I don't even know how he looks like or what his name is. I also have a half sister my dad's daughter. My mum tells me he was the reason my dad had to leave us because he loved his wife and when my mum found out they were still married behind her back he left her with his old wife. Then my mum got the news when I was one years old they had a girl.

Indeed, some students wrote pages of this kind of 'autobiography'.

These histories were supposed to serve as background information supporting the production of the class soap – in much the same way that Julia Smith and Tony Holland have recounted producing 'fact files' on characters for *EastEnders*[15]. As has been noted, one of the distinguishing features of soaps is the relationships they forge with audiences; and this is based in part on the knowledge those audiences develop of past events[16]. What we know about characters' past lives influences our understanding of their present behaviour. Although the above description might appear superficial, the author has created a perfect narrative full of hidden secrets and complex sub-plots. This is typical of soap narratives in general and would more than adequately serve as the basis for a developing serial. Although the students were not explicit about the function this kind of narrative could perform, these profiles were produced as a distinct stage in the production process; and they actually reveal a more complex understanding of the requirements of the project than might be initially assumed.

The work at this stage also reflected a detailed and sophisticated description of emotions: 'has a habit of talking back to his wife and then regretting it', 'he depends on himself'. Of course, such comments are not especially profound or insightful in their own right, but they do imply that the students have thought quite hard about this level of characterisation. The frequency of these kinds of remarks, in conjunction with the explanations of motive in the fact file biographies, would indicate that the students found this process of improvising and then creating profiles a fruitful way of creating character. The emphasis on feelings, as opposed to limited demographic detail – age, race etc.- or even physical description – height, warts on the face – is important. It suggests that making up characters through drama does encourage an empathetic mode, a way of getting into the character's deepest feelings and thoughts. And of course, as we shall see later, using empathy is one of subject's key methods of teaching and learning.

Of course, it is important to be cautious about the claim that students make a subjective 'identification' with the character they are acting. Nevertheless, the fact that the student has to *perform* their character (and then follow it through in certain plot situations), means that it is sensible to invest in the character in ways that the student will derive pleasure from as the project proceeds. In other words, if you develop a romantic or melodramatic storyline you could have a host of 'sexy' scenes to play out, whereas if you merely write a story about romance the story has a limited currency: it will only be read by a few after all. Your acting, on the other hand, can go on for weeks in front of the whole class.

From improvisation to episodes

Having developed characters and plot lines, we needed both to reduce the quantity of drama available (there were nearly 30 students in the class), and begin to structure the first episode in more detail. The class first watched each others' improvisations and were then invited to suggest ways in which characters could be doubled up: for example could the black cafe owner be married, or have been married to, the family with the daughter having a drug problem? Secondly, the soap needed a specific location around which it could function. The students had initially agreed on an inner city London locale but, as we shall see, the characters needed to develop professional or social functions in order to facilitate the naturalistic growth of the narratives. The characters needed to be rooted in geographical and social relationships, and in individualised histories. Thirdly, the form of the episode needed to be organised.

Inevitably we had to take the lead in stimulating this process of negotiation and reorganisation. The tension between a student in role as a character and a student as director/producer was both positive and negative here. On the one hand, students could use the process as a way of advancing, or in the case of shy students, killing off, their characters. On the other hand the intense focus on one or two storylines often meant that those plots would be scrupulously developed with an eye to naturalistic detail almost invisible to an 'outsiders'. For example, a 'superfluous' subplot was devised in which the boyfriend of the druggie girl had a crush on the girl's mother. Whilst it was difficult for all the students to get a grasp of the overall structure of the episode, the slow process of negotiation and development did require most of the class to take responsibility for the product. We will trace the actual growth of the finished episode below.

First of all, however, we need to describe the second important intervention we had to make at this stage: to establish camera crews and to turn the focus from live performance to filmed performance. Drama, as a subject, relies intensively on students showing work to the larger group; but in order to turn their improvisations into a soap episode we needed to introduce the idea of performing for camera and editing scenes together. This dimension of the project created significant logistical problems but, more importantly, it began to impact on the ways in which the class proceeded to develop their soap.

We ended up with two camera crews; one male, one female. As the process of consolidation took three weeks, the cast had several opportunities to rehearse their scenes. This gave the film crews similar opportunities to rehearse the filming; a process which had several effects. First, even though the cameras were present in the lessons right from the first session, the students later indicated that this didn't stop them being nervous when it came to the 'final' performance (i.e. the final take). Indeed, from the actors' point of view, it was by no means certain that they became more comfortable in front of the cameras as the unit progressed. One of them commented that acting was:

> different when you get in front of camera ... When you're doing it without people looking at you, just your friends in the class looking at you its just easy to do, 'cos you know how they're ... understand how you're not doing it right. But when you're in front of the camera it's like; 'Am I doing it right?' and stuff like that.

I was surprised by this, because from my point of view performing 'live' improvisations didn't seem that different from performing for camera. Nevertheless, whatever the actors' anxiety about performing in this way, the operators did become fluent with the equipment. We also introduced the idea of beginning each rehearsal with a deliberate clapperboard countdown in order to get the class accustomed to the idea of leaving a 10 second lead-in for the video tape (a technical necessity for editing).

Secondly, given that we aimed to produce a completed first episode, it was obvious that we were not going to script every shot. Indeed, this is a crucial distinction to make between this kind of drama work and professional media production. In principle, all filming should have camera (and lighting) positions scripted. However, this is time-consuming and creates a weight of difficulty, which is why much good video work in schools is in the form of short adverts and trailers. In this instance we wanted the project to focus on the performative aspects of the soap, so we were faced with an impossible dilemma: either to compromise on the filming or the performing. Should we, for example, cut out dialogue because of the difficulties of working out the shot/reverse shot camera positions? In the end, we decided to use two cameras, one to film medium or long establishing shots, that is setting the scene, and the other to concentrate deliberately on close ups and reaction shots. The thinking behind this set up was that we would be able to use insert editing to reproduce the naturalistic style of soaps. Characteristically, the genre intersperses close ups with two shots or medium long shots. Of course, once you start using more than one camera there is the problem of continuity on the sound track.

This was a reasonable decision to make in the circumstances, but despite the fact the crews could practise filming during rehearsals, students of this age have a tendency to use the camera to follow the action. In our experience, when young people first use video they tend to use it as a means of *recording* the action. This is directly opposed to some of the cherished principles of film theory which stress how filming *constructs* the action. There is a difference between staging events for the camera and using the camera instrumentally as a recording device. Indeed, only once did the students use the camera as a way of staging the action, when they cut the sound track of a mother beating her child over a shot of another character looking out of his window, thereby showing him listening to his neighbours (see scene 10 below). In the other scenes the action was staged as if for live performance. Since a central argument of this chapter is that acting out soaps gives students access to a meaningful study of the genre, this technical 'deficiency' should be noted as one of the contradictions that arise when replicating professional practice in schools.

The problem was further exacerbated by the dual role in which the students found themselves, as technicians and as audience. Requiring students to concentrate on a delimited task, for example just filming close ups, imposes a discipline on the camera operator. This is often resisted or ignored, especially when the technician is socially involved in the action, as we would all be watching members of our peer group perform. Students are thus drawn into the drama as members of the audience, rather than in role as camera operators. This again raises the more general issue, to which we will later return, that reproducing the divisions of labour prevalent in the media industries does not necessarily have positive implications for the *educational* nature of the activity.

The final peculiarity of filming drama work is that the conventions of 'make-believe' look rather exposed on film. Thus, for example, it is quite common in improvisations to create a space by pretending to knock on a door whilst stamping one's foot. Our students were quite happy to do this on film when they were unable to use props or real doors. Similarly they were uncritical about using white actors to play black characters, at the same time as (and in apparent contradiction to) paying scrupulous attention to the details of narrative continuity. Like the hybrid nature of the written school stories we discussed in chapter 3, school Drama makes up its own modality rules. It is quite happy to mix cinematic naturalism with the representational codes of improvised drama.

Johnswood Heights

We furnished the students with a plan of the hypothetical area in which their soap was set, and began the process of distillation. The final edited version ran as follows.

Scene 1 *Cafe*
The cafe owner (Leon) is arguing with his ex-wife (Joanne) who wants maintenance. We are introduced to his two daughters, the younger of whom (Natasha) manages to sweet-talk money out of Leon; the older does not. Natasha is friendly with Kofi, who seems to be helping out in the cafe. The argument is inter-cut with a comic routine involving an increasingly hungry customer who is trying to get served.

Scene 2 *Surgery*
The Social Worker is bringing an autistic client to see the doctor. The Social Worker explains he is going on holiday and asks the doctor to keep an eye on the client (fig. 7.1).

Scene 3 *Shop*
Panning round the shop, we see the doctor looking at magazines. The nosy shopkeeper tries to get a woman who has just arrived in the neighbourhood to talk about herself. She is curt despite the forwardness of her daughter, who is severely rebuked for her friendliness.

Scene 4 *Living Room*
The aggressive wife (Rukshana) threatens her husband (Ataur) and rants and raves at him (fig. 7.2).

Scene 5 *Living Room*
The relatives of the autistic boy await his impending arrival with argumentative trepidation. The father slips out, leaving the two brothers to greet the social worker and his client. The younger brother shows his resentment about having an autistic relative coming to live with them and the scene ends acrimoniously.

Scene 5 *Bedroom*
Natasha and Kofi are in bed having sex. Unwittingly Kofi exhales the name of Joanne in lust. He is saved from further embarrassment by the arrival of Leon. Kofi jumps out of the window.

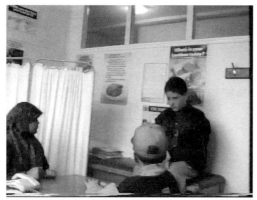

Fig. 7.1 The Surgery

Fig. 7.2 Domestic violence

Fig. 7.3 Overhearing gossip

Fig. 7.4 The laundrette

Scene 6 *Exterior*
Ataur is moaning about his wife to Rachel. She is sympathetic. Joanne walks past looking at them suspiciously (fig. 7.3).

Scene 7 *Exterior*
Natasha buys drugs from a shady dealer loitering in the park. Joanne, her mother, comes along and although she is suspicious, they go home together.

Scene 8 *Surgery*
Natasha's sister confides in the doctor that her sister is a drug user. The doctor mistakenly offers her help. The ensuing argument is calmed down.

Scene 10 *Living Room*
The new arrival from scene 3 is savagely beating her daughter. There is a cross cut to the shop keeper looking out of his window. He knocks on her door to try to intervene and is met with short shrift.

Scene 11 *Laundrette*
Joanne is 'bitchy' to Rachel and calls her a prostitute at the same time as Rachel's son walks in. Rachel admits that she is on the game; but at least she is honest about these things. There is a slanging match (fig. 7.4).

Scene 12 *Living Room*
Rachel's older son is reading the paper. The younger son comes in and wants to know what a prostitute is. The older brother wants to know where he heard the term. The younger brother's explanation leaves the older in shock.

Scene 13 *Living Room*
Rukshana explodes in jealous anger at Ataur. In her passion she knocks him unconscious to the floor. In her grief she says how much she loves him.

This is a summary of the final edited version. In fact, however, *Johnswood Heights* never existed in this shape until the actual process of editing. For three or four weeks, the episode existed as an organic, amoeba-like entity which kept changing its shape from one week to the next. This was partially the result of having lessons so far removed from each other; but it is also in the nature of improvised texts to work in this way. By definition they retain a fluidity that changes in performance. But, as we discussed in chapter 4, this kind of approach also raises questions about directorial control. In the end, it was the editors who made the final decisions, mainly on the basis of the rushes that they had in front of them at the time. Again, this was also due to problems of logistics and management: it is expecting too much for a 14-year-old to control the rest of the class[17]. Like the dilemmas identified in chapter 4, it also indicates the rather contradictory mix of values in the situation, where the 'democratic' ideals of progressive Drama seem at odds with the requirements of the task. However, from the students' point of view, the soap was owned by the class; and if actors in scenes changed bits as they went along, as long as it didn't overtly clash with developments in another scene, this was allowed to happen.

This issue of control is yet another example of the ways in which school practice appears to be diametrically opposed to conventional practice in media production. As we have observed above in relation to the differences between recording action and filming drama, school activities are anything *but* professional practice. There, the economics of production time and the solution of hierarchical job specialisation (directors, camera operators, sound operators, writers, editors etc.), results in a compartmentalised process of production. By definition, this is not a model of learning suitable for the classroom. As we saw in chapter 4, a curious educational economy of scales operate where the aim seems to be to maximise the overall opportunities for participation and learning for the greatest number of students. This equation seems to be based on an assumption that more involvement equals more learning. It is a quantitative not a qualitative model of learning. Clearly, the improvisation model of production also seems to do this: it seeks to involve more students for more of the activity. Yet one cannot ignore the fact that what students actually do in video production significantly differs from professional practice; and that key tasks, like editing, are not made equally available to all.

These differences affect how students learn about the media in a variety of ways. We will return to the larger questions about the *educational* dimensions of these modes of production in the final chapter. Initially, we want to trace some of the changes the soap went through in order to describe these differences in more detail. First of all, when it came to understanding narrative, for the class the major focus was on *content* not form: they were less concerned with the overall shape of the episode than the development of character and plot. For example, the plot line about 'the autistic relative' began in the first week with a scene depicting a family row. An elder brother with younger twins talked about having their cousin come and stay with them. The scene was broadly comic: there was much 'business' as the twins fought over computer games whilst the older brother valiantly struggled to prepare them for an arrival of an autistic child. There were two problems with this: first of all the actor playing the autistic child went on holiday; and secondly the older brother was out-acted by the comic duo of the twins. It was also pointed out in discussion that this family could not in reality be ignorant of the fact that they had an autistic relative; in which case, the comedy of winding up the older brother to explain the nature of disability just did not make any sense. This was in effect a modality judgement: because this first comic version was internally incoherent (according to the rules by which we tend to know about the mental health of our relatives), the class decided it would not fit into their drama.

To solve this problem, the professional characters, the doctor and the social worker, were invented. It should also be pointed out that because the doctor was played by a veiled Asian pupil it met the secondary need, frequently made explicit in class discussion, to have some 'positive images' to redress the perceived lack of realism of the token casting in *EastEnders*. (The contradictions here, in that they were merely reproducing the tokenism they objected to, seemed impossible to expose.) Nevertheless scene 2 (where the social worker explains to the doctor that he is going away and asks her to keep an eye on the autistic boy) was invented almost as a solution for the weaknesses of the early version of this plot line – and the twins were whittled down to one surly younger child. The earlier version had also avoided the potential conflict about having a relative to stay in favour of comedy, because in discussion the class felt that this was 'unrealistic'. We stimulated this debate because the students initially wanted a positive representation of autism without any negative aspects at all. This storyline was thus spread across two scenes, 2 and 5, and like all the storylines, set up tensions for the serial to explore. Having invented the doctor, the character could also be used in scene 8 to develop the drug habit storyline and give the 'good' sister opportunities to develop her character.

Surgeries and doctors thus have structural functions, although it should be clear by now that a large number of diverse influences went into the development of the narrative; and that decisions about it were also governed by a sense of dramatic propriety, itself subject to conceptions of realism. By contrast much media criticism and thus much media education has emphasised the formulaic and the generic as a means of explaining how soaps work[18]. This class ended up with a narrative that fulfilled the formal demands of structure and shape. However, this final version was very much 'arrived at', through a meandering process of improvisation and evolution; and it was determined by a scale of *dramatic* values. Not once during the production did the class discuss the soap in terms of generic features until we evaluated it afterwards. Indeed, I was so concerned about this that I attempted to intervene and asked whether 'a real soap would have as many storylines as this'. The retort immediately came back, 'no, but ours does'. Obviously it did not seem important in the midst of the creative chaos of production that the shape of the drama had mutated into a 'syncretic' form, mixing the genres of school drama with versions of soap. Yet despite the students' identification with the concerns of the drama throughout the production process, it would wrong to conclude that they were not also learning about media texts.

This was most apparent in the storyline about the beaten husband. Again, this emerged out of the kind of idealised 'positive images' discourse prevalent in schools: there is a strict logic which dictates that men can be victims too, and as the case of Lorena Bobbit was current in the news at the time, a wife-beater seemed an alternative but valid storyline. The problem is that any storyline which is invented to prove a theoretical nicety can become absurd in practice. In this instance, it was redeemed by the acting. Rukshana, the wife, enthralled the class with lively and energetic scenes screaming at a (giggly) husband and alternating between violent passion and angry humiliation. The interest was pure soap: intense domestic drama, a strong female role and melodrama verging on comedy. But the scene was not necessarily interpreted within the terms of this critical framework. The students were as intrigued by the qualities of the performance as by the pertinence of its style to the genre. Of course it is difficult to distinguish between the students' pleasure in the performance and the scene's function in the structure of the soap. However, their response does underline the ways in which students' interest in these kinds of activities is not going to be purely schematic. On the contrary, it is more likely to be motivated by the same dramatic pleasures that underpin the genre's popularity in the first place.

In general, the process of plot evolution was one of learning what to throw out. The genuinely experimental nature of improvisation and the tradition of informal discussion and criticism within Drama lessons meant that the 'organic' nature of the product seemed to evolve without much obvious dispute. For example, my shooting notes for the final day of filming show that the laundrette scene was in fact the elision of two scenes, that another two scenes were just not filmed at all and that an extra scene was invented. The class even deliberately filmed redundant scenes, something which would never happen professionally. In one of these, the eldest son of the prostitute talks to Joanne about her gossip concerning his mother.

The discipline of repeating performances from week to week, remembering blocking – crucial for the camera operators to reproduce successful work from earlier weeks – is quite intense; and should be balanced against any sense of failure about this erratic shooting schedule. Equally, and this is a characteristic of all successful productions, the number of happy accidents were legion. This process is not just limited to amateur work: there is the Spielberg story about the 'funny moment' where Indiana Jones uses a gun on a swordsman in an Egyptian marketplace because Harrison Ford allegedly had diarrhoea on that day. These kinds of events become incorporated into the myths that accrue around all accounts of production. In *Johnswood Heights*, the star Rukshana, who played the wife-beater, was absent when we filmed, so we used rehearsal footage instead – not that there was that much difference in quality, even if the ideas for the bloody ketchup and the cliff-hanger had to be left out. The most technically satisfactory shot was the pan around the shop, which established the location and caught the doctor skimming through the magazine rack, thus creating excellent continuity from the previous scene; yet this was completely unplanned – although it was immediately perceived as 'stylish'. For her part the doctor had just wanted to get out of PE. And so it went on.

Without labouring the point, it is difficult to know what to make of these sorts of 'mistakes'. On the one hand, purists might argue that they diminish the value of the activity, because playing at making a soap does not really put students through the real constraints of production – the overcoming of which would determine the educational success of the task. On the other hand, the speed with which students adapt and modify ideas shows that their understanding of what they want is ahead of what they are capable of making; and in any case, the broader benefit of production work is that it teaches a general level of understanding about the media, rather than specific technical skills. The intention, after all, is not to turn young people into professional producers. Traditionally, as we saw in chapters 3 and 5, this dilemma is resolved in the evaluation – in the sense students are seen to make of their own experience. In Drama, the tradition of self-assessment is different from that in Media Studies, significantly because of the credit given to discussion rather than writing. It is therefore to an account of the class's response to viewing the edited version that we will now turn.

Talking soaps

Besides ongoing talk about the project, I recorded two main discussions. One was with a small group of students which took place just after a long lesson of filming and was infused with enthusiasm about what they thought they had achieved. The second session was a whole class discussion after viewing the episode. The former was structured as an informal interview, the latter more formally organised. We had asked the class to divide into small groups and then consider *Johnswood Heights* under the following headings.

> Acting – characters, motive and status
> Realism
> Which TV soaps was it most like/unlike?
> What might happen in the next episode?
> Filming
> Storyline
> Editing – pace, cliffhanger

The groups then fed their comments into a whole class discussion. Besides these conversations, a group of students acting as editors made collective notes on the rushes which also shed light on their understanding of the whole project[19].

Although Drama is an 'older' subject than Media Studies, it has not solved the problem of how to encourage students to reflect on their learning. Like Media Studies, Drama GCSE requires the keeping of logs or diaries and suffers from similar anxieties about the weighting between reflection and product; about how to get students to develop their reflective skills; and about the place of that reflection within the learning process[20]. However, it is fair to say that Media Studies seems more obsessed with *writing down* reflective insights than Drama, where it is more common to reflect and criticise in class discussion. This may have been less of an issue with the age group we were teaching, not least because their work would not be submitted for examination purposes. As was suggested in the preceding chapter, one of the primary function of logs relates to assessment; they provide evidence for assessment when there is no shared understandings of ways to evaluate products. Nevertheless, as we have argued, reflection should be a broader process than simply writing a descriptive 'log'. In this respect the 'rigour' of the whole production described above must remain open to question. There were significant gaps in our production schedule, such as not having opportunities to look at filming in progress; and we did not build in opportunities for individual or group reflection as we went along. In addition to this, it is clear that class discussion – however perceptive the comments of some students – does not necessarily advance the learning of all students in equal ways – although the same can of course be said of writing[21].

However, one of the main virtues of discussion is that it establishes an explicit level of shared social meaning. It also encourages the use of argument and dialogue rather than description, a common failing of many logs. Nowhere was this more apparent than in the students' attempts to justify the ways in which their soap was 'true to life'. This mainly took the form of justifying 'mistakes'. Kofi, for example, pointed out that Loretta 'called me by my real name in one of the plays'. Similarly he recalled a moment where 'what she'd done once, she went, 'you're going out with my daughter, whatever her name is'. Another pupil maintained:

> Some bits that weren't convincing: you know Rukshana was hitting him on the head? The stick didn't actually make contact with his head.

A fourth 'error' noted here was the way in which one boy, Stephen, played three parts. Here, however, the students used *post hoc* rationalisations ingeniously. Because Stephen did not speak as one character, and was only an off-screen voice as another, it was possible to argue that these errors did not destroy the internal coherence of the performance. There was even a gap in continuity 'when Rukshana came home and beat up Ataur, because we didn't have that scene in'. Indeed, that scene, which importantly explained her motive for killing Ataur, was part of the elided laundrette scenes. In the end, as I said above, because Rukshana was absent, her scenes were composed of rehearsal footage. We could not, however, cut all of these into the final version because the rehearsal for the laundrette scene involved the students miming the use of washing machines (!). Therefore, the students argued, it would look odd when set against the 'real' laundrette footage.

These are all different examples of the ways in which the students measured their product implicitly against a model of soap realism. Their comments are in effect judgements about the modality both of their own and of broadcast soaps. Similar comments reflected on the quality of the lighting (on the whole poor, especially in two scenes shot against windows), and the sound, (also poor, both in technical terms, but more frequently because of poor projection and clarity from the actors). This is most apparent in the editors' notes: for example 'all the zooms are good ... light quality is very poor'. However, judgements about technical quality were inextricably bound up here with comments about the acting and staging: a comment like 'sound quality is alright, lots of energy' reflects a good mix of values. More obviously, the editors noted in relation to what became scene 12:

> Scene with David [prostitute's son]. First one is a bit too silent at times. Hunza [the younger brother] walk through the door ?!!?!! So did Joanne??!!! [here there were make-believe 'doors'].David is too calm, if someone called my Mom a prostitute I'd flip.

Here issues of filming, staging, verisimilitude and identification are all deployed to support the writer's notions of realism.

It was, however, the locations which became the most significant point of reference in what speedily became a sliding scale of reality values. These were praised or criticised in varying degrees. The surgery (the school medical room), the cafe (home economics), and the furniture in the child beater's house were all positively highlighted. In fact, a year 10 student who was watching the episode with us commented that this range of locations, rather than make-believe places within the drama studio, made the project different from their usual GCSE Drama projects. On the other hand, the tendency of Joanne to keep 'putting her hand down into the washing machines' undermined 'the way they used their body and their voices' to promote a convincing portrait. The actress's inability to use real props only showed up the limitations of her performance. By far the most damning comment came from Marcus, who in a flash of Brechtian insight, pointed out that:

> the shop scene [looked] realistic but there was one problem when that man walked through. The man sort of made it look as if we were all acting as kids.

The shop was a real shop round the corner from the school, but however convincing this might appear to be, its use was undermined by the intrusion of a *real* customer.

In general, although we had established the criteria for this discussion, the students kept on returning to this issue of reality. Of course, all these judgements belong to different repertoires of modality, or models of realism. Marcus's comment about the adult walking through a shop is on a different level from comments about the action not being realistic because the actors do not talk loudly enough. As has been noted, the term 'realism' has various meanings in different contexts[22]; it is after all, a historically loaded word[23]. However, the nature of the discussion meant that this idea could not be followed through and the criteria for judging realism were left unquestioned.

At the same time, this level of criticism is similar to the ways in which people talk about soaps in general. Although the genre has become a staple of our oral culture[24], and it features heavily in the tabloids and so on, it seems as if everyday discussion about soaps, particularly amongst young people, frequently follows the same line of debate: the extent to which episodes are or are not realistic[25]. Of course I am not suggesting that we commonly discuss the lighting or how well the actors speak, but that the 'unrealistic' nature of the storylines (or in the case of *Neighbours*, the sets), are often put forward as evidence of the genre's lack of realism. An example of this took place in the small group discussion, where Saheda commented on the current state of the marriage between the Asian couple in *EastEnders* (Sanjay and Geeta have physically separated), arguing that 'it wouldn't happen in a real [i.e. Asian] family, I can tell you from experience'.

If this is the case, then it seems clear that the same level of critical debate had been transferred to account for *Johnswood Heights*. It was interesting that even though these students totally 'made up' their soap, their critical appraisal of it was still governed by the same values adhering to 'professional' examples of the genre. This has two implications for the study of soaps in media education. The first is that, as we have seen, the composition of the students' soap is *necessarily* going to imitate the conventions of the genre. Attempts to be 'more realistic' or promote innovative storylines will inevitably become as compromised as attempts to be different are in *EastEnders* or *Brookside*. Thus, a student commented that:

> You wouldn't really see a prostitute on a real life soap like *EastEnders* and things like that. Maybe you know just a small appearance or something, but not far to show how her life's going, and you'd have kids who hate their mum being a prostitute and things like that. It's quite realistic at some points.

This is both self-contradictory and untrue. There have been similar storylines on *EastEnders* just like this: indeed, this is exactly the sort of social concern the producers use to justify the drama's wider value. This student's claim that '*our* soap is more realistic, more true to life' is very much part of the discourse of creativity that surrounds practical work: it attempts to stake a claim for originality. However, the constraints of the genre work against this. Inevitably, they limit the sort of innovations that viewers claim they want in order to make soaps more real. Ultimately, the 'more realistic' soap may be as idealistic as is the 'progressive text', beloved of seventies film theorists: they are both impossible ambitions.

Secondly, if the students' discussion about their product is similar to the sort of informal discussion they might have about real soaps, then what can we claim for the role of Media Studies here? One of the aims of the subject is to make students more 'critical' about the media. Yet the students' discussion of this project would suggest that the barrier between formal criticism and casual conversation is lower than is normally credited. Students are obviously equipped to be critical about the media through their experiences as consumers. Projects like this should be seen more as building upon that knowledge and experience rather than offering new and different perspectives. The endless microscopic analysis of modality that formed the substance of the debrief conversation does, of course, need to be taken further through the media curriculum. Yet it also needs to be taken on its own terms, as part of a popular discourse about the representation of social reality; as well as (more obviously) a constructive technical commentary on the skills (such as acting and filming) which are needed to reproduce that reality.

The final observation I want to offer on this whole class debrief is that it made obvious the partial perspectives that students necessarily adopt when reflecting upon practical work. We have already touched upon the ramifications of using simulations, with their concentration on specific roles and tasks within the larger frame. This individualistic focus is made even more extreme by the self-obsession that seems to be endemic to all kinds of performers. As the students at times rather tartly pointed out, each and every one of them paid enormous attention to the scenes they were in, at times to the exclusion of others. This again raises questions about the extent to which all the members of a group have equal opportunities to learn on this kind of project. As a method, this 'democratic' approach can have as many advantages as disadvantages in this respect. Thus, Maha quickly pointed out that in all 'the scenes I was in ... some people were shouting and it went a bit wrong'. This anxiety about her performance seemed to completely filter out her ability to talk about any other aspect of the project until very near the end of the lesson. I do not think this self-consciousness can be attributed to adolescence either: performances tend to make performers in general acutely self aware.

More positively, Natasha seemed to be the only student to point out that in the drug dealing scene the editing broke the basic rules of continuity. She walked on screen from left *and* right, although she was only making one journey. Obviously, the extreme attention we all pay to our own performances can result in more detailed observations. In this instance, these can be worked into a more general and theoretical set of principles. Watching oneself on film also foregrounds an awareness of the body, which is more evident in Drama anyway. This is perhaps also at odds with the traditional emphasis in media education on denying those same elements of self-consciousness in favour of distanced critical commentary. Altogether there is a disjuncture here between the ways in which both subjects value the learner's sense of themselves, the way that they construct their individual *subjectivity* – an argument we will take up towards the end of this chapter. Here I want simply to note that Natasha's self-awareness is the basis for further learning. 'Critical' awareness stems from it. This is quite different from a model of disengaged, dispassionate and distanced criticism. Either way, this kind of reflection on performance needs to synthesise students' strong personal identifications with individual characters and storylines with disengagement and critical impartiality. Interestingly enough, the small group discussion drew attention to this dual perspective, particularly through the ways in which students contrasted themselves as soap viewers and as soap makers; and it is to this that we now turn.

Children and adults

Marcus' amusing comment quoted above – about the real adult walking through the shop – points to a crucial element in the modality of their soap which goes to the heart of the genre's appeal amongst young people. Soaps give young people the opportunity to 'live' adult lives. Initially, Kofi countered Marcus' remark by loyally claiming that 'everyone does seem to be like an adult'; but Rukshana argued that it was simply a question of consistency: 'because we didn't have any adults in the soap, only children and that's why we never thought about [it].'

It is strange that this rather entertaining dilemma is not more common in Drama. Although I have no statistical evidence for this, I suspect that most improvisations must entail children acting as adults; and if the un-reality of this was overwhelming, Drama would seem more like make-believe play than anything worthwhile. We will be exploring in greater depth the claim that such acting develops students' understanding of the adult world; but we will begin with a lengthy section of the small group discussion which allows the students to offer their thoughts on the pertinence of this process:

Shofna:	Usually in soaps there are some good bits and some bad ones. But, I mean, in our one there's everything ...
Marcus:	And everyone's enjoying themselves.
Saheda:	Yeah.
JSG:	What do you mean?
Saheda:	They're having fun playing the characters.
JSG:	Why is that enjoyable to do?
Saheda:	Because you're playing an older person and you want to be mature. And really ... when you're playing it, you feel like, 'I can act like this, when I grow older', but maybe everything ...
Shofna:	Moving around.
JSG:	So maybe you could become a prostitute when you grow up? [general laughter]
Saheda:	No I mean like ... you have, you know, experience, experience like what's happening to a prostitute, and stuff. Maybe they don't do it because they want to do it, maybe they have a reason for doing it.
JSG:	So by acting all these roles you find these things out?
All:	Yeah, yeah
Saheda:	You find out what they really feel like inside. Because you're playing a character you have to, sort of, feel something about it ...
Shofna:	You just actually, you get your normal selves and you like, you act and do your age. But it's like, it's more fun, when you're someone older or younger.

Here the students are explicit about the fact that acting as adults is an important and significant part of the learning process. They argue that school Drama can in some way enhance their understanding of potential adult lives; although the fact that they themselves may not live these lives (for example, as a prostitute) supports the idea that such acting develops a liberal humanist understanding of other people's 'problems'- 'Maybe they don't do it because they want to do it, maybe they have a reason for doing it.'

However, they also argue that playing grown-ups is 'fun' and acts as a way of trying out adult roles: 'you feel like "I can act like this when I grow older"', or 'it's more fun when you're someone older or younger'. Here identity and certainly social interaction is conceptualised in terms of the central learning theory of Drama – which is, in essence, that we are all of social actors of one kind or another. However, it is only adults who are seen as real social actors: and childhood is, by implication, an opportunity to rehearse the roles one will occupy in later life. It is the desire of these students to play out the real dramas of adult life that lies behind much of their enthusiasm for the project. Indeed, this may explain some of the vicarious pleasure we all take in problem dramas.

On the other hand, the activity of acting established pleasures in its own right which almost stem from the process of identity management:

Saheda:	It's quite hard to take on different characters. Sometimes when you're doing acting you can forget about what's happening, you know, like, you can forget what's happening next.
JSG:	Like little children's play?
Saheda:	Wearing make-up, and clothes and high heels and things like that ...

JSG: So is what you're doing like that?

Saheda: Sort of ... yeah, but not all..

Akbar: I think everyone feels like that when they are acting another role.

Marcus: That they're all glamorous, thinking like, 'do I look good enough for this scene?'

JSG: But not everyone can be an actor in life so what do you get out of it?

Saheda: You have a thrill out of doing it because you feel like you're getting your chance to do this.

There is an important ambiguity here. On the one hand, acting is seen to be childish, 'wearing make-up, and clothes and high heels and things like that'; but on the other it is validated by the world of the theatre or Hollywood, by glamour and thrills. It gives you opportunities to explore other lives, 'the chance to do this'; but it is also confusing. As we will discuss below, it creates a 'phenomenological problem', being both yourself (the actor) and another person (the character); and it is challenging to remember all the right moves for both people, as Saheda's opening comment above suggests. On the whole, the students resisted my attempts to define what they had achieved as being a more grown-up version of childhood play, not least because the discipline of performance required adult self-control:

Akbar: It's like, when you see it, other people's [performances], you know how professional people do it. It comes like that ... not like little kids playing about with video cameras ...

JSG: What do you mean different from kids messing about with video cameras?

Akbar: You don't actually have two people, two cameras and you're showing each point of view of the other people, what one person is saying to the other person ... if you like. I used to play with cameras when I was little, just walk about pointing at everything but not specific things.

JSG: But does it look like kids playing or a real soap?

Akbar: I think it looks like a real soap 'cos everything's been planned well and connected together.

This last point was reiterated by other students at other stages in the conversation; the planning and the interconnectedness of the dramas and the process had clearly made an impact. However, Akbar's deliberate distinction between 'little kids playing about with video cameras' and our production process reinforces the same distinction between play acting and learning about adult life. It may be that this group resorted to a language of 'maturity' and adult values as a way of justifying something they found pleasurable but which did not appear to have any obvious instrumental or vocational value. It may be that they had internalised the values of the subject as a way of explaining the abstruse nature of learning in drama.

However, they also connected this dialogue between the worlds of the adult and the child with the nature of watching and following soaps:

Shofna: Another thing is, its like, you're watching all kinds of soap opera and you're thinking ... 'somehow I wish I was this, or I was doing that', but then ... you get the chance of doing it.

JSG: What do you mean, you wish -

Shofna: Sometimes you see something and you think, 'I wish I was in her place' or something like that.

When pushed for an example, Shofna gives an example of how her younger sister wanted to be like somebody in *Home and Away*, and not an anecdote from her experience. However much we identify with the roles in soaps and play with the positions the narratives offer, it is a difficult thing to admit to; far easier to blame a younger member of the family[26]. Marcus does go so far as to speculate that 'it's really fun to work as an older person seeing what it's like, how you're treated and everything'; but although this comment follows Shofna's observations here, I think he is referring to the process of acting rather than that of watching the dramas of soap. Nevertheless, the students do clearly compare the processes of identification and character modelling that are common to their experiences both of consuming and of producing imaginative fictions.

Learning through imagined experience

This phrase is taken from the title of a book on drama education at Key Stage 3[27]. It sums up the sense of mystery that seems to be embedded in many philosophies of drama education. Learning *per se* is clearly not a simple, observable phenomenon; it is, to be equally obvious, complicated. On the other hand, there is a traditional preference in writing about drama education for obscurity and quasi-mystical rhetoric. Imagined experience, is, for example, a contradiction in terms: and the actual process of learning *through* it is likened in the book and elsewhere, to a magical and transcendental moment of illumination, not something everyday and pedestrian. As the author, Jonathan Neelands, observes 'because Drama uses words and human actions for its expression there tends to be no written record or evidence of "work"' – an absence which can create no small problem for teachers. Nevertheless, in practice, both as a method of learning and as an important part of the progressive tradition within English, Drama remains a central part of all children's educational experiences. I want to end this chapter, therefore, by tracing some of the subject's theoretical principles in the context of the soap project, in order to begin a dialogue between media education and Drama that can build on the strengths of both.

We will begin with the notion of 'imagined experience' which, as the students implied above, may have explained their interest and pleasure in the project. Playing at being adults, exploring grown-up lives from grown-up points of view appears to reflect the philosophy of drama education that is apparent in the HMI report:

> [Drama] relies on the human ability to pretend to be someone or something else. Through this act of imagination, pupils can explore how people in particular circumstances might behave now and at different times and in different societies. Though imaginary, the exploration can be experienced and shared *as if real*[28].(my emphasis)

On the other hand, it could be argued that the positions Saheda, Shofna and Marcus advanced showed no more than the ability to internalise and reproduce the values of the subject. Saheda, for example, argued that when 'you're playing an older person ... you want to be mature ... when you're playing it you feel like "I can act like this when I grow older"' – which would seem to offer a perfect description of 'how people in particular circumstances might behave now'. In several respects, the students' discussion bears out ways in which such an 'exploration can be experienced and shared as if real'. The students' experience of Drama appears to have taught them its theories of learning.

Alternatively, it could be argued that our analysis of *Johnswood Heights* has demonstrated the ways in which it is imitative of the conventions of the genre; and that it merely reflects the students' ability to reproduce those conventions. In other words, it is not the students' sense of 'real life' and its problems that is being explored, but the *mediated* or *represented* nature of their conception of that reality – even though the students themselves would not conceptualise their project in these terms. To re-cast the work in this way is to move the emphasis away from a naive belief in the creativity of young people, towards an understanding of the codes or structures of dramatic forms. This is in fact very much a contemporary move in drama education, and one which has explicitly drawn on media education[29].

In summary then, there would appear to be three levels to the idea of 'learning through imagined experience'. First of all, there is the psychological dimension, in which students explore what it is like to be another person through empathy and 'identification'. Secondly, we are requiring students to develop understandings of motive and character – and even of other models of human interaction, for example those based on ideas like 'role' (itself, of course, a theatrical metaphor). As this level relies on *explanations* of human behaviour, and is essentially linguistic, it is fair to label it discursive. Thirdly we have the generic level: the reproduction of the forms and conventions of mediated realities.

Traditionally it has been the first approach which has preoccupied theorists of drama education. Bolton talks of 'the peculiar socio-psychological structure of the medium of drama ... [in which] the participants adopt an 'as-if' mental set, an imaginative frame of mind'[30]. However, it is not clear how this works; nor indeed are there substantial empirical accounts of drama education, in the mode of *Watching Media Learning*, which one might use to begin to theorise this process. Hornbrook has outlined the links between such theories and broader movements in Western philosophy; but in fact these kinds of ideas have popular currency primarily because of their connections with prevalent models of child development. Thus, Drama is seen as an extension of childhood play and an organised curriculum space in which to develop language and narrative skills. This is basically an application of Piagetian ideas that children explore the outside world through play: to quote Neelands again, 'stories and play are the natural means by which young people process abstract thought'[31]. However, although this approach is common to much English teaching, particularly of younger children, such a debate is underrepresented in discussions of media education. Not least because Media Studies initially developed as a subject for older students, the notion that it might involve 'playing' at the media, either in terms of soap or cartoon narratives or, as in this instance, playing out roles in media production itself, has rarely been explored.

In fact, it seems quite tenable to describe *Johnswood Heights* – like many other media production activities, such as the *Neighbours* photoplay in Chapter 2 – in terms of play[32]. The students are playing at filming (see Akbar's comments above on kids playing with cameras); at adult lives (see Saheda's comments on being grown up); and in putting on soaps. These are all accurate (if partial) accounts of what happened here – and indeed what happens in media production work much of the time. To pursue this analogy properly we would then have to account for the quality of the learning that has gone on in psychological terms; but there is little in the history of media education to allow for this. Learning objectives are specified in terms of 'key concepts', not in terms of the relationship of the media to the development of the child. Indeed, as we have argued, the elements of imagination and the subjective pleasures of learning are subordinated to rationalistic forms of intellectual thought. Part of the problem here is that it is difficult to make the case that media work is anything other than a sub-section of other forms of dramatic play except for the dimension of using technology. Media-play could therefore be distinguished from drama-play by virtue of the ability to record and re-present oneself and others; and in this respect, it could be argued that media technology has led to a significant change in the potential of children's play, in that it extends their ability to reflect upon their own identities and upon the genres they enjoy.

Drama education has built on notions of early play to develop a whole theory of learning. However, it can easily be made to look rather silly for its claims about *how* one learns through play as well as about precisely *what* can be learnt[33]. In particular, Hornbrook has castigated the work of Heathcote and Bolton for their mystification of drama learning: playing at being Nicaraguan peasants is not, he suggests, a reasonable way of learning anything about peasantry, Nicaragua or the unequal distribution of social power. From this point of view, one has to be sceptical about the students' claims here that they learnt about the problems of autism or prostitution and that this therefore validates their work on this project.

Hornbrook has also traced the reduction of Drama to a learning medium, a series of techniques and arcane processes, some of which (such as hotseating) we have described. This is of course the area from which media education has drawn the most. What lies at the heart of using drama as a means of learning (about almost anything) is the concept of *role*, which we have touched on throughout our discussion. This concept may offer an insight into what precisely one might be learning through play. Unfortunately however, the concept of role is extremely complicated and derives from a number of discrete areas of study which seem to have become confused in much drama education theory. First of all, there is the study of actors and acting: a body of work which is strangely absent from drama education writing[34]. As we have seen, it is a commonplace in these theories that being an actor poses a phenomenological problem, in that the actor is both themselves and the character they are performing; one cannot talk about the fictional character without taking into account the 'real' person[35]. We have described the mutated Stanislavskian model of character development we used in the soap project, which is no doubt used in Drama classes much of the time. The students were both developing themselves as performers, as comments about the rigours of acting on camera testify, as well as developing the characters themselves, as comments about the problems of being 'grown-up' indicate. Bolton describes this as being 'both participant and percipient'[36] – although while this might make a clever rhyme, it is ultimately far from illuminating. We need to develop models of learning which allow students to structure a *dialogue* between these positions – of engagement and distance – and to reflect on the ways in which they interact, if we are to give the phrase more than literary value.

Ultimately, all theories of acting have to be predicated on contemporary notions of identity and social relations if they are to be coherent. Stanislavski developed the idea of 'the through line', which refers to where the character 'came from' and how she or he possesses internal coherence. This is one of the most important markers of modality: we do not find characters who change suddenly convincing. Psychological motivation is central to all post-nineteenth century theories of realism. In effect, actors are convincing if they possess this coherence, because we expect characters to perform according to these notions of the self – as opposed to other, historical models of the actor, such as stereotypes, *Commedia del'arte* or masks, which carry with them different notions of identity. Indeed, this model has been developed further to describe 'being a person' in terms of playing a social role: from this perspective, acting is a metaphor for the ways in which we 'perform' in jobs or in the family and so on. One of the most well known and popular theories of this kind is Erving Goffman's notion of 'impression management'. These ideas have significantly influenced common sense views about what it is to be a person today[37].

To what extent did the process of character generation that our students went through actually mobilise these theories of character and identity, either implicitly or explicitly? We might well ask whether it is reasonable (or possible) to expect year 9 students to deconstruct concepts of identity so that they can be critical of the construction of characters in twentieth century soaps. At one level, this would seem absurd. However, it is possible to trace the process of character growth, which is similar to the process of debating a character's 'reality', in the debrief discussion. This is closer to Britton's notion of 'the spectator role' in children's writing. He argues that it is through the mixture of distance and engagement in writing imaginative fiction, where the writer can adopt a number of different characters and positions, that she or he develops an understanding of those positions and characters[38] – an idea that is clearly similar to that of learning through role in drama. However, the crucial point of difference must remain the element of distanciation. In media education, this takes place during the process of reflection and writing. There is no doubt that the dramatic aspect of projects like this is responsible for a significant part of their final appearance. Nevertheless, developing a product exclusively through drama education techniques runs the risk of excluding important learning outcomes that arise from the move to a more distanced perspective – such as an explicit grasp of questions about the form and style of soaps.

The second implication about roles and learning in role is more general. This project, typically, required students to learn about soaps from a range of perspectives – as actor, character, soap writer/director and student. Those perspectives were effectively constructed in terms of roles. Much of the work in this book and indeed much media education uses simulated settings as starting points for production; and inevitably these utilise models of dramatic role playing. However, many media simulations do not consistently play out roles through to the end in the way this kind of project did. Often they merely use the dramatic situation as a motivational starting point. Traditionally, drama education has not interrogated learning in role. It has been content with a romantic progressivism, in which 'true knowing is what you know you feel'[39]. However, the methodologies of simulation and the concomitant emphasis on group or team work are almost axiomatic to all forms of training, and indeed to the pedagogy of many modern academic subjects, not least Media Studies. Nevertheless, simulation is not a magical process, as much drama education seems to imagine; nor does the belief that it somehow enhances natural development help an analysis of its specific educational potential.

We have almost come full circle. At the beginning of this chapter I argued against a model of learning about soaps as generic formulae on the grounds that this approach ignored what viewers actually enjoy about the genre. The project we set up overcame these difficulties primarily through developing students' imaginative involvement in the production; and yet, as a consequence, it appears to lack a necessary degree of critical reflection and distance. Nevertheless, it may be that the practical work here was more effective in enabling students to explore the salient features of the genre – and particularly the question of realism – in a way that traditional media work is not.

However, we are still left with a series of unresolved questions about this more subjective approach. The gap remains between the kind of academic knowledge about the genre embodied in Media Studies, and the way we all learn about soaps through watching them or indeed play acting them. If there is a solution to this problem it may begin with a more integrated timetable where the techniques of studying the topic in a 'drama' or a 'media' or an 'English' way are not so isolated from one another. Practical work of the kind I have described in this chapter clearly draws upon and develops a wide range of skills, knowledge and cultural competencies – although it may well require a more general change in attitudes towards education if its potential is to be fully recognised.

Notes

1   See Richards (1990).
2   Cambridge A & B 'A' level syllabi.
3   As exemplified by Bob Ferguson's (1981) emphasis on the cognitive dimension to practical work: see Chapter 5.
4   See Ang (1985) for an academic critique of this concept.
5   The figures are summarised from Dickson (1994). Unfortunately there is no equivalent information for Drama.
6   See Willis (1990) and Buckingham (1993c).
7   Wollen (1991).
8   See Buckingham (1990), Buckingham and Sefton-Green (1994).
9   Hornbrook (1989), see Chapter 4.
10 Hornbrook *ibid.*
11 See Buckingham (1987b).
12 See Jordan (1981).
13 Hotseating probably has its origins in the formalist devices of distanciation promulgated by Brecht or in the Stanislavskian technique, but which has become standardised as one of the techniques in the Dorothy Heathcote repertoire. See Bolton (1986) or Hornbrook *op cit.* for a sympathetic and critical (respectively) explication of these techniques.
14 See Harrop (1992).
15 See Buckingham (1987b).
16 See Dyer et al (1981), Hobson (1982), Allen (1985) and Buckingham (1987b).
17 This internal 'democracy' also has to be contextualised within the power relations of the school. Potentially one of the most catastrophic problems the production faced was when we got to this stage! The group of four students who had been selected by the class teacher to act as editors, who had previewed the rushes and made detailed notes, were suddenly whittled down to two the day before we started editing because they were suddenly required to attend sports day. Of the two we were left with, one had a weak heart and one was excluded!
18 See the diagrams and charts in Geraghty (1981), Jordan (1981) and Buckingham (1987b).
19 See note 17 above. Only one of these four, Saheda, did the editing. She was joined by the excluded pupil on the day. He contributed well to the actual editing but had not been involved in the prior process of making up the edit list.
20 See Grahame (1990) and Buckingham and Sefton-Green (1994) for a detailed discussion of this problem in media education.
21 Quite how one could 'measure' the different values of talk and writing over a period of time in different kinds of production is difficult to imagine, though see Buckingham and Sefton-Green (1994), Chapter 8, for an attempt at this.
22 See Sefton-Green (1990), Jhally and Lewis (1992).

23 Williams (1976).
24 See Fiske (1987)
25 See Buckingham (1987b) and (1993b).
26 See Buckingham (1993b) for a thorough analysis of these discursive moves.
27 Neelands (1992).
28 HMI (1989) quoted in Neelands *ibid.*
29 See Hornbrook's (1991) use of media education key concepts.
30 Bolton (1989).
31 Neelands (1992).
32 The most developed study of drama and play is in Courtney (1974).
33 Hornbrook (1989).
34 Ironically Bolton (1986) does talk of using some of Stanislavski's exercises as a form of self -development. See Way (1967).
35 Harrop *op cit.*
36 Bolton (1986).
37 Goffman (1969).
38 Britton (1970).
39 The quote is Bolton's in Hornbrook (1989).

Chapter 8

Conclusion

The work we have analysed in this book has been diverse, both in terms of the age groups and curriculum contexts, and in terms of the media technologies and genres that have been employed. More fundamentally, each of the case studies has sought to address a rather different conceptual issue, or set of related issues – although there has inevitably been a degree of overlap between them.

In this concluding chapter, we seek to draw together some of the most significant themes that have arisen in the case studies. We begin by locating our approach in the context of broader debates about pedagogy; and by re-stating some of the fundamental emphases that have informed our account of teaching and learning. We then move on to a discussion of three very general themes which have traversed our otherwise quite disparate case studies. We look first at the social and political dimensions of learning through media production; secondly at the ways in which students acquire skills and competencies as users of 'media language'; and thirdly at the role of production in developing students' conceptual understandings of the media.

As with the more specific issues addressed in the case studies, this discussion raises questions and dilemmas which by their very nature are almost bound to remain unresolved. As we have indicated, it has not been our intention here to offer accounts of good practice, or a series of recipes for successful teaching. Indeed, we would argue that successful teaching is not something that can be brought about simply through the application of abstract rules or prescriptions. Nevertheless, we do feel it is possible to offer some general *principles* on which future work in this area might be based; and it is with a statement of these principles that this chapter will conclude.

Pedagogy, teaching and learning

The past two decades have been a period of growing confidence in media education. Despite tensions and occasional setbacks – most notably in relation to the National Curriculum and in teacher education – media education has continued to expand at all levels of the education system. New curriculum materials and handbooks for teachers have become available, and there are authoritative statements of the conceptual basis of the field that enjoy widespread respect. Yet as we have argued, media educators have been much slower to develop a *theory of teaching and learning* which would provide a basis for devising and evaluating classroom strategies. Books about media education have typically been preoccupied with defining the *content* of the subject, often in the form of simplified accounts of academic research. Although there has been a considerable amount of stirring rhetoric about classroom practice, much of it has been highly utopian. And while there is now almost a standard repertoire of 'effective' teaching strategies, there has been remarkably little discussion of the fundamental principles on which they might be based – or indeed, any real evidence to support the claim that such strategies do in fact represent 'good practice'.

The advent of classroom research in recent years has begun to remedy this absence. Yet this book and those that have preceded it have sought to do rather more than simply describe or document what happens in classrooms. On the contrary, they have raised fundamental questions about the aims and methods of media teaching, which in many ways challenge the positions of earlier media educators. However, in some respects, the broader debate about *pedagogy* – that is, about *theories of teaching and learning* – in media education has remained conspicuous by its absence. The often heated exchanges that surfaced in journals like *Screen* and *Screen Education* in the 1980s[1] have given way to what might easily be mistaken for consensus. Looking back, those earlier debates do appear remarkably polarised – and indeed extremely parochial. Evidence from classroom practice was at best anecdotal; and there was very little sense of a wider world of educational theory and debate. Yet, here again, we feel that there are fundamental questions to which media educators must return – even if we would wish to challenge the terms in which they were raised, and the conclusions which were reached.

In many respects, the debate about pedagogy in media education has been framed in terms of a fundamental opposition that recurs both in academic and in popular debate. Thus, in one corner, we have 'progressive pedagogy' – the 'child-centred' approach, based on notions of 'readiness' and 'discovery learning'; while in the other, we have 'traditional pedagogy' – based on the 'rote learning' of a given body of skills and information. This opposition is one that is routinely defined and reinforced through a process of mutual caricature, from which academics and teachers themselves have been far from immune. Thus, the progressive approach is condemned for its liberal sloppiness, its lazy celebration of children's experience, and ultimately for its rejection of *teaching*. Meanwhile, the traditional approach is depicted as a form of educational terrorism, in which children are 'drilled' and intimidated into acquiring arbitrary, disembodied fragments of information. If progressive pedagogy is accused of abandoning the authority of the teacher, traditional pedagogy is accused of abusing it. If traditional pedagogy is condemned for ignoring children's own perspectives, progressive pedagogy is condemned for simply leaving them where they already are. And so the debate goes on.

The problems here are not simply to do with the degree of polarisation, or with the insistence on either/or choices. We would argue that these rhetorical constructions of 'progressive' and 'traditional' pedagogy – whether positive or negative – are in fact a very inadequate representation of the nature of classroom practice. Of course, this is not to suggest that such characterisations are simply false; on the contrary, they are extremely influential, not least in terms of how teachers themselves account for what they do. Nevertheless, it is very doubtful whether 'progressive' or 'traditional' pedagogy actually *exist* in the terms in which they are typically described. There are numerous empirical studies which suggest that the realities of both approaches are much more contradictory and much less uniform than the debate itself might lead one to suppose[2]. It is not simply that, in practice, teachers will consciously combine a variety of approaches – or that their attempts to meet the needs of their students will actively require them to do this. It is also that neither position would seem to offer a theory that helps us to understand the ways in which students *learn* – and indeed, the ways in which teachers might enable this to happen. Students, we would argue, do not learn *simply* by 'doing' or 'discovering' things, any more than they learn *simply* by being instructed or told.

In the case of media education, this debate between traditional and progressive pedagogy has taken on an explicitly political form. Thus, it is possible to identify a *radical* version of traditional pedagogy, which has remained highly influential. From this perspective, the teacher's task is essentially to transmit a body of 'radical information' to the students, and thereby to alert them to the operations of the 'dominant ideology'[3]. On the other hand, there is a form of progressivism – albeit one which is often more a matter of rhetoric than reality. This approach emphasises the students' expertise as users of the media, and regards the teacher as little more than a 'senior colleague' who engages them in an 'equal dialogue'[4]. In the case of practical work, these positions give rise to two quite distinct approaches. From the radical perspective, practical work is regarded primarily as a means of demonstrating pre-determined theoretical principles – as in the case of 'deconstruction exercises'; while a progressivist approach emphasises the possibilities for creative self-expression (see Chapter 1). Yet despite their differences, advocates of both positions seem to share a faith in the ease with which teachers can 'politicise' their students – whether this is seen as a matter of rigorous training in the skills of objective analysis, or of enabling students to 'find a voice' in which they can express themselves in truly authentic ways.

In practice, however, there are often some significant contradictions here. Len Masterman's work, for example, shifts uneasily between a comparatively traditional conception of knowledge and a highly progressivist set of prescriptions for classroom practice[5]. On the one hand, the teacher is the agent of 'demystification', the bearer of 'hidden' but nevertheless objective knowledge that is apparently denied to the 'mystified' students; yet on the other, the teacher is merely a participant in an 'equal dialogue', whose perspective cannot be privileged. These tensions are partly effaced by a familiar form of rhetoric, in which the teacher is cast as the liberator, challenging the dominant ideology to which her students are helplessly enthralled – arguments which are typical of so-called 'critical pedagogy'[6]. Perhaps the abiding fantasy here is that students will somehow recognise their 'real' interests when they are revealed to them – or that when they 'find a voice' they will use it to say things that we as teachers judge to be politically correct.

As we have argued, practical work has served as a major focus of these contradictions and anxieties. Compared with the safety of critical analysis, practical work is bound to be much less controllable. It is here that teachers have to hand over the 'means of production' to their students, and to live with the consequences. As we have indicated, media educators' reluctance to cede this control has led to a widespread suspicion of practical work, and to prescriptions for classroom practice that are often highly reductive. In the process, a series of fundamental theoretical oppositions have been invoked which are profoundly problematic – oppositions between theory and practice, between rationality and emotion, between objectivity and subjectivity, between the cognitive and the experiential. Here again, the problem is not simply that these oppositions are theoretically questionable, nor indeed that the central terms are so ill-defined; it is also that they fail to provide an adequate account of what is actually taking place in students' *uses* of dominant media forms.

Towards a theory of teaching and learning

In many respects, this book is part of a continuing attempt to find a way beyond this polarisation between traditional and progressive pedagogies. Our aim has not been simply to accumulate another set of descriptive accounts, but to analyse practice in the light of broader theoretical concerns. Both implicitly and at times explicitly, this book has sought to develop a *grounded theory* of teaching and learning in media education – a theory that addresses the dilemmas and problems of everyday practice, but which also suggests potential alternatives.

The aim of any theory of teaching and learning is to explain the relationship between what learners *already* know and what it is that teachers need to teach. In the case of media education, it is fair to say that the former has largely been neglected in favour of the latter. We still understand very little about what children at different ages might 'know' about the media, and hence what they might possibly be capable of learning – although we would hazard the assertion that both have been significantly underestimated. A developmental theory of 'ages and stages' might tell us when children are ready to learn, and hence give us some idea about what we might teach at what time; and in this respect, it might provide the basis for a series of attainment targets – if indeed such statements are required.

Yet this kind of developmental theory can only ever be part of the story. As psychologists themselves have increasingly recognised, such theories are almost inevitably normative and mechanical: they do not account for the diversity of what children know at a particular age, or the different *ways* in which they can be said to know it. Perhaps more significantly, they do not address the fact that 'knowledge' is itself a social and ideological construct. In the case of media education, for example, certain kinds of knowledge are accorded privileged status, while others are implicitly rejected as somehow invalid or irrelevant. 'Popular' knowledge about the media – such as the encyclopaedic information about comics or soap opera stars which is possessed by their fans – undoubtedly has a lower status than 'academic' knowledge about the work of particular theorists or researchers, although both are clearly *forms* of knowledge. Finally, developmental theories do not in themselves necessarily illuminate the day-to-day business of *teaching*. Teaching, we would argue, is not simply about waiting until children are 'ready' – in which case they will probably learn anyway. On the contrary, it is about actively moving students on to things they do not yet know. What is needed, then, is a theory that will help us to make interventions, to structure activities and to evaluate students' work in such a way that they can revise and move beyond what they already know.

Our broader theoretical concerns in this book have converged around three fundamental themes, which will be explored in greater detail in the following three sections of this chapter. These might be summarised as follows:

1. The social dimensions of media learning.

We have assumed that learning is not merely a psychological process that happens inside individuals' heads, but on the contrary occurs within specific social contexts. These contexts are simultaneously inter-personal and institutional. They are characterised by power-relationships between students and other students; between students and teachers; and between teachers and the wider structures which determine their practice (such as the management of schools, the process of public examinations and the overall direction of educational policy). In the case of media education, as in any other area of the curriculum, these relations of power are *both* reproduced *and* challenged through specific forms of educational practice, however consciously or inadvertently on the part of those concerned.

2. Learning 'media languages'.
While we would accept that the metaphor of 'media language' is far from unproblematic, we have argued that the ability to use media technologies – and to 'write' in the verbal and visual languages of the modern media – is a fundamental dimension of any contemporary definition of literacy. Nevertheless, the question of how students might *learn* to use and control 'media language' has been an underlying focus of concern throughout our case studies. This has taken us into some highly problematic debates, for example about the relationships between technology and creativity, between linguistic form and content, and between language skills and the social purposes of language use – and in many cases, we have been led to question the terms of those debates themselves.

3. Production and conceptual understanding.
As we have argued, it is not enough that students learn to 'read' and 'write' in contemporary media forms; they also have to learn to reflect upon the nature of reading and writing themselves, and on the ways in which meanings are socially produced and circulated. While we have regarded conceptual learning of this kind as a central and indispensable aim, we have also sought to question its nature and its privileged status. As we have indicated, conceptual learning cannot be divorced from the social contexts and relationships in which it is acquired; or from the emotional investments students make, both in the media and in their relationships with others. Critical reflection must be seen as a crucial aspect of the production process, and not simply as a means of assessment; yet the question of how it is to be encouraged and achieved remains highly problematic.

These three broad themes will be developed in the following sections of this chapter. In the process, we hope to move beyond some of the rather inadequate dichotomies we have outlined, and to suggest a new agenda for future debate.

1. The social dimensions of media learning

Like many kinds of teaching in many subjects, media production activities inevitably raise larger questions about the unequal distribution of power in society – not only in terms of their overt 'content', but also in terms of the production process itself. This is, on one level, a conscious and deliberate strategy; yet it is an issue that is raised even in the most apparently 'open-ended' production activities. This is apparent, for example, in our discussion of the rap video produced in Chapter 4, not only in terms of the sexism of the rap itself but also in the sexist ways in which the young women in the group were marginalised during the production process. In that instance, our analysis of the project suggested that the apparently non-interventionist teaching strategy was partly responsible for the sense of hurt and alienation experienced by the young women in the group. In addition, we were critical of the ways in which a rather sentimental or romantic attitude towards the political values of rap ended up reinforcing what we would see as sexist attitudes towards the display of the female body.

In many ways, it is easy to pick on the kind of work described in that chapter – not least because it enables us to occupy the moral high ground. However, as we argued in our introduction, media education has been fond of presenting itself as a means of political enlightenment. The syllabi and writings of the last twenty years have vehemently proclaimed a vanguardist position in terms of the 'identity politics'[7] of 'race', gender and social class. Yet as this and previous studies have consistently shown, the claim that media education will liberate students from the oppressive power of dominant ideologies is highly questionable. One of the most difficult reflections we have all had to come to terms with is that the social relations of the classroom are bound to mediate – and can in certain situations undermine – the broader political intentions of our teaching. Analysing the sexism of teenage girls' magazines, for example, may end up simply reaffirming boys' assumption that girls only read them because they are stupid[8]. Teaching about 'positive images' of black people in inner city schools may do no more than allow black students an opportunity to adopt a self-righteous position of superiority[9]. As this and previous studies have shown, students may find it comparatively easy to reproduce 'politically correct' arguments, without necessarily questioning their own position – as in the case of the sitcom group whose work was analysed in Chapter 6.

In acknowledging these complexities, we are not of course seeking to deny that media education is an essentially *political* process – although we would argue that its political consequences may be rather less straightforward and less far-reaching than some of its more optimistic advocates have tended to assume. On the contrary, we feel that media production activities can offer a valuable perspective on these questions of power and political understanding. There seem to be three distinct issues that emerge from our case studies. First, there is the question of the differentiated knowledge about the media that students bring to media production in the first place. For example, in Chapter 5 we contrasted the detailed and almost condescending use of musical knowledge demonstrated by the boys in the class with the more experiential and perhaps 'aesthetic' approach to the topic adopted by the girls. Secondly, there is the question of students' attitudes towards, and experience of, the technology of media production. For example, in Chapter 4 the uses of technology were clearly differentiated along gender lines; and the extent to which boys tend to dominate the use of technology in classroom situations has long been an issue of concern among media teachers. Thirdly, there is the way in which the social relations of the production process – both among the students themselves, and between students and teachers – can influence or determine its outcomes. In Chapter 6, for example, the students' attitudes towards (and fears of) homosexuality were a significant issue, both within the group and in terms of the disciplinary relationship between teacher and taught. In exploring each of these issues in more detail, we shall also point to some of the dangers of an *essentialist* approach – for example, in which males and females are seen to relate to the media or to technology in inherently and unavoidably different ways. As we shall indicate, there are strategies that can actively prevent this kind of differentiation.

Knowledge about the media: gender and genre
Although gender is not by any means the only determinant in this sphere, it has been research about the gendered dimensions of media consumption which has highlighted its significance for media educators. Studies of romance novels, soaps, comics and magazines have all pointed to the ways in which reading the media is often highly determined by social factors – or at least that the *competencies* that are required to read

particular genres are not universal, but socially distributed[10]. Males and females, for example, not only tend to have different tastes and preferences, but they also tend to use the media in different ways and for different purposes. This has consequences, not only in terms of the *content* of the media curriculum, but also in terms of the general educational principles that inform it. Thus, for example, our interest in exploring 'visual literacy' in the case study described in Chapter 2 led us to devise tasks that were perceived in very different ways, and offered rather different points of entry for boys and for girls. The boys seemed to possess a more filmic, visual imagination whereas the girls seemed to begin with a stronger sense of character and narrative. Of course, we are not suggesting that either sex is *inherently* more inclined in one direction or another – even if this did appear to be the case here. Nevertheless, it is reasonable to assume that students arrive in our classrooms with differentiated knowledge and experience of the media; and that the ways in which we frame assignments and activities will enable them to use that knowledge in different ways.

One immediate effect of this process is that it can appear to 'gender' the media curriculum. Thus, in the study of music in Chapter 5 it appeared as if the early work on genre and taste was dominated by the young men in the group. The apparently 'masculine' tendency for men to list, label and categorise artists, recordings, dates and so on, enabled them to dominate the discussion and to inflect it in a particular direction. Of course, this may not reflect a more general tendency – although it is worth noting that, for example, the readership of the specialist music press is heavily skewed towards males. Nevertheless, it clearly does suggest that the media curriculum is susceptible to appropriation by 'interest groups' in particular ways. For example, the fact that the group in Chapter 4 was encouraged to make a rap video, despite the explicit reluctance of some of the older students, is another example of the ways in which certain kinds of partiality (in this case inflected by ethnicity and a particular definition of 'youth') can dominate the direction and outcomes of practical work.

The point here is not that we need to implement a 'socially neutral' curriculum – which would of course be an absurdity. It is not even that we should attempt to strike a 'balance' in our selection of *content*; although this might be one place to begin. As we have implied, the 'gendering' of the curriculum may also be reflected in the underlying *theoretical assumptions* that inform our teaching in the first place. For example, it may well be the case that an approach based on the concept of 'visual literacy' does not offer an equal point of entry to media production, however much pleasure and interest both the boys and the girls found in the project described in Chapter 2. Of course, we should be wary of jumping to facile and essentialist conclusions about the differences between boys' and girls' relationship to very broad dimensions of the media such as narrative or visual 'language'. Nevertheless, we are left with the question as to how we might teach this project again in ways that actively address the *different* knowledge and orientations of the two groups – and indeed seek to build on the strengths of both perspectives.

This question of the different cultural experiences and competencies that students bring to the media classroom is of course not confined to the area of gender. Ethnic differences were also a fundamental issue in a number of the case studies here. In Chapter 2, for example, the students' different cultural repertoires were manifested not only in their knowledge of particular texts but also in their broader orientations towards aspects such as narrative or realism. The attention in most media teaching to 'popular' or 'dominant' forms is implicitly based on the assumption that students somehow share a common culture – an assumption that in many circumstances may prove to be quite unwarranted[11]. In some instances, this can result in some highly problematic situations: teaching about the representation of women in advertising or in women's magazines, for example, has a very different significance for Muslim students as compared with their Anglo-Saxon peers. There is clearly no simple solution to these problems; although the starting point is surely to be sensitive to such differences, to the reasons why they might occur and to the potential consequences they might have in terms of students' work.

Accessing the technology
There is a substantial body of research which points to the difficulties of using any form of technology with mixed sex groups. Young women, it has been argued, have been systematically denied access and opportunities to develop technological competence within the education system. Not only do boys monopolise the scarce equipment available; but girls are socialised into opting out of technological activities. Indeed, the commonsense wisdom amongst teachers on this point is now so institutionalised that it may have become a self-fulfilling prophecy. Although not statistically significant, the work described in this book sheds an interesting light on this issue.

Thus, there were certainly instances of this pattern of male dominance, most obviously in the case of the rap video in Chapter 4, and to a lesser extent with some of the mixed groups in Chapter 6. However, in Chapter 3, we described technologically advanced work that was undertaken within an all-girls school; while the project discussed in Chapter 5 was set in the mixed sixth form of another such school. As we have noted, the sixth form work was decisively affected by the gendered nature of musical knowledge and by the ways in which the young men 'negotiated' their position in relation to the female staff. Yet the question of access to technology was not in fact an issue here: the most technically demanding work on that project was in fact produced by a young woman working alone. Similar observations could be made about the drama work described in Chapter 7. There, the class teacher had actively attempted to pre-empt such difficulties by organising two camera crews (one male, one female) right at the beginning of the project. Similarly, the division between female performers and male camera operators that we observed in Chapter 4 did not emerge as an issue because of the way in which the teacher had explicitly set out to organise the class. Furthermore, it would be impossible to say that the male students who were involved in these projects emerged as any more technologically competent than the female students.

We would not wish to become complacent about this issue; but it is perhaps reasonable to assume that women are more positive about learning to use equipment than may be commonly supposed, *particularly where opportunities are explicitly provided for them*[12]. Thus, within the all-female environment of the school in Chapter 3, attitudes towards the use of complicated equipment were uniformly positive. In Chapter 7, it was again girls who used the more technically complex equipment of the edit suite; and while this was partially a question of availability, it was also a result of the fact that the girls took a high level of responsibility in the project as a whole. In general, the most effective practice occurred when teachers had anticipated the possibility of competition over the equipment and precluded it by organising groups in advance, for example by organising single-sex groups or by carefully allocating roles in the production process.

The politics of production
As we have suggested, existing patterns of social relations within the classroom may have complex ideological consequences. Relations between students, and between the

students and the teacher, can inflect the production process in ways which teachers themselves might well regard as unwelcome or even counter-productive. The most obvious dimension of this process is that which is now popularly characterised as 'political correctness'. In using this term, we do not wish to subscribe to a kind of fashionable cynicism, in which 'political correctness' is simply a synonym for left-wing principles – as, for example, when Tony Blair, the current Labour leader, justifies his decision to send his son to an elite grant-maintained school by suggesting that 'individual choice should not be sacrificed to political correctness'. However, the notion of 'political correctness' does seem to point to some of the *pedagogical* problems of contemporary left politics – that is, its relationship with the various constituencies whose interests it purports to serve and represent.

As we have implied above, these problems have a particular resonance in media education. As with other forms of so-called 'critical pedagogy'[13], there is a danger that media education will become little more than a means of propagandising students – attempting to command their assent to political positions which we as teachers judge to be 'objectively' in their interests. Perhaps unsurprisingly, students often respond by resisting this approach. If they want good marks, or simply a quiet life, they may obediently learn to repeat the politically correct line, without any necessary commitment, or even much detailed thought. Alternatively, they may choose the more subversive option of 'winding up' the teacher, using any opportunity to say things they know will generate official disapproval – and, as often as not, approval from their peers. Neither response necessarily requires students to challenge – or indeed, even to think through – their own position; and in this respect, 'political correctness' would almost appear to guarantee a form of political superficiality.

The most obvious example of this kind of dilemma here was that which arose in relation to the sitcom production discussed in Chapter 6. While we might choose to read their work as a reflection of the insecurities of male adolescence, it clearly served a rather different function for the students themselves. The confident, perhaps smug, rationalisations of the group reflect the ease with which they are able to play what they perceive to be the teacher's game, while simultaneously subverting and mocking it. Ultimately, the whole process may simply have served to reinforce the students' sense of their own gender and class superiority. These students' articulate use of argument and counter-argument, which is deliberately mobilised against the 'politically correct' position of authority, clearly shows how transactions in the classroom are *not* politically neutral. On the contrary, they are inflected with tensions and conflicts that derive not only from the inequality between teacher and student but also from the broader relationships between the liberal position of the school and the rather different politics of the pupils' home backgrounds[14]. This latter point was particularly apparent in the 'racial politics' of Nicky, the Greek Cypriot student in that group. On the one hand, it seemed as though the position afforded by his 'Greek' identity offered a degree of power, not least in the fiction of the production itself. Yet on the other hand, the 'Greek' identity was depicted self-consciously as a *stereotype*, and lived partly as a *role* that could be assumed (ironically or seriously) for particular social purposes.

By contrast, this kind of positioning did not seem to arise in the extremely ethnically mixed classrooms observed in Chapters 2 and 7. The students there did not, at least in this context, seem to be concerned to make ethnic differences a point of contention – although this may partly derive from the fact that they definitely *were* a very problematic point of contention in the wider communities in which these schools were situated. At the same time, particularly in the case of the drama project described in Chapter 7, it may be that the work provided comparatively open opportunities for students to explore questions of identity, albeit in ways that were more invisible to us. By contrast, it was precisely Nicky's resistance to an 'assigned' identity that made the issue visible in the first place. On the other hand, in the case of the rap video, ethnicity seems to have acted as a superficially 'politically correct' way of allowing for the 'authentic expression' of identity – even if it did so in a way which we have described as almost sentimental, and at the cost of some very fundamental issues of equality and access.

What is clear throughout these projects is that questions of politics and identity cannot be divorced from the crucial dimension of *pleasure*. As we have shown, much of the pleasure of practical work depends upon its collaborative nature: being part of a team, sharing your work with peers, having a laugh, dressing up and enjoying in-jokes, are absolutely central to the activity. At the same time, there is a sense in which many of these projects reflect a kind of subversion or transgression of the rules of 'serious' educational endeavour. As we shall argue in more detail below, simulation and parody appear to allow a sanctioned space for play, in which it becomes possible to speak the unspeakable, to flirt with what may be clearly recognised as politically incorrect. However, the political *consequences* of this are inevitably complex and problematic. It may be a result of the peculiarities of London schools, but most of these students already knew the politically correct things they were expected to do and say: much of the pleasure here came from the fact that they could do and say precisely the opposite, without any necessary commitment, but also without fear of reprisal. It has not been our intention merely to celebrate this; although equally, it is not easy to see how one might intervene to prevent it. Simply policing students' behaviour in order to ensure that they produce politically correct texts is, we would argue, a futile activity that will only be counter-productive. The crucial question is how we enable students to *reflect* upon what they have done, and to evaluate the consequences of the choices they have made.

We will return to these issues in due course; but it is perhaps worth emphasising at this stage that there are no simple 'rules' about ethnicity or class or gender that could be extrapolated from our work here. As we have suggested, essentialist conceptions do not do justice to the complex ways in which identities are lived and negotiated in classrooms; but neither does the 'postmodern' argument that identity is infinitely fluid and unstable[15]. These (often contradictory) forms of *difference* are almost bound to act as fault lines within the highly charged social relationships of any classroom. Insofar as it hands over some of the control to the students, media production will almost inevitably raise questions of social inequality; and limitations of time and scarcity of resources are perhaps bound to intensify that situation. Here again, we would argue that a sensitivity to the inherently *social and political* dimensions of such work is a fundamental prerequisite for effective practice. Rather than assume that the curriculum is a neutral space, we need to plan in advance for likely conflicts of interest. Ultimately, such inequalities cannot be wished away; but it should be possible to manage them in a way that offers all students an equal, or at least an equivalent, starting point.

2. Learning 'media language'

The language analogy: 'skills' and 'creativity'
As we have indicated, the analogy between audio-visual media and verbal language is both problematic and productive. The notion of 'media literacy' can have a great

polemical value: it implies that the use and analysis of the modern media should be a central aspect of the school curriculum, alongside more traditionally privileged forms such as print. On a theoretical level, the language metaphor also has considerable potential. It is through language, broadly defined, that a great deal of social interaction is accomplished, and hence a great deal of learning occurs. Talk and writing – and, by extension, media production – can be seen as 'social modes of thinking'; and in this respect, the focus on language can enable us to move us beyond the dualistic opposition between the individual and the social that has often characterised educational debate.

Nevertheless, the notion that the media can be analysed – and indeed taught – as forms of language is one that can be interpreted in a variety of ways. On one level, it can lead to a highly mechanistic form of pedagogy, in which students are taught discrete skills in a fixed and apparently logical sequence. On another level, it can lend support to the argument that the media are simply another means of 'self-expression'. From this perspective, the camera becomes the modern equivalent of the pen; and simply placing it in students' hands will, it is argued, result in new forms of 'creative writing'. Ultimately, neither of these approaches appears to us to offer a satisfactory means of enabling students to become competent media producers. Yet as we shall argue, the notion of 'media literacy' – and in particular the analogy between media production and contemporary approaches to the teaching of writing – may suggest other, more productive perspectives.

The polarisation between traditional and progressive approaches outlined earlier in this chapter has of course had a particular significance in the teaching of print literacy. For example, the stand-off between different approaches to teaching reading – 'phonics' versus 'real books' – has been a major focus of academic and popular debate. On the one hand, we have an approach which emphasises the importance of 'decoding skills', as though these were basic 'building blocks' on which meaning was built. On the other, we have an approach which prioritises the reader's 'search for meaning', and in which the decoding of print is seen as a secondary phenomenon. In terms of the psychological jargon, meaning is seen to be produced either from the 'bottom up' or from the 'top down'. This is of course a complex debate, which we cannot afford to enter here; but it is one which has striking parallels with the debate about media production. Theoretically, the debate would appear to reflect a kind of dualism – an opposition between structure and agency – which is characteristic of theories of language, and indeed of the human sciences more broadly. On the one hand, we have the individual helplessly positioned within the objective (or at least socially determined) structure of language; while on the other, we have the individual as a free user of language, an active and creative maker of meanings.

As we have indicated, much of the criticism that has been directed against practical work in media education has been caught within the terms of this dualistic approach. In establishing the claims of Media Studies to be a rigorous academic subject, its advocates were keen to distinguish themselves from what was seen as the individualistic, 'liberal' approach of subjects like English and Art. The notion of 'creativity' and the view of practical work as a form of spontaneous 'self-expression' were condemned as simply romantic obfuscation[16]. The argument here is partly to do with whether such approaches can simply be transferred across to contemporary electronic media. While these ideas might perhaps be easier to sustain in the case of creative writing and the visual arts, there are several reasons why they seem much harder to apply to media production – not least, it is argued, because of the nature of the technology, and the reliance on group work. In fact, of course, such an individualistic, 'expressive' approach *has* been sustained throughout the history of the modern media, particularly in the *avant garde*: even high-tech media such as film and video have been used in aesthetically 'creative' ways that bear comparison with older media such as painting or poetry.

Nevertheless, there is a much more fundamental theoretical issue at stake here. Even in the case of those older media, and in the case of the *avant garde*, we would wish to challenge *individualistic* notions of creativity. As we have argued above, cultural production is an inherently *social* process, even when it appears to be simply a matter of making 'personal statements': it is based in social experience, in a social dialogue with others (real or imagined), and it uses socially-available resources for producing meaning. Whether they are using 'dominant' or 'oppositional' forms, producers do not just invent the conventions and genres they use. Both the technologies and the language that are used determine what can be said and how it can be said. In this respect, notions of 'self-expression' and 'originality', which are routinely used in relation to creative writing or children's art, remain profoundly problematic.

The danger here, of course, is that we lapse into the opposite term of the dualism, in which language is seen as something that is objectively given. From this perspective, language can simply be broken down into its component parts and then taught in a logical sequence. In terms of media production, this assumption is most apparent in two approaches which are otherwise quite opposed. A great deal of technical training – for example on pre-vocational media courses – is based on the notion that there is a given form of professional practice that can be taught as though it were a series of objective 'rules'. Teaching media production is thus a step-by-step approach, in which meaning is seen to be made through the gradual accretion and mastery of a fixed repertoire of techniques. 'Deconstruction exercises' would appear to be based on a similar belief in media language as a fixed system of rules and norms, which should be analysed and taught systematically – although from this perspective, 'dominant' forms of language are seen to be almost irredeemably tainted with ideology.

On one level, we would agree that there are 'skills' that students need to learn. Media products are constructed according to generic and linguistic conventions. All of these conventions have to be learnt – and can thus, in principle, be taught. Most of the case studies in this book have touched at some point on the 'grammatical' correctness with which various conventions have been understood and applied by students; and on the ways in which they gradually develop the ability to control the various technologies that are involved. As we have indicated (for example in Chapters 2 and 7), students' early attempts at media production are often characterised by fairly basic 'mistakes' – in the sense that what they produce does not correspond to what they intended, or indeed what they thought they 'saw'. For example, many students' early attempts at photography are often entirely in long shot: the subject they are intending to focus upon occupies only a small area of the frame. If they are to move beyond these limitations, students clearly do need a certain amount of formal instruction; and there may prove to be a 'hierarchy of skills' which might usefully be taught in some kind of logical sequence.

The dilemma, of course, is *when* and *how* that formal instruction should occur. As we have argued, skills cannot be taught in any lasting way if they are not set in the context of the students' attempt to communicate *meaning*. Decontextualised exercises in camera angles – like exercises in using prepositions or intransitive verbs – will not necessarily make very much sense, or indeed make very much difference to what students eventually produce, if they are unrelated to their own intentions and purposes. Furthermore, the ways in which we might break down these skills does not necessarily correspond to the ways in which students build them up: what appears to us to be a logical structure may well not correspond to the 'logics' with which students themselves make meaning.

A useful way of beginning to rethink this issue is in terms of the relationship between what students *already* know and what they need to know. Students of course possess large repertoires of knowledge about 'media language'. A great deal of the television they watch, for example, presumes a sophisticated (and indeed critical) knowledge of the conventions of the medium – and television itself is increasingly self-reflexive in its deliberate and conscious play with conventions. Students are, in this sense, not learning a foreign language: they are already fluent 'readers', even if they have yet to become 'writers'. Nevertheless, as language teachers would say, their existing knowledge is passive: it has to be made active in order for it to be used. They may know what a particular convention 'means', but not how that meaning is achieved. In other words, there has to be a kind of *translation* from the 'passive' knowledge that is derived from viewing or reading to the 'active' knowledge that is required for production or writing; and this process is one that perhaps inevitably requires some *teaching*. It may be impossible to learn to make television simply by studying television, or by following a series of technical exercises; but it is equally impossible to do so simply by discovery. As we have implied, there are certain aspects of media production that can only be meaningfully learnt by doing; but if students are not enabled to reflect upon what they have done, it will be impossible for them to generalise from their experience to future situations. In this respect, then, learning has to involve a dialectical relationship between doing and analysing – or, to put it in media education terminology, between 'practice' and 'theory'.

Ultimately, then, our intention here is to move beyond this dualistic approach – and hence beyond the opposition between 'skills' and 'creativity'. In a sense, we are arguing for a *social* conception of creativity, not as a process of spontaneous self-expression, nor as a replication of existing language forms, but as a means of *social dialogue*. Our central interest, therefore, is in how students might learn to 'write' media in ways that are *socially* meaningful, not just to themselves but to others.

Progression in practical work

One of the most fundamental issues here is that of *progression*. Is it possible to identify a logical sequence of production 'skills' that students should learn? To what extent do these skills transfer across media – for example, from still photography to video? And to what extent might this model of development change as the production technology itself is changing?

For example, it is traditional in most forms of media education that work on still images precedes work on moving images. The truism seems to be that one should learn how to operate still cameras first; video later. We teach framing and camera angles first; continuity editing second. The assumption here would seem to be that 'low tech' media are easier to *control* than 'high tech' media, and that they therefore enable students to acquire production skills (and potentially conceptual understandings) in a logical and manageable sequence. There is clearly an implicit hierarchy of knowledge here, which is bound up with an unspoken model of skills development.

Although we have not been able to offer a systematic analysis of these issues, several of the case studies in this book have sought to question these assumptions. Of course, there is an implicit model of progression in the activities we undertook with different age groups. We would obviously not have attempted the comparatively demanding tasks described in Chapter 5 with the much younger students we encountered in Chapter 2 – or indeed vice-versa. Yet as media education has begun to expand beyond its traditional base in the upper years of the secondary school curriculum, the lack of any shared understanding of progression has become an urgent problem. As primary school students appear to be able to engage with activities that had previously been designated as appropriate for GCSE students, it is clear that we need much more effective models of development, in relation to both practical and analytical aspects of the subject. For example, virtually all children will study and probably make newspapers at Key Stage 3 (age 11-14) within English[17]. However – and this is not a criticism of English teachers – there is no overarching reason why these particular texts should be studied and produced at this stage in students' school careers – and indeed, at an age where they may well not actually spend much time reading newspapers themselves. If part of the logic here is that students are enabled to *transfer* their knowledge as 'consumers' to their activity as 'producers', it would surely make sense for production work to focus on media forms or genres with which they are most familiar at any given age[18].

These arguments may become more acute as the technology itself develops. For example, modern video cameras are probably easier to use than single lens reflex (SLR) still cameras. Although purists are suspicious of the auto-focus, it is fairly easy for quite young students to use video to construct coherent film narratives. On the other hand, framing and composing still images is conceptually complicated. Children's earliest attempts at photography – like most domestic 'snapshots' – tend to be composed in medium/long shot, as if they were selecting stills from a sequence of moving images. In fact, of course, most narrative tension within still images is produced by the use of conventions of framing and composition; although this may be much easier to grasp when using moving images, particularly given the possibility of re-shooting and editing. As we saw in Chapter 2, children's construction of narrative may proceed *in parallel* with their ability to construct individual shots, rather than *as a consequence of* that ability. Likewise, as the projects described in Chapters 6 and 7 would suggest, students are often able to produce meaningful film narratives without necessarily beginning with technical instruction in the fundamental 'building blocks' of film art. Creating narrative cohesion does not necessarily depend on constructing a whole story mechanistically from the sum of its parts; it may depend primarily on a sense of the overall shape of the narrative, of the meanings that have to be communicated, and of the ways in which the audience will make sense of them. In terms of the debate about print literacy, then, we are suggesting that such abilities may develop from the 'top down' as well as from the 'bottom up' – in other words, from the attempt to find or communicate specific *meanings* as much as from the accumulation of 'encoding' or 'decoding' *skills*.

The storyboard

Nowhere are these difficulties more exposed than in the use of the storyboard – a technique which is commonly accepted as 'good practice' in media education at all levels of the curriculum. We have touched on this issue in a number of our case studies, but it is worth a more extended discussion here. On one level, the use of the storyboard appears to represent an attempt to replicate professional practice. Though accounts of this vary considerably, we imagine that films exist first as a treatment, which is then turned into a script; this leads in turn to a shooting script; and finally, the cinematographer might storyboard sections to assist with the positioning of the cameras and subsequently with editing[19]. In practice, of course, this procedure is not always followed, nor indeed is it relevant to all areas of the media: while storyboarding is a familiar practice in advertising, for example, it is much less frequently used in mainstream TV, even for studio-based drama. Indeed, even in the case of advertising, it is not always clear whether storyboards are produced primarily for cinematographic purposes or as presentational devices – in other words, as a means of persuading clients to finance the production. Either way, it is clear that there is no single industry practice; and certainly not one common to the range of media forms studied in media education.

The dubious status of the storyboard is further confused by its association with other graphic representations of movement like the comic or cartoon, with which students themselves are likely to be more familiar. There, the use of frames and the sequencing of images clearly draws upon filmic modes of narration. But the form also relies on highly conventionalised means of representing movement or action, from the writing of 'POW!' to the use of lines to indicate speed[20]. In practice, students will often approach the task of storyboarding as though it were a matter of producing a comic – an approach which does not necessarily help them when it comes to translating these still images into moving ones.

Despite this confused pedigree, the storyboard is very widely used within media education classrooms – albeit for a number of reasons. It may be the case that teachers use the device on the grounds that it replicates professional practice – an assumption that we have suggested may not always be correct. In many cases, however, we suspect that difficulties arise when the interim stages in the process (the treatment, the shooting script) are neglected, and students are required to go directly to the storyboard. More problematically, as we argued in Chapter 3, the storyboard may also be used as a form of classroom control in a context where it is necessary to ration students' access to scarce equipment. Indeed, in many situations, we suspect that storyboarding is used as a *substitute* for actual production.

More positively, however, we would see the most fundamental purpose of the storyboard as being to assist students in their efforts to 'think visually', and hence to develop an understanding of the conventions of film narration. Encouraging them to think through their ideas on paper first should, at least in principle, focus their attention on issues such as framing, movement, editing and the relations between sound and image in a way which is not always possible in the heat of production. While this may serve as a stage in the production process, in certain instances it can also be justified as an end in itself[21].

Yet whatever the rationale, we would suggest that storyboarding requires very particular skills and ways of thinking that are rarely explicitly addressed or taught. Storyboarding is in fact a very difficult task. It can serve several functions, albeit sometimes conflicting ones; and it can, in itself, be broken down into a number of discrete skills which may need to be addressed individually. For example, it is often unclear to students whether each frame in a storyboard represents a scene or a shot, however much one may attempt to explain this. If it is the former, then storyboards would seem to act as a kind of visual note-taking, and more detailed decisions would be made *in situ*. If it is the latter, then we need to consider how students might actually *learn* about aspects such as camera positioning, the timing of shots and editing. We would suggest that such things cannot easily be learnt in the abstract, with pencil and paper. Indeed, it may only be *after* a considerable amount of production experience that students actually learn how a storyboard might be used to represent moving images, and the functions it might serve.

In terms of production work, therefore, the storyboard should serve a primarily *supportive* function, particularly in helping students to 'think visually' about the effects they want to achieve. However, it will only do so if students are able to *use* it in this way. Making it a necessity, and indeed a chore – which it often appears to be in media classrooms – may be a waste of time, or indeed positively counter-productive. As we have shown (for example, in Chapters 2, 4 and 6), students will often ignore their carefully drawn storyboards when it comes to the experience of filming, and they frequently do so for very good reasons. In many cases, the aims of the storyboard could be much better achieved through a process of trial and error – or what English teachers would call 'drafting and re-drafting'.

If we do want students to produce storyboards, then we need to teach them how to do so – although we need to recognise that they may need a considerable amount of production experience if they are to use them effectively. Equally, if we want to devise mechanisms to support the production process, then there are alternative forms of 'note-making' that can be used, which are less reliant on 'artistic' skill and focus more on the conceptual demands of the task[22]. For example, we have undertaken successful projects where students making pop videos begin by representing the lyrics along a time line and then go back to 'fill in' the relevant images. This helps the students know how much footage they need in advance and how to build in repetitions and the other formal features of the genre. Another approach is to require students to represent the narrative in the form of a chart and to then to work backwards to devising individual shots. A third method is to use the virtual storyboard of non-linear editing, described in Chapter 3. Of course, all of these approaches are best worked out in conjunction with the students; but whichever approach is used, it is vital that students and teachers find a common language in which they can imagine and conceptualise their work *visually*, in ways that are appropriate given their previous knowledge and experience.

From storyboards to stories: the genre of 'practical work'

All the students' work described in this book, and indeed in others to which we have contributed[23], uses 'dominant' media forms and conventions. Indeed, most of the projects we devised consciously set out to encourage this. As we have indicated, this issue is one which has generated considerable mistrust and criticism in media education. Most obviously in the case of debates about imitation, discussed in Chapter 5, students' use of dominant forms has been seen as a process of ideological reproduction, which is not only educationally invalid but also politically suspect. The alternative model for production work that is often promoted in this context is that of the artistic *avant garde*: the production of experimental or 'oppositional' texts is seen to encourage an attention to formal characteristics, and to questions of representation, that may be taken for granted in dominant media genres.

Our rejection of this view has been apparent at a number of points, both in terms of the theoretical assumptions on which it is based, and in terms of the alternative classroom strategies that are prescribed. Of course, the encounter with a broad historical and cultural range of media texts – including those of the *avant garde* – is an essential element of media education. Nevertheless, we would challenge the view that the *avant garde* is any *less* generic or 'conventional' than dominant media; and we would question whether the use of such models necessarily encourages a greater degree of theoretical reflection. Indeed, many of the 'dominant' genres which are most frequently employed in practical work are precisely those which have incorporated many of the stylistic devices of the *avant garde*, such as advertisements and pop videos.

Furthermore, as we have argued, critics of practical work have often neglected the complexity of students' uses of dominant forms, and the positive functions it might serve – not least, in terms of our concerns here, in enabling them to 'learn the languages' of the media. By contrast, our analysis has pointed to the ways in which the pedagogic purpose of production work is interwoven with the *meanings* that its authors derive from it, which are in turn inextricably bound up with the *social context* and *social relations* of production. This multifaceted nature of practical work is most evident in the ways in which students actively use and appropriate dominant forms and conventions. As we have implied, these forms and conventions are neither fixed nor objective, nor do they necessarily have fixed meanings. Indeed, we would say that most practical work by young people adopts a *hybrid* generic form. Even where students are positively required to use a 'given' genre (as was the case, for example, in Chapter 6), they typically re-work the conventions of that genre, borrowing in the process from a number of other sources and forms. What is more, the hybridity almost always bears a trace of its immediate context – that is, the classroom.

The work described in this book displays this hybridity in a number of ways. On one level, it is apparent in the ways in which students combined and mutated existing forms. This was perhaps most evident in instances where students did not appear to possess – or at least use – a *single* generic 'model'. For example, the lack of an obvious model for the hypertext stories in Chapter 3 (apart perhaps from the choose-your-own-adventure stories, which these students largely avoided) led them to draw on a wide range of existing forms. Likewise, the students' lack of experience of photostories in Chapter 2 left them free to construct narratives that drew upon and combined elements of film, television, comics, horror and soap opera. Of course, genre theorists have pointed out that there is no such thing as a 'pure' genre; all cultural forms mutate as they borrow from and reference others[24]. Indeed, some critics maintain that this quick turnover of generic forms is a distinguishing feature of postmodern culture[25]. As we have suggested (Chapter 5), the notion of 'intertextuality' – rather than the reductive notion of 'imitation' – may provide the basis for a more productive account of what is taking place in students' uses of dominant forms.

At the same time, this process of generic mutation can also be traced to the influence of the social context of the classroom. Thus, the sitcom described in Chapter 6, the photostories in Chapter 2 and the soap opera in Chapter 7 all reflect the ways in which dominant forms are refracted through the students' peer group relationships and through the institutional context of schooling. The influence of 'school' genres – that is, of the discourses and values of school subjects – is also very apparent; although this is sometimes resisted (as in Chapter 6) and sometimes more enthusiastically incorporated (as in Chapter 7). This issue leads us on to broader questions about the 'reality' of school work, and about the use of simulation as a means of teaching about professional practice, which will be addressed below. At this stage, however, it is important to emphasise that this generic hybridity is partly a function of the way in which media education combines – and in some respects crosses the boundaries between – the 'official' world of the school and the 'unofficial' world of leisure and popular culture.

Writing genres: making media

In many ways, the young people whose work we have described in this book could be seen to be doing no more than 'practising' or 'playing' at making media. Their work possesses the same indeterminate status occupied by children's science experiments, or by creative writing in the English classroom. At the same time, we would argue that the social activity of media production, with its highly 'visible' end product, acts as unique form of communication within the school environment. The common feature of all of the successful projects described in this book is that they generated interest and entertainment for an *audience* of peers: they had a value and status within (and in some cases beyond) the school which the vast majority of students' work never attains. As the students here were often explicitly working within the frames of reference particular to student culture, this visibility seems to have even more resonance. It is particularly in terms of this *social* dimension that we would see the value of regarding media production as a form of 'writing'. Students have to learn to 'write' media, just as they have to learn to write in print; but having learnt how to write, they then use that writing in their own social transactions and as a means of gaining access to cultural and social worlds.

There is an interesting parallel here with the debates about 'genre' that have been advanced in relation to the teaching of writing[26]. In many respects, the arguments for and against the 'genre' approach would seem to rehearse many of the familiar debates about traditional and progressive pedagogy described above – and indeed, to do so in similarly polarised terms. The genre theorists have argued very strongly against what they have depicted as the woolly progressivism of much English teaching – for example, the notion that students will learn writing by discovery, and that dominant genres of writing should be no more privileged than any others. According to them, this approach leads to a form of institutionalised disadvantage, in which working-class students are effectively excluded from the dominant culture in the interests of a phoney relativism[27]. By contrast, the genre theorists argue, what we need to do is to identify the dominant genres of writing, analyse their rules and conventions, and then actively *teach* them. There is an interesting contrast here with traditional views in Media Studies, where dominant genres are often regarded as ideologically corrupt and hence to be avoided as models for production – although the genre theorists themselves do not of course regard dominant genres as ideologically neutral. In practice, however, genre theorists would probably favour an approach based on deconstruction exercises, in which the fundamental aim of practical work is to teach the 'grammar' of the media; and indeed, they might well appear to favour an approach which is based on vocational training – learning to make media the way the professionals do.

This critique is a powerful one; and it points to a kind of *abdication of teaching* that sometimes takes place in media production work. While this is most obviously the case with the youth work approach discussed in Chapter 4, it could be identified even in some of the more effective projects we have described. In several instances, we have pointed to the ways in which students effectively *taught themselves* the 'rules' of framing or composition – or even, in the case of Chapter 6, continuity editing – almost through a form of 'discovery'. As we have argued, students should be enabled to transfer their knowledge as consumers across to their experience of production; and it is clear that this must involve an *interaction* between 'discovery' and instruction.

While the genre theorists' emphasis on 'learning the rules' is an important one, there remain several difficulties in applying it to media production. First of all, as we have argued, students may already 'know' many of these rules, albeit implicitly[28], from their experience of watching and consuming media products – which may not be the case in relation to some written genres. Secondly, we have argued that what students actually make is not generically 'pure'; it is hybridised – and genre theory does not really allow for the ways in which students might actively *use* and appropriate dominant forms in order to communicate, for their own reasons and to their own audiences. Ultimately, the fundamental problem with the genre theorists' approach is that it has largely failed to address the central question of *learning*[29]. On the one hand, we have a highly developed theory of language – albeit a strangely fixed one, which does not always seem to allow for challenges and inconsistencies in the 'dominant' genres. Yet on the other hand, we have a view of pedagogy which seems to imply that teaching (of a highly didactic kind) leads inexorably to learning: tell them the rules, get them to practice them, and then they will learn.

Despite these important reservations, genre theory is currently reinvigorating discussion around the teaching of writing in English, and it is an approach that offers some potential for developing our understanding of media production. Perhaps most significantly, it seems to offer a framework in which media forms are set alongside, and not ranked against, written forms of communication. As we have argued, it is important that all forms of communication are discussed holistically in this fashion, and that are all considered equally. 'Making media' should, in this respect, co-exist with writing as a fundamental entitlement of contemporary literacy.

3. Production and conceptual understanding

Learning language – learning concepts

Media Studies teachers have traditionally placed a central emphasis on *conceptual understanding*. The primary aim of practical work, from this perspective, is to enable students to explore the broad theoretical issues which have arisen from critical analysis of the media. Much of the work we have described, particularly in the later chapters of the book, exemplifies this approach, with its explicit address to questions of audience, genre, representation and so on. As we have argued, practical work in media education is not simply a matter of learning 'how to' skills; it must also involve students in *reflecting* on the processes by which meanings and pleasures are made, and indeed how they might be different.

However, there are several potential problems with this emphasis, particularly if it ends up simply privileging 'theory' over 'practice'. There is a risk that practical work will become a mere illustration of theory, rather than an area in which theoretical understandings can be explored and generated. Likewise, 'reading' practical production work simply as evidence of students' theoretical understandings is both an extremely difficult and problematic process, and one which may lead us to neglect many of its most significant outcomes in terms of learning.

The relationship between the development of conceptual understanding and students' ability to *use* 'media language' is also far from straightforward or direct. Deconstruction exercises, for example, appear to be based on the assumption that 'teaching the system' will have conceptual – and indeed political – consequences. Exposing the conventions of continuity editing or the visual rhetoric of television interviews is seen as a means of exposing the ideology of dominant forms, and hence of liberating students from it. Yet it is debatable whether it does any such thing. Learning about editing in the news, for example, may make you watch it in different way: you may, albeit intermittently, find yourself noticing the number of edits or looking for the cutaways that have been inserted. Yet the notion that this in itself will lead one to question or challenge the 'dominant ideology' of the news is both theoretically and empirically very questionable.

There are also difficult questions here about the limitations and possibilities of particular forms of technology. On one level, we would want to question the idea that any given technologies are *indispensable* for media education. A great many conceptual issues can be introduced and explored using 'low tech' methods such as photomontage. Nevertheless, it is clear that certain technologies do make certain kinds of understandings possible, or at least easier to achieve, than others – although of course they do not necessarily guarantee them. As we have argued (Chapter 3), the experience of editing moving images offers a very concrete opportunity for students to grasp fundamental principles to do with selection, mediation and the construction of narrative. Editing at an edit suite, or with a vision mixer, is in this respect qualitatively different from editing in camera; and using the 'virtual storyboard' of non-linear editing can also add a further dimension of understanding to the process.

Here again, there are questions about *progression* which media educators have barely begun to address. Our case studies reflect some of our own implicit assumptions about this; but they also indicate some awkward problem areas. Thus, the kinds of questions about representation that were explicitly written in to the project undertaken by the year 13 students in Chapter 5 are only implicit in the task we set to the year 7 students in Chapter 2. Such issues do of course get raised implicitly – and sometimes explicitly – in much of the work we have described, in some instances with very problematic results. Yet here too, our responses to this also imply a recognition of the differences in terms of what students at different ages will be able to understand, or at least explicitly discuss.

For example, 'audience' is one area in which this question of progression is particularly problematic. To look again at the extremes, it is clear that the year 13 students have a fairly self-conscious understanding of audience, particularly in terms of their use of language and mode of address – even if they experienced some difficulty in explicitly reflecting upon this. By contrast, the year 7 students found it almost impossible to 'decentre' to the point where they were able to imagine a possible reader making sense of their stories – although whether this reflected an inability or a reluctance to do this is an interesting question. In the work described in Chapter 3, it is almost possible to trace a developmental progression in terms of students' ability to take up the position of an imaginary reader; although there were also significant differences *within* each age group here. While this kind of comparison between our case studies might suggest some starting points for investigation, there is a significant need for more systematic longitudinal study of this issue.

For all these reasons, the relationship between critical analysis and practical production remains a fundamental dilemma for media teachers, particularly in the context of examined Media Studies courses. Media Studies syllabuses often talk about the need to 'integrate' theory and practice, although there is very little understanding or guidance about how this might be attempted, and very little evidence that it is being successfully achieved. How do we expect theoretical understandings to be manifested and explored through practical work? How can we enable students to analyse their production work in the light of theory, and to use it as a means of generating new understandings? In this penultimate section of the chapter, we will consider two areas of media education in which these dilemmas are particularly apparent.

The first of these concerns the kinds of practical *assignments* that are typically set in Media Studies classrooms. In general terms, we would argue that many of the assignments that are being set are quite unrealistic, not so much in terms of what can be achieved with the technology but in terms of the conceptual difficulty – and indeed the internal contradictions – in the content of the tasks themselves. We routinely ask older students to produce 'alternative' soap operas or 'non-sexist' teenage magazines or even 'anti-realist' advertisements, when they have rarely had a chance to explore the possibilities of the technology, or indeed to gain some experience with the dominant forms they are supposedly expected to be challenging or moving beyond. The majority of such assignments are in the form of *simulations*; although the rationale for simulations, and the potential outcomes of this approach, are often confused and contradictory.

The second area we want to consider here is that of *evaluation and assessment*. As we have noted, students are typically required to submit a written 'log' or essay to accompany their practical productions. The log is expected to provide an analysis of the production process, but also to give a rationale and a critical evaluation of the project in the light of the theoretical issues that are addressed on the course. It is in this written self-evaluation that the integration of theory and practice is expected to be achieved – although there is good reason to conclude that it is often far from effective in this respect. There are fundamental questions to be raised, therefore, about what *kind* of reflection we are looking for; about the *form* in which it takes place; and about how we might enable it to happen more effectively.

The limits of guided discovery

In practice, a great deal of media education adopts what might be called a 'guided discovery' approach. This is the case, albeit in rather different ways, both in the analytical aspects of the subject and in practical work. Research on the use of this approach in media analysis has drawn attention to the problems of what is sometimes termed 'cued elicitation'[30]. Students analysing 'images of women' in advertisements, for example, will typically do so in response to a set of questions or categories provided by the teacher, whether in the form of whole class teaching or small-group work. Despite the repeated assertion that 'there are no right answers', such work often implicitly assumes that there are, and that the teacher's role is to guide the students in such a way that they will discover them 'spontaneously' and of their own accord. In practice, such work often becomes little more than a matter of 'guessing what's in teacher's mind': what appears to be a process of open investigation is in fact a way of commanding assent to a pre-determined (political) position.

In the case of practical work, these dilemmas are most apparent in the use of *simulation*. Many of the projects described in this book, particularly those which took place in the context of examined Media Studies courses, were explicitly defined as simulations: students were required to take on fictional roles as media production companies, and to devise products within a specified set of institutional constraints. These assignments are clearly not open invitations for students to 'express themselves'; on the contrary, they set very clear parameters on the form and content of the final product, and in some cases (for example, in the project described in Chapter 6) establish definite requirements in terms of the sequence of the production process.

Although it is a widespread practice in media classrooms, simulation has rarely been discussed as a specific teaching method in this field[31]. Of course, it is possible to argue that a great deal of learning in schools is simulated in one way or other. This is obviously true where students are undertaking science experiments or 'research' using original sources in History: while the aim of such work might be to enable students to become 'real' scientists or historians, they nevertheless remain students. Even in the case of more apparently open-ended activities such as imaginative writing, there is an inevitable element of 'unreality': children write stories, but they are not novelists, nor are their stories generally published. In the case of Media Studies, however, the essential *artificiality* of the simulation is often explicitly announced: everybody is consciously agreeing to act 'in role' in order to undertake a specified task. There are at least three possible rationales for the use of this approach.

The first is to do with the attempt to replicate what is seen as 'professional' practice – an issue that was touched upon in our discussion of storyboarding above. Of course, there are very real limitations on the extent to which any such replication is actually possible, given the constraints of time, equipment and resources; and in practice, these limitations are likely to be recognised both by teachers and by students. Students obviously know they are not advertising executives or film makers, even when they are invited to make 'real' ads or films. Even in the case of our attempts to involve a 'real' audience in the project described in Chapter 6, it was clear that everybody concerned (including the audience itself) recognised the essentially fictional nature of the activity. Nevertheless, part of the point of this approach is to learn something about 'how the professionals do it'. In media education, this is often seen as a form of 'demystification', a matter of exposing the 'hidden' economic and institutional constraints which are seen to determine media production. As we have noted, however, this can have contradictory consequences: at least initially, the students in Chapter 6 compared their own work unfavourably with that of the professionals, and expressed considerable admiration for the time and care that must go into 'the real thing'.

A second rationale for simulation relates to the issue of group work. By encouraging the students to function 'in role', and to work on a specified, collaborative task, it is argued that they will be able to develop more general social and communication skills. While we would not regard this as a *fundamental* aim of practical work, it should be seen as more than a mere by-product. As we have implied, group work is not in itself unproblematic or inherently a 'good thing': a great deal depends upon how effectively students are *enabled* to work together. Nevertheless, there is undoubtedly a sense in which the 'scaffolding' that is provided by an explicitly simulated project, in which roles and outcomes are clearly defined, can help to overcome some of the more predictable problems of group work, of the kind described in Chapter 4 – although it would be false to imply that it necessarily prevents them.

The sense in which simulation acts as a kind of 'scaffolding' also applies to our central concern here with conceptual learning. It is here, we would argue, that a third – and in our view, fundamental – rationale for simulation in media education can be found. As we have noted, each of the simulations described here was deliberately designed to enable students to explore a particular conceptual area of the media curriculum. The work on *The Outsiders* described in Chapter 3, for example, was designed to raise questions about the targeting of media audiences; the children's TV project in Chapter 6 raised similar issues, in addition to questions about genre; while the pop music simulation described in Chapter 5 also raised questions about audience, representation and the institutional context of popular music. These projects clearly set out to integrate theory and practice; and in some cases, to integrate conceptual areas of the media curriculum that are often addressed separately.

The use of simulation in this way has attracted some criticism within educational research. Atkinson and Delamont[32], for example, provide a telling analysis of the hypocrisy of science experiments which will be recognisable by anyone who ever attempted to fake the results in their school science lessons. As they argue, 'guided discovery' of this kind is often stage managed in such a way as to arrive at pre-destined conclusions: despite the rhetoric that is often used to support it, opportunities for genuine experimentation or discovery are systematically closed down. While this analysis is certainly applicable to some media education activities, there is a sense in which the outcomes of media production simulations are not quite so cut-and-dried. Not all outcomes are equally valid, in the sense that there is a set of constraints that has to be observed; but equally, there is not a *single* outcome which can be foreseen or privileged.

Edwards and Mercer[33] provide an analysis of a primary school simulation which may have more far-reaching implications here. In this case, the students were asked to imagine that they were castaways on a desert island. What for the teacher was a means of 'discovering' and exploring basic social studies concepts (co-operation, the division of labour, social structure) was read by the students as a kind of training exercise in how to survive as a castaway. The problem, Edwards and Mercer argue, is that the 'ground rules' of such activities are often not made explicit, for fear of 'putting words into the children's mouths': the theoretical principles or concepts which form the basic rationale for the activity are somehow expected to emerge of their own accord. This is, we would argue, a familiar problem with the use of such activities in media education. It is often extremely difficult for students to 'see the wood for the trees' – to detach themselves from their involvement in the concrete particulars of the simulation and to adopt a more distanced, analytical stance. The debriefing, which is a crucial means of connecting theory and practice, is often very difficult to manage successfully. Students often actively *resist* the attempt to get them to reflect upon and evaluate their work once it is, in their terms, complete.

This last point raises questions about the process of evaluation which will be considered more fully below; but it also points to some of the broader difficulties with simulation as a method. These are partly to do with the potential conflict between the three different rationales we have just outlined. As we have suggested (Chapter 4), the desire to replicate professional practice may well conflict with the need to ensure the effective functioning of a working group – or indeed, with the need to ensure equal access to learning. Perhaps more significantly, the replication of professional practice may also conflict with the insistence on conceptual learning. Setting 'realistic' institutional constraints on students' work may actively prevent them from addressing central theoretical issues, for example to do with representation[34]. Indeed, it may simply cultivate a form of cynicism about the operations of the media industries, in which political principles and the desire to innovate are simply jettisoned in favour of 'catering to the lowest common denominator'. This was clearly part of the rationale for some of the work we have described in Chapters 5 and 6: students produced material that they themselves considered patronising or even 'politically incorrect' (at least on one level), yet they were able to rationalise this on the grounds that this would be the way it would be done in real life.

This conflict of aims is particularly apparent in the tendency of many media simulations to set up what may ultimately be impossible demands. Students are frequently required to produce material that is simultaneously a replication of dominant genres *and* an ideological or formal deconstruction of them. The fantasy of the anti-sexist police series or the anti-realist soap opera is one that recurs throughout media education classrooms, although it is one that would only ever be entertained by the most *avant-garde* professional producers – or indeed by post-graduate students. However implicitly, students are being required to mimic the work of 'alternative' and 'theoretically informed' practitioners such as Jo Spence or Cindy Sherman or the Black Audio Film Collective – who together would make at least the beginnings of an alternative 'canon' for many Media Studies teachers. Of course, this is not to suggest that such things cannot be attempted, or that students should be confined merely to working within dominant forms; although it does imply that they need a firm grounding in those forms before they can be realistically expected to deconstruct or subvert them.

A second issue here concerns the relationship between the 'cognitive' and 'emotional' dimensions of simulation – and indeed, of practical work more broadly. As we have suggested, this issue has often been posed in very polarised terms. The discourse of 'objective', rationalistic analysis is consistently privileged, while students' emotional investments and pleasures in the media are seen as something to be overcome. Here again, we suspect that students may be confronting impossible demands. As we have noted, students often find it hard to abandon or step back from their involvement in a simulation. Indeed, as is very clear from the work described throughout this book, students often display very high levels of personal and emotional commitment to practical work – commitment which, in our experience, is less frequently the case with the more analytical aspects of media education. Yet in many respects, the work we have described provided students with opportunities to investigate areas of identity and subjectivity that most media education practice does not come near. Rather than being encouraged to disavow their emotional investments, they were offered the chance to explore them in a comparatively non-threatening public arena. Indeed, we would argue that much of the value of simulation derives from the way in which it creates a 'safe' space, in which it becomes possible for students to *play* with media forms. Since they are explicitly being encouraged to adopt a fictional persona, rather than to make a 'personal statement', they are sanctioned to say things without being held to account for the consequences. Simulation allows students to have their cake and eat it: they can say things without being required to make any commitment to them, and they are provided with the perfect let-out clause. Simulation is, in this sense, precisely a kind of *game*. It is at once 'real' and 'unreal' – perhaps the perfect postmodern form.

This has particular implications in terms of the *ideological* dimensions of simulations. As we have shown in Chapters 5 and 6, this approach may well result in work which the students themselves may or may not recognise as 'politically incorrect', or at least as highly ambiguous. Practical work in general, and simulation in particular, could be seen as a site for 'carnival'[35] – an opportunity for students to subvert and transgress the 'official' discourses of the school. As we have suggested, this form of resistance does not in itself necessarily possess 'progressive' political consequences. Nevertheless, we would not wish to consign this simply to the domain of the 'uncanny' or the 'unknowable', as some recent theorists have done[36]. Despite the elements of ambiguity and self-conscious subversion that are present in productions like *PMT* (Chapter 5) and *Flat Broke* (Chapter 6), they can nevertheless be read in ideological terms; and they do in some respects reflect these students' genuine positions or concerns.

The solution here, we would argue, is not simply to intensify our political policing of students – an approach which has been consistently found to be counter-productive.

On the contrary, we would suggest that these issues can be made the focus of explicit debate and reflection *by the class as a whole*, rather than simply in response to the requirements of the teacher. This was indeed partly the case with the 'audience research' dimension of the project described in Chapter 6, which effectively forced the students to justify their decisions to other students, and to respond to some very fundamental criticisms. As we have shown, this is not without its difficulties – particularly if, as in the case of *Flat Broke*, the students are able to co-opt the discourses that might be used to question them. Yet reflection and self-evaluation of this kind is a crucial and indispensable aspect of practical work; and it is accordingly to this issue that we now turn.

The problems and possibilities of reflection

The need for students to reflect systematically on their own media production work has been a recurrent emphasis throughout this book. Indeed, this emphasis could be seen as a distinctive element of media education. One of the most important limitations that we identified in the projects described in Chapters 3 and 4, for example, was the failure to build in opportunities for reflection and self-evaluation – not least because this would be seen as inappropriate or indeed in conflict with the values of the curriculum subjects or institutional locations (English and youth work, respectively) in which that work took place. Similar limitations were identified in the case of the drama work discussed in Chapter 7, although we also acknowledged the potential of some drama techniques in this respect. By contrast, the Media Studies projects discussed in Chapters 5 and 6 placed a central emphasis on theoretical reflection, primarily in written form. In both cases, the students were required to produce an evaluative account of the production process, which would make explicit the conceptual issues that were at stake. As we indicated in Chapter 6, there are significant difficulties with this approach, particularly if self-evaluation is perceived by students as simply a covert form of teacher assessment. If this kind of reflective writing is simply a matter of regurgitating 'critical' knowledge, or of deploying a particular academic vocabulary, it is almost bound to be superficial and ineffective.

Our argument here, however, is not that we should necessarily abandon written self-evaluation, let alone self-evaluation as a whole. As we have consistently argued, it is not enough for students simply to 'learn the language' – to learn to 'write' in the modern media. They must also learn to reflect upon the process of writing itself. They must come to understand the ways in which meanings and pleasures are made, and the ways in which language both constrains and creates the possibilities for social communication. We would argue that there are good reasons why this reflection should take place in *written* form, which are partly to do with the 'externalising' function of writing, and its particular status as both a private and a public form[37].

Here again, the analogy with verbal language is potentially very productive. In a sense, we are making a similar argument to that of the genre theorists – that students need to develop an explicit and systematic understanding of language itself. In practice, however, genre theory has often led to a rather mechanistic pedagogy that comes close to the grammar teaching it has supposedly moved beyond. By contrast, the notion of 'Knowledge About Language' developed in the wake of the Kingman Report on English teaching would seem to offer a more productive approach[38]. John Richmond's account of this area[39] provides a theoretical model which offers significant potential for rethinking this relationship between practical production and critical analysis – or, in 'English' terms, between *language use* and *language study*. For

Richmond, it is principally through the dynamic *interaction* between these two areas that knowledge about language is seen to be acquired. This occurs primarily as a result of a process of 'translation', as students move across language modes, using one mode as a means of reflecting on another – for example, talk about writing, or writing about reading (and, of course, we would want to include media production as another language mode here). Thus, it is through shifting between the role of writer and the role of reader that students' development as writers can be sustained: 'the eye of the reader', Richmond argues, 'informs the voice of the writer'. The 'technical' metalanguage and the conceptual knowledge that students need in order to understand the structures and functions of language is thus acquired, not through a process of direct instruction in the 'rules' (for example, through abstract grammar exercises), but through a process of *theoretical reflection upon practice*. It is in this process, Richmond argues, that students' existing, implicit knowledge of language becomes explicit, and is thereby developed and extended.

As this account implies, knowledge about language cannot be effectively communicated simply through transmission; nor is it the case that such knowledge can simply be 'discovered' through language use. The teacher plays a crucial role here, not so much as a source of superior wisdom, but in creating learning contexts and in making interventions through which students can reflect upon their work, and thereby develop their understanding. This is inevitably a recursive process, rather than a matter of arriving at insights once and for all: while teachers have to make new information and terminology available to students, they also have to provide them with opportunities to take it on and make it their own. This notion of learning as a dialectical (or dialogical) process thus effectively takes us beyond both the 'progressive' and the 'traditional' models of pedagogy with which we began. In the case of media education, and perhaps more generally, this broad approach could obviously be extended. In very general terms, learning about the media might be seen to result from a series of dialectical relationships: between practice and theory; between language use and language study; between experience and abstraction from experience; between induction and deduction; between emotion and cognition. Here again, it is in the interaction *between* these different modes of engagement that much of the most significant learning in media education may occur.

Nevertheless, it is clear that any such dialectic will only be possible if there is something at stake in it for the students themselves. In the case of media production, it requires a commitment both to the product itself (or to the 'statement' it is making) *and* to the process of reflection (in the sense that it should *matter* to the student, rather than simply to the teacher – or indeed the examiner).

This implies a need to develop alternative approaches to self-evaluation. This may be partly a question of the *context* in which it occurs, and the *audience* to whom it is addressed. As we argued in Chapter 6, students need to have opportunities for self-evaluation that are not tied to the requirements of assessment. Such opportunities may not necessarily be directed towards – or indeed even involve – the teacher; and even where they entail writing, we should give more thought to providing different audiences for that writing. Secondly, we need to consider the *medium* through which self-evaluation occurs. Even where self-evaluation is also an assessed task, we should consider alternative possibilities such as individual spoken presentations or small-group talk. We might also use further media production activities in a similar way – for example, encouraging students to reflect upon their work through producing imaginary reviews or TV interviews[40]. Finally, and perhaps most importantly, we need to consider the *process* by which self-evaluation is supported and encouraged. For all its limitations, the use of the 'real' audience in the project described in Chapter 6 did seem to play a positive role in enabling the students to distance themselves sufficiently to be able to reflect upon their work. Perhaps the most fundamental problem here – and, we would argue, with a great deal of *teacher* assessment as well[41] – is that the criteria for evaluation need to be made much more explicit and open to debate. One possibility in this respect would be for the students themselves to agree upon criteria, and then to use them as the basis for analysing each other's work[42].

Of course, none of these suggestions necessarily precludes the production of discursive writing, which (for the reasons we have noted) may well need to remain the 'end result'. Nevertheless, they could be seen to enrich and support a practice that in our view is frequently far from successful. The crucial point here, however, is that reflection should be seen as an ongoing, recursive process, which by its very nature will not always be capable of explicit *demonstration*. Many of the 'results' of reflection will, in this respect, not become apparent until students have their next opportunity of production.

Finally, this perspective implies that we may need to reconsider the *sequence* of activities in media teaching. As we have noted, Media Studies typically begins with analysis, and then moves on to production. This serves to establish a particular relationship between them, in which theory is seen as the site of truth, and practice merely as the implementation of theory. In our view, this leads to some extremely reductive versions of practice – as in the case of deconstruction exercises – or alternatively to assignments which (as we have noted) end up making impossible demands on students. In Chapter 5, for example, we argued that the analytical work on the music industry may have actively closed down opportunities for practical exploration, and thus restricted the possible learning outcomes of the project. The dialectical approach we have outlined would suggest that this sequence could profitably be reversed, at least in certain instances. Particularly in areas where we might reasonably assume that students possess a high level of existing knowledge – popular music, for example, or soap opera – it would seem reasonable to approach the topic in this much more *deductive* way. Work on areas such as documentary or 'alternative' media – both of which we would see as essential aspects of media education – might need to proceed in a more traditionally *inductive* way. The crux, however, is to ensure that in either case the movement is a dialectical one. Rather than simply moving from theory to practice or vice-versa, we need to move constantly *between* them. Theory must inform practice, but practice must also inform theory.

Conclusion: some principles for practice

It has not been our intention in this book to provide a set of prescriptions for successful media production work in classrooms. Sound guidance on the 'nuts and bolts' of classroom management, on selecting and using equipment, and on curriculum design and assessment can be found elsewhere[43]. On the contrary, our intention here has been to undertake a theoretically informed *interrogation* of practice – of a kind which is in some ways analogous to the approach we have argued for in media education itself. Nevertheless, it would be appropriate to conclude with a summary of some of the broad principles which we feel might usefully guide the development of practical work in media education. There are three major points we would like to make here.

1. Practical work has to provide students with *genuine* opportunities to develop their own insights and theories.

In criticising past approaches, we have warned against a notion of practical work as subordinate to theory, or indeed as a means of demonstrating pre-determined theoretical insights. Yet we have also challenged the view that media production should be seen as an open invitation for students to 'express themselves'. Of course, we cannot avoid setting an agenda of theoretical issues, not least in terms of how we frame and structure classroom assignments; and as we have argued, it is vital that these issues should be made explicit to students, rather than left for them to 'discover'. Yet if students are not enabled to investigate these issues on their own terms, and to draw on their existing knowledge of (and pleasures in) the media, then the outcomes of such work will be little more than trivial. If practical work is to be more than a superficial exercise in *form*, we need to enable students to develop the *content* of their work in ways that allow for genuine exploration and change. Much of the value of practical work lies in the fact that it allows students to explore their affective and subjective investments in the media, in a way which is much more difficult to achieve through critical analysis. If it is to be effective in this respect, we have to allow – and consciously construct – a space for play and experimentation, in which there are genuinely no 'right answers'.

2. Practical work must be recursive.

On one level, this simply means that there needs to be a lot of it – and with the cheapness and accessibility of the technology, this is increasingly becoming a realistic possibility. Rather than leading up to the Big Production Number (as is the case in some Media Studies syllabuses), students should be engaging in practical work on a regular basis, both in the form of longer projects and in frequent, small-scale activities, not all of which should be assessed. While these activities might take the form of 'exercises', there is an important place for unstructured social uses of the technology – or what might well resemble aimless 'messing around': this is, we would argue, a vital first step that should be built upon, rather than avoided. Equally, it is important that students have the opportunity to work across a range of media forms and technologies – photography, video, desk-top publishing and so on. At the same time, to argue that practical work should be recursive is also to imply a different relationship between process and product. As we have suggested, the product should not be seen as the end of the process, or as a summary demonstration of what has been learned, but as a stage within it – a starting point for reflection or redrafting, and the basis for future work.

3. Reflection is a central and indispensable aspect of practical work.

Although we have expressed reservations about the emphasis in media education on analysis and critique, this is not to say that it should simply be abandoned. The challenge of integrating theory and practice remains. If we are to develop the full potential of *both* kinds of work, the relationship between them needs to be equal and dialectical. This has implications, for example, in terms of how we sequence classroom activities. As we have suggested, there is a strong case in many situations for using practical work deductively, as a means of generating fresh theoretical ideas. As in the case of 'Knowledge About Language', we need to provide opportunities for students to 'translate' insights from one medium to another, and to reflect upon one mode of language through using another. At the same time, it is clear that we need to find new and more effective ways of enabling students to step back from their productions, and to reflect upon their theoretical implications. Although we do feel there is a value in insisting upon written reflection, we need to devise alternative strategies that can both stand alongside and feed into students' writing. This kind of self-evaluation has to be motivated by something more than the abstract requirements of examiners – and it too should be recursive, part of an ongoing cycle of action and reflection, and not simply a once-and-for-all activity.

Perhaps inevitably, the principles we have outlined suggest many issues for further exploration and research. We are certain that, in the coming decade, media production will occupy a much more central role in children's education. In future, it will no longer be possible to see 'making media' in isolation from children's other learning experiences, both inside and beyond the school. As we have implied, technological changes may lead to a convergence of previously discrete curriculum areas such as English, Drama, Art, Technology and Media Studies. Nevertheless, the fundamental questions we have raised about teaching and learning through media production must continue to be addressed. As the technology becomes more widely available, and as media education comes to be integrated throughout the curriculum, we will need to think much harder about *progression* – that is, about what and how we expect students to learn about the media at different stages of their school career, both in terms of practical skill and in terms of theoretical understanding. The danger, in this area as in others, is that technological developments will effectively dictate educational priorities. As media educators, we do not believe that technology is an irresistible force. On the contrary, how technology develops depends fundamentally on how (and by whom) it is *used*. If new media technologies are to be a genuine means of learning and of social empowerment, it is vital that they are used productively and creatively by the future generations whom we teach.

Notes

1 These debates have been widely summarised elsewhere: see, for example, Lusted (1986), Hartley, Goulden and O'Sullivan (1985). Key contributions to this debate would include Alvarado (1981), Masterman (1981), Williamson (1981/2; 1985), and Buckingham (1986).

2 See, for example, Willis (1977), Corrigan (1979), Sharp and Green (1975), and Edwards and Mercer (1987).

3 This position is particularly apparent in Alvarado (1981); and is directly attacked by Masterman (1981) and Williamson (1981/2).

4 This is the position espoused by Masterman (1980), from whom the quotations here are drawn - although it is one that is significantly at odds with other aspects of his argument, particularly his view of the 'power' of the media (see Buckingham, 1986, 1992). For a further discussion, see Buckingham and Sefton-Green (1994), Chapter 7.

5 The quotations here are again drawn from Masterman (1980).

6 In the US, this position is particularly associated with the writings of Henry Giroux and Peter McLaren. For critiques of this approach, see Ellsworth (1989) and Gore (1993).

7 See Hall (1992).

8 See Williamson (1981/2).

9 See Sefton-Green (1990).

10 There are several relevant studies in this area: for example, Radway (1984), Morley (1986), Longhurst (1989), Moss (1989) and Gray (1992). For a discussion relating specifically to media education, see Buckingham and Sefton-Green *op cit*, Chapters 2 and 3.

11 For a further discussion and some empirical research on this issue, see Buckingham and Sefton-Green *ibid*, Chapter 2.

12 This is borne out by empirical studies of computer game players, which suggest that girls are beginning to demand and enjoy equal access: see Cunningham (1995).

13 See Gore (1993); Buckingham (1986).

14 Similar issues are raised in Turnbull (1993).

15 A great deal of contemporary cultural theory has attempted to pick a way through this particular minefield. Hall (1992) and Gilroy (1993) represent notable recent examples.

16 This is most apparent in the arguments of Ferguson (1981), discussed in Chapters 1 and 5.

17 See Dickson (1994).

18 This is not of course to suggest that students should not study areas such as news, which is important for all sorts of reasons. It is rather to question which areas of the media might be most effective to focus upon at any given stage, particularly when it comes to practical production.

19 See Bordwell and Thompson (1993).

20 See Barker (1989).

21 In the case of English teaching, for example, producing storyboards from print texts can be a useful way of enhancing students' understanding of *narration* in both media: it does not necessarily have to result in a 'finished' production.

22 We have not dwelt on the most common difficulty with storyboards, namely the degree of artistic skill that is needed to make an effective one. Most media teachers are accustomed to circumventing that argument: it is the intention not the execution that counts. Nevertheless, the fact remains that the more artistically capable students are often the most able at conceptualising media forms.

23 Buckingham (1990), Buckingham and Sefton-Green *op cit.*

24 See Neale (1980) and Kress (1994) for this approach to different kinds of genres.

25 For example, Collins (1989).

26 For accounts of this work, see Reid (1987) and Cope and Kalantzis (1993). For an important critical view, see Barrs (1993).

27 This is, it must be emphasised, a gross caricature of the 'progressive' position, although it is one which supposedly radical genre theorists seem to share with the political right. See Cope and Kalantzis *ibid*, Chapters 2 and 3.

28 Of course, knowing rules implicitly may be how we all *use* rules in life anyway.

29 See Barrs (1993).

30 See Hudak (1987), Buckingham, Fraser and Mayman (1990), Turnbull *op cit.*

31 But see Alvarado (1975) and Buckingham (1995).

32 Atkinson and Delamont (1976).

33 Edwards and Mercer (1987).

34 See Grahame (1990).

35 This notion derives from the work of the Russian literary theorist Bakhtin (e.g. 1968). For a discussion of this in relation to students' media production, see Buckingham and Sefton-Green *op cit*, Chapter 10.

36 See, for example, Britzman (1991), Ellsworth (1989).

37 This argument is developed in Chapter 6 above; and in Buckingham and Sefton-Green *ibid*, Chapter 8.

38 For theoretical and applied accounts of this work, see Carter (1990).

39 Richmond (1990).

40 Some of these possibilities are discussed in Grahame *op cit.*. Of course, one of the problems here is that such activities remain *simulated*: the moment of 'genuine' reflection may be forever deferred, and the imperatives of the product itself may again supersede the need to reflect upon the process.

41 See Fraser (forthcoming).

42 For further suggestions in this area, see Grahame (1991a, 1991b).

43 See particularly Grahame (1991b) and Stafford (1994).

Bibliography

ALLEN, D. (1992a) Media, Arts and the Curriculum, in ALVARADO, M. & BOYD-BARRETT, O. [Eds.] *Media Education: An Introduction*, London: British Film Institute & The Open University Press.

ALLEN, D. (1992b) Media Education and the Art Curriculum, *English and Media Magazine*, No. 27. pp. 26–29.

ALLEN, D. (1994) Developing Visual Literacy – Some Reflections on the Term, *Journal of Art and Design Education*. Vol. 13 No. 2. pp. 133–143.

ALLEN, D. (forthcoming) Production in Art Education, in BOWKER, J. [Ed.] *Production Lines*, London: British Film Institute.

ALLEN, R. (1985) *Speaking of Soap Operas*, Chapel Hill: University of North Carolina Press.

ALVARADO, M. (1975) Simulation as Method, *Screen Education*, No. 14, pp. 21–26.

ALVARADO, M. (1981) Television Studies and Pedagogy, *Screen Education*, No. 38, pp. 56–67.

ALVARADO, M. & BOYD-BARRETT, O [Eds.] (1992) *Media Education: An Introduction,* London: British Film Institute & The Open University Press.

ALVARADO, M., GUTCH, R. & WOLLEN, T. (1987) *Learning the Media: An Introduction to Media Teaching,* London: Macmillan.

ANG, I. (1985) *Watching Dallas: Soap Opera and the Melodramatic Imagination*, London: Methuen.

ANG, I. (1991) *Desperately Seeking the Audience*, London: Routledge.

ARTHURS, J. (1987) Production Projects for GCSE, *In the Picture* (Yorkshire Arts), Autumn.

ATKINSON, P. & DELAMONT, S. (1976) Mock-ups and Cock-ups: The Stage Management of Guided Discovery Instruction, in WOODS, P.E. & HAMMERSLEY, M. [Eds.] *School Experience*, London: Croom Helm.

BAKHTIN, M. (1968) *Rabelais and his World*, Cambridge Mass.; M.I.T. Press.

BARKER, M. (1989) *Comics: Ideology, Power and the Critics*, Manchester: Manchester University Press.

BARNES, D., BRITTON, J. & ROSEN, H. (1969) *Language, the Learner and the School*, Harmondsworth: Penguin.

BARRS, M. (1993) Genre Theory: What's it all About? in STIERER, B. & MAYBIN, J. *Language, Literacy and Learning in Educational Practice*, Clevedon: Multilingual Matters.

BARTON, D. (1994) *Literacy: An Introduction to the Ecology of Written Language*, Oxford: Blackwell

BAZALGETTE, C. [Ed.] (1989) *Primary Media Education: A Curriculum Statement*, London: British Film Institute.

BENNETT, T., BOYD-BOWMAN, S., MERCER, C. & WOOLLACOTT, J. [Eds.] (1981) *Popular Television and Film,* London: British Film Institute & The Open University Press.

BETHELL, A. (1981) *EyeOpeners One and Two,* Cambridge: Cambridge University Press.

BLANCHARD, T. GREENLEAF, S. & SEFTON-GREEN, J. (1989) *The Music Business: A Teaching Pack*, London: Hodder & Stoughton.

BOLTON, G. [Ed.] (1986) *Gavin Bolton: Selected Writings,* Harlow: Longman.

BOLTON, G. (1989) Drama, in HARGREAVES, D. [Ed.],*Children and the Arts*, Milton Keynes: Open University.

BORDWELL, D. & THOMPSON, K. (1993) *Film Art*, Fourth Edition, New York: McGraw Hill.

BOWKER, J. [Ed.] (1991) *Secondary Media Education: A Curriculum Statement*, London: British Film Institute.

BRADEN, S. (forthcoming) Video, the Camera and the Subject: Pedagogy and Assessment, in BOWKER, J. [Ed.] *Production Lines,* London: British Film Institute.

BRITTON, J. (1970) *Language and Learning,* Harmondsworth: Penguin.

BRITTON, J., BURGESS, T., MARTIN, N. et al. (1975) *The Development of Writing Abilities 11–18,* London: Macmillan.

BRITZMAN, D. (1991) Decentering Discourses in Teacher Education: Or, the Unleashing of Unpopular Things, *Journal of Education (Boston),* Vol. 173 No. 3, pp. 60–80.

BUCKINGHAM, D. (1986) Against Demystification, *Screen,* Vol. 27 No. 5, pp. 80–95.

BUCKINGHAM, D. (1987a) *Unit 27: Media Education (EH207 Communication and Education),* Milton Keynes: Open University Press.

BUCKINGHAM, D. (1987b) *Public Secrets: 'EastEnders' and its Audience,* London: British Film Institute.

BUCKINGHAM, D. (1988) Media Studies, Cultural Studies, *Media Education Initiatives,* No. 10, pp. 11–13.

BUCKINGHAM, D. (1989) Television Literacy: A Critique, *Radical Philosophy,* No. 51, pp. 12–25.

BUCKINGHAM, D. [Ed.] (1990) *Watching Media Learning: Making Sense of Media Education,* London: Falmer Press.

BUCKINGHAM, D. (1992) Media Education: The Limits of a Discourse, *Journal of Curriculum Studies,* Vol. 24 No.4, pp. 297–313.

BUCKINGHAM, D. (1993a) *Changing Literacies: Media Education and Modern Culture,* The London File, London: The Tufnell Press.

BUCKINGHAM, D. (1993b) *Children Talking Television: The Making of Television Literacy,* London: Falmer Press.

BUCKINGHAM, D. (1993c) Re-reading Audiences, in BUCKINGHAM, D. [Ed.] *Reading Audiences: Young People and the Media,* Manchester; Manchester University Press.

BUCKINGHAM, D (1995) Media Education and the Media Industries: Bridging the Gaps? *Journal of Educational Television,* Vol. 21 No.1, pp. 7–22.

BUCKINGHAM, D., FRASER, P. & MAYMAN, N. (1990) Beginning Classroom Research in Media Education, in BUCKINGHAM, D. [Ed.] *Watching Media Learning: Making Sense of Media Education,* London: Falmer Press.

BUCKINGHAM, D. & SEFTON-GREEN, J. (1993) Towards New Literacies: Information Technology, English and Media Education, *English & Media Magazine,* No. 28, pp. 20–33.

BUCKINGHAM, D. & SEFTON-GREEN, J. (1994) *Cultural Studies Goes to School: Reading and Teaching Popular Media,* London: Taylor and Francis.

BURGESS, T. et al. (1973) *Understanding Children Writing,* Harmondsworth: Penguin.

BURNS, T. (1977) *The BBC. Public Institution and Private World,* London: Macmillan.

CARROLL, T. (1992) Photomontage: Image and Meaning, in ALVARADO, M. & BOYD-BARRETT, O. [Eds.] *Media Education: An Introduction,* London: British Film Institute & The Open University Press.

CARROLL, T. Contextualising Art Education (unpublished paper).

CARTER, R. [Ed.] (1990) *Knowledge about Language and the Curriculum: The LINC Reader,* London: Hodder & Stoughton.

CAUGHIE, J. (1980) *Theories of Authorship,* London: Routledge and Kegan Paul & British Film Institute.

CHAPPELL, C. (1984) Family Fortunes, in MCROBBIE, A. & NAVA, M. [Eds.] *Gender and Generation,* London: Macmillan

COHEN (1984) Against the New Vocationalism, in BATES, I. et al., *Schooling for the Dole?* London: Macmillan.

COHEN, P. (1990) *Really Useful Knowledge,* London: Trentham Books.

COLLEDGE, C. (1984) *Classroom Photography,* London: Ilford.

COLLINS, J. (1989) *Uncommon Cultures,* London: Routledge.

COPE, B. & KALANTZIS, M. [Eds.] (1993) *The Powers of Literacy: A Genre Approach to Teaching Writing,* London: Falmer Press.

CORRIGAN, P. (1979) *Schooling the Smash Street Kids,* London: Macmillan.

COURTNEY, R. (1974) *Play, Drama and Thought: The Intellectual Background to Drama in Education*, London: Cassell.

CUNNINGHAM, H. (1995) Moral Kombat and Computer Game Girls in Bazalgette, C. & Buckingham, D. [Eds.] *In Front of the Children. Screen Entertainment and Young Audiences*, London: British Film Institute.

DEPARTMENT FOR EDUCATION (DFE) (1994) *Art in the National Curriculum, England*, London: HMSO.

DEWDNEY, A. & LISTER M. (1988) *Youth, Culture and Photography*, London: Macmillan.

DICKSON, P. (1994) *A Survey of Media Education*. London: National Foundation for Educational Research/British Film Institute.

DONALD, J. (1977) *Media Studies: Possibilities and Limitations*, London: British Film Institute, mimeo.

DONALD, J. & RATTANSI, A. [Eds.] (1992) *'Race', Culture and Difference*, London: Sage.

DONELSON, K. (1971) Reinventing the Wheel: 10 Questions about teaching and using film being asked in the 70's that were answered in the 40's. *English Journal*.

DOWMUNT, T. (1980) *Video with Young People*, London: Interaction.

DROTNER, K. (1989) Girl Meets Boy: Aesthetic Production, Reception and Gender Identity, *Cultural Studies*, Vol. 3 No. 2, pp. 208–225.

DYER, R., et al (1981) *Coronation Street*, Television Monograph, London: British Film Institute.

ECO, U. (1979) *The Role of the Reader*, London: Hutchinson.

EDWARDS, D. & MERCER, N. (1987) *Common Knowledge: The Development of Understanding in the Classroom*, London: Methuen.

ELLIS, J. (1982) *Visible Fictions*, London: Routledge and Kegan Paul.

ELLSWORTH, E. (1989) Why Doesn't This Feel Empowering? Working Through the Repressive Myths of Critical Pedagogy, *Harvard Educational Review*, Vol. 59 No. 3, pp. 297–324.

FERGUSON, B. (1981) Practical Work and Pedagogy, *Screen Education*, No. 38, pp. 42–55.

FINEGOLD, D et al (1990) *A British Baccalaureat?: Ending the Division betwen Education and Training*, London: Institute for Public Policy Research.

FISKE, J. (1987) *Television Culture*, London: Routledge.

FRASER, P. (forthcoming) Questions of Evaluation, in BOWKER, J. [Ed.] *Production Lines*, London: British Film Institute.

FRITH, S., GOODWIN, A,. & GROSSBERG, L. [Eds.] (1993) *Sound and Vision: the Music Video Reader*, London: Routledge.

GAUTHIER, G. (n.d.) *Initiation to the Semiology of the Image*, London: BFI Education.

GERAGHTY, C. (1981) The Continuing Serial: A Defintion in DYER, R., et al, *Coronation Street*, Television Monograph, London: British Film Institute.

GILLESPIE, M. (1995) *Television, Ethnicity and Cultural Change*, London: Routledge.

GILROY, P. (1993) *The Black Atlantic*, London: Verso.

GOFFMAN, E. (1969) *The Presentation of Self in Everyday Life*, Harmondsworth: Penguin.

GOLAY, J-P. (1971) Introduction to the Language of Image and Sound, *Screen Education Notes*, No. 1.

GOODMAN, S. & TANDY, B. (1993) Portfolio Assessment: The Tape's Great, But What Did They Learn? *The Independent* August/ September.

GORE, J. (1993) *The Struggle for Pedagogies*, New York: Routledge.

GRAHAME, J. (1990) *Playtime*: Learning about Media Institutions through Practical Work, in BUCKINGHAM, D. [Ed.] *Watching Media Learning: Making Sense of Media Education*, London: Falmer Press.

GRAHAME, J. [Ed.] (1991a) *The English Curriculum: Media*, London: The English and Media Centre.

GRAHAME, J. (1991b) The Production Process, in LUSTED, D. [Ed.] *The Media Studies Book: A Guide for Teachers*, London: Routledge.

GRAHAME, J. [Ed.] (1994) *Production Practices*, London: The English and Media Centre.

GRAHAME, J. & BLANCHARD, T. (1992) Ration(alis)ing Media Studis, *English and Media Magazine*, No.27, pp. 12–13.

GRAVES, D. (1978) *Balance the Basics: Let them Write*, New York: Ford Foundation.

GRAY, A. (1992) *Video Playtime: The Gendering of a Leisure Technology*, London: Routledge.

HALL, S. (1992) The Question of Cultural Identity, in HALL, S., HELD, D. & McGREW, T. [Eds.] *Modernity and its Futures*, Cambridge: Polity Press.

HARROP, J. (1992) *Acting*, London: Routledge.

HARTLEY, J. (1987) Invisible Fictions: Television Audiences, Paedocracy, Pleasure, *Textual Practice*, Vol. 1 No. 2, pp. 121–138.

HARTLEY, J., GOULDEN, H. & O'SULLIVAN, T. (1985) *Making Sense of the Media*, London: Comedia.

HELLER, C. (1978) The Resistible Rise of Video, *Educational Broadcasting International*, Vol.11 No.3 pp. 133–135.

HOBSON, D. (1982) *Crossroads: the Drama of a Soap Opera*, London: Methuen.

HORNBROOK, D. (1989) *Education and Dramatic Art*, Oxford: Basil Blackwell.

HORNBROOK, D. (1991) *Education in Drama: Casting the Dramatic Curriculum*, London: Falmer Press.

HUDAK, G. (1987) Student Knowledge and the Formation of Academic Discourse: A Case Study, in SMYTH, J. [Ed.] *Educating Teachers: Changing the Nature of Pedagogical Knowledge*, London: Falmer Press.

JAQUES, D. (1991) *Learning in Groups*, London: Kogan Page.

JHALLY, S. & LEWIS, J. (1992) *Enlightened Racism: The Cosby Show, Audiences and the Myth of the American Dream*, Boulder: Westview Press.

JORDAN, M (1981) Realism and Convention in DYER, R., et al, *Coronation Street*, Television Monograph, London: British Film Institute.

KAPLAN, E. (1987) *Rocking around the Clock: Music Television, Postmodernism and Consumer Culture*, London: Methuen.

KNIGHT, R. (1964) Film Studies and English, in WHANNEL P. & HARCOURT P. [Eds.] *Film Teaching, Studies in the Teaching of Film Education. Four Courses Described*, London: British Film Institute.

KRESS, G. (1994) *Learning to Write*, Second Edition, London: Routledge.

LANDOW, G. (1992) *Hypertext. The Convergence of Contemporary Critical Theory and Technology*, Baltimore: John Hopkins Press.

LEAVIS, F. & THOMPSON, D. (1933) *Culture and Environment*, London: Chatto and Windus.

LONGHURST, D. [Ed.] (1989) *Gender, Genre and Narrative Pleasure*, London: Unwin Hyman.

LORAC, C. & WEISS, M. (1981) *Communication and Social Skills*, Exeter: Wheaton.

LOWNDES, D. (1968) *Film Making in Schools*, London: Batsford.

LUSTED, D. (1986) Why Pedagogy? *Screen* Vol. 27 No. 5, pp. 2–14.

MASTERMAN, L. (1980) *Teaching About Television*, London: Macmillan.

MASTERMAN, L. (1981) TV Pedagogy, *Screen Education*, No. 40, pp. 88–92.

MASTERMAN, L. (1985) *Teaching the Media*, London: Comedia.

MELLOR, B. et al (1984) *Making Stories*, London: English and Media Centre.

MESSARIS, *Visual 'Literacy': Image, Mind and Reality*, Boulder: Westview Press.

MILLER, H. (1979) *Films in the Classroom: a Practical Guide*, Metuchen, New Jersey: Scarecrow Press.

MORLEY, D. (1986) *Family Television: Cultural Power and Domestic Leisure*, London: Comedia.

MOSS, G. (1989) *Un/Popular Fictions*, London: Virago.

MOY, B. & RALEIGH, M. (1984) Comprehension: Bringing it Back Alive, in MILLER, J. [Ed.] *Eccentric Propositions. Essays on Literature and the Curriculum*, London: Routledge and Kegan Paul.

NAVA, M. (1984) Youth Service Provision, Social Order and the Question of Girls, in McROBBIE, A. & NAVA, M. [Eds.] *Gender and Generation*, London: Macmillan.

NEALE, S. (1980) *Genre*, London: British Film Institute.

NEELANDS, J. (1992) *Learning Through Imagined Experience: The Role of Drama in the National Curriculum*, Sevenoaks: Hodder & Stoughton.

PERKINS, T.E. (1979) Rethinking Stereotypes, in BARRETT, M. et al. [Eds.] *Ideology and Cultural Production*, London: Croom Helm.

PETERS, J. (1961) *Teaching about Film*, Lausanne: UNESCO.

POSTER, M. (1990) *The Mode of Information: Poststructuralism and Social Context*, Cambridge: Polity.

PUDOVKIN, V. (1929) *On Film Technique*, London: Victor Gollancz.

RADWAY, J. (1984) *Reading the Romance*, London: Verso.

REID, J-A., FORRESTAL, P. & COOK, J. (1989) *Small Group Learning in the Classroom*, Scarborough (W. Australia): Chalkface Press.

REID, I. [Ed.] (1987) *The Place of Genre in Learning: Current Debates*, Geelong: Deakin University Press.

REYNOLDS, M. (1994) *Groupwork in Education and Training*, London: Kogan Page.

RICHARDS, C. (1986) Anti-Racist Initiatives, *Screen* Vol. 27 No. 5, pp. 74–79.

RICHARDS, C. (1990) Intervening in Popular Pleasures: Media Studies and the Politics of Subjectivity, in BUCKINGHAM, D. [Ed.] *Watching Media Learning: Making Sense of Media Education*, London: Falmer Press.

RICHARDS, C. (1994) The English Curriculum: What's Music Got To Do With It? *Changing English* Vol. 1 No.2, pp. 68–83.

RICHMOND, J. (1990) What do we Mean by Knowledge about Language? in CARTER, R. [Ed.] *Knowledge about Language and the Curriculum. The LINC Reader*, London: Hodder and Stoughton.

RIMMON-KENAN, S. (1983) *Narrative Fiction*, London: Routledge.

SCHLESINGER, P. (1987) *Putting 'Reality' Together*, London: Methuen.

SEFTON-GREEN, J. (1990) Teaching and Learning about Representation: Culture and *The Cosby Show* in a North London Comprehensive, in BUCKINGHAM, D. [Ed.] *Watching Media Learning: Making Sense of Media Education*, London: Falmer Press.

SEFTON-GREEN, J. (1994) From Real Books to Play Books to Un-books, *English and Media Magazine*, No. 30, pp. 32–37.

SHARP, R. & GREEN, A. (1975) *Education and Social Control*, London: Routledge and Kegan Paul.

SMITH, A. (1988) Wings of Desire: Organising Practical Project Work, *Media Education Initiatives* No. 10, pp. 7–10.

SPENCE, J. (1986) *Putting Myself in the Picture*, London: Camden Press.

SPOURS, K. & YOUNG, M. (1990) Beyond Vocationalism: A New Perspective on the Relationship between Work and Education in GLEESON, D. [Ed.] *Training and its Alternatives*, Milton Keynes: Open University Press.

STAFFORD, R. (1990) Redefining Creativity: Extended Project Work in GCSE Media Studies, in BUCKINGHAM, D. [Ed.] *Watching Media Learning: Making Sense of Media Education*, London: Falmer Press.

STAFFORD, R. (1994) *Hands On*, London: British Film Institute.

TAYLOR, R. (1986) *Education for Art*, Harlow: Longman/SCCDC.

THOMPSON, D. [Ed.] (1964) *Discrimination and Popular Culture*, Harmondsworth: Penguin.

TURNBULL, S. (1993) The Media: Moral Lessons and Moral Careers, *Australian Journal of Education*, Vol. 37 No. 2, pp. 153–168.

TWEDDLE, S. & MOORE, P. (1993) Working within a New Literacy, in BRINDLEY, S. [Ed.] *Teaching English*, London: Routledge.

WAY, B. (1967) *Development Through Drama*, Thetford: Longman.

WHANNEL, P. & HARCOURT, P. [Ed.] (1964) *Film Teaching, Studies in the Teaching of Film Education. Four Courses Described*, London: British Film Institute.

WILLIAMS, R. (1976) *Keywords: A Vocabulary of Culture and Society*, Glasgow: Fontana.

WILLIAMSON, J. (1981/2) How Does Girl Number Twenty Understand Ideology? *Screen Education*, No. 40, pp. 80–87.

WILLIAMSON, J. (1985) Is There Anyone Here From a Classroom? *Screen*, Vol.26. No.1, pp. 90–95.

WILLIS, P. (1977) *Learning to Labour*, Farnborough: Saxon House.

WILLIS, P. (1990) *Common Culture: Symbolic Work at Play in the Everyday Cultures of the Young*, Bury St. Edmunds: Open University Press.

WILLENER, A., MILLIARD, G. & GANTY, A. (1976) *Videology and Utopia* London: Routledge and Kegan Paul

WINTER (1989) *Learning from Experience: Principles and Practice in Action Research*, London: Falmer Press.

WOLLEN, T. [Ed.] (1991) *Media in English; Classroom Materials at Key Stage 3*, London: British Film Institute.

Index

A Level Media Studies 14, 105–138, 170, 173
advertisements 55, 215
Allen, D. 19
alternative/oppositional media production 111, 122, 131, 158, 214,
Art 8, 18, 22–23, 209; history of 17; critical studies in 8; as a design subject 70
assessment 53, 70, 109, 122, 140, 142, 160, 163, 167, 171, 203, 223; see also *evaluation, log*
Atkinson, P. 221
audience 9, 14, 15, 22, 23, 37, 45, 59, 70, 121, 128–129, 140–167, 178, 217–219, 224;
audience research, 123–124, 145–153, 223
avant-garde 10, 51, 75, 111, 134, 210, 214–215

Barnes, D. 76
Barthes, R. 18
Barton, D. 20, 44–45
Boal, A. 174
Bolton, G. 194, 195
British Film Institute 2, 11, 18
Britton, J. 76, 165, 196
Bruner, J. 67
BTEC National 5
Buckingham, D. 19

camera angles–see *camera shots*
camera shots 18, 22, 23, 24, 28, 44, 78, 180, 210, 211
Carroll, T. 129
characterisation 172
children's TV 15, 27, 38, 140–167
class (social) 20, 77, 208
Cockpit Cultural Studies Department 80–82
collaborative work–see *group work*
computer games 52–53, 58
computers 47–49
conceptual learning 11–12, 20, 21, 45, 141, 147, 199, 203, 211, 217, 220

creativity 7, 13, 47, 49, 67, 108, 167, 173, 189, 194, 210; and technology 72–73, 203, 208–211
cross-curricular skills 50

de-centering 41, 58, 143, 218
deconstruction 6, 107, 108, 112, 171, 201, 210, 216, 217, 225
Delamont, D. 221
demystification 201, 219
de Saussure, F. 17
development–see *progression*
Dewdney, A. 80–82
'discovery learning' 91, 100, 105
dominant media forms 110, 112, 205, 210, 214–215, 217–219, 222
drafting 24, 34, 45, 49, 68, 214
Drama 6, 11, 15, 169–170, 223; in education 171, 177

editing 12, 68, 78, 87, 146, 180, 183, 212, 218; continuity 12, 88, 163, 211, 216; montage 88; non-linear 48, 214
Edwards, D. 221
Eisenstein, S. 18
empathy 178
English teaching 1–8, 11, 21, 17–73, 48–9, 50, 53, 112, 209, 212, 223
Enzenberger, M. 108
ethnicity 20, 23, 25, 31, 39, 45, 77, 205, 207 208
evaluation 15, 25, 39, 45, 70, 129–30, 140, 142–143, 146, 162, 163, 173, 221; self-evaluation 140, 142, 224, 227 see also *assessment, log, reflection*
EyeOpeners 18

Ferguson, B. 108, 109
Film education 47
Film Studies 4

film noir 6, 170
framing and composition 41–42, 211–212, 216; see also *camera shots*
Frith, S. 118

Gauthier, G. 18
gender 20, 23, 25, 37, 38–39, 45, 77, 86, 91, 96, 106, 115, 148 204–208
genre 6, 14, 22–24, 37, 39, 54, 110, 143, 147, 170, 185, 204–208, 212, 215, 217–219 see also *film noir, horror, situation comedy, soap opera, spy, suspense*
genre recognition 18, 22, 45
genre theory 216–217, 223
GNVQ 5
Goffman, E. 195
Golay, J-P. 18
Gombrich, E. 17
Grahame, J. 142
'grammar' of film 18, 22, 164; of the media 216
Graves, D. 143
group dynamics 14, 33, 83, 147, 166
group work 5, 14, 26, 42, 75–103, 142, 208, 222

Heathcote, D. 195
Hebdige, D. 81
Hornbrook, D. 194, 195
horror 6, 25, 38, 148, 185, 188
Hypercard 52, 53
hypertext 14. 51, 52, 55, 72, 215,

identification 20, 178, 193, 194
identity 39, 106, 177–178, 191, 204, 207, 222
ideology 7, 105, 109, 121, 127–128, 137, 153–161, 210, 214, 218
image analysis 12, 20
image manipulation 10, 14, 50–53
imitation 14, 105–138, 147, 194, 214–215
improvisation 174–177
institutions 9, 77, 81
intertextuality 107, 215

Kaplan, E. A. 118
Kingman Report 223
Knowledge About Language 6, 142, 152, 223, 226

Leavis, F. R. 6
Leigh, M. 174
LINC Project

linguistics 17–18
literacies; digital 49–50; media 18, 45, 208–211; new, 9–10; visual 17–45, 67
Lister, M. 80–82
log 12, 70, 129–130, 141, 143, 187 see also *evaluation, assessment*
Lorac, C. 5, 76
low-tech production 29, 211, 218

MacArthur, C. 110
Making Stories 52
Manpower Services Commission 5
marketing 69–71, 106
Masterman, L. 6, 7, 108–109
McCabe C. 110
Media Studies 4, 11, 21, 75; GCSE 8, 14, 65, 140–167, 212, 218
media 'effects' 111
media language 72, 78, 88, 111, 199, 203, 208–211
media production processes 11, 65, 77, 86, 98, 184, 203
Mercer, N. 221
methodology 13–15, 152
mise-en-scene 24, 29
modality 169–197 se also *realism*
Morph 50–55, 72
multimedia 10, 14, 24, 45–73
Music Business 119

narrative 14, 18, 22, 23–29, 38, 45, 52, 178, 181, 184, 205, 212, 218; of film narration 212-214
Neelands, J. 194–195

originality 105–107, 147, 160, 166, 189

Panofsky, E. 17
parody 14, 40, 60, 105–138, 208
pastiche 105–6
pedagogy 199–200, 217; 'critical' 207; 'progressive' vs 'traditional' 200–202
performance 170, 171, 178, 185
photography 5, 14, 17–45, 80, 210
photostories 17–45, 215
Piaget, J. 194
Picture Stories 18
pleasure 59, 106, 109, 169, 171, 173, 208, 222
'political correctness' 207–208
pop video 14, 53, 83, 214–215
popular music 14, 105–138, 220, 225; see also *rap*

post-modernism 9, 25, 215, 222
post-structuralist 82, 107
posters 61–72
pre-vocational –see *vocationalism*
process and product 76, 79, 140–141
progression 45, 50, 173, 202, 211–212, 218, 227
Pudovkin, V. I., 3, 67–68

rap video 83, 85, 88, 203, 205–207
'reading' the media 11, 12, 17, 36, 41, 45, 203, 210
Reading Pictures 18
realism 31, 169, 174, 205 see also *modality,*
reflection 13, 25, 33, 45, 55, 70, 79, 82, 111, 142, 152, 172, 187, 197, 203, 208, 214, 217–219, 221, 227 see also *evaluation*
representation 81, 158, 161, 206, 214, 217–219, 221; 'positive images' 184–185, 204
Richards, C. 170
Richmond, J. 142, 223–224
role-play 105, 177

scaffolding 44, 67, 220
School Council Project on Communication and Social Skills 76
Screen 200
Screen Education 7, 109, 110, 200
scripting 24
self expression 3–6, 47, 108, 177, 209
Selling Pictures 18
semiology 6, 14, 17–45
semiotics 44, 82
sexism 116–117, 203
simulation 60, 63, 70, 105, 119–121, 147, 159, 170, 172–173, 177, 196, 208, 218, 219–222
situation comedy 140–167, 215
skills–decoding 209; in media production 11, 41; social and communication 5, 75, 220; technical 43, 45, 78, 140, 141, 160, 208–211

soap opera 15, 26, 169–197, 202, 215, 225
social relations–in production 202, 204, 206, 208, 215
sound technology 83–84
spy genre 109
Stanislavski, K. 174, 177, 195
stereotyping 158, 207
storyboard 14, 20, 22, 45, 67–68, 90, 212–214, 219
subjectivity 201, 222
suspense 27

technology 9, 11, 47–48, 55, 204, 226–227; and creativity 72–73, 203, 208–211; digital 25, 61, 75; and gender 204, 206; information 50, 61, 70–71; new 9–11, 25, 47–73 see also *multimedia*
theory and practice 12–16, 72, 105–138, 201, 211, 217–219, 220, 221, 2224
trailers 14–15, 61–72, 147
training –see *vocationalism*

video games 50
video production 5, 44, 84, 169–197
visual conventions 17, 18, 20–21, 43–44, 65–67, 205 see also *literacies – visual*
vocationalism 4, 5, 7, 48, 91, 101 216;
Vygotsky, L. 67, 142

Weiss, M. 5, 76
Willis, P. 81
writing–media production as 9, 11, 14, 17, 20, 41, 45, 49, 142, 174, 203, 209, 211, 216, 223

Youth Work 5, 13, 75–103, 216